PETER MARTELL

First Raise A Flag

How South Sudan Won the Longest War but Lost the Peace

OXFORD
UNIVERSITY PRESS

OXFORD
UNIVERSITY PRESS

Oxford University Press is a department of the
University of Oxford. It furthers the University's objective
of excellence in research, scholarship, and education
by publishing worldwide.

Oxford   New York
Auckland   Cape Town   Dar es Salaam   Hong Kong   Karachi
Kuala Lumpur   Madrid   Melbourne   Mexico City   Nairobi
New Delhi   Shanghai   Taipei   Toronto

With offices in
Argentina   Austria   Brazil   Chile   Czech Republic   France   Greece
Guatemala   Hungary   Italy   Japan   Poland   Portugal   Singapore
South Korea   Switzerland   Thailand   Turkey   Ukraine   Vietnam

Oxford is a registered trade mark of Oxford University Press
in the UK and certain other countries.

Published in the United States of America by
Oxford University Press
198 Madison Avenue, New York, NY 10016

Library of Congress Cataloging-in-Publication Data is available
Peter Martell.
First Raise A Flag: How South Sudan Won the Longest War
but Lost the Peace.
ISBN: 9780190052706

Printed in India on acid-free paper

To the new mothers of South Sudan, in whose arms the future must lie. And to my mother, whose love meant I could travel far, because there was a happy home to come back to.

CONTENTS

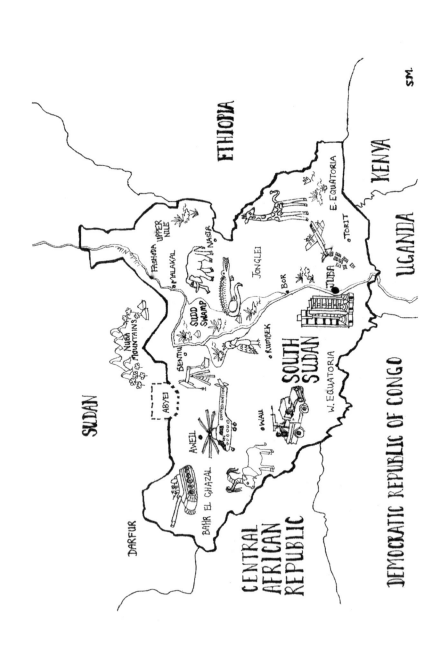

CHRONOLOGY

2500 BCE	Kingdom of Kush expands in modern-day North Sudan.
61 AD	Roman expedition up the Nile.
6th century	Kushite kingdoms in Nubia convert to Christianity.
8th century	Islam arrives, and Christian kingdoms of Nubia slowly convert.
15th century	Migration of Dinka and Nuer into the South, until 17th century.
16th century	Shilluk Kingdom founded. Azande Empire later develops.
1820	Slave raids. Ottoman 'Turkiya' forces start the South's '191-year struggle'.
1841	The Sudd is breached, and slavery escalates.
1870s	Britain expands control of Egypt, then Sudan.
1881	The Mahdi's war begins. In 1885, British-held Khartoum falls.
1898	Britain defeats Mahdists at Omdurman. France retreats from Fashoda.
1899	Anglo-Egyptian Sudan rules for the next 57 years.
1930	Closed Door. The Southern Policy blocks Northerners from travelling into the South, until 1946.
1947	Juba Conference. Talks on the South's future, as Britain pushes unity.
1955	Torit Mutiny. Southern soldiers rebel on 18 August.
1956	Independence of Sudan from Britain and Egypt on 1 January.

CHRONOLOGY

1963	The First War. Anya-Nya rebellion.
1972	Peace. Addis Ababa agreement ends seventeen years of war.
1979	Oil. Major finds announced around Bentiu. Jonglei Canal begins.
1983	The Second War. Fighting breaks out in Bor on 16 May. Rebels form the Sudan People's Liberation Army, SPLA.
1989	President Omar al-Bashir seizes power in military coup.
1991	South–South War. Mengistu falls and SPLA flee Ethiopia; the rebels splinter after Riek Machar launches a coup. Khartoum advances.
2002	Talks. Khartoum and SPLA meet in Kenya. Riek Machar rejoins SPLA. Meanwhile, war in Darfur escalates.
2005	Peace. The 9 January deal ends 21 years of war.
2011	Referendum. 98.83 percent choose a separate nation.
2011	Independence of South Sudan declared on 9 July.
2012	Oil War. Juba stops production in January, fighting erupts in March, with a deal signed in September.
2013	Civil War. Fighting breaks out in Juba on 15 December.
2014	War. Major towns swap hands multiple times.
2015	Peace ignored. An August peace deal is celebrated, and broken.
2016	Collapse. Machar returns in April, but flees fighting in July.
2017	Famine declared in February. Warnings of genocide.
2018	War continues. Peace efforts stall, again.

A NOTE ON NAMES

North and South

The history of Sudan—or The Sudan, or the two Sudans—is one of contested identities. Geographical descriptions are always political. Academics argue any concept of 'South Sudan' before the mid-20th century, or even for many decades later, is inaccurate. Before independence in 2011, the bottom half of Sudan was referred to as southern Sudan. As the days towards separation narrowed, that became Southern Sudan, and then finally, South Sudan. After independence, the rump state in the north was known simply as Sudan. I have used the terms North and South even before they became separate states, for sake of clarity.

People, Tribes and Clans

The terms are not interchangeable and have been intensely debated, not least because 'tribe' has pejorative connotations of colonial classification. It is, however, what many call themselves. In swift summary, 'people' refers to a wider ethnic group with shared language and culture, as well as potentially referring to all member citizens of a formal sovereign state. 'Tribe', and the smaller subset of clan within that, is a political grouping—but one rooted in geography and ethnicity.

AUTHOR'S NOTE

This is the history of how a country was made, but I did not set out to write that story. I came to South Sudan as a reporter, a bystander covering the end of one long war who became caught up in a new one.

Writing such a narrative history brings with it many challenges. There is the obligation to record; I have seen how factual reports I made just a few years ago have subsequently become twisted into new and dangerous narratives. Memories are not fixed, but can change in time as a consequence of the suffering people have endured.

But the story is also a personal one; I wanted to share what I saw and heard. The stories told are selective and subjective. I recorded eye witness testimonies of key events—often for the first time—but there are still so many voices missing. This is the story of what I witnessed and the people I was privileged to meet.

Recording such stories meant including graphic violence of the most brutal kind. Retelling them risks reliving the trauma for those who have suffered. Yet to gloss over the details would be a betrayal of the courage of those who came forward to entrust a stranger with the darkest moments of their lives. To understand what has happened is the only way there can be hope of solutions. Reconciliation requires forgiveness, forgiveness an acknowledgement of what happened.

For South Sudan, the legacy of the last few years will echo far into the future. The understanding of those years will define what the very nature of the country means to its people.

PREFACE

In the dry season, when the grass grew yellow and thin and crackled underfoot, the bones bleached under the sun poked through the undergrowth. Twisted creepers curled up between the eye sockets of the skulls, some so small they must have been children.

It was July 2011, days before South Sudan would declare independence as the world's newest nation. I had come to the army barracks in Juba, the capital-to-be, to see the place that for so many symbolised why they voted overwhelmingly to split from Khartoum in the North, to divide Sudan and form their own country.

People called the barracks the White House, and there were few places in South Sudan that evoked as much terror. For over two decades, this was the government in Khartoum's main torture and execution site in the South. It was where it dealt with those it believed supported rebel forces: activists and aid workers, priests and nuns, doctors and nurses, academics, students, civilians and soldiers. Security officers would march them out of their work, homes, or off the streets. They were removed without question, trial, or need to account for them. Thousands vanished.

The bones were left where the bodies had been dragged and dumped. You could see them from the edge of the dirt track that wound its way along the gentle sloping hillside. Soldiers said there were more piles deeper into the field, but you couldn't go further, even if you wanted to. Red skull and crossbones signs tied onto thin poles were pushed into the hard earth. They warned of landmines once laid to defend the base, or artillery and mortar shells which had failed to explode.

'That was the place of our nightmares,' college student Mabil William had told me before I visited the barracks, as we drank tea on a roadside stall. 'If you heard someone was taken there, you had said goodbye to them already. They were not coming back.' William's father, a teacher, had been accused of backing the rebels and was taken at night by soldiers. He was bundled into a pickup truck that was last seen heading towards the White House. He was never heard of again.

'When I voted for separation, to say bye-bye to Khartoum, it was places like that we were waving an end to,' William added, a quiet and shy young man. He wanted to be a teacher like his father had been.

Northern soldiers had left the White House only weeks before, the last units to depart before the division of Africa's biggest nation. For the first time, Southern soldiers—and a journalist—accessed the complex; I had spent several hot days persuading the men in black suits from national security to allow me in.

The barracks are a scattered collection of low brick buildings with tin roofs on a wide hillside a short walk from the University of Juba, just south of the city centre. The official title of the barracks is *Giada*—derived from the Arabic for 'the commanders'—but the entirety of the feared complex gained its popular name from the feature most visible from the vantage point of the road, a couple of two-storey white-painted hospital buildings. I was taken to a low, grass-covered bunker. Our shoulders pushed the heavy metal door open, and I used my phone to light the steep concrete steps down into the darkness. The air was chokingly hot. It took time to see into the gloom, before someone found the switch to turn on a bare hanging bulb, pulsing with the erratic surge of electricity from a generator.

The soldiers and security men who supervised me were as grimly interested in seeing these rooms as I was. As Southerners, they had not been here during the torture, but had heard the stories. The air was thick and intense, heavy with fuel fumes. The burly national security minder rested his hand on my shoulder and peered over my head. Large sacks of rubble lay in the corner. 'These ones they used when you were brought here,' he said, prodding one of the bags with his shiny long-pointed shoes. 'They would lie you down, and then put this one on your back, maybe two of them, maybe even three,' he added, trying to heave one up in his hand, but finding it too heavy.

xvi

'The only time the door opened was when somebody was being taken out to be killed,' he said, turning to me with a strange grin. Then he pointed upwards. A pair of handcuffs still dangled from the metal girder in the roof, and he moved them open and closed like a jaw, with a grating squeak. 'They would hang you here for days,' he said. 'I doubt if any other journalist has ever been down here before.'

His companion, silent until then, chipped in. 'If they did, they didn't come out alive,' he said.

We left minutes later, glad for the fresh air outside. Eyes adjusting to the bright sunlight, we walked the short distance through the barracks to another building, a whitewashed series of fetid storerooms, now used as basic dormitories for soldiers, where grey mosquito nets were draped over simple metal cots. The paint was peeling and smeared with dark stains. When the North was in charge, prisoners dragged out of the dungeon would be taken here and executed. For the soon-to-be independent South Sudan, the torture chambers offered the starkest of warnings that the future must not be like the past.

Major-General Marial Chanuong Yol Mangok was the new commander of the barracks, a towering man with a shaved head, dressed smartly in a scarlet beret and broad epaulettes with loops of gold wire on his uniform. His fleshy hand gripped mine in welcome, and he continued to hold onto it as he guided my tour around the buildings. 'In the past, this place was a place of torture, of pain,' Mangok said. 'They killed a lot of our people here.'

He looked straight at me, staring uncomfortably and holding my gaze, saying the barracks should be set up as a memorial to remember the crimes of the past. Hundreds if not thousands of bodies lay here, too many for anyone to know, he said. 'This is a graveyard—a mass graveyard. We need it to be kept as a historical place in the future,' he said. 'No more White Houses in the South, so that it will be a free country, where justice and freedom is everywhere.'

I believed him. At the time, there was hope. You heard optimism at every corner, a sense that change had come at last. The dead lying in the grass around the White House might have had their names forgotten and their deaths unmarked, but perhaps they had not suffered in vain.

* * *

Two and a half years later, I tried to visit the White House again. Soldiers at a roadblock pointed guns at my motorbike long before I could even reach the gates of the barracks. A stench of rotting flesh drifted on the wind. Smoke rose above the buildings.

On 15 December 2013, after simmering arguments within the ruling party erupted into fury, fighting broke out in the same barracks between Dinka and Nuer members of the presidential guard. The White House, where the torture that had blighted South Sudan was meant to end, would be where the next round of war would start— and this time it was a battle of Southerner against Southerner.

The battles kicked off a civil war of horrific proportions. Revenge and retribution forced people to divide along ethnic lines. Scores were shot in the streets, bodies lay scattered on the roads. Hundreds were rounded up and forced into a room in a police station. The officers opened fire with AK-47 assault rifles.

I'd also hear Mangok's name again. Now head of the Presidential Guard, a 4,000-man strong Special Forces unit known as the Tiger Division with distinctive striped camouflage uniforms, he led Dinka troops in massacres against Nuer comrades. 'He executed orders to disarm Nuer soldiers and then ordered the use of tanks to target political figures in Juba,' the United Nations Security Council wrote as they ordered sanctions against him, including freezing his bank accounts and a travel ban. 'In the initial operations in Juba, by numerous and credible accounts, Mangok's Presidential Guard led the slaughter of Nuer civilians in and around Juba, many who were buried in mass graves. One such grave was purported to contain 200–300 civilians.'[1]

That was just the start. The people fled massacres, ethnic killings and deliberate starvation. A man-made famine was declared. The UN warned of the risk of genocide. It has become one of the most dramatic failures of the international community's efforts at state-building. Just three years after independence, South Sudan was ranked worst in the world in the list of failed states.[2] The war would descend to levels of depravity few could ever have imagined.

Independence was won but freedom was lost, for the new leaders repeated the crimes of those they had ousted. The unity of purpose to achieve separation broke down, and divisions and hatreds were unleashed. Hope turned to disaster. Euphoric ideals collapsed with the bloody, bitter reality of their implementation.

This is the history of a dream. Many have fought. South Sudan did the impossible and won.

It is also the story of a nightmare. For countries are forged not born, and making a nation takes more than unfurling a flag.

* * *

'*Khawaja!*' shouted Joseph Bading, calling out the Sudanese name for foreigner as he beckoned me over, waving a carved ebony stick. An elderly gentleman with thin white hair, the primary school teacher was dressed in a ragged yet neatly pressed shirt.

The civil war that had begun in 2013 was raging, and I was lost. It was three years after South Sudan had declared independence and the world had celebrated. The memories of joining the crowds on the streets dancing in delight at their new nation seemed so far away. Now I stood filthy and knee-deep in the stinking sewage that washed down a side street of the UN base in Bentiu, a camp city of thatch and plastic shacks housing over 125,000 South Sudanese civilians. They were crammed together, sheltering from the violence outside, protected by high earth walls topped with razor wire. UN peacekeepers in watchtowers stood guard with machine guns. It felt like a prison.

'*Khawaja*,' he called again. 'Why do you write? You make the reports, and then you go, but nothing changes,' he said wearily. 'We need more food, more medicine. We need all this to end, so tell them that.'

I mumbled the foreign correspondent's awkward mantra: that I had no power to make change, but those who read the story would understand the situation better, and that might help. He had already been in the camp for more than a year, and he sighed with a deep seen-it-all-before tiredness. 'It is okay,' he said, softening his speech. 'The *khawaja* are always writing, it is what they do. We need someone to write all this down, so that what has happened is not forgotten.'

Sometimes the stories of suffering you are told can merge into one, and past pains bleed into the present. The horrors done are recounted with a sickening, resigned shrug of exhaustion: this has been done before; now it has happened to me; it will happen again. Tales are told as though in a cave crowded with echoes. Old histories reverberate in the politics, psyche and power struggles of today.

Khawaja, as Joseph Bading dubbed me, is a word taken from the 19th century Ottoman slave raiders for 'master'.

PREFACE

So much of the story of South Sudan has been one of violence. Far into the past, great leaders rose and fell, as people migrated into new lands and built communities, jostling against each other for control. Then came waves of outsiders.

In the 19th century, foreign forces led large-scale slave raids, treating the people of the South as a raw resource to exploit. The slave raiders set up fortress camps from which to attack, and then to control. They laid the groundwork for rule by a repressive minority whose power was based on using the human capital of people, swapping slaves to purchase loyalty and expand their personal empires of blood.

Next came British officers. They too used military force to break those who opposed them. In speeches they spoke of offering protection, but they subjugated the people to do their will for London's imperial dreams, and expand hardnosed geo-political ambitions to yoke Africa under their control. The paternalistic colonial policies treated the South like a land unchanged since time began, as though it were a living museum—or more darkly, a human zoo—to be preserved.

The British handed power to an elite in Khartoum. In turn, they built on that repressive state with staggering cruelty, developing a leadership whose survival depended on using the people and land for their narrow pursuit of power. Such dark history cannot simply be buried and forgotten.

Yet at independence, international experts came bearing proposals and plans to fix a land as though it was a blank slate to write upon, swept up in the euphoria of hope for the future. A new round of foreign forces arrived, once again looking at the land either as a wilderness to be explored and exploited, or the canvas upon which to paint themselves as the heroes who saved it.

For while South Sudan was a new nation in name, the past cast a long shadow. It struggled to make a fresh start, and the new leaders followed in old footsteps. Generals who had led the long fight on slogans of freedom bartered the future of the people for themselves. They used them as pawns for their own goals.

Beneath the rhetoric of democracy, freedom, equality and justice, there was no social contract between the government and the people. Instead, there was a simple system where the military men in charge bought the loyalties and services they needed from cash taken from oil.

That money should have developed the nation for all. Instead, it funded a brutal capitalist dictatorship of greed where the people's dreams were squandered for power. It was less of a government, more of a business conglomerate.[3]

For a while, the system seemed to work. Yet appetites expanded as the men gorged at the feast. The numbers of people to be paid off grew, as did their expectations and demands. The system that once made South Sudan's leaders strong would also be their undoing. The resources were finite, and when the cash ran out and people grew angry, the house of cards collapsed. Those left outside the luxuries of power rose up to take what they needed by force.

Today, leaders and rebels alike look to see what they can sell or loot to fund their constituency and keep their power afloat.

* * *

For three years, in the run-up to separation in 2011, my sign-off went out across the fledgling nation-to-be on crackly shortwave radios: 'For the BBC, this is Peter Martell in Juba, South Sudan.' Technically, the script sent to London was 'south Sudan'—without a capital letter—to ensure the BBC remained impartial in the independence referendum. Yet such nuances are lost on radio, and Southerners who tuned in heard it very differently. The BBC, they said, backed their dream of a separate nation. In the newspaper debates on what the new nation might be called—Azania, Juwama, Kush, Nile Republic and New Sudan were all suggested—editorials said that if a BBC correspondent called it South Sudan, then that name seemed a sound choice too.

In Juba, I first lived in an oven-like canvas tent that leaked in the rain. Then I moved to a crumbling tin-roof bungalow without electricity or running water, shared with a dozen others. In the day, it served to amplify the hot sun beating down. In the sweats of the night, I'd wake to the thump of plump mangoes hurtling onto the roof, thinking it was gunfire.

I stayed in some of the dustier corners: decaying hotels, army tents, hospitals, aid agency offices and thatch huts. I was sheltered from the sun in mosques and churches. At times, I slept simply on the ground beneath the moon, the curling smoke from cattle dung fires keeping the mosquitoes away. I travelled by motorbike, truck and foot, by battered boat and canoe, barely-there airplanes and terrifying helicopters. I met leaders and guerrillas, ate with rich and poor, stayed with fighters and farmers. I heard how they saw this land, and how they dreamed it could be.

Today, the foreigners who come to South Sudan stay for ever shorter periods. Institutional knowledge and experience shrink. Even the aid workers with their branded utility vest uniforms and flags have adopted the language of the military and speak of being 'on mission in the field'. They cross days off the calendar until they jet back out on leave or the next R&R ('Rest and Recuperation') holiday cycle. A rare few say they actually live in South Sudan.

For outsiders, it can be hard to see where one round of violence ends and another one starts. The seemingly endless cycle of violence can make it appear that the problems of the South are unsolvable. People call it a 'tribal' battle as a lazy shorthand explanation, as though it were a primordial conflict from time immemorial. Yet the reliance that people have on their community is not the cause of violence but, rather, because of it. It is the only security network that is durable enough to survive. Without a government who offer support, people have to care for themselves.

Increasingly, security fears mean that many foreigners rarely venture far beyond the bubble of guarded compounds, except for the briefest of trips. When the UN peacekeepers emerge from their base in their blue helmets and flak jackets, they peer out from the slits of armoured combat vehicles. The visiting diplomatic envoys stepping out from air-conditioned Land Cruisers come with analyses written by foreigners, based on security reports of the previous few months. The technocrats who make the decisions on policy and aid sit in Nairobi, Washington or New York. The businessmen who buy the oil, the politicians who pocket the money, or those who sell the guns drink the profits in far-away luxury homes.

I am an outsider too, of course. Strict word limits or two minutes on air meant my stories often provided simplistic summaries: a war between tribes; a rivalry between two men; a conflict between an Arab Muslim north and African south of traditional belief and Christianity, fought over race, religion, land and oil.

Yet as a foreign reporter, I was also privileged with access many did not have. I was able to cross front lines to interview those in power and their victims, to travel both to war zones and the extravagant hotels of peace talks. I could open the door to other foreigners, whose aid, money, weapons and diplomacy—deliberately or not—helped sustain the conflict. I gathered the stories of those who have not spoken of them before.

Most of all I met ordinary people, the kind men and women who shared their food, offered me shelter, and looked after an outsider in their land. For the grim lists of statistics fail to mention that in the midst of gloomy broad brushstroke assessments there are children who grow up happy and live life with a smile, men who don't kill, women who die in peace. There is suffering, yes, but people also live. Parents raise families, go to work, make love, drink and laugh.

The story of South Sudan is not only one of war. I have wanted to show, through laying out the long history, that peace is possible. These are horrifying times today, but there have been horrifying times in the past. They too were overcome. This is not a definitive history; that must be told by the South Sudanese themselves. It does, however, tell the story of how a nation emerged, and of how, for a moment, there was hope.

1

JUST DIVORCED

'A long journey of more than 5,000 years.'
John Garang, 2005 peace agreement.

Freedom came at midnight and the people went wild. Tens of thousands of people crammed the streets. Cars careered down potholed tracks of the new capital Juba hooting horns, and arcs of flames spewed out from aerosol cans. Gunfire rattled the hot night with shot after shot aimed at the moon. 'We are free! We are free!' screamed mother-of-four Mary Okach, waving a flag around her head, the material swirling. She gave a high-pitched ululating cry of joy. It was 8 July 2011, and rule imposed from Sudan's faraway capital was coming to an end. 'Bye-bye Khartoum, hello happiness!' she wailed. She danced holding hands with her sister, spinning in the centre of the main road.

Next to them was soldier Daniel Bol, dressed in green army fatigues and thumping a makeshift drum of an empty cooking oil can, leaping from one foot to another. 'Fifty years fighting for independence and if this is freedom, then this is great,' Bol said, a barrel-chested 30-year-old captain who grew up fighting in war. He bent down to me, offering a beer-soaked bear hug. Down the road came men carrying a giant flag stitched out of bed-sheets in front of a convoy of buses blaring raucous rumba music, the green, red and black rippling as they danced. *'Junub Sudan, oyee!'* they shouted. 'South Sudan, oh yes!'

An electronic countdown sign mounted on a metal telegraph pole on a roundabout in the city centre flashed out succinct but misspelled messages in red lights: 'CONGRATULATION. FREE AT LAST. SOUTH SUDAN.' One car dragged tin cans on strings, carrying a sign on its back bumper that read: 'Just divorced.'

Dancing at the base of the countdown clock, 67-year-old mechanic Andrew Amum was breathless in the sweltering night, panting his words out in euphoria, as cars hooted around him and people sang. 'We have struggled for so many years and this is our day,' Amum said. 'You cannot imagine how good it feels.' Like tens of thousands of the millions who had fled war, Amum had come back after decades abroad to celebrate independence and rebuild his long destroyed home. He'd returned from a Kenyan refugee camp in time to vote in the referendum for independence, which saw a landslide 98.83 percent choose to separate from Sudan. More and more joined the party on the street, shouting in the darkness at the spreading trees above. 'THANK YOU FOR FREEDOM,' the flickering screen now read, with a computer-generated flag flapping alongside.

As the people danced, the faraway voice on the faint phone line I'd hooked up via satellite dish to the BBC's World Service radio could hardly make out a word I said. The final minutes crept towards the first strokes of 9 July when after the longest of wars, Africa's biggest nation would become two. Not since the age of empires had a new African nation been so created—and none with such international goodwill.

'What is the mood? Have celebrations begun?' asked the calm BBC presenter in London. There was only one possible answer; broadcasting the screams of joy live to the world. I held my microphone up to the crowd. The seconds edged towards the pips at midnight, and the countdown clocked ticked to zero. The street exploded in cries.

'Freedom!' shouted a man in a military smock festooned with ammunition pouches, clutching one-handed the back of a packed pickup truck speeding past, a beer in his other fist. 'South Sudan! South Sudan!' Midnight had come, and a new nation was made.

* * *

A few hours later, my motorbike's weak headlights picked the way home carefully through the capital's Hai Malakal district, a series of decrepit bungalows and occasional mud and thatch hut compounds. Only the curious fox-like street dogs seemed awake, the road theirs for now, padding quietly along, scavenging for scraps. I followed them on my bike, bouncing down the bumpy, sandy backstreets to avoid the worst of the drunken soldiers on the checkpoints posted on the main roads. The night air was cooler, though it was still some time off dawn. Formal independence would be later in the day, when the flag of Sudan was lowered at a ceremony with heads of states, marching bands and military parades.

Softly, in the darkness, the candle stubs flickered. Away from the parties, each candle was lit in a spontaneous, unorganised memorial for the millions who had died, placed outside homes on the edge of the track. They offered a more sombre memory of the war's cost. They were a remembrance of the past, and prayers for the future.

South Sudan had been at war for as long as most people could remember. With each round of conflict, the weaponry and devastation it caused became more intense, from spears to rifles, to artillery, then tanks, fighter jets and helicopter gunships. As I pushed my motorbike into the sandy courtyard of my tin-roof home, the deserted street outside was marked by a line of glittering flames.

* * *

President Salva Kiir pushed his black cowboy hat up and rubbed his forehead wearily when I asked about the challenges ahead. There was a deep sigh, then a long pause. South Sudan's first independent leader, an ex-rebel general who had fought two civil wars to reach this point, looked exhausted before the task of forging a nation had even begun. Decades of war had left everything broken. He stared back at me from the head of the enormous table of the Council of Ministers, deflecting questions as to whether the land was ready to break free. 'We are not rebuilding this country,' Kiir said, through his thick beard. 'We are building it from the beginning.'

The UN creates long lists of indicators of a country: health, economic, education and development rankings. At freedom, South Sudan shot straight to the bottom rung of almost all, with some of the worst development indicators of any nation on earth. The wars had forced millions of people into exile and left those who stayed destitute.

When the country split, the rump state of Sudan in the north saw its position on paper move upwards. The situation in the South was so bad that it had dropped beneath a nation accused of carrying out genocide in Darfur. A 15-year-old girl in the South had a higher chance of dying in childbirth than completing school. In fact, if you looked at statistics of how many mothers died in childbirth, conditions were actually significantly better in Afghanistan under the Taliban.[1]

With oil providing 98 percent of government income, South Sudan was the most oil-dependent nation in the world. Yet there was little infrastructure beyond wells and pipelines. For the 10 million people, just one percent had access to a regular electricity supply. Even in Juba, power came from smoky diesel generators or solar panels.[2] For villages in the oil zones, often the only impact they saw was the filthy drinking water covered in scum, that tests showed to be riddled with toxins.

'When the assembled presidents and prime ministers board their official planes to return home, the challenges that remain will be daunting indeed,' UN Secretary-General Ban Ki-moon said, hours before the flag of the united Sudan was lowered and South Sudan's was raised. 'On the day of its birth, South Sudan will rank near the bottom of all recognised human development indices. The statistics are truly humbling.'

Those in South Sudan at independence could see the risks ahead. 'The world's first pre-failed state,' cynics quipped. For there were few places on earth as badly damaged, undeveloped and destroyed as South Sudan.

Yet the warnings didn't put off the people; this was a party a long time coming. 'When you're being beaten by your husband, you have to leave the marriage,' said Mercy Zamoi, a single mother who, after the new flag was raised, gave birth to a tiny, struggling, wailing baby. She called her daughter Independence.

* * *

It is a vast land. The two Sudans, North and South together, are the size of the United States east of the Mississippi. Transpose a map of the Sudans onto Europe, and they stretch from France to Russia, Norway to Turkey. The South alone, which made up about a quarter of the total of a united Sudan, is the same as Spain and Portugal combined.

Distances become multiplied by difficulty. Going by road from Khartoum in the North to Juba in the South isn't really viable, except for the most determined. Imagine the distance from London to Madrid, or Washington to Ottawa, but on the roughest of tracks. For almost half the year, torrential rains make three-fifths of roads near impassable with tyre-sucking mud.[3]

The South was nothing like what I'd imagined from schoolboy geography lessons about 'The Sudan' of deserts, pyramids and camel caravans. It could not have been more different. I travelled from the rivers of Ethiopia in the east, through the marshes and on the slow waters of the White Nile. I floated on boats down the beautifully named River of Gazelles and River of Giraffe—in Arabic, the *Bahr el Ghazal* and *Bahr el Zeraf*—and drove across wide plains of dry grasslands that stretched to the horizon. I bumped on tracks through the green farms of Equatoria out to rainy jungles in the west.

At night, viewed from airliners, the orange haze of street light sprawl fades south from Cairo. Then the skies go dark over South Sudan. In the day, look down from the belly-churning tin-can airplanes coughing their way from Khartoum to Juba, and you'll see the land change colour from yellow-brown to iridescent green as you pass over the immense papyrus swamps of the White Nile. On a map, the border between North and South follows the dry scrubland belt of the Sahel, the division that separates North Africa and the deserts of the Sahara from the rest of the continent to the south.

The land is a crossing point and melting pot of people; between the continent and the Middle East, it is a bridge between African and Arab, Muslim and Christian. North and South: this is where two worlds collide. At the best of times, they blend together. At the worst—and there have been a lot of bad times—they fray and split, turning differences of race, religion, language and ways of life into violence.

* * *

The South still managed to have traffic chaos despite the barely-there roads. Zooming on a motorbike through Juba late at night, I could cover most of the country's tarmac in half an hour. There were some useless roads faraway that crossed over from the North—the failed legacy of those who had hoped for unity—now dead-ends that would disappear into the grass. At independence, almost all the others were in Juba, a ramshackle town of rapid construction, guns, thatch huts and dust strung out along the steamy river banks. By the time you'd made it to the bridge across the Nile at the edge of the city, the tarmac had already turned back to the teeth-chattering, rust-coloured earth.

The narrow bridge spanned the length of two football fields, a decades-old pre-fabricated relic with worryingly patched holes. Overloaded trucks squeezed past bicycles on the clanking span over water inhabited by occasional hungry crocodiles. It had collapsed a couple times, but was always lifted back up, hammered into shape and opened again, wobbling. It was the only bridge to cross a wide river that neatly divides the country east from west.

On quiet days, I would take my motorbike across the bridge, swinging up the main road north. Then I'd peel off on thin tracks through the trees, taking the hot helmet off and putting on a pair of swimming goggles to keep out the dust, weaving eastwards through the high grass that whipped the bike on either side. I would screw my face up to the burning sun, feeling like I was flying down the animal tracks. The roads in the end would peter out, and I'd stop the engine, listening to the calling cicadas and smelling the rustling grass that reminded me of hay on the farm at home.

From there until Ethiopia—a journey with few roads that could take weeks to cross through the forest of the Boma plateau—there were a handful of villages. It is one of the continent's greatest wildernesses, the largest area of intact savannah eco-system left in East Africa, where antelope, elephant, buffalo and giraffe roam. Some were convinced a lonely white rhino might be left, if the reports from cattle herders of occasional sightings were true.

The giant herds of elephants have been massacred, but I had still seen the heart-stopping magic of the survivors stampeding through swampland, as the terrifying Ukrainian pilots flying the UN helicopter swooped us down the Nile for a better look. The animals were a fraction of what there had been once, a time when colonial officers found plains crowded with antelope and giraffe unafraid of man, where 'game was to be seen as thick as the blades of grass in a field.'[4] Even Ernest Hemingway had written of the South as a legendary land for big game.[5] The epic migrations of antelope, the Sudanese topi or tiang and the white-eared kob, had been badly hit in the war. Yet more than a million antelope and gazelle still travelled in giant herds, rivalling the legendary Serengeti and Maasai Mara in the size of migration. 'Like Jurassic Park,' said one conservationist, who flew aerial surveys to assess animal numbers.

* * *

Everyone wanted to come and give their plan on how to make a country. The crowds of foreigners saw the South as a new land on which they could test the theories they had studied, with blueprints drawn up by policy experts on far away desks. Here was a chance to atone for the failures of the past and, by being the ones who could bring a hopeful future, seek validation for themselves. The long history of the South was brushed over. Many mistook the absence of roads and infrastructure to mean the South also lacked its own old ways of governance—or believed what it had was so ruined that it should be swept away and replaced.

At independence, one of the scores of earnest, eager American graduates readying laws for the new nation had cornered me at a crowded aid agency party in Juba, expounding loudly on his work to help draft a constitution. Sweat washed down my body as the heat of the day radiated out in the evening from the concrete walls of the compound.

The young American I was chatting to leaned uncomfortably close towards me, speaking over the brain-thumping beat of the diesel generator that powered a couple of slow fans and tinny laptop speakers blaring out hip hop. He waved a bottle of White Bull, South Sudan's first commercially-produced beer, launched just months before. 'The Taste of Progress,' the label read.

'Nip the shoots of arbitrary power in the bud, man,' he told me, paraphrasing John Adams, fresh from his political science degree. He pulled out a chunky penknife from khaki safari trousers with zip-off legs and plenty of pockets, popping the cap off another beer. 'It is the only way to preserve the freedom of the people.' America, he told me, had a responsibility to ensure the young nation would succeed. 'We're midwifing this country's birth,' he said. The American was euphoric at the opportunities that he saw. 'You can't have a country without a constitution,' he said. 'This place is unique. We have a chance of getting a place right from the very beginning.'

Despite his unbridled optimism, I feared it would be a harder task. My own home, far away in constitution-less Britain, was a small rain-swept archipelago where over three centuries since the Act of Union amalgamated our multiple nations, we still struggled with contested identities. Europe had needed centuries of savagery to carve out its sovereign nations and resolve borders in peace, including the two great wars that exported its slaughter across the world. As for that old European colony, the USA, it had fixed its frontiers on the bones of the peoples the new arrivals had destroyed, then fought again to unify the warring settlers.

A nation is a mental and physical construct, not just a border line on a map. Violence in the process of state formation is the norm, not an aberration. What is strange is that anyone helping create South Sudan should have thought it would be any different.

That morning, I had driven by motorbike an hour out of Juba, where I had been given a bleak sense of the challenge of building a nation. Refugees returning after two decades away were hacking holes in the ground to put up the first wooden poles of a hut. The forest had reclaimed the land, and there was the terror of landmines as they cleared thick grass to plant the food to survive. It was frightening, back-breaking work.

The political slogans and rhetoric of freedom in the capital could seem very far away. In the weeks before, I had seen villages torched and destroyed in raids. On one trip, I woke at dawn to the magical sight of a cattle camp, watching the dozens of fires of cow dung rising in wreathes of blue smoke. The guards scooped up the remaining white ash as soft as talcum powder, rubbing it on their bodies to stop the biting mosquitoes. Some swirled in decorations, using their skin as a canvas. Many were as tall as international basketball players. In the morning mist, the ash-covered men appeared like ghosts.

Then they did the same to protect their beloved cows. As the ash was rubbed in, the animals lowed in delight, moving their sweeping horns. Their keepers had shaped them into dramatic curves with knives, and then dressed the tips with tassels from buffalo tails. The cows are their fortunes, their mobile bank accounts and the source of war. They are their obsessions, the inspiration of poetry, and the muses for music. Each of the men were named after a special ox, identified through its colours and shape of horns. They were names of poetry, reflecting the natural world around. The common man's name Makwei, for example, describes a special pattern of a black cow with a white head, but also echoed the cry of the soaring black and white *kwei* fish eagles who hunt above the cattle camps. Another man might take the name Makuac, describing a black-spotted pattern on the bull, but also a name rooted in the word for leopard, or *kuac*.[6] The herders moved across the land with their cows, experts in knowing when the rains would fall, of when to plant crops, and when to seek new grass.

The cattle keepers I was staying with were from the Dinka people, the largest group in the South, but there was no one 'Dinka nation'. They themselves were split into multiple clans. This group was from the Dinka Bor, and they had been fighting neighbouring raiders from the Murle people. Each had an AK-47 rifle slung on their shoulders, or if they were grooming their cows, dangling from a nearby tree branch. The men here would die to defend each other, and to protect their wider family in the clan, where marriage networks meant that all were connected through blood and payments of cows. In a land where government social security was an abstract concept, people depended on their clan for protection. When it was threatened, they pulled together. When an individual needed help, the community came to support. Through their stories they shared their long history that bound them together, and in their songs, their collective future. The sense of a wider nation seemed far away.

Across the foreheads of all the men were drawn four deep scars, sweeping in a V-shape down to the top of the nose. They had been made to mark a boy from a man, the skin sliced and then permanent welts raised by rubbing in ash. Other groups had parallel lines that wrapped around the skull, swirling dots across the face, or bodies scarred like a living pointillist painting. It marked people out; all know where the other is from. For there were so many other groups in the South. It is one of the most diverse lands in Africa—around 70 ethnic groups, most with their own language. There is no majority people. The Dinka make up around a third of the population, followed by the many Nuer groups, totalling about half that in terms of numbers.[7]

Those outside the big cities rarely talked of grand plans of a new nation. Their talk was of survival. The many peoples sometimes seemed united by little more than a shared history of oppression from outside.

9

There was a long journey still to go before the people of the South saw each other as people of one country.

* * *

The hope in the roar of the crowd as the giant flag of South Sudan rose on Independence Day in 2011 still overwhelms me when I remember it. Women sang with joy. Soldiers wept.

Yet South Sudan's history did not start that day. When does the story of a nation begin? The oldest usually were formed by geography: isolated as islands or divided by rivers, mountains or jungle—natural divides that pushed together a people with a common language and past. Others emerged from war, the collapse of empires and the breakup of larger nations into blocs of language and people.

In Africa, colonial cartographers drew ruler-straight lines. Unified peoples were divided, and scores that were different were pressed together. The name 'Sudan' comes from the Arabic Bilad al-Sudan, the 'Land of the Blacks'. It was a loose term for everything south of Egypt, not a coherent state with fixed borders.

History is so often written by the winners, and those outsiders who conquered the South assumed that because its past was not on paper, it did not exist. 'What is known as the Southern Sudan today has no history before AD 1821,' British colonial officer and archaeologist A.J. Arkell wrote, dismissing a past before foreigners invaded.[8]

Even the names the foreigners have given are wrong. The Dinka call themselves the *Jieng*, the Nuer, the *Naath*, and the Shilluk, the *Chollo*. The Bari people tell a fireside legend of how when explorers came up the White Nile, they were greeted by villagers on the riverbank. They screamed at the foreigners for news of the daughter of their chief, Jubek, captured by slavers in a recent raid. 'Jubek, Jubek,' they cried in desperation at the boat, hoping somehow she'd reply. At the same time, the explorers were shouting to shore asking the name of the riverside village. 'Juba,' the explorers duly noted on their sketch map—and so it was that the future capital of South Sudan was named.

South Sudan's own voices were silenced. The official accounts are the voices of the rulers, not the ruled; the general not the soldier, the politician not the people. The voices of women are almost absent from archives, for those who held power dominate the story. The voices left are whispered ghosts in the gaps.

* * *

So I went looking for the earliest record I could find. I was back in London, and headed to the giant halls of the British Museum. A teacher shouted at the children to stop running as they charged past me through Room 65, the Sudan, Egypt and Nubia gallery. They were headed to see the Roman gladiator helmets and swords.

I was looking at a fragment of wall painting from a tomb at Thebes in 1,400 BC, today the Egyptian city of Luxor. Lines of men walk in relief bearing gifts and tributes to the pharaoh: nuggets of gold, jewels and rings of metal, then the more exotic giraffe tails, ostrich feathers, incense and ivory. Three and half millennia old, and you can still see the mud and straw base onto which the plaster had been smoothed before being painted.

'The presentation of African products to the pharaoh,' the museum caption said. Egypt's power reached far, bringing slaves to toil on the building of its grand pyramids. These men paying tribute had come down a trade route of the Nile that stretched far south into the centre of Africa. 'The men of the south are painted brown or black, and wear large earrings and animal skin kilts,' it read. 'Their offerings include gold nuggets and rings, ebony rings, a monkey, a baboon, giraffe tails and a leopard skin.'

Only one figure stood out to me. A century before Tutankhamun was born, a man stands in line wearing a leopard skin around his waist, and a single string necklace of black and white beads. It was a portrait of a South Sudanese warrior. It was a drawing that could have been done today.

* * *

Most countries have a foundation legend of how they began. Out in the cooler green forests west along the border with Congo, I was camping in the grounds of a mission near Yambio. Philip Ladu, a trainee-priest with a smiling face and generously-sized belly that almost squeezed into his shirt, had come to investigate who the grubby foreigner was.

He brought with him a plate of sweet potato he had roasted in the fire to share, and settled down on a creaking plastic chair.

'Every tribe has their belief of where they came from,' he said. 'Some say they were born from a great cow, others that God moulded them from the clay.'

He told me how the Dinka and Nuer were once one family. The Dinka, who call themselves *Jieng*, or 'the men among men', was brother to the Nuer, or *Naath*, the 'original people'. A father had two sons, Naath, to whom he promised a calf, and Jieng, who would get an adult cow. However, Jieng tricked the father and took the calf, splitting the brothers. For the priest, the story helped explain why two cattle-herding peoples with so much in common so often fight.

Another Dinka tale narrates how God offered the people a gift: a choice between cattle or a mystery present called 'what'. The Dinka tasted milk first and chose the cow, without finding out about the other gift. Europeans and Arabs chose the secret gift, which some see as the skill of reading and the technology of guns.[9]

I asked Ladu which story he believed. 'Those are just legends we are told around the fire as children,' he laughed. 'I'm a Christian. Our history has been written from the very beginning.' Islam dominated the North, but Christianity is the main organised religion in the South, although belief remains strong in the spirits and gods of old. For the Dinka, it was *Nhialic*, the sky god, for the Nuer, the spirit *Kwoth*.

Ladu dismissed those. He pulled out a well-thumbed Bible, and read me a passage from the prophecies of Isaiah. 'Woe to the land shadowing with wings, which is beyond the rivers of Ethiopia,' he read. 'Go, ye swift messengers, to a nation scattered and peeled, to a people terrible from their beginning hitherto; a nation meted out and trodden down, whose land the rivers have spoiled.' He looked up. 'You see?' he said. 'It is written. That's us. That's South Sudan.'[10]

Then he told me that the first Gentile to convert to Christianity was from Sudan. Ladu read of a treasury official who travelled to Jerusalem just a few years after Christ's crucifixion. The official, a eunuch, converted and returned home to preach. He was, therefore, according to Ladu, also the first missionary to Africa.[11]

Dusk had crept up. We stared at the dark shadows of soaring trees above us, thick with creepers and noisy with roosting birds and chattering monkeys. Then Ladu opened the Bible again at Genesis, and read to me how the river that watered Eden split into four. One of them, he read, flows around a country called Kush.[12] 'This is the oldest Christian country,' Ladu said proudly. 'Here was the Garden of Eden.'

Legends are powerful. Kush, or Cush, was an ancient kingdom of Nubia with its capital at Meroe, just north of Khartoum. Now it is a haunting place, an Ozymandias-style city of eerie magnificence with 200 pyramids scattered in empty desert sands. At its peak, a time when Rome was a village on the muddy banks of the Tiber and fledgling Greek city states controlled tiny territories, the Black Pharaohs of Kush stretched their power both north to the Mediterranean and far to the swamps in the south.[13] The deserts around Kush were once green, for rock paintings and carvings show long-horned cattle and farmland.

For several centuries, the kingdoms of Nubia that succeeded Kush were Christian, but from the seventh century on, from across the Red Sea and from Egypt, the Arab people arrived and Islam slowly became the dominant religion. Meanwhile, large parts of once lush land dried into desert, and as the green shrank and violence grew, some of the people were pushed southwards.[14]

So in the South, people said they were the descendants of Kush. They pointed to what they saw as their ancient roots, in the construction of a soaring earthen conical mound covered in gleaming elephant ivory, on which their prophets would stand. The British had blown that up last century and stolen the tusks.

It was no pyramid, but myths hold magic. For the South, or New Kush as some called it, the legends showed they were not destined to be slaves. They had been kings once, and they could rise again.

* * *

The rebel movement turned new national government had another answer for the start of history.

Behind a chunky mahogany desk, the Minister of Culture, Gabriel Changson Chang, told me of plans to create a hero's State Medal, to honour those who had fought for freedom. 'It has been a very long battle,' Changson said, a heavy-set man with a deep furrowed brow.

He reached forward from a deep leather armchair, pushing a design suggestion across the table. It showed the emblem of the new country,

13

a fish eagle with outspread wings and sharp pointed talons. A new coat of arms for a new nation, with a motto of optimism: Justice, Liberty, Prosperity. Apart from the addition of a crossed spear and spade in front of a shield, the design bore similarities to the US presidential seal—and claimed a national history almost as old. 'The struggle for independence,' Changson said with immense pride. The medal was to carry the date of when the struggle began: 1820, and the date it ended: Independence Day, 2011. 'After 191 years, freedom,' he said.

Historians penning long papers say the government's 1820 start date of war is a stretch, arguing that this dating serves as ideological rhetoric against old enemies in Khartoum rather than forming an accurate estimate. There was little if any concept of Sudan, let alone South Sudan, when the slave traders swept in to set the land on fire. Yet that does mark the start of the South's common experience of oppression by outsiders.

At independence, Southerners were in little doubt about the epic nature of their shared struggle. It is a history of victimhood that began when the warriors of the South with their spears first confronted raiders from the North and found their hippo hide shields did nothing to stop the gunfire. The struggle was seen in near mythic terms, with events from distant history told in stories as though they happened just a few years before. Southerners fought for freedom against the invading outsiders: from Turks to Egyptians, Arabs, North Sudanese and the British. Yet outsiders also often persuaded those they met to fight for them against each other: Southerner versus Southerner, tribe against tribe.

Sudan was the first country in Africa to win independence when European nations began pulling out of their colonies in the second half of the 20th century, the lowering of Britain's Union Jack and Egypt's flag on New Year's Day 1956 marking the end of Anglo-Egyptian Sudan. South Sudan, 55 years later, would be the last in a much-delayed liberation from colonial rule.[15]

More than a million people died in guerrilla battles fighting against Khartoum's domination from 1955 to 1972, Southerners estimated. A second and more deadly war against government oppression broke out in 1983, lasting until 2005. More than two million died in those battles, the South's leaders said. There were lulls of fighting and patches of peace, but most saw the wars as blurred acts in one long conflict.

Southerners were deeply aware that their struggle against oppression was not years, nor decades, but rather centuries old. The stories of war, slavery, violence, defiance and rebellion were handed down through the generations in fireside fables. Yet the stories had also been repeated and reinforced with new rounds of brutality. In an oral culture, exact dates slipped. History as a linear narrative was distorted, because the stories were as alive today as they ever had been. These were not the dry, dull dates of faded textbooks. They were the events that had shaped life, and had been fused into the history with blood.

2

THE CATTLE PEN COMMANDERS

'Religion in the Sudan, as far as my experience goes, is governed by the principle that the end justifies the means.'

Rudolf Carl Slatin, escaped prisoner of the Mahdi, 1896[1]

Rainbow coloured bee-eaters zoomed between the bushes, and elegant, long-necked white cranes rose in front of us, wide wings flapping slowly. The dugout canoe made barely a sound through the narrow channel, the papyrus and reeds rising twice the height of a man on either side, with a sweet smell of rotting grass. There was a rustling in the reeds, a soft splash, and I feared a hippo or a crocodile. Instead, out peered a giant shoebill, a grey prehistoric-looking bird the height of a man's chest with a beak that could swallow a baby. The fisherman steering the boat said that when he nets extra fish, he throws a fat one to the birds as a gift so they won't attack him.

The Sudd, from the Arabic for barrier, is an awesome sight. One of the world's great freshwater swamps, it swells to twice the size of Belgium or three times Florida's Everglades after the rains. Herds of elephants live in the safe isolation of the maze of lagoons. The channel narrowed, turned, and stopped. We paddled back down the route we had come, looking for another way through. Eventually, we waded out into waist-deep water. Thick, cool mud oozed between the toes. We pushed our way through the final stretch to the small village on a rare area of raised land. The clouds of mosquitoes covered us like fog.

* * *

When our ancient ancestors marched out of East Africa on their migration across the world, the land that is now South Sudan was a first stop. Millennia later, waves of people came from other directions. As the Sahara extended its grip and green fields dried, some pushed into the wetlands and vast grazing lands of the South.[2]

Some, such as the Dinka and Nuer, built societies around their cattle, largely egalitarian systems. Others created more centralised authority, such as the powerful Azande empire that stretched deep into what is now Congo. On the White Nile, the Shilluk Kingdom was founded in 1545 by Nyikang, the first king or *Reth*, a man who claimed to be half-crocodile with the power to make the rains fall, and who eventually vanished in battle in a whirlwind. His power was passed down a line of Reths still running today. At its peak in the 18th century, the Shilluk Kingdom stretched far into the north towards modern-day Khartoum. Their fierce resistance kept outsiders away. The South remained unknown to the wider world.

In London, I dug through old atlases in a dusty shop off Portobello Road. I pulled out one map dated 1802, the smell fusty, and held it up to the light to read the spider-like ink descriptions. I traced my finger south up the Nile. The paper was crowded with details and names from the Mediterranean, through Egypt and south to Khartoum, then east along the Blue Nile into Ethiopia. The details of that tributary's source was first explored by foreigners as early as 1618—by Portuguese priest Pedro Páez—and later by Scottish explorer James Bruce in 1770. Even in the far west, the Sultanate of Darfur is well marked.

Yet the White Nile in South Sudan fades out just below where Khartoum is today. It is tracked to its source in an imaginary, jagged semicircle of snowy peaks marked as the mysterious Mountains of the Moon.[3] 'UNEXPLORED', the inscription beneath read. Beyond that, the map was empty, a giant expanse of *terra incognita*.

Over three centuries since the Amazon had been crossed by explorers, the Nile remained a mystery. The source of the world's longest river remained one of the last, great geographical riddles. Outside knowledge was still rooted in Greek and Roman stories, coloured with the wild imaginations of Herodotus and Pliny, and medieval flights of fancy. It was a lost world with tales of monstrous creatures, men with dog-heads, people with faces in their chests, or a single giant foot so big they used it as an umbrella from the sun.[4] For outsiders, it was seen as a place to be explored, then captured and dominated.

* * *

The swamps, impenetrable to armies, had shielded the river route to the South from most outsiders. The South was as distant and remote as almost anywhere on the planet. The swamps blocked the Romans in 61 AD, when Emperor Nero sent a force of Praetorian Guards to explore new lands, find trade routes and secure the source of the Nile. They made it as far south as possibly Malakal, several days sailing south up the White Nile. 'We came to immense marshes, the outcome of which, neither the inhabitants knew nor anyone hoped to know,' the historian Seneca wrote. 'The plants were so entangled with the waters that they were impenetrable except, perhaps, to a one-man canoe.'[5]

I grew up on a hill farm in Northumberland, on the English side of Hadrian's Wall, that epic barrier marking the furthest north the Roman Empire stretched. In the Nile swamps, so very far away, the marshes demarcate the furthest point south the Romans reached. I just can't shake from my mind the image of a centurion in his shining armour with horse-hair mane helmet, hitching up his flowing toga out of the mud of the marsh, that for him marked the very ends of the earth.

The Romans were stopped, but it did not halt people trekking north, for the routes were open on the ground and people mingled. Today, the Nile is still the great way deep into the heart of Africa. There is no reason the South could not have been a supplier of the wild beasts sent to the slaughter for Rome's gladiator fights in the Colosseum, be that rhino, elephant or lion. After all, the kings of Kush rode elephants at their court north of Khartoum, tuskers that could have come as infants down the Nile from the Sudd marshes. They exported them via the Red Sea. Perhaps even Hannibal of Carthage marched some across the Alps to invade Rome in 218 BC, or they were among those according to legend, the Romans took on their invasion of Britain in 43 AD.[6]

Little had changed when the first giraffes in the modern era to reach Europe arrived from Sudan, travelling down the Nile and across the seas by boat before walking the final stretches. One, the wondrous Zarafa, stunned the court of France's Charles X in 1827. '*La Belle Africaine*' sparked an outlandish fashion craze with spotted fabric and towering hair-dos piled up '*à la giraffe*'. Another was sent shivering to Britain, where Londoners were amazed at the '*cameleopard*' living at Windsor Castle and doted on by George IV. Later, more Sudanese giraffes—and a hippo from the Nile—were among the first animals housed at London Regent's Park, the world's oldest scientific zoo.[7]

Still, the Sudd blocked travellers, the reeds far higher than the deck of the boat. 'It is, of course, as difficult to judge what is going on in the Upper Nile as it is to judge what is going on the other side of the moon,' the Victorian Prime Minister Lord Salisbury wrote. Some explorers trekked in overland, but it remained as isolated and unknown to outsiders as it had been to the Romans nearly two millennia before. 'Heaven for mosquitoes, and a damp hell for man,' wrote British explorer Sir Samuel Baker as he tried to hack his way through the 'fever-stricken wilderness' to find the source of the Nile.[8] Sometimes an opening would appear, then close again without warning. Boats could disappear into the morass like into pack ice in the Arctic. Their remains were sometimes found years later, the passengers long dead from starvation or eaten by crocodiles.

Yet it would not remain a barrier forever. The immense marshes would be breached. The invasions that followed would leave the South in ruins.

* * *

Far to the north at the start of the 19th century, in the ever-constant chaos that is Cairo, the viceroy eyed the riches up the Nile for himself. Ruthless and power-hungry, Muhammad Ali came to Cairo as the Ottoman's deputy army commander. Soon he controlled Egypt and paid only token obedience to Constantinople. He wanted Sudan as his own, coveting the reports of lucrative gold mines and piles of ivory for the taking. He also wanted men, and lots of them, to fight and die as soldiers in an army of slaves to expand his lands.

In 1820, he dispatched thousands of troops south into Sudan. There was little resistance. Five years later, Ottoman troops had built a fort at Khartoum, controlling the strategic confluence of the White and Blue Nile. The era of the 'Turkiya' rule had begun. 'You are aware that the end of all our efforts and this expense is to procure Negroes,' Ali told his commander. 'Please show zeal in carrying out our wishes.'[9]

The first slave raid on the Shilluk people was recorded in 1826. A year later the Dinka were attacked, and 500 people taken as slaves.[10] Wave after wave of large-scale military raids soon followed. In 1839, Ali ordered Captain Salim Qapudan to find the source of the Nile, to open new routes for trade and plunder deep into the heart of Africa. Salim, a tough sailor from Crete, reached somewhere near today's town of Bor. The next year he tried again, with a flotilla of ten boats loaded with cannon and over 350 well-armed men.

The force was a motley expedition. Sent by Ali, the Greek-born Albanian adventurer who became the ruler of the Turkish empire in Egypt, the soldiers were Egyptian, Syrian and Sudanese, while the officers and others included a Turk from Constantinople itself, two Kurds, a Russian, an Albanian, a Persian, and three Frenchmen. It also included German adventurer Ferdinand Werne, a hapless explorer who forgot his mosquito net, and thus spent much of the expedition puffing a pipe and sweltering under a woollen hooded cloak in a vain bid to escape the relentless mosquitos, whilst ordering a servant to fan him constantly with ostrich feathers to cool him down.[11]

Southerners were rightly fearful. They staged warning war dances, the thumping sounds echoing across the flat plains. 'We sailed through a sea of green grass or reeds, where we saw over the extensive verdant plain on the gently rising right shore a large city of the Dinkas,' wrote Werne. 'The Dinkas were seen at a distance, jumping in the air whilst they raised one arm, and struck their shields with their spears.' Others ran inland, driving their cows ahead of them to safety.

The response was a wise one. Looking out at the passing villages, Werne asked his travel companions who the people were on shore. '*Kullu abid*,' the ship's crew replied greedily. 'All slaves.'[12]

The Dinka warriors knew the threat of slavers already. This was the first river expedition to reach so far into the Sudd, but smaller-scale slave raiders from Khartoum had already struck overland into the South for generations.[13] There had been an ancient history of slavery, and the hatred of Arab raiders was already intense. Werne described the brutal punishment the Shilluk people reserved for an Arab slave raider they had captured. 'They beat him to death with cudgels, death by the spear being considered too honourable,' Werne wrote.[14]

As they travelled further southwards, the people they met saw foreigners for the first time. The soldiers fired their guns into the air to impress with the explosions and muzzle flames, but the people on shore did not comprehend their real, murderous power. 'They feared only the thunder and lightning of them,' Werne said. 'They knew not the melancholy truth that our shots would hit at a distance.'

They soon learned. An argument as the soldiers bartered for ivory spiralled into violence. 'All three vessels fired away, as though they were beset by the devil,' Werne wrote. He described the horror as the bullets smashed into the crowd, killing a dozen immediately and wounding scores. 'An old woman was shot down by an Egyptian standing near me, and yet he boasted of this heroic deed, as did all the others,' Werne wrote in disgust, staring back to shore through the clouds of gun smoke as the boats left the bloody massacre behind. The survivors on shore wailed in grief.

'Relatives of the slain came closer to the border of the shore, laid their hands flat together, raised them above their head, slid upon their knees nearer to us, and sprang again high in the air with their compressed hands stretched aloft, as if to invoke the pity of heaven and to implore mercy of us. A slim young man was so conspicuous by his passionate grief that it cut to my heart,' Werne said. 'Our barbarians laughed with all their might.'[15]

The expedition pushed on, finding a gap in the marsh, and eventually, in 1841, reaching up to about where the city of Juba lies today. The Sudd was breached. So began the long and terrible exploitation of the South by outside forces.

* * *

In West Africa, the Atlantic slave trade was coming to an end. After building its empire on their backs, Britain abolished the trade in slaves, and then ended slavery itself in 1838. Royal Navy warships blocked the East African slave trade from Zanzibar to Arabian markets. It was exactly a year after the ban that Captain Salim set out to open up slave markets beyond the Sudd.

In Sudan, the traders were only just getting warmed up. The numbers are sickening. A decade after Captain Salim led the way, a dozen expeditions were raiding up the Nile. By 1863, 120 private armies set sail every year. Their annual haul of human cargo sent to Khartoum totalled at least 12,000–15,000 slaves—some suggested double that—with many others dying in the terrible conditions on the way.[16]

'The Sudan supplies slaves,' British explorer Sir Samuel Baker wrote. 'Without the White Nile trade, Khartoum would almost cease to exist; and that trade is kidnapping and murder.'[17]

A single expedition could involve a dozen gunboats and 300 soldiers, and the attacks were carried out with military precision. 'Quietly surrounding the village while its occupants are still sleeping, they fire the grass huts in all directions and pour volleys of musketry through the flaming thatch,' Baker wrote, describing in disgust how men were shot 'like pheasants' as they fled, as though it was a hunt for sport. The women and children were kidnapped, the great herds of cattle rounded up. Everything was taken, nothing was left. Homes were torched, and granaries looted or destroyed. 'The hands are cut off the bodies of the slain, the more easily to detach the copper or iron bracelets that are usually worn,' Baker added.[18]

As the village burned, the living were led away. With guns trained on them, the women's necks were forced and bound into tight wooden V-shaped poles. 'The wrists, brought together in advance of the body, are tied to the pole,' Baker wrote. 'The children are then fastened by their necks with a rope attached to the women, and thus form a living chain.'

The enslaved were forced to carry the stolen ivory and grain. Those with babies watched their children beaten to death so they could bear more loads.[19] Anybody who tried to escape counted themselves lucky if they got off with a flogging. Many were hanged as a warning. 'They were driven through the country like herds of cattle,' one witness said. 'When the poor wretches could go no further, their ears were cut off, as a proof to the owner that his property had died on the road.'[20]

Gross fortunes were made. Baker described in detail the planning for each raid. 'A piratical expedition,' he called it. They were commercial enterprises, funded by business loans and banks and paid back by the ivory carried out by the captured slaves. The tusks were shipped to Europe, where supply could not keep up with high-society's demand for tusks for trinkets, piano keys and billiard balls. The slaves were for pure profit.[21]

Southerners fought back, but it was a losing battle. 'Most people are bad; if they are strong they take from the weak,' Kamiru, an elder of the Lotuka people, told Baker. 'The good people are all weak; they are good because they are not strong enough to be bad.'[22]

* * *

Slavers set up a long-reaching network of fortified camps known as *zariba*, from the Arabic for cattle pens. Instead of housing cows, the thick earth walls topped with thorns became slave cages. Organised government had arrived in the South through the barrel of a gun. They were cruel and parasitical enterprises that laid claim not only to the land, but to the very people themselves. First the people were attacked, then the survivors were forced into launching raids against their rival neighbours. The violent cattle pen government of the *zariba*, established not to serve the people but to exploit and subjugate them, set the tone for the South's relationship with the outside world.[23]

For communities co-opted to help the slavers, there was little reward: the defeat of their rivals, and a paltry pay-off of a few dozen cattle. 'In his turn he is murdered and plundered by the trader, his women and children naturally becoming slaves,' Baker wrote.[24]

Former French diplomat Alphonse de Malzac, a self-styled count who proclaimed himself 'King of the White Nile', hanged his enemies on the trees around his *zariba* camp and stuck their skulls on stakes. His business model was barbaric: seize men to make them slave-soldiers, then send that army out to capture more. He refined the system with deadly efficiency, writing down laws for his realm of terror which were copied by other commercial companies. It was a self-perpetuating trade of doom that depended on destruction for growth; the greater the blood profits, the more the raids increased. 'He plundered, wasted, consumed everything far and wide round his settlement, shooting down all who resisted him,' wrote one contemporary.[25]

The fresh slaves he exchanged for ivory and used as salaries to pay his soldiers. One slave was three-months wage. A single slave chain could see as many as 500 men each hauling a tusk of ivory to his boats. When de Malzac visited Khartoum to relax, he used the basement of his home as slave-holding cells for a hundred people, chained in the darkness, awaiting sale.

One rare account by a freed slave, Hatashil Masha Kathish, described the horror of the system. 'When the slave dealers have desolated a district they often set up a despotic kind of government over the people that have been spared slavery or the sword, exacting from these poor wretches such a heavy tribute in grain, cattle, and other things, that death might be preferred to life,' he wrote. Taken as a boy, Masha—or Machar, to give him his Dinka name—was forced to take part in slave raids himself. 'Those fare best who volunteer to become fighting men in their service,' he wrote, adding that in desperate hunger, his fellow slaves would at times resort to cannibalism to survive. 'They learnt to plunder their neighbours, and to cut the throats of their prisoners just like the Arabs themselves,' he added.[26]

His story is only known because he survived. Sold onwards for a roll of cloth three-men-long, he was later rescued and looked after by an English missionary who took him to Britain. There he became an anti-slavery preacher, settling in the tough northern industrial town of Scunthorpe. He renamed himself Selim Wilson, married his landlady, and worked as a grocer. He outlived World War Two, dying aged 86 in 1946.[27]

'It often enters my waking thoughts, and is present to my dreams,' he wrote of his lost homeland with nostalgia, describing the family huts beside a slow river. 'Many a hut was over-shadowed by some fruit-bearing tree, such as the fig,' he recalled. 'The surrounding scenery was such as only Africa can show, and as I remember it, my old home, for beauty of situation, might have been in paradise.'

For almost all the other slaves taken from the South, their stories simply faded into the dust.

* * *

The Dinka called it 'the time when the world was spoiled.' It created deep divisions on all sides—between the South and the North, and with tribe set against tribe, within the South itself. The legacy echoes down the centuries.

'I have seen the destruction that came to our people,' Chief Makuei Bilkuei said, who witnessed slave raids as a child at the end of the 19th century. He recalled with hatred how the attackers shouted the Islamic creed of faith. 'They said, "*La Illah, ila Allah, Muhammad Rasul Allah*",' he said; there is no god but God, and Muhammad is the messenger of God. 'That was the way they chanted while they slaughtered and slaughtered and slaughtered.'[28]

So many from the South came through for sale in Khartoum that soon the very appearance of a Southerner became associated with that of being a slave. It left a dangerous legacy of the bitter belief in racial superiority. Some were sold in North Sudan, others on to Red Sea ports for export to Arabia and Persia, or down the Nile to Cairo. Women were taken as cooks and cleaners, or raped repeatedly. 'Those put up for sale are carefully examined from head to foot, without the least restriction, just as if they were animals,' one eyewitness described the human markets.[29]

Thousands of the strongest men were taken for the army in Egypt, and forced to fight for the masters who had captured them. They ended up scattered across the world, rented out as a slave army for hire, fighting for colonial powers, and helping in their conquests from Kenya to Congo to Uganda. Some went further, to the Middle East, the Crimean Wars against Russia, and even to Mexico to fight for French Emperor Napoleon III, returning to parades in Paris and awarded the Légion d'Honneur.[30] They became a lost tribe, fighting far from home.[31]

* * *

When the heat of the dry season became too intense and the dust too heavy in Juba, I'd drive north out of town, and hitch a lift on a canoe across a narrow channel to a long, shady island in the Nile. It was a good place to walk, away from the smoky trucks of the city, weaving past small plots of maize and pumpkin beneath trees. The farmers would wave hello at the stranger, and I'd often come back with a couple of avocados they'd given me stuffed into my bag. Sometimes I'd jump into the water to cool off, swim down with the current, then take a motorbike taxi back.

In the 1860s, it was a grim place. 'A perfect hell,' British explorer Baker called the grubby port on the river island of Gondokoro, which he first visited on his search for the source of the Nile. 'A colony of cut-throats.' The island was the base of some 600 slave and ivory traders, who had little else to do but drink and fight. In 1869, Baker received orders from Egypt to become the governor of Equatoria with his base on the island, as Cairo extended its control ever further south. Egypt was under increasing European pressure to be seen to at least try to stop the worst excesses of slavery. They brought in Western officers, but they had little or no success. For Baker, the very base he commanded was a slave centre, ringing to the sound of shuffling slaves clanking their heavy leg irons. 'From morning till night, guns were popping in all quarters, and the bullets humming through the air sometimes close to our ears, and on more than one occasion they struck up the dust at my feet,' he wrote. [32]

The Bari people, whose home it was, had been beaten into fearful obedience. 'The traders' people, in order to terrify them into submission, were in the habit of binding them, hands and feet, and carrying them to the edge of a cliff,' Baker wrote. 'Beneath this cliff the river boils in a deep eddy; into this watery grave the victims were remorselessly hurled as food for crocodiles. It appeared that this punishment was dreaded by the natives more than the bullet or rope.'

The slave traffickers came from all over: Sudanese, Turks, Syrians, Europeans and Egyptians. Slavers used Islamic law to justify their plunder of non-believers', flying black flags painted with Koranic exhortations to jihad or holy war. There was no attempt to convert people to Islam—for if the slaves were Muslim, that would prohibit their capture and so stop the dark trade. Christian slave traders joined in and raised the black banners of jihad for convenience too. [33] Flags from many nations flew—alongside the Islamist banners also fluttered the US Stars and Stripes. 'To my surprise, I saw the vessels full of brigands arrive at Gondokoro with the American flag flying at the mast-head,' Baker wrote. [34]

Yet with the slavers also came religion. The first Catholic missionaries headed South in 1849, and a brick church was built on Gondokoro. Reports of slavery from explorers and freed slaves filtered back to Britain, sparking intense anger among abolitionists. Missionaries faced deep hostility from the traffickers, fearing they would stop the trade. So the slavers told people the missionaries were sorcerers who liked to 'feed on the flesh of their children.' [35] People understandably fled as the priests approached, though Italian Catholic priest Father Angelo Vinco slowly won the trust of those he met, celebrating when he was finally accepted by a welcome ceremony, where he was anointed with liquid from a bowl containing cow urine into which the crowd had spat.[36] He died of fever soon after in 1853, aged 34.

Many followed, for at least 46 missionaries died in just 14 years, riddled by disease. By 1862, they were recalled and the mission at Gondokoro was closed. When explorer John Hanning Speke passed by a year later, he found the church bricks collapsing back into the earth. 'Not one convert had been made by them,' Speke wrote.[37]

Religion, however, was about to become a major force.

* * *

It was a grey, winter's day on London's Embankment alongside the brown waters of the Thames. A wind wet with sleet whipped yellow sycamore leaves against the ancient stone hieroglyphs on the pillar of Cleopatra's Needle. I shivered as soon as I stopped walking. A tourist with newly bought 'I ♥ LONDON' scarf wrapped around her took photos of her son looking miserable between the paws of a metal Sphinx. The stone at its base is pockmarked from a German bombing raid in World War One, but London's oldest structure, carved in Egypt in 1,500 BC, has seen far more history than that.

Dug out from the sands where it had fallen at Alexandria, the Ottoman viceroy Muhammad Ali sent it to London in 1819 as a three millennia-old megalith thank you for Britain's defeat of Napoleon's forces at Alexandria. London was keen to safeguard its power base in Egypt. The Suez Canal opened in 1869, becoming the key trade route to Britain's imperial jewel in India.

Britain, with its huge empire straddling the globe, had no qualms about taking territory it coveted. In other lands it set out to conquer, it did so determinedly with all guns blazing. In 1882, with Cairo in political and financial turmoil, British warships simply bombarded Alexandria and sent troops ashore, swiftly seizing Egypt for herself.

Sudan however, which now fell under its control, was a mistake. London never meant to get involved, at least not in the way it was dragged in. It did want to secure control of the Nile—the waters upon which all Egypt depended—and ensure no other European power could stake a claim. The government was also pressured to stop the slave trade, but it did not particularly want another land to rule, and certainly not a white elephant that would chew up men and money for little reward.

Things were about to change dramatically. In 1881, Muhammad Ahmad, the son of a humble boat builder from north of Khartoum, claimed to be the Mahdi, 'The Guided One', sent to restore order before the Day of Judgement. A religious visionary and skilled military tactician, the Mahdi called for jihad against the foreign invaders, who lived luxurious lives in Khartoum while imposing crippling taxes on the people. His followers grew from a handful of believers into a huge force of tens of thousands. It was an army of patched clothes, chainmail and swords, but they were driven with passion and righteous belief. Town after town fell to the Mahdists.

Stopping the slavery in the South, however, was not part of the Mahdi's plan of freedom. Efforts by European governors to stem the slave trade had caused anger among powerful merchants in Khartoum, and many threw their lot in with the Mahdists. So the slave boats kept coming. 'Hundreds died from suffocation and overcrowding,' wrote Rudolf Slatin, an Anglo-Austrian officer captured by the Mahdists, who witnessed the slaves dragged out from the boats. Many of those who survived were so weak even the slave buyers rejected them. 'Wearily they dragged their emaciated bodies to the river bank, where they died,' Slatin wrote. 'As nobody would take the trouble to bury them, the corpses were pushed into the river and swept away.'[38]

A British-led force of 10,000 men was sent to crush the rebellion in 1883, but they were almost all slaughtered or captured. Now garrisons stationed across the South were marooned, and fear grew that it was a matter only of time before they would be killed. So a veteran soldier was brought in to save the men; Major-General Charles Gordon, a British colonial hero who had already served in Sudan as a governor.

Once in Khartoum, however, Gordon decided to stay. There was no way to move the men out from the furthest flung forts and, like the captain on a sinking ship, he defied orders and refused to leave his men while garrisons in the South and Darfur were stranded. London had wanted no more part in Sudan, but the intensely religious Gordon would disobey orders for a principle, a moral duty that dragged Britain in deeper than ever before. Far from being the saviour of Sudan, Gordon would become the casualty.

On 13 March 1884, the Mahdists arrived at the walls of Khartoum. For almost a year, Gordon stood his ground from the city walls, writing for help from Cairo, as a relief column fought its way painfully slowly to Khartoum. On 25 January 1885, after a 320-day siege, two days before British reinforcements arrived, the city fell.

'Before dawn we rushed in and overcame the defenders,' said Ibrahim Sabir, a soldier with the Mahdi. 'There was scarcely light to see, but we could dimly discern a figure standing on the steps leading up to a roof and gazing intently at the troops who were rushing into the town.' A Mahdist soldier raised his gun and fired. 'The man was hit and fell down,' Sabir said. 'His body rolled down the stairs to the ground, staining the steps with blood.'[39]

Gordon of Khartoum, stoically walking out to face his enemies without fear, became the ultimate martyred hero, a Christian warrior whose death became the stuff of Victorian legend. Gordon was shot through the chest, then his head was chopped off and taken to the Mahdi. It was one of the British Empire's most dramatic defeats, and the soldiers who killed him were the first to topple a European-backed government and establish an Islamic state.

Gordon's memorial stands lonely in London, just down the Embankment from the Needle, beneath the grey hulk of the Ministry of Defence. He stares morosely with chin in his hand across at the giant Ferris wheel of the London Eye, swagger stick under his left arm, a Bible in his hand. 'Right fears no might,' the inscription reads, but this is no statue of victory. If the Needle column symbolises the ties that bound Egypt and Britain, the statue across the road to Gordon marks a death that would enrage an imperial Britain. It would commit it to a full-scale invasion of Sudan.

* * *

After Khartoum's fall, the garrisons of soldiers in the far South were now cut off entirely. The commander in Equatoria was Emin Pasha, a small bespectacled German-born scientist-turned-explorer. The British newspapers feared he would suffer the same fate as Gordon, and demanded his rescue. For that task, only one man would do: Henry Morton Stanley, the brash explorer who tracked down David Livingstone years before. So in 1887, two years after Gordon's death and with the Nile route blocked at Khartoum by Mahdist forces, Stanley dusted off his pith helmet and began the long march in across Congo.

It was a disaster. The expedition got lost in the forests, one officer was accused of cannibalism, and the commander of the rearguard column took to biting, beating or murdering those he met, providing one inspiration for Kurtz in Joseph Conrad's *Heart of Darkness*.[40] Stanley called his memoirs of the fateful expedition 'In Darkest Africa', popularising the pernicious stereotype of a continent for generations to come.[41] When they finally stumbled into Emin's camp a year later, he told them he was fine and didn't need rescuing.

The plan to take back Khartoum was better prepared—building an entire railway line for a new invasion. London wanted to crush the Mahdists and ensure Sudan was then theirs to exploit. The railway across the desert bypassed rocky rapids of the Nile to ensure troops could never be cut off again. They gathered their forces outside the thick mud walls of Omdurman, the Mahdists' capital just across the Nile from Khartoum. On 2 September 1898, the assault began.

'Nothing like the Battle of Omdurman will ever be seen again,' wrote Winston Churchill, the future prime minster. He was then a 23-year-old war reporter who swapped his pen for a pistol, galloping on horseback to take part in one of Britain's last major cavalry charges. The Mahdists, dressed in chain mail with swords and spears, faced the overwhelming firepower of a military with machine guns. Artillery on land and gunboats on the river fired barrages of shells into the Mahdists.

'From the direction of the enemy there came a succession of grisly apparitions,' Churchill wrote. 'Horses spouting blood, struggling on three legs, men staggering on foot, men bleeding from terrible wounds, fish-hook spears stuck right through them, arms and faces cut to pieces, bowels protruding, men gasping, crying, collapsing, expiring.'[42] Some 10,000 Mahdists were massacred. The British force lost 48. The Mahdi's bones were scattered. His skull was taken, some said to be made into a wine goblet.[43] After 13 years, Britain had avenged Gordon's death with the bloodiest of battles.

* * *

The boat had seen better days. I sat at sunset listening to the call to prayer echo out from the mosques across Khartoum. My legs dangled off the top deck of the *Melik*, a British gunboat twice the length of a bus. She had come by rail across the desert, then sailed up the Nile to bombard the Mahdists, bristling with cannon and machine guns. Two days after the battle in 1898, the boat took the victorious General Horatio Herbert Kitchener from Omdurman across the Nile to Gordon's ruined governor's palace in Khartoum.

Now the boat rotted slowly in the Blue Nile yacht club, a handy place to sit and contemplate the passing waters. Washed onto shore in a flood, the sides of the boat had merged into the bank, the purple bougainvillea creeper offering shade and curling around the still mounted cannon. My companions were insect-chasing swallows. Today, the silver dome of the Mahdi's tomb has been restored. A short walk away beside it every Friday sunset, the Sufi whirling dervishes swirl and spin to drums and cymbals, dressed in patched white robes with green and red in a graveyard, chanting and singing as the scent of burning frankincense drifts sweetly in the air. Each year, the *Melik* gunboat sinks deeper into the dust.

* * *

The Mahdists had been defeated. Britain basked in the glory of victory, but they could not relax. The scramble for Africa was in full swing, and European powers were vying for control of the key trade routes. Britain saw securing control of the mighty Nile as all important, so it set out to conquer it from either end.

From the Nile's mouth in the north, it had taken Britain years to battle to Khartoum. To secure the headwaters in the south, Britain had begun the massive project of constructing an East African railway from the Kenyan coast to Lake Victoria in Uganda, an epic feat of engineering dubbed the 'Lunatic Express' for its sheer scale, notable for the number of workers gobbled by lions. Before they could meet, those expensive and well-laid plans would be turned upside by a challenger from a most unexpected corner, beating the British at their own ploy of planting a flag, claiming the critical land between the two sides as theirs.

Five days after the battle at Omdurman, a steamer arrived in Khartoum. The sailors spoke of being attacked by white soldiers commanding African troops under a 'strange flag'. The shots were dug out of the boat's hull. They were not the rough scrap metal blasted by a blunderbuss from a fleeing Mahdist soldier, but the nickel-covered bullets fired by a European force.

While Britain was fighting, someone else had slipped in and taken the Nile. 'An incident which might easily have convulsed Europe,' Churchill said.[44]

* * *

We flew in low with wobbling wings that appeared to nearly scrape the top of the palm trees. The small Twin Otter airplane roared down the shining waters on the west bank of Nile, before swinging over and down onto a bumpy airstrip. The riverside town of Kodok was little more than a grid of a dozen dust tracks. A few administrative tin-roofed buildings marked the centre, surrounded by scattered thatch hut compounds. Kodok is the capital of the ancient kingdom of the Shilluk.

Donkey carts and pickup trucks met us at the arrival as medical supplies were offloaded, boxes of sweet peanut-flavoured formula food for starving children. They took us to the hospital, a handful of one-storey whitewashed buildings with a large Red Cross painted on the roof to warn off aircraft. The air stank of a strange mix of drying fish and mud, half masked by the buckets of antiseptic used to mop down the hospital floors.

It was 2014, the midst of civil war, and women lay on stretchers on the ground. The doctors struggled to cope with a never-ending backlog of cases. Complicated childbirth and gunshot wounds, life and death, kept the exhausted surgeons busy.

I watched people pass by outside the hospital through a car-sized hole ripped in the blue fence from rocket fire, the metal crumpled like paper. Half a dozen men, one carrying a machine gun and draped in belts of bullets, wandered past. They wore flip-flops or had bare feet, and their uniforms were a mismatch of ragged army jackets, police uniforms and T-shirts. One wore a bright yellow cowboy Stetson, and another, a fur trapper hat. It was not clear who commanded their loyalties.

Fist-sized bullet holes were punched into the buildings. 'Fighting, so much fighting,' said Dak Nyikango, the hospital's chief doctor, a tall man with wire-rim glasses, dressed in a white coat gleaming in the fierce sun. 'No one benefits. The people just suffer.'

Kodok seemed a distinctly unprepossessing town to die for. Still, the Upper Nile oil fields are not far across the other side of the river. Being a militia commander in control of these lands can pay.

* * *

In 1898, the town of Kodok was called Fashoda. I doubt it looked hugely different when Major Jean-Baptiste Marchand arrived after a marathon march across the width of Africa, taking two years with 120 Senegalese troops to paddle and then drag a collapsible metal boat from Congo-Brazzaville. By crossing overland in a daring trek, as far as from Paris to Moscow, the French had stolen a march on the British. Exhausted but overjoyed, Marchand arrived in Fashoda on 10 July 1898. I imagined the bemusement of the Shilluk warriors, watching as Marchand, a slender man with excellent whiskers wearing a neat kepi cap, planted the Tricolour in the earth of their ancient capital and claimed it for France. Marchand called it Fort St. Louis du Nil.

France wanted to connect their empire across the continent from west to east. Britain dreamed of stretching their empire north to south, to build the great railway from Cape to Cairo. Fashoda was where those great transects crossed, and the two powerful empires would come face-to-face. Claiming Africa's largest land and the world's longest river was the biggest of prizes. 'When suspense ended in the certainty that eight French adventurers were in occupation of Fashoda and claimed a territory twice as large as France, it gave place to a deep and bitter anger,' Churchill wrote. 'A "friendly power" had, unprovoked, endeavoured to rob them of the fruits of their victories.'[45]

So Britain sent gunboats. Messages were sent to Paris and London for orders, and the soldiers awaited the return of their messages nervously.

The French, since they arrived first, put their camp on about the only small hill around. They grew vegetables and watched, from a distance of three football pitches away, the British suffer in the swamp. Rushing to the fight, the British were still dressed in their desert kit, and came without waterproofs, tents or mosquito nets.[46] The French sent over champagne and delicacies from their gardens to share.

The French were sitting comfy in Fashoda, but their little empire on the Nile was hopelessly outgunned. 'Our poor Froggies are virtually our prisoners, they cannot budge a step,' wrote Colonel Reginald

Wingate, the British intelligence chief in Sudan, in a letter to his wife. 'Personally one cannot help having a regard for the pluck of these men, who in face of fearful natural obstacles, have gone to the place where their insane government told them to go.'[47]

Yet while a battle at Fashoda would not last long, a war in Europe could. It was the closest European powers came to war in Africa before World War One.

'Marchez! Marchand!' a pith-helmet-wearing John Bull tells a little Frenchman in a cartoon in London's *Punch* magazine.[48] France blinked. In December, five months after arriving, Marchand packed up his kit. Defeated after the hardest of journeys, Marchand refused to travel home via the easier but ignominious route down the British-controlled Nile, choosing instead to trek eastwards through Ethiopia to the Red Sea.

For the British, it was soon forgotten; they changed the now rather sensitive name of Fashoda to Kodok, to salve hurt French pride.[49] In the end, Fashoda contributed to the Entente Cordiale between Paris and London, the 1904 deal of alliance of friendship after centuries of rivalry. After Fashoda, it would take another 16 years before Europe would rip herself apart in a war just as idiotic, but by that time France and Britain were on the same side.

The French remember it a little differently, retelling the defeat as a public humiliation, a cautionary tale that has influenced France's policy towards Africa to ensure the devious British never impinge on their influence again. 'The Fashoda Complex,' some call it.

The sun was so bright off the water it hurt my eyes. I sat above the mud bank where the Shilluk fishermen had beached their canoes. They were dragging a giant catfish the size of 10-year-old child out from the water lilies. They beat it to death with a rock. I went looking, but nothing remains of the rival camps now, for the mud bricks had long since crumbled and washed back into the river.[50] No one in Kodok I met knew the story of how France and Britain almost fought over the town. No one, after all, had ever asked them what they might want. The land here has seen so much war that a squabble between foreigners—the threat of battle over a century ago that didn't actually happen—pales into insignificance.

* * *

35

Now victorious, Britain set about securing the new imperial possession. They had not come to build a new state, nor to care for the people. They had come to exploit it. To do that, the British needed to open up the White Nile into the South once and for all. Cutting a permanent path through the shifting swamps was a herculean task. In 1899, a year after Fashoda, a Sudd clearing team was put together consisting of five steamers, 100 soldiers and 800 Mahdist prisoners of war. They hacked and burned their way through the huge blocks—just one key section was the width of the English Channel, and there more than two dozen of comparable size to chop through. It was dangerous work, for the weeds acted as dams for the water. When the cutters broke through, a wall of water surged downstream sweeping boats and hippos in its path.

Progress was slow, for the swamps closed in behind the routes cleared. Sudd-cutting chief Major Malcolm Peake wrote to Khartoum saying the task was too big, for he would need an army of more workers to break through. 'Arrest 500 suspicious characters and complete the work,' the reply from Khartoum returned.[51] The usual suspects were duly rounded up and set to work and so the White Nile, at long last, was smashed open.

* * *

Yet as one door opens, another closes. After so long at war, the legacy of hate resulting from centuries of raiding meant colonial officers thought it better for a time that the two lands remain separate. The Closed Districts Ordinances for the South were first introduced in 1922, limiting contact between North and South. The modern world that had devastated the South would be shut out. It was meant to be for its protection, but it would forge a two-track system, developing the North but leaving the South in limbo. It was a boxing bell break that did nothing to stop the fight.

3

THE BOG BARONS

'Southern Sudan was conquered with force and is ruled by force, the threat of force and the memory of force.'

E.E. Evans-Pritchard, 1938[1]

John Hannah rubbed his hands to warm them after returning from teaching a French lesson. It was an icy November morning, and the 91-year-old sat wrapped up warm in a thick jumper, corduroy trousers and neat red wool tie in his cozy centuries-old home in Burford, a sleepy, picture-postcard Oxfordshire market town. He was among a handful of officers left who had served in Britain's administration in Sudan, one of the most prestigious imperial services of all. 'It was bloody tough, but then they were such delightful people,' he said, speaking in the clipped military tones of a long past era. 'Although of course I was only there from '50 to '55. Not long at all.'

Five years as Assistant District Commissioner in Juba with the power of life or death as a magistrate; I thought of UN staff with a six-weeks-on, one-week-off holiday rotation schedule who believed their two-year stint managing spreadsheets in air-conditioned units inside a gigantic guarded compound qualified them as experts.

For 57 years, a grand total of 393 men in the Sudan Political Service instilled their rough rule in the tenth biggest country in the world. Most of the time, there were hardly a hundred officers keeping the bare-bones, scattered cogs of government moving.

Hannah appeared fragile in his armchair, but the old fierce spark was still there. 'To control a country with so few people,' he said, passing me a plate of home-baked ginger biscuits. 'Do you think that could be done now?'

The system they worked for necessitated control, and that required violence. They were there to execute the authoritarian rule of imperial despotism, not establish social services for the greater good.

Yet years in the country also meant men like Hannah developed a deep understanding of the people and land. Many became fluent not only in the largest spoken languages of Dinka and Nuer, but also in Zande, Murle and Shilluk. It meant they could foresee all too well the chaos that would come when they left.

* * *

Hannah searched through long bookshelves, pulling out the account of 31 years in Sudan by the top British bureaucrat in Khartoum. 'It is true that the assumptions on which we worked were based on a paternalistic outlook towards the peoples we ruled,' wrote Sir James Robertson in the book. 'The changes that we sought for them were what we, and not they, thought were good.'[2] On his arrival in 1922, officers told him to act like a 'genial baron'. Some did rule with misplaced benevolence. Others were cruel, vicious and brutal.

Sudan was a hard place, and London knew they needed men able to cope. Hannah had pulled out another dusty book, and read of the dangers the officers faced. Malaria, tick-bite fever, cholera and typhus struck down many. 'The outlook was grim if, with only the simplest medicines in their boxes, they fell dangerously sick hundreds of miles from the next outpost,' wrote Lord Robert Vansittart, the Foreign Office chief. 'For in those days, miles counted painfully. At best they might be traversed on camel or pony; often they had to be walked. Weeks would be consumed by distances now covered in hours. In return, they got to know their people better than their successors can do by motor or plane.'[3]

The majority came from Britain's elite public schools—Winchester, Eton, Rugby and Marlborough sent the most—an education designed to create the officers of empire.[4] The majority had studied at Oxford or Cambridge, where several had won sporting Blues. Others had gone further; officers included England cricketers and rugby players, a Scotland rugby captain, and Olympic gold medallists. Even the football skills of the first Bishop of Khartoum were impressive; Llewellyn Gwynne had been instrumental in the 1880s in taking Derby County to the FA Cup semi-finals. Sporting prowess was seen as a good indication of leadership and confidence, as well as the much needed physical strength needed to trek for weeks and survive on one's own. It earned Sudan a dubious epithet: a country of 'Blacks ruled by Blues'.[5]

The young officers were appointed as District Commissioners, known more simply as DCs. In isolated lands, they operated independently like lords. One DC, who spent his time constantly on trek to control a land the size of Belgium, likened the peripatetic rule to that of the medieval English monarchy.[6] In the South, they were given another nickname: 'The Bog Barons'.[7]

* * *

In the North, slavery not only continued, but remained the backbone of the economy, though it was branded 'bonded labour' to make it more palatable on paper. The British needed the mass workforce that it provided. Officers busily signed 'freedom papers' for slaves who asked to be released, but they knew it was little more than window-dressing.[8]

In the South, slavery was pushed underground. The British said limiting access was the only way to stop the centuries of hate and exploitation, so the Closed Districts Ordinances restricted Northerners travelling to the South. They began in 1922, with Passport and Permits Ordinances requiring traders from Khartoum to have visa-like permission to travel South, as though they were separate nations. That was later expanded and formalised into the Southern Policy to limit the spread of Islam and the Arabic language, running from 1930 to 1946. The complicated pass system blocked most Northern merchants, although along much of the border people still came and went as they had always done, moving with the seasons and following grazing for their cattle. Trade was taken over by Syrian, Greek and Coptic businessmen.

'The aim was to create a barrier against exploitation of the simple, uneducated inhabitants of the South by an astute and untrustworthy people, and thus prevent the continuation of the hatred between North and South,' Robertson wrote. 'It was hoped that behind such a barrier the Southern peoples would develop until they were able to stand on their own two feet, and meet the Northerners on equal terms.'[9]

In places, the border was enforced with violence. The far western Kafia Kingi area was razed to ensure separation between North and South, and the people deliberately driven away from each other to halt contact.[10] One DC even banned the sale of flowing *jellabiya* robes. 'Large quantities of 'Arab' clothing are still being made and sold,' an order to merchants read. 'Please note that, in future, it is FORBIDDEN to make or sell such clothes. Shirts should be made short with a collar and opening down the front in the European fashion.'[11] While such orders were at the extreme end of the policy, deeper in the South Northerners were rarely seen anyway. Behind the barrier, the South stagnated.

Many officers romanticised the people as untouched, seeing them as 'noble savages' who needed to be protected from the modern world. Perhaps the officers found their roles easier to justify that way, to impose their mistaken model of order on a land somehow unchanged by time, but it didn't help the people. 'I doubt if anyone is very clear in his mind as to the exact reasons for which we administer large tracts of the African continent,' wrote Chauncey Stigand in 1914, an elephant-hunter who became governor of Upper Nile.[12]

Critics say the restrictions were a misjudged policy of divide and rule. By keeping the South languishing in unnatural isolation as the North developed, it exacerbated differences. 'The British administrative policy... prevented the Sudanese from knowing each other, feeling from each other, working with each other, and learning from each other,' a British government report later read. 'This marked difference in development between two so different people of one country inevitably creates a feeling in the underdeveloped people, that they are being cheated, exploited and dominated.'[13]

Belief, culture, economy, education, language and religion; all are key foundation pillars of identity. Before the British, the concept of Sudan had been the loosest of terms. The lands of the many different peoples bled into each other with blurred, shifting boundaries. Now the differences were formalised and entrenched. The formal policy lasted only for 16 years, but its impact resonated far longer.

In Sudan, divisions grew on all sides. There was no unified system of administration, not even in the army. Southerners enlisted in their own, separate regiment, called the Equatoria Corps. Britain had removed Northern and Egyptian officers from the South in 1910. The one institution usually relied upon to lead a country's visible display of nationalism was divided.

Britain ruled the land, but responsibility for basic services including health and education in the South was left to missionaries. It remained the most basic of provisions—almost entirely village primary schools—but even the limited spread of Christianity that came with education drove a wedge with the Muslim North. While the North spoke Arabic, the language of instruction in the South was English.

At independence, there were 30 times more pupils in government-schools in the North than the South.[14] The policy officially endorsed grossly unequal development that compounded the bitterest of legacies of separation and suspicion. The British sought to protect the South. In the end, they steered it towards disaster.

* * *

Pax Britannica was a very bloody affair. To control the land, the British needed roads built, and to do that, they needed labour. There was a key problem. 'There is no money amongst them and they do not understand its use, and so they would not thank you for small round discs of metal, unless, indeed, they immediately become popular as ornaments,' wrote British officer Chauncey Stigand. 'Where the natives are quite naked, they are usually quite content and happy in that state, and do not immediately see any advantage in changing it, especially when such change will involve extra work.'[15]

So to instil control, they broke the people by force. It was dangerous, crooked logic: make peace with war. The British set out to crush the people; there were battles against the Dinka, the Zande, and then the Nuer. Southerners fought back, but using spears to fight artillery was suicidal. In the first three decades of British rule to 1930, there was an average of more than one campaign or military patrol a year.[16] The violence unleashed was some of the worst seen anywhere under British imperial rule.

In 1925, Vere Fergusson, DC in the Western Nuer district, led an armed column of men into northern Jonglei. 'They gave us a bit of a shock by opening fire on us with their old rifles,' the officer wrote, in an unsettling account more akin to boyish bragging about a cricket match than mass slaughter. 'Most of the shots came uncomfortably close until we got the machine gun going and silenced the gunmen,' he added. 'The spearmen kept pushing forward and dancing about like madmen, and did not clear off until a good few of them had been blotted.' Fergusson was speared to death in 1927.[17]

Britain sent in the Royal Air Force, a terrifying new tactic to wipe out entire villages.[18] The airplanes pursued people deep into the heart of the once safe haven of the swamps, dropping bombs and strafing those huddling among the reeds. On the ground, troops burned villages, and destroyed the symbols of power, including the great monumental mound of the Nuer prophets, an earth hill covered in elephant ivory. The last leopard-skin wearing prophet who foresaw the future from its peak was killed in 1929, with RAF planes murdering the surrounding worshippers. Then soldiers looted the tusks and dynamited the hill.[19] The Nuer were driven into 'concentration' zones to isolate and weaken them. Memories last long; when Britain eventually began to withdraw, few wanted to take part in the politics and voice criticism.[20]

Britain's implementation of the Southern Policy tried to block out the North, but it could not keep the South frozen in time. The foreigners themselves were agents of change. Officers deposed those leaders viewed as too powerful and a challenge to their rule—killing, jailing or exiling them instead. They refused to accept the looser, spiritual power wielded by the old leaders: the powerful prophets, the rainmakers, and the warrior commanders called Spear Masters. Instead, the British wanted chiefs they could control under a straight hierarchical order often alien to the people. So they created new systems by raising up the men they believed should rule; now the power of the new and secular chiefs rested ultimately not on their authority and personal strength, but on foreign guns. In so doing British officers badly damaged, indeed often destroyed, existing systems of rule and authority.

Britain's brutal enforced pacification largely put a stop to fighting between tribes, but people remained at peace through threat of outside force. People were held in place, but there was no wider move to generate a unifying identity. Before, neighbouring peoples pushed back against each other with raids and violence, but conflict ended eventually with reconciliation and settlement. Now those old ways were dismantled.

* * *

The British government eventually realised brute force alone could not succeed: they needed to understand the people. Edward Evans-Pritchard, a British anthropologist researching the Zande, was funded to go and understand the Nuer. London hoped it would help them govern.

To colonial officers, the Nuer were warriors who refused to accept their rule. To Evans-Pritchard, they were a fascinating and complex society. 'The government was more or less at war with the Nuer at the time, and I was dumped down there among them,' Evans-Pritchard said, who arrived soon after RAF bombing raids on cattle camps. 'The Nuer saw—being intelligent and charitable people—that I was all alone and helpless, and they just accepted me as a guest.'[21] Living alone among the people, he studied the people for who they were—making the anthropologist a neutral observer, and not an interpreter laying social judgements on their society. His work helped show Nuer society's complexity and organisation, despite the absence of regimented political institutions that foreigners might recognise.

His work would become instrumental in the development of social anthropology, but colonial officers found his work little help for their rule—they wanted practical tips for command and control. They called him 'The Poet'. Yet for most outsiders coming to South Sudan, perhaps his work holds a simpler lesson: to listen in order to understand, and not just impose the foreigner's impression of what is thought to be best without asking.

* * *

After war, there was peace, of sorts. Such a small number of officers meant their rule depended on the cooperation of the chiefs, and that meant they needed to understand those they ruled.

'Numerous attempted murders on both sides, much shouting and spear shaking,' wrote Dick Lyth in his diaries, a young officer posted to eastern plateau of Boma. I imagined the fear the lone officer felt as he stood between the massed ranks of rival spearmen he had brought together. 'Today I have been holding a peace ceremony between the two tribes, which will, I hope, prove binding,' Lyth wrote, who took off his clothes and smeared himself in excrement to join the ceremony, something I cannot imagine many UN negotiators would do for peace today. 'It has been held on the boundary between the tribes, and accompanied with all the traditional ceremony—slaying of white sheep, smearing bodies (including mine) with dung, and spearing the ground.'[22]

In time, there was respect, and even friendship. Yet, as single officers sympathised, the wider British system destroyed. 'When they tie your hands, they tie you with silk, not with iron chains,' one chief said of later British rule.[23]

* * *

Such a life attracted those who came for their own adventures. Wilfred Thesiger came for the big game. At his London interview in 1934, he was asked why he wanted to join. 'I very nearly said, "because I want to shoot a lion",' Thesiger recalled. 'It was on the tip of my tongue.'[24] He used hunting as a way to earn the respect of the people he was governing. 'I had no idea till then how huge a hippo is,' Thesiger wrote after he joined a hunt in Upper Nile. 'Once he came for our raft. He rose out of the water at my feet, a vast cavern of a mouth and two angry pig eyes. I sent my spear home into his mouth and rolled out of reach.'

It was not uncommon to march for a dozen days to reach a village, hear court cases, and then trek back. When not splashing through the marshes, Thesiger used a steamer with a paddlewheel like a miniature Mississippi ferry as a mobile headquarters, a double-storey barge packed with porters, police and prisoners—as well as horses, sheep, goats, chickens and cattle. 'Conditions aboard it were crowded and chaotic, but no one seems to mind,' he wrote.[25]

The men were strong—they had to be. When DC Jack Wilson was speared in the chest by a woman furious at his ruling concerning her stolen goat, he barely survived the trek to hospital.[26] His old Cambridge rowing partner Ran Laurie, another DC, rushed as fast as he could to see him, but he feared he would arrive too late to say goodbye. By the time he burst into the hospital, the hospital bed was empty. Distraught, he asked the medical orderly what had happened. 'Out playing tennis, sir,' the reply came.[27]

Laurie later returned with Wilson to London. 'Desert Pair Set Thames on Fire', the headlines read, as they won Olympic gold in the double sculls in the 1948 London games, before returning to a slower style of boat back on the canoes of the Sudd.[28] They were typically modest: Ran's son, the actor Hugh Laurie, only discovered his father's success years later when he found the gold medal in a sock drawer.

Officers kept up appearances. The annual government handbook ranged from history to tax rules, emergency medicine to tribal law, but also devoted an entire page to the correct size of tennis, football and hockey pitches.[29] Officers would spend weeks training their ponies for the Christmas polo match at Malakal, crafting mallets out of tree branches and galloping in circles around the villages to the laughter of children. Several brought their families. One officer, Ted Nightingale, would go on horseback treks lasting weeks with his wife, and their one-year-old son slung in a hammock on a pole carried by porters behind. To complete the family they wanted a pet, but with fear of rabies, dogs were considered too dangerous. Instead, they had a pet cheetah who trotted alongside, called Swan. 'She was a delightful pet,' Nightingale remembered. 'Very affectionate, definitely more cat than dog in temperament, but impossible to house train.'[30]

Irish-American photographer Radclyffe Dugmore was impressed when he travelled through the rugged Nuba Mountains in 1924. At dinner, long tables were laid outside decked with porcelain as the candlelight glinted off silver tableware. 'We sat down about 30 in number to a most excellent dinner, while the regimental band played, and played very well too,' Dugmore wrote. 'They had no lights or music, but played from memory. It was altogether a strange experience listening to selections from the Gilbert and Sullivan and other light operas played by natives and sitting down to well-appointed tables.'[31]

Dugmore borrowed a dinner jacket from the governor. Officers dressed for dinner, but given the heat, a summer kit of white linen shirt with a black silk cummerbund was quite acceptable. 'You could quite easily become so slack that you could almost become a castaway,' remembered Geoffrey Pett, a flying boat officer in the 1930s, who described cooling off in the bright green waters of the swimming pool in Juba.[32] 'You've got to have certain disciplines that you carry out, and one of them was you always changed for dinner.'

There were the eccentrics too. Richard Owen lived for years in Wau with the unruly Marcus, a pet parrot who delighted in interrupting speeches by screaming 'Shut up, yer ba-a-astrd.' Church services were a favourite of Marcus, requiring each Sunday that he be caught and removed to a far-away tree.

Years of experience meant Owen worked out the best suited punishments for a range of crimes. 'Cattle thieves were the best choice for looking after a herd of dairy cows, but for tending one's garden one normally chose a murderer,' he advised. 'A recruit from a tribal fight was the surest man to water one's petunias tenderly, and even to grow successful lettuces. They seemed to be crisper and to have better hearts when tendered by a hand which had shed blood.'[33]

Faraway diktats from Khartoum or London thought irrelevant were ignored—or replied to with rambling verses of Latin doggerel. One DC posted scouts to give a warning signal for him to scarper safely away if visitors from Khartoum ever came.[34] David Bethell, posted to perhaps the most remote outpost of Raja by a frustrated bureaucracy in Khartoum, would be on trek nearly constantly to avoid meeting officials from Khartoum. He finally died of blood poisoning by refusing medical attention in his haste to leave Wau to escape the governor.[35]

The men knew the land. Once in Juba waiting for a police immigration stamp, I passed several sweaty hours reading the limited literature in the book case. I dug out a termite-chewed, crumbling, blue-covered paperback, 'The Report on the Administration of the Sudan, 1948'. It was the driest of reading, with almost 300 pages listing detailed economic statistics, from the exports of animal hides and gum to the imports of tractor parts. I looked out the broken glass window to the chaos on the dust road outside. Times had changed so much it felt like a different country.

* * *

Southerners were bemused at the strange, white foreigners who came unasked into their lands. 'The British seemed to some as phantoms who rode through towns on white horses, leaving children standing beside the road in wonderment,' wrote academic Francis Deng, reminiscing on his childhood. 'The British were regarded with a mixture of superstition, awe, fear, respect and admiration.'[36]

In the early 1950s, journalist Jacob Akol remembered meeting the priest who would take him to school. 'His whole face was covered with thick red hair with his big nose protruding out of it,' Akol said.[37] 'His mouth and the red lips looked like a red smear on a bird's grass nest. He smelled awful, a combination of soap and cigarette, odours with which we were not yet familiar. Where he parted his lips to smile and speak, we saw a row of teeth both up and down. A cannibal we thought! So we ran off.'

There was a gulf of difference between the two sides. Hannah told me how he had looked after three chiefs who had come for the 1953 Coronation of Queen Elizabeth II in London. He showed them around and visited a former DC, who had become a cattle farmer outside London. When the chiefs returned home, they told stories of the staircases that go underground and trains at the bottom. 'People thought they'd been drinking, but they insisted it was true,' Hannah said. 'But then they spoke of cows that produced half a dozen big buckets of milk a day, and everyone laughed. That really was beyond the pale.'

* * *

In time, South Sudan settled to British rule, but war outside brought change. In June 1940, the war storms of Europe rolled out over Africa. Germany controlled nearly all of Europe, Britain was reeling from Dunkirk, and then Benito Mussolini joined the fight. Italy's forces in East Africa were gigantic: at least 300,000 men backed by modern tanks and aircraft.[38] The Sudan Defence Force totalled just 4,500 men led by a sprinkling of British officers, troops trained for quelling tribal battles not war. The only heavy guns they had were four antique ceremonial cannons at the palace in Khartoum.[39] If Sudan was lost, sandwiched between Italian-held Libya and Ethiopia, it would cut vital Allied supply lines through the Middle East and Red Sea.[40]

On 4 July 1940, a 10,000-strong Italian-led force with tanks and warplanes launched a probing attack. They outnumbered the Sudanese defenders sixteen-to-one.[41] Italian aircraft later bombed Khartoum, Malakal and a clinic in Upper Nile, killing two American missionary doctors despite their frantic waving of the Stars and Stripes to signal neutrality.[42] In panic, a ramshackle force was drafted in; everyone who could be spared was recruited. 'As disorderly a troupe of performers as ever took the stage,' veteran Sudan officer Henry Jackson called it, with some pride.[43] 'It was an amateurish production in which District

Commissioners, railway officials, clerks, cotton-growers and many others suddenly found themselves in uniform.' They were sent to raise their own guerrilla armies. 'UNDER NO CIRCUMSTANCES DO I WANT UNNECESSARY RISKS TAKEN DURING WAR TIME,' Khartoum thundered in a telegram.[44]

The Bog Barons took no notice, of course. Thesiger and Laurie claimed to have fired the first shots; after hearing news that Mussolini had joined the war, they leapt about in a war dance before rattling off their guns across the border into Italian Abyssinia.[45] Others went further. Decorated World War One veterans, Captain Arthur Alban and Captain Herbrand Romilly, were now DCs among the Nuer and Anyuak. Itching for a fight, they crossed into Abyssinia to destroy an Italian post at Tirgol in June 1940. By leading troops into Ethiopia, they claimed to have been the first Allied force in World War Two to have taken Axis territory. 'Schoolboys,' Khartoum fumed.[46]

Even Evans-Pritchard donned khaki and led a force of Anyuak warriors. 'They are brave, but become very excited and expose themselves unnecessarily,' the anthropologist-turned-officer wrote of the guerrillas he led behind enemy lines. 'They like to fire from the hip, and when firing from the shoulder do not use the sights, so to conduct a successful skirmish it is necessary to take them right up to the enemy and let them shoot at point-blank range.'[47]

* * *

I opened the photo album of Dick Lyth, a fresh-faced British missionary who had arrived in South Sudan in 1938 aged 22 as a teacher, but who volunteered to fight Italian forces. Lyth, like other Britons in Sudan, was pulled into an extraordinary war. He was ordered to raise recruits to guard a frontier the distance of Berlin to Moscow, to stop Italy 'by whatever means possible'. His selection criteria of some 120 men included who could throw a spear the furthest. He made them swear an oath to the King using their old ceremony of licking a blade.

In one photograph, a new recruit daubed in neat lines of ash stares at the camera defiantly, naked save for a brass bangle. 'Before enlistment,' Lyth has written beneath the photograph. A second shot shows the soldier dressed in neat-pressed khaki uniform with a bush hat, rifle and bayonet—though still barefoot. 'And after,' Lyth has written. More photographs show the fresh recruits training to shoot down aircraft, aiming their rifles at a model airplane carried on a long stick by a comrade far in the distance.

They would trek for months surviving on what they could hunt, staging daring hit-and-run attacks on Italian-led Ethiopian troops. Lyth used hippo fat and mud as camouflage paint to cover his white skin as he led the men in commando raids on Italian bases. 'Somewhere away up in the foothills a lion grunted as he drove game to his waiting mate,' Lyth wrote in his diaries, describing how the soldiers lay around him, using piles of leaves as a bed. They had shot a gazelle, and the men had feasted on venison roasted on sticks over the fire. 'And so I sat on through the early night, until a double span of the finger and thumb against the moon's silver track told me that two hours had passed away, and I shook the shoulder of the man next to me.'[48]

He built a series of fake forts along the Ethiopian border, each manned by a lonely pair of soldiers. They lit roaring bonfires each night. The Italians, watching through binoculars, thought the area was crawling with troops, not just the tiny force. The bluff worked.

The Italians were pushed back, and soldiers chased them to Addis Ababa. The official report heaped praise on them. 'They deserve in the Battle of Africa the same tribute as the Prime Minister paid to the fighter pilots of the RAF in the Battle of Britain,' it read. 'For rarely has "so much been owed by so many to so few".'[49]

* * *

The war ended, and for South Sudan, life rolled on much as normal. The DCs continued their command, organising court hearings and settling disputes. In lands where calendars were measured in seasons, day-to-day time mattered little. Bog Barons like Lyth would send a rope tied with knots to the village he was due to visit. Each night a knot would be untied until, on the day the last knot was undone, the DC would ride in on horseback to hear the court case.

Yet the world outside had changed forever. Britain was victorious but broken, and the empire was ending. In South Sudan, the Closed Door was opening, with the restrictions of the Southern Policy lifted in 1946. The DCs had expected to be in command until the end of the century, but independence was coming. It was too soon for their plans for a slow handover.

A frantic development drive was launched to bring the South into the modern world. The difference was staggering. In the North, long railways had been laid down, and a giant dam had been built across the Blue Nile for one of the world's largest irrigation projects supplying vast cotton farmlands.

The South was starting at zero. 'The Southern Sudan had to be opened up and brought into touch with reality,' James Robertson said in Khartoum, the top bureaucrat overseeing the transition to independence and Britain's withdrawal. 'The people there could not be segregated any longer into a kind of human zoo.'[50]

* * *

The British began drawing back, with a policy of 'Sudanisation' to replace them. For Southerners, that meant 'Northernisation'.[51] The one secondary school for all the South had only opened in 1949, and pupils still studying were not ready for posts of power. So with almost no Southerners trained in positions of government, it was Northerners who got the top jobs. Even the government admitted it was an 'increasingly raw deal' for the South. 'Even if they were to go all out now, the South could never hope to catch up on the North,' official reports from London read. 'Consequently it would be bullied by the North in an independent Sudan.'[52]

The warnings were clear. 'It had not been envisaged that independence would be thrust upon the Sudan at such an early stage,' wrote Ted Nightingale, Governor of Equatoria. 'The Southerners' fear of being dominated by the North was so great that some of their leaders warned me that their people would revolt rather than submit to rule by the North. I reported to Khartoum that I put the chance of this happening after independence at nearly 50 percent, a risk which I considered too great, but the Foreign Office decided to ignore it.'[53]

* * *

Lunch was coming to a close. Hannah's wife Mary served a slice of treacle tart. 'It's lovely to talk about the old days,' she said, pouring cream. Colonialism was gone, condemned and castigated. She and her husband had spent the best part of their lives working as administrators across Africa. I thought of the 393 men of the Sudan Political Service. The old officers believed they had left a positive legacy of justice and fair play, but if they had, it was all destroyed now. Grey rain spattered against the window. 'You see, when you come back to England, no one is interested,' Mary said. 'You must talk about the crops and the weather. You have to draw a line and move on.'

* * *

When Hannah left, he handed his duties over to his chief clerk, a Northerner. 'I remember him saying to me, 'I do the work. I type the letter, I put a stamp on it. What do you do? You sit and appear important in your uniform.' I replied that there is such a thing as the confidence of people,' Hannah said. He was silent for a moment. 'Anyhow, he became a DC. He was killed within six months.' The storm was coming, just as predicted. 'It was like telling the people to stand on the edge of a precipice and take one step forward,' Hannah said. 'We knew there was going to be trouble.'

In 1954, he wrote a warning note to the governor. 'We told him we were convinced there was going to be an uprising. It was going to be in our district, and it was going to be in a year's time,' Hannah said. 'We were right about the timing, but the war broke out in the district next door.'

4

A POSTMAN AND AN ARROW

'The south is afraid of being overrun by the north.'

CIA, November 1954.[1]

Thumping pop beat hymns played out on crackling speakers, as a
Dinka-language weekday service finished up in the church. The songs
echoed in the tall hall, bright with white-painted walls. Deng Kooch,
a slender, soft-spoken and earnest man in neatly pressed shirt and trousers, leant towards me. 'This was where the British decided our fate,'
Deng said. 'We warned them of what would happen in a united Sudan.'

We had met at breakfast at one the best stalls in Juba for *fuul*, bowls
of slow cooked beans mixed with cumin, garlic and chili, topped with
egg and crumbled cheese, then scooped up with soft bread hot from
the bakery. I had shared a table with Deng, who wanted to be a teacher
but could not find a job. 'Or at least, one that will pay me,' he said
glumly. Deng was 22 and from the Dinka grasslands of Twic, but had
fled fighting and grew up as a refugee in Uganda. Then, as a teenager,
he returned to South Sudan into the liberated areas wrested from the
government by rebels. He spoke of carrying pumpkins on his head to
the frontlines for the fighters to eat.

The shadow of war hung heavy around his narrow shoulders, for he
spoke of his three brothers and two sisters as though alive, but they all
had died or disappeared in the fighting. The wounds in his heart

53

remained raw. Between bites of bread and beans, and sips of scalding sweet tea, we talked history. From the restaurant, he pointed towards a half-built memorial in the centre of a busy roundabout, where dates were inscribed on the edge to mark the key events of the nation.

The first date he had pointed to was South Sudan's Independence, 2011; I knew that one. Deng explained the second date on the roundabout. In a country of battles, it marked a meeting: the Juba Conference, 1947. 'The British brought together the chiefs to discuss the future of South Sudan,' Deng said. 'They asked what should be done, but they did not listen to what the chiefs said.' The conference had been held in town's only cinema, then one of the few buildings large enough to hold hundreds of people. When I had first seen it soon after the end of the war in 2005 it was in ruins, but it had since been renovated, with a sign outside noting proudly it had been converted into the Emmanuel Jieng Parish Church. It was a short walk away. Deng worshipped there, and since we had finished our beans, he asked to show it to me.

From the entrance hall of the church, we slipped up the stairs to where the projector once screened films, a balcony overlooking the main hall. The few clunking fans working were slowly turning, but moments after we sat down, our shirts clung damp to our backs against the plastic chairs. Mosquitoes whined. 'No one knew the British would leave so soon,' Deng said. 'We were not ready for it.'

* * *

After a century of outside rule, the June 1947 conference was the first time anyone had asked the South Sudanese what they wanted. The British brought in chiefs from the across the South, as well as a small but vocal crowd of the educated, including teachers and government clerks.

The problem was the deal was already done. It was simply window dressing. Three months before the conference an internal report put forward a clear recommendation; the South would join the North. 'We are of the opinion that the future of the Sudan depends on welding together the people of the whole country,' the report read. 'Through the representation of the Southern Provinces on a Legislative Assembly responsible to the whole country, the unification of the Sudanese peoples will more quickly be achieved.'[2]

Some British officers had suggested the South could be independent or be combined with Britain's East African colonies. Still, joining its neighbour Uganda was no easy alternative; South Sudan is more than two and a half times the size. As for an independent South, the practical matter was cash, officers said. The South could be developed—but it would need to be financed, and it already sucked up money for no return.

'During all the time I have been Civil Secretary, I have never seen anyone proposing to help find this money,' top government administrator Sir James Robertson said. For every pound South Sudan brought in as revenue to government coffers, at least four were spent.[3] 'The Northern Sudanese have been financing the South and look upon it as a sort of El Dorado, and would not be very keen to see it go off somewhere else,' he said. 'They would want their money back.'

So unification was the chosen route. The meeting was a rubber-stamp formality to strong-arm enough delegates into showing support for the plan.

The chiefs were unaware. At the conference, debate was fierce as to what they thought should happen. There was, however, one thing they could agree on: a common fear of Khartoum. 'The ancestors of the Northern Sudanese were not peace-loving and domesticated like cows,' Lolik Lado, a leader of the Lokoya people, warned the hall. 'The younger generation claim they mean no harm, but time will show what they will in fact do.'[4]

As talks in the cinema dragged, pressure grew. Overnight, Northern officials pushed delegates to support sending Southern members to a national legislative assembly. In the end, the chiefs were worn down.

'Gentlemen, we now have stayed too long,' Dinka elder Cyer Rehan finally said. The chiefs had grown tired at the pressure. 'Why should we be afraid of the Northerners?' Rehan added. 'If anything happens, if the Northerners want to make injustice to us, well, we have young children, young men. They will take up the response and fight them.'[5]

The chiefs accepted they could send representatives to Khartoum. No bigger decision or formal vote was made, nor was it explained what agreeing to send leaders to the North really meant.

So the British had what they needed. 'A representative body of Southerners endorsed the view that they should not be administered separately from the Northern Sudan, but emphasised their backwardness and their fears of Northern domination and infiltration,' Robertson wrote to London.[6]

Southerners later called it 'The Abominable Conference'.[7]

* * *

Still, Britain could not make a decision on its own. As the joint Anglo-Egyptian Sudan, a condominium of two powers, Sudan was unique in the vast portfolio of colonial possessions. Britain had sidelined Egypt's claims for years, but Cairo was now flexing its muscles. London was fearful of the charismatic pan-Arabist and populist military leader Gamal Abdul Nasser, who wanted the whole of Sudan to be part of Egypt.

In Juba, there was a small but energetic political class, with growing activism, nascent parties, and fledgling unions. They watched the rising strength of Cairo and decline of London warily, fearful of what it meant for the future of the South. In 1952, a group calling themselves the Southern Intellectuals Organisation, including some of the 13 senators appointed after the 1947 conference to a national assembly in Khartoum, telegrammed Winston Churchill directly. The former foreign correspondent who once charged into the Mahdi's spearmen was now prime minister. 'As human beings Southern peoples determined decide their future,' the message read in telegram staccato language, sent by Paulo Logali, a politician from the Bari people in Juba. 'You fought the battle of Omdurman to save Sudan and earnestly hope you not help sell us.'[8] Receipt was acknowledged, but no reply came.

In his bullish fashion, Churchill wanted a blunter approach: to send a British battalion to Khartoum, 'thus imprinting on the minds of the Egyptian dictators the fact that we can quite easily cut them off entirely from the Sudan out of which they hope to talk, bribe and swindle us.'[9]

Yet these were different times, for Britain was far from the power of old. London was paranoid Egypt would block the Suez Canal and cut its crucial sea route to Asia. Cairo was fearful that if Britain supported the South's separation from the North then it would lose control over the Nile waters, upon which it depended. Diplomacy won, a deal was done, and the South was the pawn sacrificed for greater *Realpolitik* ambitions. British officers would leave within three years, and Sudan's parliament would be given a vote to choose to be part of Egypt or become independent. Either way, North and South would be one.

It was a cold, grey Thursday in February 1953 when the agreement was announced in the wood-panelled hall of the House of Commons. 'I am sure that the good wishes of the whole House will go out to the people of the Sudan,' the Foreign Secretary Anthony Eden told parliament. 'These notable developments have been warmly welcomed by the Sudanese themselves.'[10] The South, it seemed, had simply been ignored.

* * *

The next year, in October 1954, 250 leaders from across the South crammed once again into the Juba cinema. They included chiefs from far-flung rural areas, urban Southerners living in Khartoum, and seven Southern members of the ruling party in Khartoum. This time they had organised the meeting themselves, and debate was on their own terms. 'Gentlemen, chiefs of all tribes, elders, citizens present in this house,' politician Buth Diu said in an impassioned speech. 'I should like to know whether you in this house want to be slaves—or it will be better for you to be poor and free and happy?'[11]

For four days they debated, concluding with a vote on two key issues. First, they chose independence from Egypt. Britain was leaving, but the South did not want rule from Cairo. Secondly, they would only be part of a united Sudan if they had autonomy for the South under a federal system. If that was not possible, leaders called for Sudan to be divided and for a separate South to be forged. The vote was passed unanimously, by 227 to zero. Only the seven government party delegates abstained.

They pointed to the 1947 division of Pakistan and India, a separation still horribly fresh. One might have imagined that the slaughter of a million people there would have provided a clear example of the risks. Yet the South was determined. 'We firmly believe in our right as a distinct race from the people in the Northern Sudan,' conference chairman Benjamin Lwoki wrote in a letter to London, Khartoum and Cairo, informing them of the decisions. 'We must determine the future of the South in the way we think suits us.'[12]

The South had voted for its future, but its fate was already sealed. When that became clear to the people, it would be disastrous.

* * *

Sarah Okuye jumped down a hopscotch grid scratched into the red earth, singing softly. The air was sweet with the scent of rotting fruit that had fallen from the wide shade of the mango tree, beside where the 12-year-old whistled a tune. She spun like a ballet dancer to twirl her bright red wax print dress. I was in the small eastern town of Torit. I had hitched a lift there, squeezed in the back of a pickup for six long hours of bumping road from Juba through wild, green forest.

Sarah's mother, Mary Okuye, sat close by, boiling water for tea in a large pot on a smoky fire beneath a tin-roof awning tacked onto a brick building. It was tall for a single roomed house, with a rickety, rusted iron ladder leading onto its flat roof. Under the British, it had been the army's signal station. The one-room building had been at the heart of the headquarters of the colonial Equatoria Corps, the Southern regiment of 1,400 men. In 1955, the parade ground here would be the site of the first shot of the war. The 'Torit Liberation Mutiny' was another date I had seen on the commemoration on the roundabout.

Now it was 2009, two years before the South's independence. Mary told me how she had returned home after years as a refugee. The 45-year-old widow, whose soldier husband had been killed, struggled to survive. Mary, a mother of three, had also been a soldier fighting in the war that began in 1983, a battle that many saw as beginning here in Torit nearly three decades earlier. She had carried ammunition and food up to the frontline under bombardment, where she then tended the wounded and dragged them out of the fight. 'We have had enough of war,' Mary said with a slow, tired sigh.

She had joined the mass return of the 2.5 million people who came back to South Sudan following a 2005 peace deal. The UN called it the biggest peacetime movement of population since World War Two. Some two-thirds of them were children and, like Sarah, many were going to ancestral homes for the first time. Mary had given birth to all her children outside South Sudan. In the two decades of war, she had fled east across the wilderness to reach Ethiopia, then west to Uganda, before coming back after the peace deal was signed. She was searching for the family she had lost contact with years before in the war, and hoped were still alive. It was a hard homecoming.

'Everything has been destroyed,' Mary said, as she stirred a thin porridge for supper for her three children. Home now was the half shelter of the brick house, dark and smoky, its windows shuttered with wooden slats and scrap metal sheeting. Tiny dots of light streamed through, the metal rusted with age, or bullet holes. She offered me tea. 'When we came back, there was nothing,' she added, waving at her few possessions—a plastic bucket for washing, a battered tin pot blackened from years of cooking on open fires, and a couple of blankets. 'I had what I carried.'

I scrambled up the wobbly metal rungs to the flat roof looking out over the barracks and the town, home to a few thousand people. The town had been heavily fought over in the 1983–2005 war. Years of abandonment meant once neat huts with grass roofs had been munched away by termites, and their mud walls had crumbled away in the rains. Around the brick building, soldiers sat beside low foxholes scraped into the dirt. I sat with my legs dangling down from the building's edge. The dry season was ending, and the Lotuko herders were burning the pastures outside town to encourage a fresh growth of grass for their cattle. The fragile stems of charred grass settled on the roof beside me. The feathery blades of ash left a smear of soot. The looming range of thick forested hills on the horizon, the high and misty Imatong Mountains, turned darker blue in the lowering light. Afternoon crept towards sunset.

* * *

Every war begins with a first shot. Often, in that moment, it is not known that it has triggered something more, for conflicts are messy and take on lives of their own. Some historians argue that the root causes bringing the crisis to breaking point are what is important, not the spark to the flame. Yet it does matter, for history is made up of stories. The tale of how the war in Sudan began, a conflict that would rage off and on for half a century, destroy a land and devastate a people but pave the way to independence—that is one worth telling. For sometimes wars do begin when one person decides that enough is enough, and takes up a weapon. In South Sudan's case, it was a bow and arrow, and it was not a glorious beginning.

As Britain prepared to leave, fear grew. There had already been riots at Nzara and Yambio in the far west, when striking workers were shot dead by police. People believed that when the British left, then

Southerners would be crushed. Rumours swirled of a return to the days of slavery; some were determined to strike first.

In Torit, Sergeant Saturlino Oboyo plotted revolution. He sent messages to conspirators across the South. The killings were to start an hour before dawn. A small gang of Southern soldiers would herald the mutiny with the murder of Northern officers as they slept. Then they would seize the garrisons, airstrips and river ports. 'There is war tomorrow at five o'clock in the morning,' Oboyo wrote in a cable to the plotters. 'Don't be late.'[13] It was not clear if the others got the message, but on 6 August 1955, Oboyo set out to spark a war on his own by assassinating his commanding officer, a Northerner. Oboyo's plan was riddled with problems, the first being that all the guns were locked up in the armoury; Oboyo borrowed a bow and arrow from a friend. Problem number two: the commanding general was out of town; Oboyo set out to kill the first Northern official he could find: an assistant postmaster. Finally: he was useless at archery. Oboyo drew the bow and fired the arrow, but missed and wounded a passing Southern soldier instead.[14]

'He appears to us to have been a fanatic in his hatred to the Northern Sudanese,' the government report on the violence read. 'He decided to murder any Northerner that he could see.'[15] Promptly arrested, when police searched him they found a list of two dozen co-conspirators in his pocket. Those named in Oboyo's list were summoned to Juba for apparently bureaucratic errands—and then arrested. 'The plan itself was clumsy, haphazard and unorganised,' the report concluded. It was not a promising start to a decades-long fight for freedom.

The arrests were only the beginning. Northern troops were flown in as reinforcements, and Southern troops were ordered to head to Khartoum. They were told they were going take part in celebrations to mark the departure of British officers ahead of independence, but the move whipped up fear.

'Rumour got around that the Equatoria Corps was going to be sent to the North, and all the soldiers would be made to become Muslims,' said John Hannah, the British number two in Juba. Like the rest of the British officers, he had been sent home under Egyptian pressure just before the violence began. He looked up sadly at me, swallowing a low, despondent laugh, the tragedy of remembrance at what could have been done. 'The officers, who were all Muslim, said this was so ridiculous we won't even deny it. The soldiers said: "They're not denying it, therefore it must be true." You see? So it sparked the uprising.'

* * *

Twelve days after the 'Arrow Incident', as Oboyo's attack was officially termed, Southern troops were ordered north. An hour after dawn on 18 August, soldiers stood on the same parade ground that spread out beneath my feet, a large, open sandy area surrounded by scattered trees.

In front of me now, the soldiers ambled across the earth, relaxing as the dusk air cooled, wearing flip-flops, combat trousers and faded T-shirts, battered AK-47 rifles slung with a strap on their back. In 1955, those on parade here were in smarter kit, standing to attention in ranks with neat pressed khaki uniforms and bush hats pinned up at the side. They were due to board trucks for Juba, and then take a steamer down the Nile to Khartoum.

As they marched past, they saluted the commanding officer smartly. Then, like a wave, there was a murmur among the troops, and ranks broke. Chaos erupted. Northern colleagues were shot or hacked to death. Two were killed cowering in their offices. Troops went on the rampage, breaking open the armoury and handing out weapons.

'The mutineers appear to have been under the command of nobody, and chaos and disorder prevailed everywhere,' the report into the violence read, as troops and civilians ran into town looting stores run by Northern merchants.[16] A panicked telegram was sent to London. 'Communications with Torit have been cut,' it warned. Terrified Northerners ran to the only place they thought safe, the police station cells. The police opened the gates, putting men in one cramped cell and women and children together next door. They hoped the solid walls would deter the rebels and stop the whizzing bullets. One of the women was heavily pregnant, giving birth early on the concrete floor in the chaos.

On the second day of fighting, a truck careered into the prison yard, packed with soldiers brandishing rifles and Bren machine guns. The police sergeant refused to hand over the keys, but the soldiers demanded blood. Pushing the police aside, they killed the cowering civilians cornered in the cells. 'Two mutineers climbed to a ventilation window in the men's cell and shot at the Northern merchants, while others directed Bren gun fire at the cell door,' a report detailed, recording nine merchants killed, and five wounded. 'At the same time a barrage of Bren gun fire was directed at the women's cell.' In there, four women and eight children were shot dead. Those killed included the one-day-old baby.

Survivors were pulled out of the cells and ordered to drag the bleeding corpses of their families to a truck. They headed outside town. Soldiers formed a semicircle around them, pointing guns as they carried the bodies off into the bush. 'We knew what was going to happen, and we tried to slow the process of unloading, so the darkness would fall and then we should have a little chance to escape into the bush,' one survivor said.[17] 'Then the soldiers and policemen loaded their rifles, and as soon as this movement started we ran away. Fire was opened on us.' Nine were massacred, but three escaped.

Of those killed in Torit town, only a handful were soldiers. Many were women and children. The rest are a depressing list of traders, teachers, a couple of carpenters, an agricultural inspector, and a road construction foreman.

This flows w. "Don't back"

* * *

Grim massacres followed in other towns as the mutiny spread.[18] Garrisons across Equatoria and in Malakal rose up, but there was no coordination, nor any clear political programme. In Yei, many Northerners sheltered in the home of a Greek trader, before missionaries accompanied them to safety into nearby Congo. 'War started in the Southern Sudan,' wrote Michael Watta, head of Yei council, in an emergency telegram to London. Lines had been cut so two policemen ran with the message, one to Uganda and the other to Congo. 'All shops burnt and goods looted,' Watta cabled. 'People started robbing each other.'[19]

In Terekeka, a two-day march north of Juba, police led nine Northerners to the river bank and opened fire. One leapt into the water and escaped, another was wounded and survived by feigning death. Nearby in Tali, a medical assistant grabbed an 11-month-old baby boy of a Northern merchant from the arms of his mother. He swung him by the leg, beating him to death on the ground.[20]

South Sudan marks the outbreak of the mutiny on 18 August as Heroes Day.

* * *

Ten days later it was over. Leaderless, disorganised and outgunned, the mutineers ran out of steam. They conceded defeat on 27 August. 'Please send British troops immediately to safeguard Southern troops when arms are surrendered,' they begged. Four days later, Northern soldiers cautiously entered Torit, advancing down the ransacked empty streets fearing attack. They need not have worried. The mutineers had long fled into the bush.

A handful of survivors stumbled out from church mission buildings. 'The bodies of some Northerners had not been buried, and the town stank with a foul smell and noise of howling dogs,' officers reported. 'All soldiers and civilians had evacuated the town completely as the surrender negotiations were going on. They were convinced that Northern troops were going to kill them.'[21]

A total of 261 Northerners were listed as killed across the South.[22]

* * *

The mutiny shocked the British. 'What happens here will set the pace for us all over Africa and the Middle East,' Churchill warned.[23] The people were claiming back their land, and the end of Britain's empire would be swift. The violence made London determined to pull out as quickly as possible. Sudan was one of the first dominos of independence that would reverberate around the world.

'Deep bitterness is a fact, and the recent events must greatly delay the realisation of a really united Sudan. They may well have destroyed any sound hope of it that ever existed,' Governor Sir Knox Helm wrote to the Foreign Office after the mutiny.[24] 'It has been far more than a military revolt and, though most Sudanese here, including the government, will try to delude themselves that with the Torit surrender the troubles are over, this is certainly not the case. The military revolt was simply an open expression of the South's inborn suspicion, fear and hatred of the North, and there can be no doubt that the entire South was solidly behind the revolt.'

Washington was worried too. A CIA briefing days after the mutiny warned that the long-term impacts were 'likely to be serious for

relations between the northern-dominated government and the southern tribesman.'[25]

The Bog Barons could see the disaster coming all too clearly. In
1951, as Major Hilary Hook left his command in the Equatoria Corps,
his sergeant-major bid farewell to the 'Ingliz' officer with ominous
words. 'On the day that the Ingliz leave us there will be bloodshed and
more bloodshed,' he told Hook. 'You will hear of it in Ingliterra and be
sad, they will never govern us from Khartoum—never.'[26] As Hook flew
home, he brooded on the warning. 'The old man was seldom wrong,'
Hook said.

The officers were furious. Men who had dedicated their lives in
government service to Britain and Sudan, found their loyalties now lay
with the people of the South. They wanted British officers to stay on as
'guardians' to run the South as a trusteeship before full independence
in ten, perhaps twenty years. Britain's Southern Policy had been a mistake, so the very least they could do would be to try to fix that, they
argued. It was not to be.

Some resigned on principle: men who had won medals for their courage in defending Britain in the past. Ranald Boyle, DC in Bahr el Ghazal,
was a former naval officer and war hero. London 'sold the Southern
Sudanese down the river' to appease Egypt, he said. 'Britain refused to
listen, abandoned safeguards, gave in to outside pressures and deserted
her friends,' he wrote. He called the deal 'The Great Betrayal'.[27]

As Boyle feared, Britain's abandoning of the South in a trade-off with
Cairo to safeguard the Suez Canal would be pointless. In 1956, less
than a year after Sudan's independence, British paratroopers, along
with French and Israeli commandos, tried to capture Suez by force.
Egypt celebrated their humiliating defeat.

Richard Owen, the Governor of Bahr el Ghazal, handed in his notice.
'The most contemptible renunciation of responsibility in our history,'
wrote the man who had served twenty-seven years in Sudan, warning it
would relegate the people 'to neglect and exploitation, and in time (have
no doubt) to the recrudescence of the slave trade.'[28] He died in 1982, all
too tragically aware his worst fears had been realised. 'Years of tragedy,
oppression, revolt, racial hatred and horror,' he wrote.

* * *

I sat behind Justin Lodinga, a soldier-turned-farmer, weaving our way down the dirt track half an hour outside Torit on his smoky Chinese-built 125cc motorbike taxi, which coughed and lurched its way along with a bundle of firewood on its back. Lodinga, a solidly-built 35-year-old wearing his old army T-shirt, headed down a thin gap in the yellow grass by a battered metal signpost with a faded painted flag of South Sudan. The sign said it was a memorial shrine to the revolution.

Soon there was a clearing. I had come to see the site of the mass graves of the mutineers who died in the fighting, or were executed afterwards. I sat in the shade of the tree as Lodinga chatted to me, but he did not know how many were buried here. He too had fled the war to Uganda, returning months before with his belongings and family balanced precariously on his motorbike. The mutiny happened in the days of his father, and the stories of that violence were muddled in the madness of the years of war that were to follow. He shrugged with a smile, snapping a stick of sugar cane in two and offering me half to chew.

After their surrender, Southern soldiers were rounded up. Some 147 were sentenced to death, a mix of soldiers, police and civilians. Around a thousand were jailed.[29] There was no conciliatory approach, rather a heavy-handed crackdown to instil order and punish the rebels, without addressing the fundamental fears that had sparked the violence.

Colonial putdowns of rebellion had been ruthless. The new masters in Khartoum would simply put those lessons into practice, to deadly effect. Khartoum—soon to be free of British oversight—directed efforts not into encouraging democratic reforms and economic development to woo the South and persuade it union was best, but rather into crushing opposition with force. After the mutiny, Khartoum could not trust Southern troops, and the loyalties of police were seen as 'unreliable'.[30] For many communities, the only sign of government action would be the army imposing its control. It provided ample motivation for the next generation of fighters.

Alison Magaya, who had spend much of the second half of the 20th century fighting Khartoum as rebel, was only 10 when the mutiny broke out. Still, he spoke emotionally about how his uncle Bullen Ngangi Kpasuwa was hanged for opposing the government. As the rope was put around his neck, he screamed out to the crowd. 'Even if I die, one day you Arabs will still leave Southern Sudan,' he shouted.[31] There may have been little consciousness of a separate 'Southern' identity, but the songs in the cattle camps found a common cause across the many peoples—they sang of anger and hostility towards 'Arabs'.[32]

As for Oboyo, the man with the bow and arrow who sparked it all, it was never clear what happened. His fate is shrouded in the confusion of the times, polished by legend. Arrested after his arrow attack, he escaped when he was released by mutineers who stormed the prison. One said he was later recaptured and executed, but another described how he fled to the bush to fight for the next three decades, dying in battle in 1986.[33]

* * *

In later years, both North and South have backed the impression that a unified Sudan was doomed from the start, and mark 1955 as the starting date for war. For the North, it exonerated their failure to create peace by blaming the 'evil colonial policies' they inherited.[34] The South was rotten when they got it, they argued, so it was not their fault unity collapsed. For the South, those who believed independence was inevitable saw it as a sign that unity was always fundamentally flawed.

Yet conflict was not inevitable, and the mutiny in Torit did not lead immediately to war. Mutineers escaped to the bush to stage guerrilla attacks, but Southern politicians still tried to implement a programme of federalisation they had decided the year before. The efforts were quashed: Khartoum saw federation as a step towards separation, and those who campaigned for it, guilty of sedition.[35] Options were closed, and the South was pushed towards breaking point.

'The Arabs, it appeared to us, had not merely stepped into the English shoes, they were bent on bringing back slavery,' journalist Jacob Akol said. He remembered tales of 'diabolical and cowardly' Northern revenge after Torit that he heard as a schoolboy. 'True or false, we believed it,' Akol said. 'Being a "Southerner" was becoming a solid concept in our minds—we were not as yet clear on the limits of the Dinka territory.'[36]

The mutiny was a messy failure, but romanticised hindsight describes it as the pivotal moment that kicked off the struggle for the nation. When the South's rebel chief John Garang signed the peace deal in 2005 from that round of conflict, he marked the war as beginning with the Torit Mutiny.[37]

'They are our heroes,' said Lodinga, as he drove me back to town on his bike, leaning around to chat to me, and waving one hand for emphasis as he weaved between potholes at speed. 'They fired the shots for freedom.'

* * *

On New Year's Day 1956, Britain's Union Jack and Egypt's flag were lowered and the flag of an independent Sudan was raised. 'The world has gained a new nation,' the British newsreader on the Pathé news broadcast narrated over dramatic music. 'The Sudan, for 58 years under the joint rule of Britain and Egypt, becomes an independent republic.' The crowds cheered in excited hope. Within the next five years, over two dozen African nations would win independence. 'The wind of change is blowing through this continent,' Britain's Prime Minister Harold Macmillan said.

Over half a century later, I stared at the flag in the Presidential Palace in Khartoum where those independence celebrations had taken place. Now the flag drooped limply from the pole. In fact, everything drooped limply. Not only was it boiling hot, and the gaggle of reporters had been waiting for hours for the president to speak, but people were fasting for Ramadan. We hadn't drunk water all day. A palace waiter in thickly starched white uniform offered a jug of deliciously scented *karkadi* hibiscus juice to me as a non-Muslim. Droplets ran down the ice-cold jug, but it seemed wrong to drink in front of the thirsty stares of a crowd of colleagues, and I declined. My friend Abdelmoneim Abu Idris, another journalist, shook his head and went after the waiter, bringing me back a glass of the ruby-coloured juice. We peered down into the courtyard at the elegant white colonnaded arches as I gulped it down. This was the colonial rebuilding of the palace where Gordon's head was hacked off.

It was 2010, months before South Sudan would vote on independence. I had just come from Juba. The mood there was exuberant, the people actually dancing in the streets at rally after rally campaigning for separation. People there were counting down the days until they believed South Sudan's flag would replace that of the united North and South.

The mood was entirely the opposite in Khartoum. 'I'm worried for the future,' Abdulmoneim said glumly. 'Completely worried. I understand why they would vote for independence, I do. If the South goes, there will be economic, security, border problems, but also, I just don't want them to go. It makes me sad if we divide into two. We are all Sudanese. I wish we could make it work.'

I thought of what might have been: if, when the flag of an independent Sudan was raised in Khartoum all those decades before, a flag of a separate South had been lifted too, what would South Sudan look like today?

Instead, the South would have to fight for their nation. It would be a struggle that would last just as long as British rule.

5

THE VENOM REBELLION

'*Whatever happens, they have machine guns, and we have not.*'
South Sudan rebel newspaper, 1963[1]

General Joseph Lagu can list the entire armoury with which he started a war for freedom: three antique guns and a rusty machete. 'We began fighting for our independence with our bare hands,' said Lagu, who mutinied in 1963 as a 32-year lieutenant, while home on leave. 'We knew our cause was right, but we lacked the tools to do it with.'

Half a century later, Lagu spooned sugar after sugar into my thick coffee strong with ginger and cardamom. We sat on the small veranda of his simple bungalow, down a rutted backstreet in the rundown Hai Jalaba district of Juba. Rusted rain gutters lay where they had fallen years before, and paint peeled in long strips off the walls. In the fierce heat of the midday sun, the lizards made gentle sounds as their tiny feet pattered across the hot tin roof above.

A fading photograph behind him on a dusty shelf showed him in his prime, a thickset and powerful man with a small, neatly groomed moustache staring angrily at the camera. Back then he wore a sharply-ironed army uniform, with the wide gold embroidered epaulettes showing the crossed sword and baton of a general. It exuded power and authority.

Much had changed, and the octogenarian's eyes were now almost blue at the edges, hazy with age and cataracts. Grey ran from the stubble on his chin into his thin hair. His shirt was frayed at the collar, the colour faded. Yet his mind was still sharp with details, and he described with vigour the guns the men with him took into the bush to begin the fight.

First, there was an ancient muzzleloader. It was the sort you'd pack with powder and homemade metal scraps, blasting wildly and hoping that if it actually did fire, it didn't simply explode back in your own face. He counted the weapons on his fingers, as though preparing for a long list.

Secondly, there was a decrepit hunting rifle, firing large calibre .404 bullets that had been popular decades before with pith-helmet-wearing big-game hunters seeking elephant, lion or rhino. That rifle fired thumb-sized bullets strong enough to knock down a buffalo. Lagu's, however, had a broken extractor. 'After you fired, you had to hit the bullet casing out with a rock,' Lagu said. 'That's just not the sort of thing you want to be doing in a close fight.'

Thirdly and finally, they had a colonial-era gun dating from the 19th century: a Martini-Henry rifle, a British army relic like those carried by the soldiers who died alongside Gordon in 1885. 'I, myself?' Lagu said, opening his hands wide, then bringing them together with a clap and a grin. 'I carried a machete.'

It was a pathetic arsenal to take on the army of Africa's biggest nation, well-equipped with troops, tanks, airplanes and helicopters. Lagu leaned forward, his face serious now, his brow furrowed. 'We saw no other option than to fight for the right of our people to live in freedom,' he said.

* * *

Lagu was born in 1931, in a village among rolling green hills covered in banana trees, some three days walk south of Juba. His father had worked as a clerk for the British, which meant Lagu was sent to the South's only secondary school in Rumbek. There, the boy from the Madi people studied alongside those from the bigger Dinka and Nuer groups. Colonial officers grandly called the tin-roof college the 'Eton of the South' or 'Dinkchester', referring to the influence its old boys later wielded in politics, the army or business. For Lagu, it was a ticket to army officer training college in Khartoum.

In the years after the British left, Khartoum tightened its control over the South. The government clamped down on outside influences, especially foreign missionaries. Removing them was shaking off colonialism, Khartoum said. They were cast as corrupting forces converting Muslims to Christians.

However, they still provided education, the only healthcare for vast areas, and even emergency food aid across the South. In 1962, the Missionary Societies Act tightly restricted their activities. Eventually, all foreign missionaries would be expelled—and that meant independent witnesses of army crackdowns vanished. 'Once the foreign missionaries had gone, the North could do what it liked with the South,' journalist Jacob Akol remembered.[2] 'There would be no foreigners to witness what was going on.' The language of instruction in schools switched to Arabic, a step many saw as Islamising the South.[3]

By 1963, anger was growing, and the politicians demanded change. 'Open segregation marks the relationship between Northern and Southern,' wrote opposition leaders Joseph Oduho and William Deng. 'We demand nothing short of self-determination, after which we shall be good friends.'[4]

Oduho, a former schoolmaster, and Deng, an ex-civil servant, fled with other leaders into exile in neighbouring Uganda, a motley mix including policeman Gordon Muortat and Saturnino Lohure, a Catholic priest. The briefcase rebels dreamed up names and drafted policies. One suggested the Pan-African Freedom Fighters; a rival proposed the Southern Sudan Liberation Movement; another the Azania Secret Army.

On paper, the South's leaders called for political solutions. Behind the scenes, they planned for war.

'I was assigned the duty to found South Sudan's army to challenge the North, because it was no longer a national army but rather one of repression,' Lagu said. 'I organised the men. They were a collection of ex-soldiers, ex-policeman and schoolboys.' Many of the men went barefoot, most at first carried spears or bows and arrows.

'We wanted freedom. The North refused the option of federation; they wanted to rule us as a colony they had inherited,' Lagu told me. 'We said, if you are coming as another imperialist, we cannot accept you. We fought to have the South as an independent country.'

* * *

US troops were heading to Vietnam, and Martin Luther King had just delivered his 'I have a dream' speech. The world's attention was far away when Lagu launched his war on 19 September 1963.

'Our patience has now come to an end and we are convinced that only the use of force will bring a decision,' the rebel manifesto read as they announced their army.[5] 'We do not want mercy and are not prepared to give it.'

Lagu called the force the 'Anya-Nya', the name for snake venom, a title that brought with it powerful associations of death, magic and strength. Hunters from his Madi people used the poison extracted from the glands of a cobra to make deadly arrows, while potion-makers added drops to brews. Lagu liked the way the Anya-Nya name echoed the hugely feared Mau Mau in neighbouring Kenya, the anti-colonial guerrillas who had just helped pave the way for Kenya's independence. 'Even if it falls on your body through the pores of the skin, the poison will penetrate,' Lagu said. 'There is no cure on earth for it, you just have to die. So the name was chosen to indicate our determination.'[6]

His first attack was to plant explosives to blow up a bridge outside the town of Yei. It was not an auspicious start: the charges failed to destroy the bridge. 'It only caused some cracks in the concrete surface,' Lagu admitted. It did, however, draw troops out to investigate. Lagu's strike force, a gang of ex-soldiers, schoolboys and a wayward Catholic priest, crouched in the grass. 'I only had the machete in my hand, but I was at the lead with the men to direct their fire. We waited for the army patrol to pass, and then the three gunmen and the men with bows and arrows opened fire on the final vehicle,' he said. 'Unfortunately, the muzzleloader misfired, but the others shot, and then we ran. We could hear them firing back at us as we took to our heels.'

That night, celebrating the first attack, the rebel camp was stormed and the men scattered. Later they discovered it had not been soldiers, but rather a herd of buffalo. 'What laughter when we realised the truth!' Lagu said. Still, some of the men took the chance and fled for good. Only three-quarters of the force regrouped.[7]

They had courage, but their arsenal was little more sophisticated than the poisoned arrows of their name. Crude petrol bombs were about their most dramatic weapon. 'We did not have landmines at the time, so we'd use road obstacles such as digging holes, planting nails or chopping down trees in narrow places to block roads,' Lagu said. 'We organised ambushes. We could not attack them in their strongholds where they were dug in, because our army was still weak. But we'd wait for them, hide in the bushes, and destroy them.'

* * *

The call to arms found willing listeners, even if most were driven by fury at Khartoum for injustices done, rather than being a politically conscious class clearly fighting for separation.

The rebels gathered guns as best they could. Rifles came from raids on police or army posts, or from defecting soldiers. One Anya-Nya recruit called Noel connived with a 'patriotic girl' to seduce a policeman. 'After they were served with local drinks, Noel pretended that he was going outside for refreshments, and left his friend inside the hut,' historian Arop Madut-Arop recalled. 'While the policeman stripped off his clothes, having put away his gun and was about to have his time with the girl, Noel rushed in.' He snatched the gun, firing it into the air as he ran.[8] Another rebel took a cow's jawbone and wrapped it up in cloth, pushing it into the back of a policeman. The policeman, thinking it was a pistol, laid down his rifle, leaving the rebel to grab the gun and scamper off.

Lagu was not the only one fighting; some soldiers had been carrying out bandit-style ambushes ever since escaping after the mutiny in Torit. Rival factions carried out scrappy, uncoordinated attacks. Without guns, however, the rebels posed little threat. 'You scorn the Anya-Nya as though they were wet hens,' the rebels sang.[9] 'You call them bow and arrow people, but they will kill you like chickens.' Yet they needed far more than scary songs to have any hope of victory. A war next door would give Lagu the weapons to fight.

* * *

'The ill wind that blew over the Congo, blew good over the Southern Sudan,' Lagu said, rocking back into the deep chair, and wistfully remembering the guns he gained from a neighbour's war. 'It gave us the guns we needed.' The air was hot and sleepy in the afternoon sun of Juba. He held his hands across his belly, and gave a deep sigh.

It was the height of the Cold War, but the rival ideologies of capital-ism and communism as dreamed in Washington and Moscow transformed into something very different on the ground. Congo's first democratically elected leader, Patrice Lumumba, had been assassinated months after independence in 1961 with the backing of the CIA and Belgian security forces, and replaced with a more Western-friendly government. They brought in Belgian commandos and a 300-strong army of mercenary misfits led by ex-British army Major 'Mad Mike' Hoare to defend it, a mob of former French Foreign legionaries and SAS soldiers dubbed 'The Wild Geese'.

Moscow backed Congo's Simba rebels, 'The Lions', sending in weapons via allies in Khartoum. Russian cargo planes flew guns to Juba, which were then loaded onto Sudan army convoys going into Congo. The trucks, trundling along slow mud tracks, cut through elephant grass that stood higher than a man; they were perfect targets for an ambush.[10] 'Weapons manufactured in China and Russia were brought through Sudan,' Lagu said with a chuckle. 'They were never meant for us, but we attacked them on the way.' It caught the attention of spies far away.

Fresh from napalm bombing runs against the Viet Cong in Laos, CIA agent Dick Holm arrived in Congo in 1964. He applied the same ruthless tactics along the Sudan border.[11] Hunting rebels scattered over forest the size of France, the CIA used nimble two-seater T-28 airplanes to swoop down, bombard remote camps and machine gun those fleeing. Lagu's men became his eyes on the ground.

It was a strange band. The war not only pitched Congolese against Congolese and Sudanese against Sudanese, but also Cuban against Cuban. Che Guevara and a 200-strong Cuban guerrilla force were also in Congo with the Simba, hoping to spark an African revolution. The CIA used scores of anti-Castro Cuban paramilitaries, unable to fight on home turf after the failed Bay of Pigs invasion.[12] 'We knew there were Cubans from Fidel… and we went to fight them,' said CIA pilot Juan Peron, who flew bombing raids along the Congo-Sudan border. 'I was happy about it.'[13]

Lagu's men were in the forests amid the elephants and rhino of Congo's Garamba national park, tracking the weapon convoys. 'I worked with the Americans, the Congolese air force, and Cuban pilots who came there as exiles,' Lagu said, describing how the CIA taught him to mark out drop zones for weapons. 'When we learned of a convoy we'd alert the Congo government, and the airplanes would come and bomb them. In return they'd drop us weapons.'

Congo is a tough place to operate. In the thick jungles the humidity is like mist, while on the plains, the crackling elephant grass is yellowed by intense sun. It was a grim war. 'Dreadful and brutal,' Anya-Nya veteran Alison Magaya called it.[14] When one Cuban CIA pilot crashed in a bombing raid, he vanished. 'Months later, missionary reports confirmed that he had been captured, killed, and eaten by the Simba,' Holm said. When Holm himself was severely burned in a plane crash, he knew that escape was the only option; he hacked off the charred flesh from his fingers and paddled out on canoes down the river for days.

Slowly, the Simba retreated, splitting into bandit gangs and slipping into the forests. The Congolese fought for their interests, not the grand ideologies of the outsiders. 'This is the history of a failure,' Che Guevara wrote in his diaries in 1965, wet and miserable in the Congo jungle. The Cubans packed up, their dreams dashed. 'Numbers are not what matters,' Che said in a morose letter to Castro. 'We can't liberate by ourselves a country that does not want to fight; you've got to create a fighting spirit and look for soldiers with the torch of Diogenes and the patience of Job—a task that becomes more difficult, the more shits there are doing things along the way.'[15]

Khartoum, keen not to isolate itself but to maintain relations with Western powers, eased its Soviet links. In turn, the CIA flow of guns for the Anya-Nya stopped. Distant geopolitics impacted the South. 'Since whatever we were getting from Congo was masterminded by America, when a pro-Western party came to power in Khartoum, that supply dried up,' Lagu said.

Yet for now, the rebels had what they needed. There were enough guns to fuel the war.

* * *

The Anya-Nya drew up a flag for the new country they fought for; a wild buffalo stomping its feet signified strength, a snake and arrow poison, against a background of horizontal stripes. Green was for the land they battled for; black was for Africa; red symbolised the blood sacrifice being spilt and white was the hope the South would one day be at peace. That, however, was still far off.

Weapons in hand, the rebels escalated raids. Some forces were organised, others emerged spontaneously, as communities decided they too had had enough, and came to join in the fight. Rebels ambushed Khartoum's convoys, hurling petrol bombs to torch those inside. Civilians were targeted too. 'You have permitted your own government to mobilise you against our people,' the rebels said in a public threat to anyone seen as from the North, or of Arab descent. 'You have confirmed this death sentence by your continuing to oppress and exploit our people… from now on your lot shall be misery.'[16]

Lagu looked back with remorse on those attacks. 'There was racial hatred on both sides, for I hated the Northern Sudanese, I regret to say, but this sprang from the injury they had done to us,' he said. 'Later, I realised that the massacre of Northern civilians, simply because of their difference in colour of skin and appearance, was wrong. For that, we in South Sudan were also guilty of racism.'

* * *

Khartoum was merciless in retaliation. Captured fighters were hanged or shot, and whole villages were burned. Hundreds were arrested, people disappeared and suspected fighters were tortured. 'I was stripped naked, feet tied and hanged upside down,' captured rebel Philip Lomodong said. He was taken to the 'torture zone' in the town of Kodok. Bodies hung from trees along the banks of the Nile.[17] 'The soldiers jumped on my chest, kicking me several times while lashing with whips made of hippo skin,' Lomodong added. 'We were left for several days without food, water and medical attention. Our wounds were treated only by using hot pepper.'

Horrific torture took place in the military prison in Wau. 'A metal ring was placed around the head of the prisoners,' one priest wrote, after talking to survivors.[18] 'Two small balls of some hard material were then placed against his temples. Then the ring was tightened, forcing the balls further and further into his temple until the eyes were almost pushed out.'

* * *

Some said the shooting started with a fight over a woman. A Southerner stabbed a Northern soldier, whose comrades then fought back. Others said it was an attack long in the making.

The evening of 8 July 1965 was a Thursday—the night before the weekend, now that Friday rather than Sunday had been made the weekly holiday as part of Khartoum's Islamisation of the South. The heat of the day had faded, and the soldiers went to the cinema. The streets outside were packed with tea stalls, women selling roasted corn and bowls of beans.

That night, the soldiers carried their rifles. Three hours after sunset, they marched back to the barracks, singing war songs. Then the shooting started. 'We jumped out of bed, but I told my wife and children to lie down on the floor,' one witness told rebels later. 'We stayed there while shooting and screaming went on around us... We could hear the roar of flames and see their reflections flickering on the walls.'[19] Whole districts were torched. People fled, many seeking shelter in churches or mosques. They were not safe even there. 'Some ten people were taken out of the Protestant Cathedral and shot dead,' another witness said. 'Soldiers shooting in the mosques told the Southern Sudanese that they do not resemble Muslims.' Educated Southerners were targeted and hunted down in such numbers that many believed there was a detailed kill list.[20] When people ventured out at dawn, corpses lined the streets.

Troops also went to Juba hospital. 'The army went there and shot at the doctors who were operating in the theatre,' another witness said. 'They managed to escape through the back windows. The army then shot all the wounded who were waiting to be operated on, including the ones left by the doctors on the theatre table.'

No one knows the exact figure of how many died, but few dispute the severity of the killings. Most agree at least 1,400 were killed, though the rebels claimed many more.[21] The killings spread. Two days later, a wedding party in Wau was attacked, leaving 76 dead. There were more shootings in Yambio, Maridi, Torit and Bor. It was a turning point in the conflict.

'The Juba massacre marks a decisive stage,' South Sudanese students at Khartoum University wrote in a protest letter. 'The Arab forces in Juba, on no grounds, butchered defenceless, law-abiding Southerners—women, men, children, young and old.'[22]

* * *

Khartoum had all the cards. At the crossroads between the Arab and African worlds, the continent's biggest nation stretched from Kenya to

Egypt to Congo, controlled the world's longest river and had key Red Sea access. Khartoum played both sides in the Cold War, and weapons poured in. Western nations wanted to ensure Sudan remained on the right side of communism, so ex-rulers Britain sent supplies and aid, and the US sent helicopters.[23] So did the Soviet Union, East Germany, Yugoslavia, and China. Arab nations sent guns too.

The rebels had no one. They called their isolation the 'Grass Curtain', comparing the South being shuttered from the world to Eastern Europe behind the Iron Curtain. African nations did not want to help. The Organisation of African Unity, the forerunner of the African Union, supported liberation movements across the continent—but only if they maintained colonial borders. African nations did not want to set a precedent to inspire independence movements inside their own country, and the Anya-Nya's rebellion was secessionist. 'What prevails in the South today is Arab colonialism pure and simple,' the Anya-Nya argued. 'It is a system based on racial superiority, political dominance and economic subjection.'[24] The appeal was ignored.

Without supplies, they would have to surrender. Lagu had another idea. Sitting in the bush, hunted by an Arab enemy, his eye turned north to seek help from a country with similar challenges. Israel was celebrating success in the 1967 Six Day War, a pre-emptive strike that smashed Egypt's air force and seized the Sinai Peninsula. Sudan had sent troops north to help Egypt defend the Suez Canal, facing Israeli soldiers across the waters.

'The enemy of my enemy is my friend,' Lagu said with a broad smile, describing how he wrote a letter to the Israeli Prime Minister Levi Eshkol.

'Well, of course, I flattered him in the letter,' Lagu said, giving me a wink. 'I wrote, "Ooh, I am happy that you, the Chosen People of God Almighty, you have beaten the Arabs! For I am fighting those very same Arabs myself. So if you support me, Mr Prime Minister, there is one thing I will do well. I will tie down the Sudanese army and prevent them from going north to fight you alongside the Egyptians."'

The next phase of the war was about to begin.

6

TARZAN AND THE ZEBRA BUS

'In the name of Peace, let your skulls be heaped to ashes. In the name of Progress, may the mortars demolish your homes.'

Anya-Nya leaflet, 1971.[1]

Tumbling high from the blue sky, the wooden crates slid out from the back of the airplane. The engines growled as the propellers pulled it out of a sharp dive. Seconds later, a line of white parachutes punched open behind. Boxes floated down onto the dirt airstrip, hacked out by hand from head-high elephant grass. Inside were the weapons that would create an effective guerrilla army to end seventeen years of conflict. It was 1969, a time of love and drugs at Woodstock and Neil Armstrong bouncing on the moon. Yet there were few signs of the outside world in the remote rebel headquarters at Owiny-Kibul, in the tangled forests along the Ugandan border. In the local Acholi language, Owiny-Kibul means 'you will hear the drums'. It is a lonely, wild place that even today takes days of bone-shaking driving down tracks smashed through the scrub.

Only a radio antenna stretching out from the roof of a grass hut, the hissing smoke of a red signal flare and the three Israeli commandos cheering along with the hundreds of rebels gave clues to the operation about to unfold. It would change the fate of South Sudan forever.

'Will we have peace with Sudan? How long will the war go on?' the women sang, clapping and dancing with high-pitched wailing ululations, swaying to the beat of the song and calling on their rebel chief. 'Joseph Lagu, you have guns, fight the Arabs! Our children are dying, Joseph Lagu, fight!'

The plane made a second pass, with another load of crates drifting down to the celebrating crowds. 'It was a beautiful sight,' said Mossad commander David Ben-Uziel. Both he and Lagu were lifted onto the shoulders of the troops as they danced. 'The men all gathered around, staring at the equipment and the guns,' Ben-Uziel said. 'They'd never seen such a large quantity of arms.' Shouting to the troops, the officers barked orders to ensure the crates were dragged away to safety under trees. The rebels were terrified the airdrop would catch the attention of government troops in Juba. They sent lumbering aircraft on daily reconnaissance flights, rolling out bombs from the bay doors if they spotted rebel camps below.

The arsenal was so huge it took two hours to clear the weapons from the field and into the camp. One by one, the crates were prised open; machine guns, mortars, rifles, bazookas, bombs and landmines. There were uniforms to replace tattered shirts, crates of medicine with vaccines on ice, and radio transmitters. It would allow the ragged rebels to operate as an army. A new batch of foreigners had come to the South, bringing another round of change.

'We were on the brink of commencing operations that would impact the entire region, influence international relations and draw the world's attention to this god-forsaken wilderness,' Ben-Uziel told me. 'I came to assist these people to stand on their feet, and I came to beat those who made them suffer.'

* * *

Five decades later, streams of people pushed through the security barriers in the blinding Mediterranean sunshine outside Tel Aviv's Azrieli train station. It was an eclectic mix: platinum-blonde women in skin tight white jeans walking sausage dogs; beefy security men with ear pieces; hipsters with flowing beards pushing tiny bicycles. A crew of teenage girls in army uniform, fingernails painted sparkly pink, stood laughing as they shouldered heavy rifles. I scoured the crowds, but I was not sure who I was looking for—I didn't know what a top Mossad spy would look like. As a veteran secret agent, Ben-Uziel had been reassuringly traditional in the meeting arrangements he provided by telephone. 'By the main train station exit at 11 o'clock,' he said. 'I'll find you.'

The 81-year-old former Israeli paratrooper colonel came towards me, a tall imposing man with craggy features, neatly cut grey hair and rimless glasses, dressed in a well-ironed blue checked shirt. He was an Israeli commando legend, twice decorated by the age of only 12, when he joined Jewish insurgent Irgun guerrillas fighting British troops ahead of Israel's 1948 declaration of independence. Back then, my grandfather was his enemy—a naval captain serving the British Mandate for Palestine, ordered to stop the boatloads of Jewish refugees fleeing Europe's horrors to create a new nation. He was posted to Ben-Uziel's birthplace, the port of Haifa. With a hand crushing grip and an unblinking stare Ben-Uziel said to me simply: 'Call me Tarzan.'

Tarzan was a nickname he was given aged 14—when the jungle films were popular—after he saved a friend from drowning. The South Sudanese rebels called him by the code name 'Mister John'. Later, after Lagu formally named him 'architect of the Anya-Nya', he was given the rebel rank of colonel.

To the Israelis, however, he was one of their greatest war heroes, a special forces assassin who risked all in raids against Arab forces. He fought deep behind the lines in Gaza and Jordan, as part of the Unit 101 commandos, a feared 50-man operation led by Ariel Sharon in the early 1950s. Feted at home, it was hated by Palestinians, after they massacred scores in the West Bank village of Qibya in 1953.

The unit was disbanded after Qibya. Its members were sent to turn the fledgling army into the powerful Israel Defence Forces of today, inspiring the soldiers with the ferocious can-do spirit of the 101. 'The unit changed the army,' he said. It forged the backbone—and in many ways helped mould the modern identity—of a nation. He wanted to do the same in South Sudan.

* * *

Mossad had received Lagu's letter. They sent a team to see what they could do, and Tarzan was named mission commander. He knew first-hand how to forge an army with a dedicated band of fighters and a handful of guns. He had also spent time operating on the continent, including two years in South Africa working for the Zionist Youth Movement. The apartheid system there horrified him, and he delighted in riling white bus passengers by a stubborn refusal to obey segregation rules. Mossad then sent him to Ethiopia, where he trained death squads for Emperor Haile Selassie to carry out assassinations and bomb attacks in neighbouring Somalia. He was one of the toughest soldiers Israel had produced, but the initial three-week mission to South Sudan would stretch him to breaking point.

In May 1969, a Mossad team of three flew to the Kenyan capital Nairobi, before heading for South Sudan. Each man brought with them a special belt carrying 50 gold sovereigns sewn in, but since they arrived in Kenya posing as tourists, their military kit had to be left behind. Their first task in Nairobi was therefore shopping, but the Israelis found that there were few stores able to supply men about to embark on a secret mission to back a rebel army fighting for a new country. 'We could only buy colourful children's school water bottles, the kind that have a sticker where you fill in your child's name and classroom,' Tarzan said. 'They were ridiculous, but that was all we could find.'

They drove west along the Equator on a two-day road trip to neighbouring Uganda, through the lush tea farms and thick banana plantations on rolling hills. The team headed north. After hours of driving, they cut off onto thin, dirt roads to meet a rebel platoon led by Lagu himself, waving a flashing light. A team of thirty rebels waited to carry the kit and sneak across the border into Sudan.

The jungles there are thick and twisted, the sun fierce. Where there are trails, they are narrow and weave through dense thorn trees. They knit together above the route, cutting out any chance of cooling breezes. Clouds of whining mosquitoes hang above the head. There are no bridges to cross the rushing rivers of thick and muddy water. Each time, the troops had to strip down to carry their guns and radio kit precariously on their heads.

* * *

It took three days of marching before they stumbled exhausted into the rebel headquarters at Owiny-Kibul. Men blew cow horns in welcome. 'The soldiers stood to attention, fully aware of the fact that they were representing the Anya-Nya,' Tarzan said. 'They conducted a changing of the guard parade with typical British pageantry, despite the fact that most of them were wearing rags. They were a quiet people—disciplined, polite, and shy in a way.'

The land there is fertile, with lush fields of cassava and groundnut, vegetables and fruit trees. Beyond that, there was little else. Its only strategic defence was remoteness. Gloomily, Tarzan realised that the stronghold of rebel defence was a clearing in the trees, and they were unable to defend even that. Lagu said he had a tiny force of a few hundred men with guns, each having only a few bullets per weapon. 'No one is bothered by a baby's bite because babies don't have teeth,' Lagu told Tarzan. 'Once we have teeth, we'll be able to make a statement and they'll have to take us seriously.' The teeth he wanted were Israel's guns.

Mossad called it 'the periphery doctrine', and Sudan was only one piece of the jigsaw. With limited cash and resources, and surrounded by hostile Arab neighbours furious at the loss of land, Israel developed a sweeping strategy. Mossad made unlikely allies with the opposition of its enemies; to the north, secret missions went to Turkey, Iran and Iraq. To the south, the policy focused on the Horn of Africa, ensuring allies controlled the vital shipping lane for Israel's access to the Red Sea through the Bab el Mandab—the 'Gate of Tears'—the narrow and rocky stretch of sea between Africa and Arabia. Mossad agents slipped into Ethiopia, Yemen, Somalia and Kenya.

In Sudan, Mossad chief Zvi Zamir had three goals.[2] 'The first was to prevent the integration of the Sudanese military units in the Egyptian force deployed on the Israeli-Egyptian border, by keeping Sudan's army occupied,' Zamir said. 'Our second goal was to strengthen operative ties with Kenya and Ethiopia, nations we considered Israel's periphery and known as the "outer ring".' The final mission objective aimed for something far more ambitious: 'To extend aid to a nation fighting for its independence and liberation from Islamic tyranny,' Zamir said.

Sudanese troops faced Israeli soldiers in the Sinai Peninsula. There were tens of thousands of soldiers on that frontline. Now a new battle zone was being opened up. In South Sudan, the Israeli force was a total of three.

* * *

The Anya-Nya took the Israelis on a marathon trek deep into the misty mountains and forests of the southeast. 'We saw a people who seemed to have no right to exist other than as slaves, because the north could do what they wanted,' said Tarzan. 'We met with villagers whose very survival was at stake.'

One elderly chief recounted how his village was torched for harbouring suspected Anya-Nya fighters, the men killed and crops destroyed. Government soldiers swept the land in a scorched earth policy, forcing villagers at gunpoint to leave their homes. Huts were burned and crops destroyed, to leave nothing to help the rebels. Villagers were then ordered to build new huts, surrounding army barracks as human shields. They were little more than forced labour camps, designed to divide the Anya-Nya from ordinary civilians. Anyone found outside was considered a rebel. Khartoum called them 'peace villages'.

'We'd been set down in a region that geographically was on Earth, but when it came to the people living there, it was like another planet,' Tarzan said. 'Political considerations, our periphery policy, none of that interested the people we'd met. What mattered was whether anyone was going to help them extricate themselves from their dire situation, whether their children might have a chance to live rather than suffer the slow death that faced them.' People were struggling for the most basic of freedoms. 'The common man didn't think about a state of independence,' Tarzan said. 'They were fighting for survival.'

He was startled at just how dire the conditions were. Tarzan had come in the expectation that by giving a little in terms of weapons and aid, he could help tip the balance of an ongoing war. He found a people in rags with machetes and a few guns facing a heavily armed and well-equipped modern army with fighter jets, tanks and helicopters. 'Khartoum had an army of so many men with airplanes—why didn't they simply wipe the Southerners out? It was a no man's land: you can come, you can rape, you can kill. Whatever you do, no one knows. Who else would have come? The UN? Hah! What would they have done with all their cars?' Tarzan said. 'The Anya-Nya had nothing, *nothing*,' he said, shaking his head. Then he rubbed his fingers together with a flourish. 'Yet the Anya-Nya had...' he said pausing, looking for the correct word, then adding with force: 'They had spirit.'

The rest of the first mission was spent trekking through the forests, then scrambling up into the mountains, rocky peaks that rise high over the jungles. When there was not torrential rain, there was burning sun. The long loping legs of their South Sudanese hosts meant they marched at a terrific pace, and the Israelis struggled to keep up. At night, sleeping in ruined villages, the mosquitoes feasted on them. They ate little: bowls of orange-coloured mashed termites, cassava, handfuls of roasted sesame seeds, and for meat, lumps of smoke-dried buffalo and elephant, boiled to an edible softness. 'It looked like a chunk of coal, but the smoky flavour wasn't bad at all,' Tarzan said. As they lost weight, the secret belts of gold coins they carried slipped beneath their hips, dragging their trousers down.

They searched for landing strips and drop zones for parachuting in arms. 'Our plan was to have hundreds of soldiers compact the earth by marching back and forth,' Tarzan added. 'Or a war dance from one end of the field to the other.'

* * *

We'd been talking for hours in a café. Tarzan paused as a man riding a floor-cleaning machine crawled past, its high-pitched alarm beeping. 'I could shoot this man, I have a pistol just here,' Tarzan said, tapping his bag in frustration. There was an uncomfortable silence as he eyed the shoppers wandering past, his back to the wall so he could see those approaching. 'My wife says I am a suspicious person. She is not, and it is a good thing to trust people,' Tarzan said, staring at me intensely. 'I trust only my dog, for she will never lie to me. I look at people's eyes. I want to feel; who are you? If you think you can convince me by smiling, you will do the opposite. If I sense that you will do the job, we will assist you, but it must be you who does the fighting.' I smiled nervously, then looked down at my notes to stop myself, pretending to think of the next question.

'I was not going to involve Israel in South Sudan just because I hated what the Northerners were doing,' Tarzan said. 'I had to put aside all my feelings.' He pulled out a bundle of photographs he had taken. There were burned villages, and thin children with ribs sticking out. 'I was watching the South Sudanese,' he said. 'I had criteria. Do they argue with officers? How do they behave when they get food, do they share? Are we supplying separate tribes, and would we be the ones who added to the chaos? When I assessed all these things, I came to the conclusion: these people are disciplined. Once given weapons, they would fight.'

As the Mossad team prepared to leave, Lagu appealed in desperation to them to return. He recalled the 'similarities between the situation facing the South Sudanese and that of the Jewish people throughout the ages,' Tarzan said. The decision rested in Tel Aviv, but as Tarzan crossed back across the border into Uganda, he knew what he would recommend.

As soft rock ballads blared out from the café, Tarzan's voice rose with anger in recalling the memory of what he saw on that first trip to the Anya-Nya. 'These people were massacred, and I hate evil, I hate it,' the veteran spy said, leaning forward across the table, tapping the table with his fingers. 'When it is done to people who could not fight back, well, I knew then that I had to be involved. It was also the Arabs who were doing it, and I have my own account with Arabs. "I am going to change it," I said, "and these Northerners will pay for all the evils they did for so long." They sold them, they raped them, they burned them. Someday it will be stopped, and that day arrived.'

* * *

'I was smuggled into Israel with forged passports,' Lagu said, giggling at the memory of the adventure. After Tarzan returned to Tel Aviv and submitted his report to Mossad chiefs, they summoned Lagu to meet Prime Minister Golda Meir. Lagu gave a blunt assessment; the rebels would fail without help. 'I told them exactly my military capabilities; I had left the army as a lieutenant, and that was that,' Lagu said. 'They were happy that I was honest with them.' It convinced the Israeli generals, who provided a crash course in leadership and guerrilla warfare before sending him back. 'They told me: "You are going to be the commander of an insurgent force,"' Lagu said.

A few weeks later, a Mossad team followed to raise an army. 'What we had in mind was continuous guerrilla warfare to undermine Khartoum's control of South Sudan, rather than conquering specific targets such as settlements or military bases,' Tarzan said. 'Our mission was complex; we had to make arrangements for the airdrops, prepare a landing strip for light planes, to train and equip a thousand men.'

Landing in Kenya, they arrived with twenty-five heavy kit bags. Needing a car to get them to the Ugandan border, they hired the sort of van tourists usually took to watch the migration in the Maasai Mara. 'The only vehicles available for hire in Nairobi at that time were mini-vans painted with black and white stripes, which reached a maximum speed of 30 miles per hour uphill—or 60 down,' Tarzan said. Mossad went to war in a zebra safari bus.

Soon after sneaking into Sudan, fresh arms drops were made. Training was rigorous, ranging from ambushes to target practice, explosives and landmines. 'It was very intensive, 18 hours a day training in drills, weapons and demolition,' Anya-Nya fighter Alison Magaya said. 'There could be no complaints, no fuss and no pretence of sickness.'[3] The commandos squeezed a two-year course of basic infantry skills and guerrilla tactics into weeks.

Mossad medic Emanuel Shapira asked Tarzan how to select recruits. 'Ability to speak English, and anyone who has actually seen a hospital,' Tarzan said. Everything needed to be started from scratch. Mud and thatch huts were built to serve as ammunition stores and a clinic. The operation base and radio room for the landing strip was a grass-roofed shelter.

The Israelis endured the same hardships as the men they trained. 'For me, it was not a question of "how much ammunition do you need?" and then going out of the country to sit by a pool in a hotel in Kampala,' Tarzan said. 'For people who had suffered every kind of abuse all their lives, suddenly someone came with a different attitude. No one in history had looked at them as equals; not the Turks, not the British, not the Arabs. Those were colonial powers, and their attitude was looking down on them as "natives". Our attitude was that they were equals.'

* * *

Sitting around a campfire, Tarzan and an Anya-Nya officer tuned their crackling shortwave radio to the BBC. A rocket had just taken off for the moon. 'We are in the Stone Age,' the officer told Tarzan morosely, as they stared together at the stars above. The Anya-Nya was a forgotten war, and without their message reaching a wider audience to have an impact politically, the ambushes were just another round of bloody killings on a jungle track.

'The South had been sealed off by the Sudanese government for years,' said Allan Reed, one of the rare few who came to report on the war. 'Hardly any foreign observers could go in, especially beyond the main towns.' Reed, who had befriended Anya-Nya refugees in Ethiopia as an American Peace Corps volunteer, spent much of 1969 trekking across the South making a documentary for NBC news.[4] 'Egyptian MiGs were bombing the cattle camps in Upper Nile,' Reed described, noting reports of Soviet helicopter gunships, Libyan paratroopers and East German agents.[5] 'I passed through villages that were totally levelled.'

Reed's film of burned-out villages and barefoot fighters taking on heavy weaponry with spears shocked many. When he left, he was determined to help the rebels make another, so left his cameras with two rebels. The men were keen to learn, but training was complicated because the new cameramen had never seen moving images before, so Reed slipped into Uganda to take them to the cinema. Unfortunately, the only film showing was a gun-slinging Clint Eastwood epic, *Two Mules for Sister Sara*. 'The deadliest man alive takes on a whole army with two guns and a fistful of dynamite,' the film poster boasts, with a cowboy and nun sidekick blowing up a railway bridge before storming a fortress. Much of the battle scenes are close-quarter fighting, as Clint takes on the Mexican army solo. The trainees returned terrified, imagining they now had to be stuck in the thick of such derring-do firefights to document their war.

Yet even with Israel's guns, Tarzan knew the motley collection of rebels had no hope of defeating the government militarily. Winning wider support was critical, and that had to include persuading African nations that a separatist rebellion was a good cause. So Mossad added a propaganda wing.

'I created a kind of bush newspaper,' said Yossi Alpher, a Mossad agent. 'The idea was to boost the armed struggle in the bush by putting the Anya-Nya "on the map", with no traces whatsoever of Israel.'[6] The paper cobbled together photographs of ripped scraps of handwritten messages and reports apparently hammered out on battered typewriters. 'Everything was produced in Tel Aviv and rendered as authentic as possible,' Alpher said. 'I copied the idiomatic English, the typefaces, and the format of African newspapers.' Paper and crayons were also handed out to children in the war zones. 'This exercise produced horrific drawings of murder and castration at the hands of the Sudanese army,' Alpher said.[7] Mossad's technique of children's art to show the impact of war on the innocent remains popular among rights activists and aid workers.

The propaganda highlighted the foreign forces fighting for Khartoum in a bid to win support from other African nations.[8] 'Soviet tanks with Russian drivers are rumbling through our villages, killing and maiming our defenceless people,' Lagu said in one appeal.[9] 'Jets with Soviet pilots overhead smash our bodies and our buildings with bombs, searing our flesh and our souls with their napalm.'[10]

* * *

In the tit-for-tat chaos of the 'enemy of my enemy is my friend' politics, regional nations were dragged in. Ethiopia provided support, including space for training camps, in revenge for Khartoum's backing of Eritrean guerrillas fighting for independence. Kenya also offered aid; quietly supporting the Anya-Nya meant it could worry less about a powerful Sudanese army on its northern frontier. 'The contribution was a few bags of corn for the soldiers to eat, dropped from the airplane without parachutes, so it was not too expensive,' Tarzan said. 'By us occupying the time of Sudan, Kenya was sitting pretty. Khartoum could not have any time for attention towards Kenya.'[11]

Uganda, for a time, also backed the Anya-Nya. Idi Amin came to visit in July 1970 when he was army chief, taking part in a target practice. He missed every shot, forcing Tarzan to step in and pretend the rifle's sights were askew. 'Idi Amin was a clown, but a dangerous and a cunning one,' said Tarzan. 'Clever he was not.' However, once Amin seized power in a coup in 1971 and found few friends to fund his despotism, he sidled up to Libya's Muammar Gadhafi. That shut down Mossad's route in via Uganda.

There was little other outside backing. The US and Britain were wary of pushing the government further into the arms of the Soviet Union. 'Still, the Americans were happy with what we did, since we were disturbing the Russians' plans in Khartoum,' Tarzan said.

* * *

The rebels, now numbering some 18,000 fighters, began major attacks, marching out on patrols lasting weeks to stage ambushes and blow up bridges. The campaign had a dramatic effect. Government troops moved in convoy, with troops walking on both sides of road as the long lines of lorries rumbled painfully slowly in first gear. A journey of a few hours became one of several days. There was panic in Khartoum and Cairo when Mossad tried to sink a large convoy of Nile barges; they feared Mossad wanted to seize control of the vital river. 'What is amazing is the idea that they had of us,' Tarzan said. 'Three Israelis in the bush with blisters, and the Egyptians believed that we were threatening the Nile.' Khartoum wanted to crush the rebels for good. Aircraft bombed Anya-Nya camps, with paratroopers dropping in from helicopter gunships. They captured the headquarters at Owiny-Kibul, with the rebels withdrawing into rugged mountains.

Eventually, the rebels sunk a boat. They hit a ferry with bazookas, and the metal barge was swept downstream. Tarzan was convinced it was that shipwreck which lay off the bank in Juba, a sun spot for young crocodiles, a useful perch for fishermen and a photo backdrop for aid workers drinking at the bar on the riverbank, a decaying reminder of a long-ago war when Israel came to fight in South Sudan.

* * *

Beyond the symbols of independence—a flag, passport, currency, army and national anthem—what makes a country? I watched the blue waves of the Mediterranean rush past as I took the train northwards up Israel's coast to Haifa, Tarzan's birthplace, a green port city of tower blocks clinging to steep hillsides. It was where my grandfather served as a British naval officer before David Ben-Gurion declared the formation of the state of Israel in 1948.

The afternoon sun was warm outside the naval museum dedicated to the Jewish struggle to defy British blockades on migration. I sat beside a boat used to flee the ruins of Europe and to build Israel as a country. I pulled out copies of watercolour sketches my grandfather had painted on the deck of a destroyer, pictures showing the Royal Naval white ensign flag fluttering, and wrecks of Jewish boats seized and scuttled. The passengers were deported, the dreams of the most desperate sunk. I thought of Tarzan fighting my grandfather as a boy. He had fought all his life to defend his homeland even before its birth, then risking so much to help fight for the freedom of South Sudan. Both were nations born, against the odds, out of the worst horrors. Neither were creations that would end conflict.

Israel was created by a people with the skills and education needed to forge a nation, but who—until 1948—did not have the land. Instead, they were unified by a common experience of oppression in exile.

In contrast, South Sudan was a place of many peoples spread across a land they had never left, but who had been starved of the education and skills needed to run a nation. They were unified by the common experience of oppression. For Tarzan, that struck a chord. 'The South Sudanese, they had nothing, and you know what the Northerners called them? Slaves!' Tarzan said, jabbing angrily into the air. 'So when I got that mission, I didn't see it at as just part of my career. Rather, it was to ensure that they would be able to fight, so the North would see that there was a change taking place.'

The next day I squeezed into a shared taxi from Nazareth to the border with the West Bank, walking through prison-like separation walls with Israel. A burly soldier stared down morosely from metal walkways on the concrete tower above. He waved his rifle at me to make sure I kept moving, as I thumbed down a car heading south to Jenin and into Palestine. I thought again of what it is that makes one land recognised as a country, and what it is that means another—one with all the trappings of a state—is not.

A few days later, drinking a beer on a rooftop bar overlooking the chaos of a Ramallah fluttering with Palestinian flags, I listened to the frustrations of young Palestinians calling their state an open-air prison. If the situation in South Sudan bore similarities to the struggles Israel had faced to become a physical country, then the parallels in South Sudan's long battles with Khartoum and Palestine's still ongoing fight for recognition were all too clear.

After crossing the ring of steel back into Israel, I asked Tarzan if he agreed. His eyes flashed with anger at me. 'When we, in Israel, pull the ear of an Arab, all the bastards on this planet say: "Look at them,"' he told me. 'No, no. We did not sell them for slavery. We did not burn their food. We did not rape their wives. You cannot compare. You cannot.'

* * *

Tarzan was not, however, the only one to come to the South. 'I was no mercenary,' Rolf Steiner barked at me, a man used to giving orders.

'That is a lie. What I did, I did for the people. It was not for the money; it was for the cause.' Steiner was a lieutenant-colonel and top foreign commander for the Biafran rebels in the 1967–1970 Nigerian civil war. It was his choice that a skull and crossbones was used as the insignia for the much feared 4,000-strong Commando Brigade. It was, he insisted, a symbol of defiance to death and not a reference to when he fought as a boy for the Nazis in the dying days of World War Two. He too would come to South Sudan.

A powerful, imposing man with wild eyes staring from sunken cheeks, the French Foreign Legion sergeant was one of the original infamous gang of white soldiers of fortune in 1960s Africa. They battled across the continent propping up rebel armies, backing bids for freedom, rescuing or toppling presidents. Comrades included Frenchmen Bob Denard, a former policeman who took part in no less than four coup attempts to take the white sand beaches of the Indian Ocean archipelago of the Comoros, and 'Mad Mike' Hoare who, after battles in the Congo, staged a coup bid in the Seychelles with more panache than planning, his soldiers arriving at the airport posing as a beer drinking society on a rugby tour. 'Be aggressive in action, chivalrous in victory, stubborn in defence,' Hoare gave as his commando rules for war.[12] 'Take pride in your appearance; even in the midst of battle, shave every day.' The French called them *les affreux*: 'The Terrible Ones'.

Yet Steiner was different, for he genuinely believed his battles were for a greater cause than for cash. 'A self-appointed messiah,' one old comrade called him.[13] He saw himself more as Che Guevara or Marquis de Lafayette than the mercenaries he called the 'scum of the earth'.[14] Too wild to conform to the rigid authority of a formal army, he found comfort in violence, and meaning in the adrenalin of battle and the regularity of uniform. Born in Munich in 1933 and growing up in Germany through World War Two, he skipped seminary school for the Foreign Legion, the corps of expendable misfits carrying out the sharp end of Paris' dirtiest foreign policy.

He was rarely a winner. He fought at Dien Bien Phu when the Vietnamese routed the French, parachuted into Suez during the 1956 crisis and battled in Algeria, but left to fight causes of his own choosing he believed were noble. He headed to Nigeria, but his luck failed there too. 'Steiner was good once, but deteriorated,' wrote British writer

Frederick Forsyth, who knew him in Biafra. 'The press publicity got to him, and that's always bad for a mercenary.'[15] Forsyth used Steiner as inspiration for a character in his Africa coup book *The Dogs of War*: the German mercenary Kurt Semmler, who marks out frontline positions by skewering enemy heads on stakes like Kurtz, before storming the presidential palace and heading off to 'another war' in South Sudan. In Forsyth's story, he dies laying a landmine to blow up a Sudanese armoured car.[16]

The reality was more pitiful. Steiner spiralled out of control, hijacking Red Cross cars, and when called to State House for a reprimand, got into a drunken brawl. The rebels expelled him in 1968. Biafran commanders loathed the 'pompous' German and the white mercenaries. 'They were merely drawn from the market pool of those who trade in death,' Biafran rebel officer Fola Oyewole said. 'Steiner's departure from Biafra removed the shine from the white mercenaries, the myth of white man's superiority in the art of soldiering.'[17]

Humiliated and rejected, Steiner chose a new cause to fight. In 1969, he headed for South Sudan, a man broken by the horror he had seen. He was one more foreigner lost in the jungles believing he could make a difference in another country's war.

* * *

'He wanted to be the king,' American filmmaker Allan Reed said, recalling how they met after stumbling by accident into his lonely compound of scattered thatch huts in the jungles of Equatoria. Steiner, the Vietnam veteran turned rebel colonel, channelled his own Kurtz in the jungle.

'We found him sitting on the ground in this little hut, and he was patching up some infected wounds that some kids had, there was a whole long line of them,' Reed remembers. 'He said that the only time he was ever happy was when he went into battle. His eyes lit up when he talked about it. He told me that he thinks of himself as a 17th century man. It seemed to me that he was there building himself a little kingdom.'[18]

He boasted of ties with the CIA and MI6, but it was not clear what Steiner thought he could achieve. 'He didn't deliver any goods,' Reed said. 'Any major Western intelligence agency from the Israelis to the Americans could get him at least machine guns or munitions.' He had been there for almost a year when Reed ran into him in the wilds close to the Uganda border. 'It is really strange. It was quite a pathetic look- ing place,' Reed said, recalling how Steiner had boasted to villagers of 'planeloads of arms and relief aid' from Europe. 'So the people chopped down the trees and built a grass runway,' Reed said, who trekked to see the airfield for himself. 'It was completely overrun with weeds. The people said that no planes had ever come.'[19]

Steiner would make the young recruits leap on rope swings over roaring fires in tough commando training. 'Sometimes we threw petrol bombs,' Paul Garang Deng told me, who had joined the rebels after government troops hunting Anya-Nya fighters had killed his mother. 'But all we had for guns were branches we had ripped off the trees.'

Steiner would wake sleeping sentries by firing bullets into the ground at their feet. Others recounted terrifying tales of how he would train soldiers to remain calm under fire by ordering men to sit in a circle with their feet facing a mortar tube pointed straight into the air, before firing a bomb up it. He'd laugh as the men scattered in terror.[20] 'I'm an extrem- ist,' he told one journalist in 1971, as his troops trained in camouflage hats made of cabbage leaves. 'The Africans need my help.'[21]

Steiner, a soldier who fought before large-scale private security con- tractors became a common, if not acceptable, face of war, believed that being called a 'soldier of fortune' was an insult. He offered to fight for Lagu for free. 'When a man fights for what he truly believes, he is not a mercenary,' he told me, his voice trembling with anger.[22] In his hand- written letters to me, half a century since he left Foreign Legion, he still quoted the rallying cry shouted by legionnaires: *Legio Patria Nostra*; The Legion is our Fatherland. He was addicted to the thrill of com- bat—or at least, to bask in the reputation of that. Coupled with a love of guns and an arrogant political naivety that he could make a change, it was a dangerous mix.

* * *

The German blundered into a war with multiple, loosely aligned groups. Steiner joined an Anya-Nya faction led by Emilio Tafeng, an ex-soldier who had served seven years of hard labour after taking part in the Torit Mutiny. Some had even declared their own states. Ex-policeman Gordon Muortat announced he had founded the new

nation of the Nile Republic, rejecting the name South Sudan as a colo-
nialist imposition.[23] Footage from the time shows his republic's capital,
a basic camp of scattered huts. 'A million patriotic dead separate us and
the Arabs forever,' said Muortat, smartly dressed in a sharp suit, trilby
and rolled umbrella as he inspected a parade of his soldiers in 1971.[24]
The men are barefoot and salute with wooden dummy guns.

Israel's weapons meant Lagu's force soon dominated. However, the
Israelis had no desire to incorporate a loose cannon like Steiner, especially with his Nazi past. 'I told Lagu, either Steiner leaves or we get out,'
Tarzan said. 'So he was taken to Kampala, and Idi Amin handed him to
Khartoum, and they interrogated him—badly.' Steiner's base was seized
by Sudanese troops and Libyan paratroopers.[25] Steiner, in jail in
Khartoum, was interrogated by East Germany's Stasi secret police and
subjected to mock executions by Sudanese security forces. 'They put him
in the sun so that he would burn from the outside, and made him drink
chilli to cook from the inside,' Tarzan said. He looked up at me with a
rare apology in his voice. 'If I had known he would have been tortured
like this I would not have let it happen,' he said. Then he shrugged. 'What
is the point to torture this person? He did nothing bad.'

Beaten to breaking point, Steiner was put on trial. Television footage
shows a gaunt figure with close-shaved head, staring defiantly out at the
crowded courtroom and armed guards.[26] He cut a strange figure.
German newspapers dismissed him as an 'adventurer with Napoleonic
delusions of grandeur'.[27] For Khartoum, it was a propaganda coup,
portraying the Anya-Nya as puppets of outside powers, not a home-
grown revolution with justified grievances.

Steiner was sentenced to death. His mission was a failure, a foreigner hiding behind a gun, confusing his own desire to seek a meaning
in life with that of a people he never really knew. After three years, a
deal was cut and he was released, a broken man. Today, he remains
defiant. 'I did what I did because I believed the cause,' he told me.

*he pretended
to train
armies?*

* * *

The Anya-Nya war fought itself to exhausted stalemate. In Khartoum,
Sudanese President Jaafar Nimeiri needed peace. He had seized power
in 1969, but had since faced down two coup attempts against himself.
'Unrelenting guerrilla warfare is forcing Nimeiri to station a sizeable

portion of the army in the major cities,' the CIA wrote. 'Military leaders are frustrated by their inability to take effective action against an opponent that appears and disappears quickly into the jungle.'[28] Nimeiri suggested talks. 'They couldn't continue fighting for forever,' Tarzan said. 'In the end, they would lose spirit. You can keep people going with high morale to a certain point, but in the end there had to be a political solution.'

Mossad had achieved all it had come to do. For Israel, strategic gains mattered less than the deterrent message it sent to its enemies that it could strike anywhere. Some even argue that the war in South Sudan helped towards peace between Egypt and Israel. Yossi Alpher, the Mossad operative who created the Anya-Nya newspapers, later heading Israel's top security think-tank centre at Tel Aviv University, believed the mission pushed Egypt's President Anwar al-Sadat towards a 1978 peace agreement with Israeli Prime Minister Menachem Begin, a deal that won them the Nobel Peace Prize. 'He had to realise that… the Israelis are in my deep rear, and they're sitting on my water, and I can't beat them, so I'm going to have to make peace with them,' Alpher said.[29]

* * *

For South Sudan, the support Israel gave helped lay the foundation for a new nation. When war returned, the veterans remembered Tarzan's lessons of how he turned a ragtag force into an army.

'The support gave Southerners the hope and determination needed to oppose oppression,' said Aleu Ayieny Aleu, a veteran fighter, later a minister of interior after independence. 'The Israeli support provided the basic tools needed that made it possible for people to do the rest in the years to come. The Anya-Nya commanders trained by Israel became the future leaders.'

John Garang, the rebel chief of the next war, was just a junior Anya-Nya officer among hundreds being trained at the time, but Tarzan said he stood out from the crowd. 'He had all the qualifications to be leader,' he said.

Tarzan returned to Sudan on commando operations in 1984, to coordinate Operation Solomon, Mossad's airlift of thousands of Ethiopian Jews to Israel, but the very first time he visited Juba was in 2010, where he was received by former Anya-Nya officer President Salva Kiir. 'It is because of you we stand here today,' Kiir told him.

Tarzan pushed across the table to me a copy of a letter Lagu had written to him. 'My friend John,' Lagu wrote, still using his codename. 'Whatever will become of the Anya-Nya, you have been the architect. You have raised an army out of nothing. We remember all that you have done to bring about this great change in the history of Anya-Nya, giving hope of survival and eventual success.'

* * *

It was a sunny late February afternoon in Addis Ababa, and the lions lazed on the grass licking their paws. The Imperial Palace in Ethiopia looked like a grand English stately home, a dank colonial-era building flanked by colonnaded pillars, cut off from sight from the bustle of Addis Ababa's chaotic streets by a thick wood of conifers. Prowling through the trees are the famed black-maned Abyssinian big cats, the beasts Bob Marley sang about in 'Iron Lion Zion', the symbol of the Lion of Judah, Emperor Haile Selassie.

In 1971, Selassie brought together the Sudanese rebels and government. In a twist, Khartoum had appointed Southern lawyer Abel Alier as vice-president, and then sent him to lead government negotiations. The rebels saw him as Khartoum's stooge who had sold out to the North. Distrust ran deep, and church leaders shuttled back and forth between the sides. The government refused talk of independence, and blocked rebel hopes for a separate Southern army. The skills needed for guerrilla combat were not those needed in negotiation, and the rebels were bullied to agree. Haile Selassie wanted a deal.

'The Emperor abruptly came to the point,' Abel Alier wrote later. 'He said any united country should have one army with one overall command. The Sudan should not be an exception to this world-wide accepted practice.'

The South could fight no more, and was forced to take the deal in good faith. After so many years fighting for their own nation, independence was shelved. A self-governing 'Southern Region' was agreed, with limited tax-raising powers, and autonomy over education, health and police. Defence, foreign policy and economic policy remained in the hands of Khartoum, and the rebels would be integrated into the army. Arabic remained the national language, but English the principal language of the South.

Yet the deal contained basic structural failures that sowed the seeds for the next conflict. The same divisions that started the war remained. The costs were horrific; some estimate between half a million and a million dead. In March 1972 the deal was signed. The 'Seventeen-Year War' had come to an end.

There was genuine optimism as Nimeiri and Lagu toured the South. 'People came on foot from long distances in the hot, blazing sun of March to receive him,' Alier wrote.[30] 'Anya-Nya soldiers slipped into reception lines in plain clothes to join in the celebration, side by side with citizens released from long detention for crimes connected with the rebellion.' There was, for the first in a very long time, a taste of peace. 'In Torit, where the first gun signalling the civil war was fired in 1955, Latuko warriors came to Nimeiri, and before a huge gathering symbolically laid down their traditional arms, spears, shields, clubs and war drums,' Alier added.

Others were more cautious. 'We, the leaders on either side in the conflict, lacked honesty at the peace settlement,' Lagu later admitted.[31] The promises on paper rarely, if ever, materialised. Rebels joined the army, but were then sidelined. The same divisions that started the war remained.

The Snake Venom rebels put their guns down for now, but the cause they had fought and dreamed of remained in their hearts. 'We pretended, and only shed old skins as snakes do,' Lagu said. 'Each group hoped to cheat the other in the course of time. That type of change is temporary, just as the new skin of a snake is smooth and shines only briefly, and shortly becomes coarse again.'

The warnings were there. Rebels wanted to keep their guns as insurance if the deal was not followed through. 'We must not be tricked into committing suicide to lay down our instruments of liberation,' wrote a young Anya-Nya captain, a certain John Garang.[32] He warned that a deal now would result in war tomorrow. 'Unless a correct consistent social democratic solution is found to the central question—i.e., to the problem of economic and political domination of Arab Nationalism over other nationalities—then, any attempts at solving the war in Sudan, no matter how refined and logical on paper, will always end in certain failure.'

His predictions would haunt the South.

7

THE MEN TOO TALL FOR TANKS

'I do not know how exactly the war began, it was so long ago. Did soldiers from the government forces steal a cow from the Dinka? Did the Dinka set out to retrieve it? Did shooting break out? Were there casualties? It must have happened something like that.'
Ryszard Kapuscinski[1]

Major-General Paul Garang Deng knows how the next war started. After all, he fired the first shots. I was squeezed beside him, careering in a pickup truck which weaved through a herd of long-horned cattle, then bounced down a backstreet in Bor, the main town on the east bank of the Nile, half a day's drive north of Juba. We screeched around a tractor tyre that served as the main roundabout in town, then pulled up at speed in a cloud of dust outside a row of shacks blaring Juba synthesiser dance beats.

'We knew war was coming,' Deng told me, after leaping out the vehicle, and tucking his commander's baton of ebony and elephant ivory under his arm. He was surprisingly nimble for a commando chief in his late seventies, still riddled with bullets and shrapnel. 'We had prepared,' he said. 'We were ready to fight.'

Deng led me down a track to meet three fellow generals dressed in bright patterned shirts sitting in the shade of tree, deep in a domino tournament. We waited for his old comrades to finish their game. All were veteran rebel fighters who had fought in the 1960s with the Anya-Nya. In 1972, at the peace deal, the old guerrilla officers joined the national army, but soon they would be sidelined. So, after a decade of relative peace, tensions rose again in the early 1980s.

'They said that Southerners could not be leaders, for they must be the ones to command,' said Brigadier-General Moses Ngoth Jok. A slender 72-year-old man wearing a tweed flat cap, we chatted as the clicking domino tiles were shuffled for a final game. 'Why should they decide over us?' he said. 'We are men, they are men. Our guns are the same guns that they have. Why should we be lesser?'

Dominos over, we all packed into the truck again, off to see another general. We shared a bowl of thick green okra stew scooped up with our hands in thin sorghum pancakes. 'It was the Arabs who attacked first,' Deng said. 'We were not afraid. You see, people who are used to being paid salaries to fight are not men to be scared of in battle. In war, there are only two choices. To live, or to die.'

* * *

There had been hope. There had been a time when schools had opened, buildings were constructed, and people recovered from the dark years. 'For a decade, we were at peace, and we had a taste of freedom,' said John Akec, Vice-Chancellor of the University of Juba, one of the generation who gained an education in a time without war.[2] 'Really, we were free. The army moved away, the police were moved, and we only had South Sudanese ruling over us.' The return to peace was not easy, however. A fifth of the population had fled their homes in the war, and now they were returning with trepidation.[3]

'Looming ahead are massive problems of resettling a million or more southerners, now abroad or in the bush far from their old villages,' the CIA wrote in a 1972 assessment.[4] 'Before the South can begin to participate in national life, it will require help in devising political forms and economic infrastructure.' People should have gone home, but the houses had been destroyed. So the war-time 'peace villages' that Khartoum had forced civilians into were now expanded for the influx returning.

The ink was barely dry on the deal, but the spies gave a gloomy assessment that peace was built on shaky foundations. 'There is widespread relief in the South that the shooting has stopped, but it is too early to judge whether or not there is enough momentum to carry through a real reconciliation,' the CIA wrote, warning that the meagre resources of Khartoum's government were woefully inadequate. 'It is clear from the reluctance of refugees to return that there is very little mutual trust and confidence. At best it will be an uneasy truce, endangered by efforts of recalcitrants to stir up trouble.'

Still, farmers in the far south could plant their fields in peace. The South had huge untilled expanses, and immense supplies of water from the Sudd. It was dreamed it could become the breadbasket not only for all Sudan, but also the Middle East.[5] It had the fertile grasslands and forests to succeed. Coffee plantations in the cooler uplands were revived.

Ethiopia boasts it is the birthplace of coffee, but its southwest highlands are not the only place in the world where *coffea arabica* grows naturally. Wild plants are also found across the border on South Sudan's Boma plateau, and both nations can claim rightfully to be the origin of coffee.[6] South Sudan could also have capitalised on being the source of the beautiful brew. There was a chance of a different future, a means of living away from war.

* * *

I leafed through old documents left over after the war, digging into mountains of yellowing papers in a giant plastic tent in the garden of a government office in Juba. They were the fragments of administrative records saved from decaying basements. There were dozens of brown cloth sacks stuffed full of brittle papers, metal cupboards bulging open with sketch maps drawn by colonial officers, years of budgets and security reports. The fledging national archives were a librarian's nightmare of random documents, ranging from the mundane to the precious. Hidden within them was the record of South Sudan's formation as a nation, the crumbling paper minutiae that detailed the decades of violence upon which Africa's youngest nation planned to forge its identity.

The archivist, Youssef Onyalla, mopping his head with a handkerchief in the steamy heat of the greenhouse-like tent, took a break from photographing the latest batch of papers. He showed me an unusual document he'd dug out, a poster advert from the late 1970s. The corners were tatty and nibbled by termites, but it offered a slice of hope for a different future. The picture was crammed with cheerful ink drawings of elephant, rhino, antelope and giraffe, the animals that roam the immense wilderness regions. 'Tourism is Yourism—the Southern Region is a Paradise of Wildlife Conservation,' it read. 'Wide-ranging scenes of tourist attractions and unique hospitality.'

In the 1970s, the new autonomous Southern government dreamed of boosting its income with tourist dollars. Buffalo and elephant used to wander into Juba; in 1972, one elephant was shot where parliament now stands.[7] South Sudan has had very few years when a tourist might think of visiting, but in the late 1970s it was opening up. It was no hippie trail stopover, but backpackers made their way through. Onyalla, showing me the wildlife poster in the euphoria of the run-up to independence in 2011, suggested it could be reissued to attract new visitors to the South.

* * *

Skimming above the sweeping grasslands turned yellow from the fierce dry-season sun, the UN helicopter slowly curled out north from the dusty town of Bentiu with a deafening whump-whump-whump of its rotors. Then it nosed east towards the White Nile and glinting blue lakes of the Sudd, the marsh islands luminous green below. I twisted my head out of the porthole to escape the head-aching fuel fumes, and watched the land below slip by. Apart from scattered villages, the land was empty. Later, heading towards Upper Nile, we passed over a field of oil wells and pipelines running north. There was a small fortified base of shipping containers and razor wire where oil workers lived. Seemingly never-ending seismic mapping tracks that smashed through the grasslands stretched to the horizon. Development, roads, infrastructure; other than what was connected to oil, there was next to nothing.

Oil had been discovered in the late 1970s in the north of Sudan, but in 1979, the US oil giant Chevron made a major find in the South around Bentiu. More was soon found near Melut in Upper Nile, while France's Total won rights to an exploratory bloc bigger than Bulgaria in Jonglei. Oil changed the dynamics of power. The sudden arrival of such a valuable resource sharply increased the risk of violence. When the Anya-Nya took up arms in the 1960s, they did so for principles of freedom and rights. Now, there was a resource worth billions to fight for too—and fuel the war. When it started, it would fund the violence for longer than ever before.

Oil would bring Khartoum into Washington's arms. President Jaafar Nimeiri, who took power in a 1969 coup, had begun with speeches of revolutionary socialism and pan-Arabism. An abortive Libyan-backed Communist plot to topple him in 1971 put paid to that. American oilman George H.W. Bush, later to become president, had toured Sudan in 1972 as US ambassador to the UN and became a key advocate for boosting ties. Nimeiri, who had spent a year at a US military college at Fort Leavenworth in Kansas, warmed to Washington. He portrayed Sudan as a stable bulwark state on the strategic Red Sea, sandwiched between the dangerous Soviet satellite of Libya and the volatile Horn of Africa.

Oil prices soared in 1973, after Arab nations blocked crude oil from nations supporting Israel after the Yom Kippur war. Washington was desperate for friendly nations in the Middle East, especially one like Sudan that offered an alternative supply of oil. Washington ramped up support, both economic and military. 'Nimeiri has played an important role that supports US efforts to prevent the further growth of Libyan and Soviet influence in the region, and to protect US access to vital oil supply routes,' the CIA wrote in 1983.[8] 'American firms are deeply involved in exploration and development in the petroleum sector.' Sudan allowed US military bases, with a large CIA operations centre set up in the heart of Khartoum. Nimeiri knew he would earn the anger of some Arab nations, but he obliged Washington for a price. Sudan became one of the largest recipients of US military aid in the world, many times larger than any other nation in sub-Saharan Africa.[9] Tanks, F-5 fighter jets, and artillery were sent.

The lion's share of oil reserves was in the South, but an emboldened Khartoum wanted to make sure it controlled all the promised petrodollars. So Khartoum redrew borders of the key oil zone around Bentiu to prise it away from the South's semi-autonomous rule. They called it 'Unity' state. Oil fields were given official Arabic names, not the local titles of the land. 'Southerners do not want "us" to have anything to do with "their" oil,' Nimeiri told army chiefs bluntly, as he ordered Northern troops to Southern oil zones to put down growing protest. The cash would revolutionise the economy and pour billions into the hands of the elite.

'Oil had emerged as the economic aspect of an internationalised North-South conflict,' wrote Abel Alier, Vice President of Sudan.[10] It was not the only factor that would push the South back to war, but it fuelled the bubbling anger.

* * *

South Sudan had another key resource that attracted interest: water. The world's longest river meanders sleepily into the morass of the Sudd swamp, the elevation dropping so slowly that the brown waters spill out sideways into immense marshes. It is a haven for wildlife, with herds of grey elephant and hippo finding the isolated islands a perfect place for some peace amongst war. The maze of channels and islands have also been a refuge for those fleeing violence. By the time the river emerges from the Sudd, half of the water has been lost to evaporation.

Egypt's population was booming in the 1970s, extracting ever more water from the Nile. With Khartoum, Cairo launched in the South's Jonglei and Upper Nile regions the ambitious and controversial Jonglei Canal, to divert the Nile and, alongside the new channel, water one of the largest irrigation schemes ever planned in the world. The canal was to stretch the distance of Paris to London, and suck out the water from a swamp larger than the Netherlands.

The bucket wheel digger, with a dozen formidable rotating slicing scoops each the size of a car, was the largest excavator in the world. When it previously operated in Pakistan, it dug a boat-wide channel as long as 200 football pitches every week. Reassembled in South Sudan, the progress was slower. The thick black soil clogged the digger like treacle in the rains and concrete in the dry season. Still, by the early 1980s, they had ploughed the way through two-thirds of the distance, already the length of the Suez and Panama canals combined.[11]

John Garang, the rebel captain who wanted to fight on in 1972, was deeply suspicious. He was now in the national army, but his distrust of Khartoum had not lessened. His old rebel commander, Joseph Lagu, now president of the Southern Region, tried to temper his anger. 'Don't drag us into trouble prematurely,' Lagu said he told him, as he approved Garang's sabbatical at Iowa State University in the US, believing the break would calm him down. 'Behave yourself and prepare for the future.'[12]

Garang focused his economics doctorate on the canal, and came to the conclusion that Khartoum was, yet again, exploiting the South.

'The canal project is pregnant with serious political implications,' he warned.[13] Such large-scale projects, like the Aral Sea or the draining of Iraq's marshlands, have repeatedly been ecological disasters. The canal would damage the seasonal cattle grazing of his homeland, the grasslands of Twic, and slice the great antelope migration in two. Rumours that two million Egyptian farmers would set up irrigated plantations along the canal zone sparked deadly rioting in Juba. Sudan had just emerged from a war fought against the marginalisation of the South, but the lessons had not been learned. 'The country cannot afford to foster further inequitable development,' Garang wrote. The digger was one of the first sites attacked and destroyed when war broke out.

Today, it sits abandoned. It rears up out of the head-high trees like a crashed space ship, a forgotten prop from an apocalyptic science fiction film. Last time I visited, I started to scramble up the rusted metal frame for the view, but then worried about explosives from old battles. An elderly lady who lived in its shadow said leopards used the driver's cabin as a hunting lookout for antelope. Around the decay of that colossal wreck, the lone and level grasslands stretched far away.

* * *

Back on the streets of Bor, the old generals talked for hours of how the war clouds had gathered. General Deng had taken me to see his old comrade Reuben Thiong, another general in his late seventies.

There was a fatalistic sense that the 1972 agreement had been only a breathing space for both sides to recover their strengths. People were frustrated that nothing had changed. 'It was about ending marginalisation by the Arabs,' said Thiong, sitting on a plastic chair beneath the thin shade of a tree. 'That was why I fought. They treated us as inferior. There was forced labour and if you refused, people were beaten, sometimes even killed.' Among the 6,000 ex-rebels who had been officially integrated to make up a tenth of the national army, anger was rising. Demoted from their rebel ranks to lower positions in the regular army, they were then blocked from promotions. Deng tapped three fingers on his arm to show his soldier's stripes; he had been a lieutenant when a rebel, but dropped to a sergeant in peace.

There was little, if any, investment in the South. Instead, there were fears about Khartoum's steps towards greater Islamisation. Mosques were built, but not schools or hospitals, they said. Islamic rules were being pushed as national law, and for both beer-loving Southerners and those who went to church that was a growing worry.

As a final death knell to the peace deal, Khartoum pushed for dividing the single Southern Region into three, revoking its autonomous powers. Bitter divisions grew between North and South, but also within the South. It was a divide and rule policy that encouraged Southerners to jostle amongst themselves for power. 'They dishonoured what we had fought for,' Thiong said. 'Nimeiri said that the agreement was neither a Koran nor a Bible, so it could be changed. We said, no, what was signed in Addis Ababa had to be implemented.'

Violence grew. The economy was in ruins. In Khartoum, there were several failed coup attempts. In the South, mutinies by soldiers were crushed. Small units of veterans from the last war rebelled, calling their forces Anya-Nya II. Fighting broke out in Abyei, the grasslands straddling the North–South border. Both the Ngok Dinka cattle keepers and the Arab Misseriya horsemen claimed it as their own. It was meant to have held a vote to choose whether it would be controlled by North or South, but that was scrapped.[14] The bonfire was doused in fuel. Only a match was needed to set Sudan alight.

* * *

Steiner II
very
bad

Major Kerubino Kuanyin Bol simply could not wait for the war to begin. He wore a pistol cowboy-style on each hip, and strapped hand grenades to his legs. He would announce his arrival in villages by firing a stream of bullets into the air, and wake sleeping soldiers by shooting into the ground between their feet or hurling a grenade so the blast only just missed them—a terrifying trick he learned from training with Anya-Nya rebels under Rolf Steiner in the 1960s. 'All he would talk about was fighting,' said Deng, who was then Kerubino's senior sergeant. 'However it started, any conversation would end up about war.'

The missionaries who baptised Kerubino 'Cherub' would have been alarmed if they had met him as an adult. He once told Deng how to beat a dog to death. 'He said: "Put your hand out with food and call it, but keep a stick behind you,"' Deng recalled, leaning forward towards me and rubbing his fingers together, making an unnerving kissing sound with his lips, just as Kerubino had done to him. Then he thumped his fist down on the table. "'This is how we will kill the Arabs,'" Deng said with a grin. 'That was the Kerubino way.' I mopped up the tea I'd spilt when I jumped in shock.

Swiss journalist Oswald Iten met Kerubino while reporting on the slaughter of elephants by hunters and poachers in the South in 1982. Hearing his interest, Kerubino helpfully dragged a pile of enormous elephant tusks out of his hut. 'I'm selling the tusks to buy guns,' Kerubino had told the reporter. 'I want to start the revolution.' Iten showed me the photograph he had taken. Kerubino, dressed in flares and cowboy boots, stares defiantly into the camera lens. The curved tusks to fuel a new war are nonchalantly propped alongside him.[15]

'People wanted to fight, but there was a plan for an uprising,' Deng told me. 'We had to take the Arabs by surprise and rise up together.' It was, he said, set for the anniversary of the Torit Mutiny, 18 August 1983. Those preparing for a fight included John Garang, an army colonel teaching economics at the University of Khartoum, back in Khartoum after his US studies. He ingratiated himself with the army chiefs. 'When you're planning an illegal or underground activity it is always best to be close to the authorities,' Garang said. 'My calculation was that if there were intelligence reports about my activities, these generals would dismiss the reports saying: "John is a good boy and it is not possible for him to do such things."'[16] Events, however, would soon outrun the plotters.[17]

In Khartoum, Garang realised that the powder keg was about to explode. He convinced army commanders to grant him leave to ensure that his family, who were living on his farm near Bor, were safe. Brian D'Silva, a quiet American who had befriended him in Iowa, was now a professor with him at the university in Khartoum. He had planned to join Garang on his Easter holidays, to see his home. 'John came by and said that plans had changed,' D'Silva said. 'He did not tell me what was going to happen.' Before he left, Garang worked late. 'He was a very conscientious professor,' D'Silva said, recalling how Garang sat up to finish marking a thick pile of exam papers.[18]

In the morning, Garang left for Bor. The next time he would return to Khartoum would be in triumph in 2005, after decades of a war he would lead.[19]

* * *

Initially, it was insubordination, not open revolt. In Bor, Kerubino took command of Southern troops, the 105th battalion. Kerubino was himself wanted for questioning at army headquarters over missing salary payments and reports of his elephant poaching. When a government spy was sent to Bor to investigate, Kerubino hanged him from a tree.

Tempers were rising to breaking point. The troops, who came from across the South, were ordered to go North. They refused, fearing that if they did go they would be arrested—or worse. 'The Northern officers shouted to us on parade: "Why must you rebel all the time? Are you wild animals?"' Thiong said. 'Our officers said: "Do not be transferred, or you will lose your lives."'

The main garrison in Bor was a collection of thatch huts by the river just south of the town, where a clearing had been hacked out of scrubland. People called it Malual-Chat; in Dinka, the 'place of the red bull'. There were no solid walls, so men dug defensive fox holes. The men waited, for they knew the battle of Bor was coming.

The first shots fired, however, would come from Khartoum. Commanders ordered an all-out pre-dawn assault on 16 May 1983. It was set for a Monday morning. 'They knew the South Sudanese always drank on the weekend,' said General Alfred Okwoch, then a lieutenant in Bor. 'Early on a Monday morning they would still be struggling.'

To the army chiefs in faraway headquarters, the troubles in Bor seemed like another grumble among soldiers they could easily crush. Some just wanted to send a cold-blooded message and cut the troublesome ex-rebels down to size. Others perhaps wanted more, initiating a full frontal attack as a calculated scheme to ensure the irksome 1972 peace deal was killed off for good, and usher in an era of Islamic fundamentalism.[20]

Some dreamed of a swift victory. It would ignite a rebellion that would engulf all of Sudan and bring Khartoum to its knees. This war would last 21 years.

* * *

It was a cold, lonely morning a couple hours from dawn, and Lance-Corporal Gabriel Mabior Nyang stood guard outside the armoury. The night had been quiet, the men wrapped up against the start of the rainy season. Then madness erupted. There were terrifying flames of tanks firing shells that lit up the gloom, thunderous machine guns, the whistling of mortar rounds as they streamed down into the barracks, and the brain-bending thumps as they exploded into fire. 'Everyone was shooting,' he told me. 'It was chaos.' The memory of what he saw that night is still tough. He was the first to see the tanks smashing through the trees with machine gun muzzles flashing. Behind them followed lines of trucks packed with a thousand government troops. He shook his head when I asked how many tanks he had faced. The terrifying, overwhelming terror of the blazing barrels and tons of armour advancing to crush him was still too much. 'Young man,' he said sternly. 'If you had been there facing such tanks, you do not remember such details.'

He does remember, however, that as shells pounded into the thin protection of the shallow trenches, the soldiers grabbed their guns and fired back. The 200 Southern soldiers were hopelessly outgunned by as many as five to one. They had neither tanks nor heavy artillery. The Southerners knew there would be no mercy shown if they were captured. The soldiers were pinned down, and ammunition was running out fast.

Then, over their heads ran Major Kerubino, pistols firing in each hand. 'Stand with me,' Kerubino shouted. 'Fight! Now we face the enemy.'[21] Kerubino was shot in the arm, and was dragged back out of the frontline. Fortune may favour the brave, but courage can only go so far.

The gunfire woke those in nearby Bor town. Roused from sleep, Southern soldiers grabbed their guns. They hunted down their Northern comrades and killed them. Then they ran towards the bigger battle at the barracks. Some with the wildlife service carried with them elephant rifles, firing giant bullets far more powerful than regular army rifles. They held the guns at their hips and charged. 'They didn't stop the tanks,' said General Moses Ngoth Jok, then a sergeant in the wildlife service who joined the assault. 'But what choice did we have?'

Yet the World War Two-era Soviet T-55 tanks had a key flaw; they could not shoot accurately while moving. When they stopped to fire their cannon at the charging soldiers, others sprinted forward to hurl grenades. 'We destroyed one,' Jok said.

Fighting stretched into a second day, and more government troops were reported to be on their way from Juba. Soon the men were down to the last few bullets, and as heavy rains poured down, they took the

109

chance to escape. Some slipped out to hide in the swamps, creeping away later to join their comrades. In Bor town, the people fled whichever way they could, piling children and the food they could carry onto bicycles, or running away on foot. On the third day since the battle began, the main body of troops met with John Garang outside Bor.

'Give me something to drink and celebrate the start of the revolution,' Kerubino told him, with his arm smashed by bullets. 'Take over the command from here, now my work is finished.'[22]

Garang ordered a withdrawal, and the men marched out through the plains and woods of Jonglei, joining other soldiers—now rebels—who had mutinied in garrisons elsewhere. Their wives and children followed.

'It was terrifying, because we did not know exactly what was going on, and I had the little children with me,' Sarah Nyakuoth told me, whose husband William Nyuon Bany led a mutiny in Ayod soon after the battle at Bor, killing Northern officers and throwing them down a well. Sarah, a nurse in Malakal, had to flee for fear she would be executed in revenge. 'Friends said: "Your husband is a well-known man," and I was told that if I was caught I would be killed,' she said. 'So that night I slept for safety in the church, then I escaped the next day on foot. I walked with my children all the way.'

Long columns of men, women and children stumbled exhausted across the border into Ethiopia. They got a warm welcome.

* * *

South Sudanese rebels were an ideal pawn for Ethiopian President Hailemariam Mengistu. A ruthless Marxist army officer who had deposed Emperor Haile Selassie in 1974—likely stuffing the Rastafarians' messiah beneath a palace toilet—Mengistu was responsible for the slaughter of tens of thousands of his countrymen. His foreign policy was just as violent, based on the explosive principle of supporting enemies of his enemies. Mengistu was fighting separatist guerrillas in Eritrea, who were backed by Khartoum. So Mengistu leapt at the opportunity to attack Khartoum through the use of rebels from the South.

'Nimeiri was not only attacking the South, his own country, but he also was the main supporter of the Eritrean rebels,' Mengistu said. 'He was the enemy of our revolution. He joined the United States and the rest of the West by attacking us.'[23] So the arrival of South Sudanese rebels in Ethiopia was a useful opportunity. 'I said to them: "We will do anything we can in our power,"' Mengistu said. '"We will even share bread."' Mengistu could afford to be generous, for he simply ignored the death of a million of his own people from a famine he had caused, a nightmare that BBC reporter Michael Buerk described as 'the closest thing to hell on earth'. Mengistu happily left Band Aid celebrities to provide the cash for food, while he got on with helping his new friends become a formidable, well-equipped rebel army.

Soviet-backed Mengistu would bring in Communist supporters for the South Sudan rebels. There were military trainers from East Germany, and advisors and doctors sent by Fidel Castro. Cuba took in children to train in medicine and other skills, with over 600 teenagers travelling by sea to a new life in the hope that when the revolution was over, they would be the vanguard to rebuild the nation.

Most importantly, support came from Libya. Moammer Gadhafi hated the Khartoum regime for its ties to Washington and support for Cairo following the Egypt–Israel 1978 peace accords. 'Gadhafi was very happy and cooperative to give us his support,' Mengistu said. 'He had very good oil money. He agreed to establish the liberation army with me.'

Unlike the first war, this time the continent offered support. 'Many Africans were with us,' Mengistu said, naming Kenya, Uganda, Zambia and Zimbabwe. 'We had a lot of support—morally, politically, materially.'

* * *

Settled deep into a sofa covered with a floral embroidered silk cloth, Brigadier-General Malaak Ayuen rested one hand on my shoulder and with the other pointed excitedly to the flickering television screen. Malaak, the army's Director of Information, is well known for his bellicose broadcasts on state television, narrating gory combat footage as he exhorts soldiers to defeat rebels. This time he had changed from his uniform into a colourful, open-necked shirt. I was in his living room in Juba, curtains drawn against the ferocious heat of a late afternoon sun, watching the archive of footage he had filmed as a rebel cameraman.

To the sound of a military bugle and men chanting war songs, we watched as tanks smashed through scrubby trees while soldiers ran behind with AK-47s. It is the early 1980s, and the war is in full swing. There are dead bodies with crushed heads lying on the earth, streams of civilians fleeing the other way, and terrified looking Northern prisoners of war throwing down their guns.

The commander stands out of the tank turret, his entire top half sticking out like a crazed jack-in-the-box. The Soviet T-55 tanks were designed to offer as small a target as possible to enemy gunners, so the Russians specially recruited small soldiers for the four-man crew to fit in the cramped space. With the height of basketball players, this was a little more of a problem for the South Sudanese. Their legs simply could not fold over themselves to fit into the baking hot metal box. So commanders threw open the hatches and stood up straight as the tanks hurtled into battle, pistols in hand and machine guns blazing. 'The men were too tall for tanks,' Malaak said. 'It wasn't very easy for them.'

Malaak reached forward to play another film, with grainy, wobbling footage, from the very beginning of the rebellion in July 1983. 'It is the first meeting,' said Malaak, as we watched half a dozen Southerners clambering onto a military helicopter as they are flown to Addis Ababa, then standing awkwardly in line for the camera on green manicured lawns. Half are young officers; Garang, dressed in a powder blue safari suit, stands alongside Salva Kiir, a military intelligence captain who, when fighting had erupted in Bor, had led his troops out of Malakal to join the rebellion in Ethiopia. Whippet-thin and dressed in flares and wide collared shirts, the men look more Saturday Night Fever than bush rebels.

Alongside them, the older generation stand with walking sticks. They are the veteran commanders of the last war, including Samuel Gai Tut, who had already been fighting with Nuer guerrillas for a year by 1983, commanding the rebels he called Anya-Nya II. The film shifts inside to an oval dining table, where the leaders speak earnestly about the formation of a manifesto and detailed structures of the army units, making notes on a bundle of papers. Garang dominates, and the older generation are sidelined.

Many other African revolutions emerged when long-debated student political movements were repressed, and their leaders took up arms.

Their rhetoric and policies were already well-formed when the time of the gun came. In the South, oppression created anger that drove rebellion, but the uprising was not born as a single force. The rebels had competing dreams of a solution for the South, and it would lead to divisions from the very beginning.

* * *

There could be no revolution without weapons. Garang knew that to get the guns, he had to say what his backers wanted to hear. His only choice was to say that he fought to topple the regime in Khartoum, not to build a new nation. Ethiopia was fighting separatist rebels in Eritrea, so Mengistu would not be seen to back other rebels wanting to split an African state in two. Libya also gave support only because it wanted a new regime in Khartoum. Gadhafi had absolutely no desire for an independent, Christian-dominated and free South Sudan.

Garang's orders were therefore for revolution—but not separation of the South. 'The movement that started in the South has been called a secessionist movement, a religious movement, a "this and that" movement,' Garang said. 'Our objectives are very clear: we are fighting for a united Sudan within a democratic context.'

Garang called his vision 'New Sudan', and the rebel force for all the country 'The Sudan People's Liberation Army', or SPLA. 'It is not a war that can be fought by the South alone,' he said. 'It is a war that will need the participation of all the oppressed Sudanese people,' Garang added. He wanted the support of struggling lands in the North too, from Darfur in the west, to the Nuba Mountains and rebels of the east. 'Let us fight for the liberation of the whole country, a victory that will restore the rights and dignity of all oppressed people,' Garang said.[24]

The war was fratricidal from the start. Garang first had to silence those who wanted an independent South. There were ruthless purges of those who opposed Garang's leadership, including the killing of Anya-Nya II commander Samuel Gai Tut. 'Long rows of naked cadavers were floating toward us, with blown-up bellies, dispersed or in small groups,' wrote Swiss anthropologist Conradin Perner. In June 1984, he was by the banks of Nile in Malakal. For hours, he watched hundreds of corpses float downstream 'like long black logs of wood peeled off from their bark.' They had been massacred in the fighting in Upper Nile

this feels like it would benefit Khartoum

between Anya-Nya II and the SPLA. 'Whenever some of the bodies got close to the shore, some men tried to pull the corpses onto land, using long bamboo sticks,' Perner wrote. 'The White Nile had turned red.'[25]

The earliest battles for control of the revolution would be some of the bloodiest. Outside guns gave Garang the control he needed. 'Ethiopian, Soviet, and Libyan support to Garang has at least temporarily unified the insurgents under his leadership and guaranteed them ready access to modern arms,' the CIA noted.[26] 'There are sharper tribal and ideological differences among dissidents, however, and Garang's leadership is only grudgingly accepted by some of them.'

* * *

My eyes on Malaak's film, I watch as Garang peers at a map of border regions with Ethiopia and South Sudan, circling possible places to set up training camps for recruits and rebel headquarters. He draws wide lines into the South where battalions would push in. 'We will conduct limited operations against police stations and isolated enemy platoons while our training is going on,' Garang says as the camera zooms in. 'This will keep the enemy occupied, so that they don't detect what we are doing.' Garang's deception seemed to work; in the beginning, the revolution did not seem to spark much worry. There had been rebellions before, and they had fizzled out. Khartoum thought the mutinies had been crushed, and was in fighting mood too. Nimeiri, with other troubles at home, had turned to religion as a tool to win popularity and drum up support.

'From now on, there will no longer be any death for a soldier in the Holy War in the South, but martyrdom,' Nimeiri told soldiers. 'Those of you who will fall as martyrs in the war against the infidels in the southern part of our beloved nation will go straight to heaven.'[27]

Nimeiri pushed ahead by declaring Sharia law, announcing amputations and the flogging of adulterers and thieves. Despite the reputation of having been a hard drinking youth, Nimeiri now staged elaborate ceremonies, pouring tens of thousands of bottles of whisky, wine and beer into the Nile.

If he had thought his strongman show would scare off troublesome troops in the South, he was horribly wrong. It would push a mutiny into all-out rebellion. 'Sudan has been declared an Islamic Republic and the Arabs are organising a religious war against the Southern Sudanese armed rebellion,' wrote veteran fighter and academic Elia Duang Arop. 'The war has become now as it was before 1972; the Arab North against Black African South.'[28]

Still, Nimeiri had allies, for now. His declaration of Islamic laws brought him closer to Arab nations. In time, Egypt, Iraq and Jordan would send military support. Since Khartoum backed the Egyptian–Israeli peace deal, this time Mossad had no interest in sending support to Southern rebels. Nimeiri still had the Americans too. In November 1983, as the South Sudanese rebels in Ethiopia readied their troops, Nimeiri travelled to Washington. There, President Ronald Reagan gushed with praise for a man he called his friend. 'Few can match your courage and foresight as a peacemaker in Africa and in the Middle East,' Reagan told him.[29]

* * *

Malaak had dug out another film. Jerky footage showed soldiers putting on a display of unarmed combat at a graduation ceremony in late 1984. 'SPLA! SPLA!' the men chant. 'We have struggled a long time, a very long time, from the last century and before,' Garang tells the graduating officers. 'We are only continuing that. Our objectives are clearly written: we shall achieve them through protracted revolutionary armed struggle.'

Garang is now dressed in the uniform of a general. He is firmly in charge, and the other leaders do not appear. Garang appears confident, boasting of taking the war to the North too. 'We have fought major battles, we have shot down planes,' he said. 'It is out of necessity the revolution started in the South, but it will engulf all of the Sudan.'

The rebels were well equipped. They used surface-to-air missiles to shoot down several fighter jets and helicopter gunships, and in 1986 a civilian airliner, killing 60 people.[30] 'When I went to Tripoli, Brother Gadhafi said that he considered the SPLA as one of the divisions of the Libyan army,' Garang said. Still, the SPLA feared Libya's arms flow might dry up. Officers therefore claimed to be training a battalion of a thousand men every month, so that Tripoli would send new guns to equip them. Libyan officials came to each graduation ceremony to gift their guns, but often handed them to the same recruits as last time. It allowed the rebels to rapidly stockpile enough weapons for a full-scale military campaign.[31]

In the film, the young recruits start singing. First there are war ballads hailing the SPLA, bloodthirsty chants for violence. 'Students, leave the school, pens can no longer liberate the Sudan,' went one song broadcast from the rebel's station, Radio SPLA, praising instead the new supplies of AK-47 rifles that even a child could fire. 'Garang will liberate the country with blood.'[32]

Then the new recruits sing another song, one taught to children when a guest comes to school. 'Welcome to the guests who have come today,' they sing, chests puffed up and smiling, their fearsome façade of commando killers melting away. 'Welcome, welcome.'

The song ached with deep sadness. As the camera panned down the line of young-faced recruits, I wondered how many would have still been boys singing that in school themselves if war hadn't broken out. Many likely died in the first few months of battle.

As the soldiers sang on screen, the generator ran out of diesel, turning off the power in Malaak's house. The television screen went blank and the music cut. As the fans stopped and heat returned, I realised a woman was sobbing quietly in a chair in the corner. The old footage had been just too much.

* * *

As for the men who started the war, they still sit in Bor, hoping for better times and clinging to the old glory fading into dust. They have no medals to show. General John Chol Mabior, another veteran who fought in Bor in 1983, instead came bearing an X-ray of the bullet still inside his knee cap. He showed the photograph proudly as proof of his years of battles. 'Look at us, we who fought the longest war,' he said sadly. 'We are forgotten.' Their salaries had evaporated into hyperinflation. Their savings of cattle were killed or stolen in the civil war that erupted again in 2013, when the town of Bor was razed to the ground. 'It is about respect,' he said. 'It is about recognition for what we did.'

Yet he was not worried for the future. 'God gives, and God takes life. In war, the only principle you need to know is kill first, or they kill you,' he said. 'As long as you fight for what you believe, you fight for your rights, and follow that rule, then you do not need to fear anything more.'

Brigadier-General Reuben Thiong sighed. He looked quietly into the distance, a sandy track lined with sausage trees, where piglets scratched in burned grass. He had been shot four times—in both arms, his left leg and in the back—and the bullets lodged inside old wounds ached. Beside him stood the battered metal of an ancient walking frame, its wheels clogged. When the rains came and the town turned to mud, it would be utterly useless. His neighbour's children scampered around the old man's home, a simple tin roof hut. All his seven children have been killed or scattered by the war.

He sat alone, staring at the grave of his son in his yard. Was it worth it all, I ask, in the end, all the fighting? All the pain and loss? He looked at me and held my gaze. 'Oh, it was worth it,' he said firmly. 'Now we have a country.'

8

THE WAR OF THE EDUCATED

'Even your mother, give her a bullet.'
SPLA graduation song, 1991.[1]

Squinting against the fierce sun from beneath the shade of the tree, the children scouted the sky. I crouched alongside them, after they'd beckoned me frantically into a scrape of earth. We stared up through the leaves for the source of the high whine of an aircraft engine. I was walking through fields of maize outside Kauda, in the rebel-controlled Nuba Mountains. The chain of green hills rise out of the hot plains on the border with North and South, where the people have been fighting the government in Khartoum in recurrent wars for as long as most could remember.

I had hoped the aircraft was the missionary flight I'd been promised I could hitch a ride home on. It was already a day late, so I was grinning idiotically and searching for it from the rocky track. To me, it sounded like the propeller airplanes I had taken a hundred times, that bounced across Sudan on dirt airstrips, picking up aid workers and delivering basic supplies. The children knew better, and called the strange man over to them to hide.

To 13-year-old Salamah Afahal and her two friends lying flat alongside me in the dust, they heard the terrifying whine of a hulking Soviet-era Antonov. Khartoum converted the cargo planes into bombers, rolling out barrels packed with explosives, fuel and scrap metal. The bombs were indiscriminate weapons, killing those in the open with broad arcs of red hot metal splinters, ripping trees out from their roots. People used caves as bomb shelters, and schools dug foxholes in the playground.

'Listen,' said Salamah, briefly propping herself up out of the dirt on her elbow, then pursing her lips and making a whining noise that mimicked the plane. 'The Antonov, it has a sound like this, like metal, not like the others.' The children had learned the hard way that the engines of the small planes brought aid, and the large ones brought death. Knowing when the Antonov had gone for good and when it was circling for a second bombing run was a matter of survival. The air attacks were crude, but Khartoum didn't care about who they targeted. The very fact they spread fear was what made them effective.

The Nuba Mountains have been a natural refuge for centuries for those fleeing the slave raids of Khartoum, becoming home to dozens of different peoples. There were some seventy languages here, many unrelated. Isolation once protected them, but from the 1980s on, even the remotest valley was within the terrible reach of the bombers above. They became a particularly punishing battleground in the war with Khartoum, and the Nuba people became a core part of the SPLA. The war here, after a break of a brief few years, continued after South Sudan's independence. I'd been there in quieter times, hiking from hill to hill and sleeping in the thick-walled stone huts with thatch roofs. It made me sick to the stomach to realise that peace was the anomaly here, not war.

This time the bomber was a false alarm—for us at least. It passed on its way, perhaps to another target. Other times, there were multiple attacks a day. Salamah brushed the dust from her floral print dress. Skipping down the track, she showed me to my guesthouse.

* * *

As it was unable to send in enough troops to crush the rebellion, the Antonovs became a favourite weapon for Khartoum, not only in the Nuba Mountains, but all across the South. Khartoum had fighter jets and helicopter gunships too. Air superiority was crucial, since so much of the South was without roads, and they were used with deadly impact.

[handwritten margin note: This is a reminder of why they didn't unify + defeat earlier]

120

Government helicopters spent much of their time simply resupplying outlying garrisons. Still, they could strafe those on the ground or, if the people hid, carve through the herds of cattle with machine guns in order to cause starvation. The government was accused of using more deadly weapons too: bombs whose clouds of gas made people vomit blood and women miscarry.[2]

With the rebel bases hidden deep under trees, the bombers attacked more obvious civilian targets. Hospitals, schools and churches were hit.[3] Their tin roofs were punched by bombs, and the people abandoned them. Brick walls crumbled back to earth. Instead, the spreading shade of majestic fig trees was used: priests prayed for peace using their branches as an open air cathedral; children sat on their thick roots for school benches.

[handwritten margin note: would like this increase enmity]

'We operated under trees,' said battlefield surgeon Major-General Peter Ajak Bullen. 'We wanted to go where the buildings were, but the enemy bombed those.' He and a handful of colleagues tried to patch up the wounded as best they could. Half a dozen doctors with the most limited supplies tried to save the lives of hundreds of bleeding soldiers. The work was never ending: pulling bullets out from where they had smashed bones inside bodies; amputating the hanging stumps of legs shattered by landmines; stitching up missing parts; cutting out oozing colons after shots to the stomach. An orderly swatted away whining clouds of black flies swollen fat on blood. Bullen was lucky if he had ketamine to sedate soldiers, while antibiotics to prevent infection were rare. There were few surgical instruments, and no blood banks. 'We had to make do with what we had,' the surgeon said, now commander of the army's medical corps. 'You do what you can, where you are.'

* * *

Still, Khartoum knew it could not win by bombing raids alone. They destroyed and created fear, but airplanes couldn't hold the ground. 'When the planes came we would blow the whistles—wheep, wheep, wheep!' said John Chol Mabior, flapping his arms at me and wailing. Mabior, a general in the prison service, was another veteran who had rebelled in Bor. He and his comrades used their military experience to train new generations in war. 'People were killed by the bombs, but not everyone,' said Mabior. 'John Garang would stand and shake his fists, shouting to the airplanes overhead: "You will not capture us from the sky!" To defeat us, they had to fight us on the ground. And there, well, we could fight.'

Fight they did. By 1984, the SPLA was launching battalion-sized assaults. Often, it matched government forces man-for-man. Road convoys and railway trains were ambushed, and attacks were even launched into the North.[4] The army's few tanks were used in defence of isolated forts. In contrast, the rebels now boasted new assault rifles, and with Ethiopia providing transport planes and helicopters, they could stage daring guerrilla hit-and-run attacks. The rebels took swathes of land. There was optimism.[5]

'Our feeling was that we'd liberate South Sudan very soon,' said, Deng Dau Deng, a giant of a man, now heading South Sudan's National Commission for War Disabled, Widows and Orphans. He grunted as he shifted a heavy-sounding prosthetic limb under the table. His right leg had been obliterated from the thigh down by an artillery shell. Aged 21, he ran off from university in Juba to join the rebels.[6] 'It was to be a quick war,' he said.

* * *

A year in, Khartoum's soldiers were struggling. Government troops dug in defensive positions, but rarely ventured outside to fight. Conditions were tough. 'Garang's forces are conducting increasingly sophisticated assaults,' the CIA wrote, noting that army recruits from the South made up more than a third of government soldiers, and they were deserting in droves. 'Rebel successes have eroded morale in the Sudanese military.' Pilots even sabotaged two of their own fighter planes to avoid having to fly their dangerous missions.[7]

In the dark, rebels would creep around to encircle a fort. 'You exhaust the enemy with an artillery barrage just before dawn,' said Deng, who became an anti-aircraft gunner. 'Then after half an hour, the soldiers attack.' Deng manned a twin-barrelled cannon, providing a terrifying blaze of fire against government jets or helicopters.

Yet the early successes were not to last. Government troops soon learned, and as the artillery barrage rained down, they sheltered in trenches. When the rebels charged across the open plains, the machine-gunners fired. The war would be harder than the rebels had hoped.

'In December 1983 we said, "By Christmas next year, we'll be free," but it didn't happen,' said Deng. 'In 1984, then we said, "We'll win in 1985." Well, that didn't happen. The war expanded, and the realities of the war on the ground became clearer.'

* * *

Kerubino Kuanyin Bol relaxed on a double bed covered in leopard skins beneath the early stars. He surveyed the curling smoke from the scores of cooking fires of his troops. Beside him stood a drinks cabinet, a pirate's chest heavy with bottles of Scotch and gin, and alongside, a large black typewriter sat on an office table. Around him there were more than a thousand men, hundreds of young recruits, wives and families, and giant herds of stolen cattle to feed them all. It was February 1984. Kerubino, rebel codename 'The Dragon', now Lieutenant-Colonel Kerubino, SPLA Deputy Commander-in-Chief, had recovered from his wounds at Bor.

Kerubino marched across Jonglei and Upper Nile, leading the SPLA's Buffalo Battalion and waging wild war on his terms. His specialty was spectacular all-out frontal assaults. Waves of troops overran enemy posts, killing with gun and spear. Victories were barbaric. Retreats were bloody and chaotic, sometimes disastrous.

'If we were lucky and he was in a good mood, he would call us around the bed and offer us a drink,' said Till Lincke, a Swiss journalist kidnapped in 1984 along with his girlfriend Astrid Hollenstein. 'If we were unlucky, if he had lost badly in a battle, he would be in a black mood for days. He could pull his gun out on anybody, or throw grenades around to get attention. He threatened to kill me too.'

The Swiss couple, who had come to report on the nascent rebellion, had carried with them letters for the SPLA from Southern leaders in exile in Europe, including audio messages recorded in Dinka and Nuer saying they were friends of the rebels. They had snuck through government lines near Malakal. Then a priest sympathising with the rebels had taken them across the Nile on a dugout canoe, leaving them on the other bank. They trekked inland to meet Kerubino.

'He just took us captive,' said Lincke. The hostages were sent to the back of the great column on its war march across the country. 'We were made to walk for weeks as they fought their way across South

123

Sudan,' said Lincke, pausing as he recalled the tough time of his nearly year-long captivity. 'We were kept with the worst wounded at the back, those too badly hurt to walk and who had to be carried on stretchers,' he said, rolling a cigarette as his last still smouldered in the ashtray. 'In the beginning we'd help them with bandages, but our medical kit soon ran out.' They trekked all the way across the east of the country, through the thick bush and across the rivers. The winding marathon took months, with the column fighting as it went.

'My military experience was from Hollywood films, but I could see they didn't prepare anything about defence,' Lincke said. 'So when we were attacked, everyone was out in the open, and everyone was shooting everywhere. It was madness.'

The Swiss had walked into trouble. Yet other foreigners would be deliberately targeted, for the rebels wanted to stop foreign investment, in order to hit Khartoum. So they attacked the oil fields and the Jonglei Canal.

* * *

'Hundreds of rounds were going through the walls of the sleeping quarters,' said British oil worker Steve Morters, whose leg was smashed by a bullet when gunmen stormed the base of the US oil company Chevron near Bentiu in February 1984. 'They were shooting my friends in the corridor and their bedrooms.'[8] Three foreign workers were killed—a Briton, a Filipino and a Kenyan—and several others wounded. The rebels said oil profits were used by Khartoum to underwrite the cost of the war.

Khartoum had hoped the oil fields would be pumping 100,000 barrels per day by 1986, earning hundreds of millions of dollars each year.[9] The attack was a clear message from the rebels; the oil companies were not welcome.

Sudanese troops were flown in to belatedly secure the base. That, however, was proof for the rebels that Chevron was working with government forces against them. Chevron called in ex-US army soldiers, Vietnam veterans who knew the limitations of a regular army against rebel attacks. They said they could not secure the oil fields.[10] Khartoum responded by equipping its own guerrillas. They shipped weapons to Arab Misseriya herdsmen, who swept down on horseback from the North into the oil fields. Helicopter gunships cleared the way, and as the people fled the machine guns, the militias moved in behind to burn the villages and take the land. They were battles with no prisoners.

Khartoum also backed Southern rebel factions opposing Garang. New Southern militias were used as proxies, given weapons and encouraged to fight. There had always been tit-for-tat cattle raids, for cows were the lifeblood of the economy, the heart of the community, and fighting for them was proof of manhood. Yet the cattle raids had been self-regulating in their intensity, and limited by the weaponry available. Traditional rules of authority would stop the fights when the bloodshed had gone too far. Now killings were not only sanctioned by government, but aggressively cheered on. Ethnic differences were encouraged.

For Khartoum, it was counterinsurgency on the cheap to 'drain the sea' of rebel support.[11] If Khartoum couldn't beat the rebels, they could divide them. It devastated the South, for the violence only expanded the war. Once the genie of such intense bloodshed was unleashed, Khartoum found it impossible to assert control.

[handwritten margin note: This is vil[l]anous bad imagery]

Soon Chevron would pull out, just as the rebels had hoped. 'The history of oil exploitation in Sudan,' American diplomats wrote later, 'has been marked by Northern domination, killings, displacement, community destruction, environmental degradation, arms purchases and accusations of cheating.'[12] Others would replace them, but the war would grow ever worse.

A week after the Chevron killings, there was a second attack. Kerubino's commandos stormed the base of the Jonglei Canal. They killed an Australian pilot and took six foreigners hostage, from Britain, France, Germany and Ireland. A heavily-pregnant German woman and her toddler were released after a month's trek across the South, but the remaining four would spend a year in SPLA hands.

[handwritten margin note: a lot of pregnancy & birth stories]

'We have shut down two major economic projects: oil and water,' boasted Garang. 'Every day they are losing money.'

* * *

The new hostages from the canal joined the Swiss journalists. Limping and sick, they stumbled across the border into Ethiopia about four months later. Their prison was underneath a tree; they initially slept outside, then later in basic huts. 'Every day I thought, we could be free tomorrow,' said Astrid Hollenstein, the other Swiss hostage. 'Then I thought, we could be killed tomorrow too.' Malnourished and sick, she suffered ferocious fevers, so bad at times that she had to be carried unconscious on a stretcher. One soldier trekked for six days to find roots with quinine when she was hit by a particularly hard bout of malaria. 'I was very near death at one point,' she said.

An empty ammunition box was their cooking pot, and they were handed basic supplies of rice, and sometimes a rare lump of bony beef. Mosquito nets doubled to catch tiny fish for protein, while occasional mangos from the trees staved off scurvy. The British pilot made himself a fly swat with a flap of scrap rubber, becoming an expert killer of the thick clouds of insects that buzzed around. He became so proficient that he cut a hole in the rubber flap. 'He needed a challenge,' Lincke said. 'So he gave them a sporting chance.'

Lincke dreamed of escape. He made a compass from magnets prized out of a travel chess set, but they had no maps, nor any real idea where they were. Still, Lincke spent days in a muddy pond teaching the Irish engineer to swim, in case the chance came to cross the crocodile-infested river at night.

Millions of dollars were demanded for the Jonglei canal hostages, but no ransom was ever demanded for the Swiss.[13] 'If they had released us, we could have given information about the other hostages, so we had to wait,' Lincke said. 'That took almost a year.' The four emaciated canal hostages were finally released for a reported ransom of 'hundreds of thousands of dollars' in radio equipment.[14] The Swiss journalists were kept an extra week. They were handed a camera and notebooks so they could complete the report they had come to do a year before. It was perhaps the longest the SPLA have made a journalist wait for an interview.

Across the table in his apartment in Zurich, Lincke passed me photographs taken just before his release. In one, the crowds of recruits sit on the forest floor as far as the camera lens can see, thousands of young men stretching back into the gloom. In another, Lincke stands alongside the SPLA chiefs—Garang in a floppy bush hat, Kerubino and Salva Kiir. 'I crossed my hands to show that I was a captive,' he said. 'That was the time when we were most scared, as we thought we might be killed at the end. No one told us what was happening.' In another, Garang appears as the revolutionary rebel leader with a red beret jauntily on his head. He still wears a US army belt around his waist, a memento of his year at Fort Benning infantry college in Georgia.

Lincke, who has since swapped journalism to sail boats in the Arctic, shakes his head at the memories sparked from a sheaf of photos he'd dug out. He handed them to his old friend Hollenstein, now a homeopath in Zurich. 'I experienced something close to death,' she said. Then she paused to look at the photographs.

'There were some incredibly beautiful moments,' she added quietly. Together, they slowly described the better memories of their time in the South: the dramatic sunsets and sparkling stars at night; the slow rivers and grasslands; the unexpected sudden kindness of ordinary soldiers. 'When I was a child I loved Robinson Crusoe,' she said. 'It was like that. We had nothing, just nature and the wild. It might sound strange, but I wouldn't have missed that.'

* * *

In Khartoum, the pain of war seemed far away. The government soldiers killed came from the poorest parts, often economic conscripts from Darfur. Yet the financial burden began to bite. War in the South cost some $500,000 every day; the economy was in ruins; inflation soared and anger grew. Foreign debt ran into the billions of dollars.[15] In 1985, Nimeiri went to Washington to plead for more aid.

He lost the presidency in the same way he took it; sixteen years since his coup, military officers seized power. Former prime minister Sadiq al-Mahdi took over, and swiftly reached out to Gadhafi. He owed him for Libya's backing of his past coup attempts, and now Sudan and Libya made up.

With Khartoum and Tripoli friends again, Gadhafi's support for the SPLA was cut. The rebels had only been his proxy, for he had no sympathy for the cause. First he stopped his supply of guns, then he sent MiG fighter jets to bomb the bases he'd set up.[16] 'Garang used to be our ally. We trained him and armed him because he was launching a revolution,' Gadhafi said, visiting Khartoum for the first time since the overthrow of the 'filthy puppet-rule' of the US ally Nimeiri.[17] 'We will press Garang until he lays down his arms.'

Sadiq wooed Arab nations to boost support, managing to win backing from both Iran and Iraq. Egypt and Jordan too sent military hardware. Sadiq, great-grandson of the Mahdi, would use the fresh supplies of arms to equip the fearsome *Murahaleen* horsemen, who would sweep far into the South on killing raids. In 1987, government-sponsored raids drove the starving, fleeing people of Bahr el Ghazal into famine.[18] Instead of allowing aid workers to bring in food, Khartoum blocked access. The famished died in their thousands. Those who had the strength fled their homes.

In turn, Sadiq was himself deposed in 1989 by Omar al-Bashir, a beefy paratrooper colonel. The attacks continued. Armoured railway trains and mobile fortresses bristling with machine guns were sent into the South, with thousands of horseback fighters and infantry on foot alongside, carving a path of destruction.[19] Villages were burned, and crops destroyed. Those civilians who could not flee were either killed or forcibly taken back to the North. Tens of thousands of civilians were forced onto trucks. It was ethnic cleansing, emptying lands of rebel supporters.[20]

Bashir escalated the jihad against the South, making sharia law more severe than ever before. Armed robbers were sentenced to execution by crucifixion, adulterers faced death by stoning. Thieves had their hands amputated, drinkers of alcohol were given 40 lashes.[21] Bashir appeared at rallies with a Koran in one hand and an AK-47 rifle in the other.

Key towns including Juba became isolated government pockets of control, accessible only by armoured convoys or by air. Towns were ringed with landmines—first encircled by government soldiers to defend against attack, and then by rebels to starve the besieged garrisons into submission. Food was scarce, but soldiers blocked civilians from leaving—even to farm—fearing they would join the rebels. Islamic law was imposed, and there were forced conversions. National security officers ran a series of torture centres in ordinary houses, notable from the outside only for the strange activities late at night, and for curtains that never opened. Suspected rebel supporters were dragged in and, almost always, never seen again. People called them 'ghost houses'.

* * *

For the SPLA, the war was going largely its way. It controlled most of the South, including the key supply routes across the borders with Ethiopia, Kenya, Uganda and Congo. While Khartoum courted Arab nations, the rebels now looked to the African continent for support. The new support bases helped divide North and South even further. 'The government's open call for military support from Arab nations makes the war appear as one between black Africa and the Arab world,' Abel Alier, the former president of the South, wrote. [22]

With African allies fearful of encouraging separatist groups in their own nations, Garang made clear he was fighting for regime change, not the separation of the South. 'The SPLA irrevocably believes in the unity of the Sudanese people,' Garang kept repeating. [23]

Yet for the huge majority of ordinary, illiterate SPLA soldiers, it was a matter of fighting for their land. The Marxist talk of bourgeoisie, revolutionaries, and comrades meant nothing to most. 'While the leadership was talking of a united socialist Sudan, the people were talking of secession of South Sudan. For the people, the enemy was the "Arab North",' said Peter Adwok, an academic-turned-rebel captain, whose leg was blown off in combat. [24] 'Much time, energy and blood of the people has been wasted simply because of this discrepancy.'

Garang's command tolerated no dissent. Those seen as posing a threat were arrested or simply killed. CIA assessments praised Garang as charismatic and an adept tactician, but warned of the 'internecine strife' ahead. 'Garang's insurgent movement suffers from many of the same internal tensions that have reduced the cohesion of earlier southern dissident movements,' the CIA wrote. 'Personal rivalries and tribal and ideological differences cause infighting.' [25]

It went right to the very top. Even Kerubino, the SPLA's deputy commander, was not safe. In 1987, he was arrested along with some 40 of his officers, taken without trial and tortured. They were lashed with hippo hide whips that slice the flesh. Others were left for days in punishing positions with their hands and feet tied together, or forced into deep pits with neck-deep cold water. Anger festered, waiting to burst. [26]

'There is no clean revolution,' said Brigadier-General Daniel Abudhok Apiokuach, an SPLA veteran with a guerrilla's wild beard. 'That is what I told Garang after he released me.' Apiokuach had been a student leader before becoming an eager SPLA political commissar, quoting Che Guevara and Fidel Castro. He was arrested in 1987 for plotting a coup against Garang, and held in foul prisons for almost five years without trial. 'We are all Sudanese, so we don't believe in separation,' said Apiokuach. 'The problem was that I knew that the government of the Arabs would not change, so they left us no choice and forced us to leave. It was Khartoum who made us separate as South Sudanese. Independence was the only solution.'

It was not an opinion Garang wanted to hear. Sometimes Apiokuach was held in solitary confinement, other times he was rammed into horrendously cramped cells with 30 other political prisoners. The cells were baking hot tin huts infested with lice. Some prisoners were thrown into open-air pits. Others had their fingernails ripped out. 'I thought I would die there,' Apiokuach said. 'They wrote my name on the list of dead people.' Even priests were not safe, despite the Church being about the only organisation staying to help the poorest, in the lands where few others dared to go.

Apiokuach, now director of the army's historical archives, sat surrounded by old photographs of the war. He shuffled through them, pointing to comrades who died in battle, and those killed at the hands of their comrades. He sighed. Then he shrugged, apparently not bitter at his treatment. 'Every revolution has its own power struggle within itself,' he said. 'What is important is to reconcile.'

* * *

Disaster came from afar. The USSR was disintegrating, and Mengistu no longer had the ally he needed to fight off his own rebels. The dictatorship in Ethiopia was overthrown and in May 1991, Mengistu fled. For the SPLA, that meant they were no longer welcome in Ethiopia. The new leaders had no love for the old regime's allies, and Khartoum had a free hand to attack. Soldiers stormed the SPLA's rear-guard bases, forcing over a quarter of a million Southerners to trek to find safety, starving without supplies. The columns were bombed from the air.

The children ran too. Khartoum hunted them down in order to wipe out the next generation of rebels, and as they crossed the river from Ethiopia back into South Sudan, soldiers opened fire. Scores drowned, and the crocodiles feasted.[27]

'One morning the children appeared, thousands of them,' said Conradin Perner, from the International Committee of the Red Cross.

'Then thousands more came each day, coming on foot, starving and desperate.' Perner, a Swiss ethnographer who had spent years in the borderlands of South Sudan with Ethiopia, was sent to the frontlines at Pochalla. 'They had nothing,' said Perner, who moved them as fast as they could from the frontlines. First, he loaded the weakest onto planes. Then, as the numbers swelled, he organised trucks to provide food and support for them on their epic march out, away from the fighting to the west that was weeks away. The children set out alone on a march through a wilderness and war zone the length of England. It was just in time.

'They attacked us,' Perner said, shaking his head, describing how he and Red Cross colleagues sheltered some twenty-five of the sickest children as the gunfire shook the building. It soon became clear they would be killed if they did not flee, and they crammed into a car that swerved and skidded away, windows shattered. 'They hit it everywhere,' he said. 'Somehow they just missed the tyres.'

Perner and his colleagues were credited with rescuing the lives of at least 10,000 children. Years later, after South Sudan won independence, Perner was invited to the presidential palace. He was granted honorary citizenship for his work.

* * *

Riek Machar smoothed the wrinkles in his cream linen jacket down over his wobbling belly, and inspected the sheen on his leather shoes. I huddled closer to the smoky campfire beside him. It was early 2006, and he was the Vice President of the South. The war had ended a year before, and he was touring battle-hit villages to promote the peace deal. I'd followed, squeezing into a battered pickup with his bodyguards. We pushed through roads swallowed by head-high bushes, camping with mosquito nets strung up under trees. For many of the villages we rattled through, Machar was the first senior government official they'd seen to tell them what the 2005 peace deal meant.

I watched as Machar told me of the war, smiling and erudite, a man of education. He was affable and easy to talk to; he wanted to be liked. He was charming if he chose to be, with a friendly gap-toothed smile. That is, of course, if you didn't know his past. In English, he appeared softly spoken, measured and careful when his words were being recorded. I had also seen his speeches in Nuer, and he was a different man: ferocious, angry and powerful.

'We were all fighting for freedom,' he said. 'But the freedom we fought for was undermined by others in South Sudan.' Born as the British left Sudan, Machar is the son of a Nuer chief from the oil zone of Leer. It is a beautiful if hard land, where the thin grass runs into the wide swamps of the Sudd, and the fierce blue skies seem like a bowl over the thatch huts of the town. That was not to be his future though. Sent to school and not the cattle camps, Machar completed a doctorate in strategic planning at Britain's Bradford University. When the war broke out, Machar returned and rose rapidly up the rebel ranks. The ambitious young officer grew deeply disillusioned with Garang, and began plotting a coup to take over power.

In June 1991, Machar and Lam Akol, a Shilluk academic with a doctorate in chemical engineering from Imperial College London, met to plot action to topple Garang. They claimed they wanted to democratise the SPLA and stop human rights abuses. 'For the last eight years, John Garang has been running the movement in a most dictatorial and autocratic manner,' the conspirators wrote. 'He turned a popular struggle into warlordism and a reign of terror.'[28]

In the afternoon, having kick-started plans for a new round of war, Machar married his second wife. His choice shocked some: an English aid worker, Emma McCune. 'Emma was barefoot, her white garments spattered with mud, and thorns caught her shoulders,' her mother wrote of their wedding in the mud of Nasir.[29] 'She remained radiant.'

Her marriage sparked scandal. Even Lam Akol said he was unaware Machar was to marry her until moments before. 'I was wondering to myself, how, on the very day we have taken such a serious decision, Machar could be getting married to an English lady?' the best man Akol wrote. Machar did not seem to care. 'If loving you is wrong, I don't wanna be right—if being right means being without you,' a besotted Machar wrote to his new wife, quoting crooner Tom Jones.[30] Emma was writing a book on her new life. 'Wedded to the Cause: Living with the War in the Sudan', it was called. She never finished it, because the dream crumbled.

Ten weeks later, in August 1991, Machar and Akol made their coup against Garang public. It would lead to disaster. All were ambitious, all believed their vision for South Sudan was the better one. All were also utterly ruthless. They were some of the best educated in the land, representing three of the great peoples of the South: Machar from the Nuer, Akol from the Shilluk, and Garang, the Dinka. Garang, with his PhD in economics from Iowa, dismissed them as the 'gang of two doctors'. It led to some of the most catastrophic divisions and bloodshed the South had ever seen. 'The War of the Educated', some called it.[31]

It turned the SPLA against itself. If the split was ideological at the start, it would soon divide the people along bitter ethnic lines. Critics said it had nothing to do with democracy but everything to do with ambition. 'They will be known in history as the people who stabbed the movement in Southern Sudan in the back,' Garang said.

The coup plotters were accused of being in the pay of foreigners, and supported by Islamists in Khartoum. Even Machar's marriage was exploited and portrayed as a part of a plot against Garang.

Power corrupts. Of all leaders in South Sudan, Machar has divided opinion more than any other. He split the rebels, swapped sides to join hands with the enemy, and signed deals with the hard-line Islamists he said he hated. He is accused of dividing the South, of turning the war against the Arabs in the North into one of Southerner against Southerner, and setting tribe against tribe. Needing men, Machar equipped and armed the Nuer youth, co-opting the old militia called the White Army as his force. They were named for the glinting light on their shining spears and the white ash that fighters covered themselves in, carrying only belts of ammunition draped around their necks, and a gun or a knife in their hands. With ash covering them like war paint, their attacks were utterly terrifying.

* * *

Journalists wrote that it was a war of medieval brutality. It was not. It was a war of medieval brutality fought with the modern efficiency of machine guns and rocket-propelled grenades. In 1991, Machar's largely Nuer forces attacked the Dinka town of Bor, the people of Garang. It was one of the worst atrocities of the war, and it was carried out by Southerner against Southerner.

The White Army went on the rampage, massacring all those they found in the town and surrounding villages in three months of blood-

Don't Look Back

shed that left thousands dead. Many villages attacked did not even have any rival SPLA troops based there, only civilians. The bones were scattered and unburied in the long grass, lying where villagers had been shot or hacked to death. The reports are grotesque: of children burned alive, of women raped, then disembowelled and hanged from trees. Men were castrated and left for dead.[32] 'Unfortunate excesses,' Akol said. 'Propaganda,' Machar fumed.[33]

Revenge attacks by Garang forces were launched: ruthless killings that included the burning of dozens of civilians inside a church in Ayod, a Nuer town. 'It had been wiped off the face of the earth,' journalist Rory Nugent told me, who in 1993 was among the first to arrive in the empty wreckage of the town, finding piles of skulls. Every home had been burned. The circles and rectangles of charred earth were all that remained. 'Many were burnt alive as their houses were set alight, others were tied and shot or hacked to death,' the UN said. 'Ayod was left burnt down, surrounded by mines and with corpses said to have been thrown in a well, infecting the main water source.'[34]

Elsewhere, Nugent found lines of women, their corpses lying where they had been executed. 'I took pictures of what was left of massacre victims, most of them women split in half by a machete, their legs spread apart and sticks from the baskets they used to carry on their heads shoved up their vaginas,' he wrote. 'As we kept walking, more and more bodies littered the way. Famine victims were usually found singly under a tree; war casualties were grouped together, their bones picked clean and then bleached by an unblinking equatorial sun,'[35]

By 1993, famine had broken out in Upper Nile, the land between the villages of Kongor, Ayod, and Waat. Aid workers called it the 'Hunger Triangle'. Thousands starved to death. It was in the village of Ayod that South African photographer Kevin Carter took his iconic photograph of a fly-covered baby crawling on the baked earth watched by a vulture. The traumatic image won Carter a Pulitzer Prize, and for many outside became a lasting representation of the war. He faced intense criticism for not helping the child. He committed suicide soon after.

* * *

It hadn't always been this way. 'Chanting their battle cantos as they went, they would rush forward a few paces all together, halt, step back as if rallying, and then surge forward once again,' British district officer Colin Borradaile wrote of a Shilluk battle in the 1920s, describing how it was more about intimidation than killing. 'Each warrior held his hippo shield aloft, and with his spear poised gracefully in the other hand, gave himself up to rhythmic caperings.'[36]

There were rules. Women would accompany men onto the battlefield to support the wounded, but killing them intentionally was taboo.[37] When there was fighting, men would line up as though standing on the sidelines of a football pitch, hurling spears across the width. 'Spears were thrown across the intervening space,' wrote Richard Owen, the last British governor of Bahr el Ghazal, describing a pitched battle between a thousand rival Dinka forces. Men at the front threw heavy sticks high in the air at the opposition's heads, while those in the rows behind hurled spears directly at opponents' bodies. When a policeman tried to break up the fight by firing shots into the air, the fighters paused politely—then carried on as before. 'This had been going on for two hours when the officer arrived,' Owen wrote. 'And it continued for three more, until sundown, when bad light stopped play.'[38]

* * *

In the past, the power of a spear thrust came from the muscles of a man. The path of death was clear. There was responsibility for each killing, and blood payments and animal sacrifices to make amends, under the watch of leaders who arbitrated peace and instilled laws— a post half-way between priest and judge. For the Dinka, that role was led by the Spear Masters, while for the Nuer, it was the 'Earth Guardians'—or, as the British called them, the leopard-skin wearing chiefs.

The young snatched power from the elders through the terrible, easy authority of a gun. The old laws could not cope, for who was responsible when death came from guns, each firing a hundred lightning strikes? Even a child can fire thirty bullets from an AK-47 in a matter of seconds. The moral brake was released for butchery.

The war within a war destroyed the South. It broke communities. Those old leaders who tried to stop the violence were killed themselves. Those who turned their authority into joining the war entered a strange world of dark spirituality, merging Biblical stories of apoca-

135

lypse with ancient vendettas. Prophets led ash-covered fighters on rampages of grotesque cruelty. It set a terrifying precedent for South Sudan's future. 'Our battalion has no mercy,' soldiers in the training camps sang. 'Even our fathers deserve to be shot.'[39]

* * *

For generations, the multiple clans that made up the two biggest peoples of South Sudan, the Dinka and Nuer, were not clearly separated. They were, rather, overlapping peoples from the same ancient roots. Their languages now were different, but the peoples still intermarried and shared much of the same culture.[40] Indeed, sometimes there was more difference between two distant Nuer clans, split by the great waters of the Sudd, than with a neighbouring Dinka clan. Extreme violence would change that, cementing differences into rival peoples.[41]

Violence in the 1990s descended into spirals of revenge. Some said more died in the battles between the South's factions than at the hands of troops from the North. Women, children and the old were now seen as acceptable targets. Soldiers who once would torch a village and set grain stores on fire then leave, would now herd children inside huts before setting them on fire. Captured fighters were executed on the battlefield. If that had started as a practical tactic by a guerrilla force with few rations and which needed to remain always mobile, then the practice fuelled the worst atrocities. Children were press-ganged to fight alongside adult soldiers. In the early battles, they were massacred as cannon fodder.

Mao's basic revolutionary doctrines of not stealing from the people were ignored, for a rifle and bullets were the only supplies soldiers would be given to survive. 'Your gun is your food; your gun is your wife,' recruits were made to sing in a graduation ceremony, when they would be handed their AK-47 rifles.[42] They became not a liberation army of the people, but an occupying force. Such glorification and encouragement of violence and death cannot simply be reeled back in when the time for war has passed. Generations were taught to kill without consequence.

'We were told to raise food rations for your army,' one elder from the Mundari people said, who had welcomed a unit of rebels seeking supplies from his village near Terekeka. 'We knew our bulls, rams,

136

grain and groundnuts were going to be your food. This is because you are our sons, our army.' The soldiers, however, demanded more. They wanted the women, and fighting broke out as their families tried to defend them. Several were killed. 'Have the private parts of our daughters, our wives, also become rations for your army?' the chief said. 'You have betrayed and abused our generosity.'[43]

* * *

Khartoum was quick to exploit such divisions as a potent recruiting tool, and the government made their first major advances for years. They persuaded Riek Machar to their side, using his forces to fight those of Garang. On paper, the politics made no sense, but the reality was about powers not true policy. Machar claimed to fight for the independence of South Sudan, but was backed by Khartoum, which fought for unity. Khartoum did not care about Machar's call for independence, for they knew a people divided posed only half the threat. Garang, who claimed to be fighting for a unified New Sudan, was their enemy. The war splinted the rebels into a messy alphabet soup of acronyms, as Machar's SPLA-United battled Garang's SPLA-Mainstream.[44]

'The leaders of the SPLA factions must address their own human rights problems and correct their own abuses, or risk a continuation of the war on tribal or political grounds in the future,' the researcher Jemera Rone wrote in a 1994 report for Human Rights Watch, documenting horrendous atrocities. It included the account of one man whose village in Equatoria was torched by the men who said they were his liberators. 'These are the ones who want to rule us in future!' he said.[45]

People calculated that over a million people had died. There was no sign of peace.[46]

9

THE MAN WHO FELL TO EARTH

'Use a slave to kill a slave.'

North Sudanese saying

Hassan al-Turabi gave a high-pitched giggle and stroked his close-cropped grey beard. 'Fighting has become a way of life for the Sudanese,' Turabi said, shrugging his shoulders, dressed in spotless, white robes. 'It is unfortunate, but when you have a dictatorship, it means you have a monopoly over power and over wealth. So what do you expect?'

His eyes twinkled with a grin. It was deeply unnerving, and not what I had expected from a man Western journalists once dubbed the 'Pope of Terror'. One of the most influential men in Sudanese politics, Turabi moulded Sudan's shift towards radical Islam, becoming puppet-master behind the throne to help Bashir seize power in 1989. His National Islamic Front party, later renamed the National Congress Party, was the preeminent force in Sudanese politics for decades. As attorney general, he oversaw some of the harshest forms of Islamic justice. He dreamed it would provide inspiration for the creation of a caliphate on the African continent.[1] He was happy to host Osama Bin Laden after he was expelled from Saudi Arabia in 1991, offering the Al-Qaeda chief a base to raise his fledgling group for five years.

Turabi reportedly fainted at the sight of blood the first time he witnessed a punishment amputation. Still, his thirst for violence towards the South remained undiminished, and in the 1990s his policies made the war bloodier than ever.[2] 'Africa is fertile, ripe for the Islamic seed,' Turabi told journalist Rory Nugent, who shared an awkward lunch of fruit and cheese with him and Bin Laden in Khartoum in 1994. 'Africa is our greatest challenge.' Turabi described his recruitment of legions of jihadi militia forces as a plan to instil 'culture' in the South. 'We wanted to plant civilisation in Southern Sudan and beyond,' he said derogatorily. 'They need one.'[3]

His mind was fiercely sharp; he had degrees in law from Khartoum and King's College London, and a doctorate from the Sorbonne. In 1991, Turabi set up the 'Popular Arab and Islamic Conference', a get-together of all sorts, from Bin Laden's Al-Qaeda *mujahedeen* Arabs, fresh from fighting Russians in Afghanistan, to Iraqi Baathists and Iranian Revolutionary Guards, and members of Hamas and Hezbollah. Egyptian Islamic Jihad used Khartoum as a launch pad for an assassination attempt on Hosni Mubarak in Ethiopia. Even the Venezuelan self-proclaimed 'professional revolutionary' Carlos the Jackal made Khartoum his base.

Turabi came to power as the Soviet bloc collapsed, but with communism in retreat, he saw a new enemy rise. Fury grew at American troops in Saudi Arabia, who came in 1990 to fight Saddam Hussein in Kuwait. When US Black Hawk helicopters were shot down in Somalia in 1993 and the body of a soldier dragged through the streets, the Islamists in Khartoum celebrated, and prepared a new front of their own. Jihadi training camps were set up outside Khartoum, including on the sprawling farms that Bin Laden ran.

[margin note: He's wrong but also right]

When I met Turabi, times had changed. It was months before Sudan split in 2011, and he had fallen out with the government in Khartoum. Yet time had not softened his racist contempt for the South. 'There is too much tribalism there,' he said. 'Once there is no common enemy to fight against, once they have passed self-determination, then they will look to themselves.'

* * *

The violence grew worse. Khartoum wanted the oil lands cleared of people; drilling operations were expanded as quickly as possible. As profits grew, Khartoum enjoyed funding for more war. Northern horsemen, the Rizeigat and Misseriya, had always come South to graze their cattle. In the 1980s, Khartoum armed them as a proxy force against rebels in the South.

In the 1990s, weapons shipments increased again. The government actively encouraged them, aiming to drive the people off the land and push people into famine. Helicopter gunships and airplanes bombed the villages before now well-armed militia units swept into the ruins to destroy what remained. Then landmines were scattered so no one came back.[4] Thousands of Southerners fled, many running to wretched camps in the North known as 'The Black Belt' by the elite in Khartoum. Shanty towns of ragged cloth tents ringed the outskirts of the capital.

The extreme violence was entirely deliberate; one commander earned a reputation for crucifying SPLA prisoners.[5] In 1994, UN teams were sent to investigate violence in the South, as disturbing reports of cruelty grew. 'Grave violations and abuses are being committed against women and children,' the UN report read, adding it had gathered 'reports of abduction, traffic, enslavement and rape carried out by persons acting as agents of the government.'[6] Women and children were separated from their families and dragged away. 'The mass abduction and traffic (including sale) seem to be an organised and politically motivated activity,' the UN wrote.

Violent, largescale enslavement of the South was back, and it was backed by the government. Children were ripped away from their parents, or rounded up in the camps and streets, forced onto trucks and taken to military barracks. Old identities were erased. 'Children of the Sudan' was written in red on their military uniforms. 'These children are transported to special camps… and are subjected to religious conversion and ideological indoctrination,' the UN said. 'There they are made to convert to Islam, and given Arabic names.' Those who resisted were starved or beaten.[7] Training began two hours before dawn with recitations of the Koran. After that came army drills. 'The physical exercises required to be performed are the same as those of the military,' the UN said. 'During this training, the idea of martyrdom for the state is given central importance.'

Months later, they would return back to the South as cannon-fodder, an expendable attack force to destroy their own people. 'The Popular Defence Forces', Khartoum called the new army.

* * *

141

A commanding voice rose above the lunchtime chatter and clink of silver cutlery in the Peers' Dining Room of British Parliament. Baroness Cox of Queensbury tapped her finger firmly on the crisp white table cloth as she made a point. I'd last met Caroline Cox, a former nurse who was now in her eighties, in a grubby bar in Juba. Here, in the House of Lords, we discussed her long role in Sudan over smoked sea trout salad and white wine. 'It was barbaric. Quite, quite barbaric,' the cross-bench peer said, a formidable campaigner who gave blistering speeches in parliament against Turabi's 'international terrorism empire' and his jihadi training schools. 'There was indescribable suffering,' she said. 'I was determined to stamp out the scourge of slavery for good.' Cox, a staunch Christian who spoke out fiercely against religious persecution, went to Sudan and clashed with Turabi face-to-face. 'By one's fruits shall you know them,' Cox said. 'In Khartoum, they appear awfully polite and charming. They'd tell me, "We want peace." I'd say to them, "Stop killing people with barrel bombs then."'

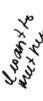

Dressed in a trouser suit, her hair pinned back with a neat band, she looked more likely to organise coffee and cake fundraising mornings than dozens of trips into rebel-held Sudan during the worst times of war. She spoke swiftly, with a quiet fury driven by moral indignation. She was a politician who not only spoke out on the wrongs she saw, but who also acted on what she believed. In the 1990s, that meant becoming an active abolitionist—raising cash for what she called the 'sad, macabre business' of buying slaves in order to set them free.

This conjured up images of lines of women and children begging slavers to be saved, as white, foreign Christians swooped in with suitcases full of money. More cash to free more slaves rolled in. Some estimated millions of dollars traded hands. The main redemption group, Christian Solidarity International, generated huge sums in fundraising from US churches and African American groups for their 'underground railroad'. A slave cost $50, the value of about two goats; CSI claimed they alone had helped rescue 80,000 slaves.

Many said such high numbers were impossible, and that while slavery was real, some abolitionists were taken in by stage-managed fakes. Critics said it added to the wider suffering by making a business out of redemption, boosting the market price beyond that which ordinary

Southerners could afford to buy back their family, and encouraging more attacks. It also pumped in hard currency that meant the very men responsible could expand their grim operations.[8]

'Of course buying freedom is not the solution,' Cox told parliament after a trip in 2000, when she had bought and freed 353 women and children. 'The solution must be to stop the slavery. But while slavery exists, I defy anyone to hear the women and children tell of their experiences as slaves, to hear them say, "If you were not here, we would not be here—we would still be slaves," and then to say to them, "I am sorry, you are going to have to remain in slavery."'[9]

As she walked me out of the House of Lords, we paused in the grand surroundings of a debating chamber dominated by a giant fresco depicting Moses and the Ten Commandments. I thought of the abolitionist William Wilberforce, who pushed to end slavery on this site two centuries before. 'I'm just one person, but you must do what you can,' she said, apologising for rushing as she said goodbye. 'I've got to get on—I'm giving a speech on Syria to get it recognised as genocide. Of course, they won't, but they should. You see, you have to try.'

* * *

The North and South are deeply intertwined. Southerners have long lived far beyond the borders defined today, and simplistic geographical divisions of sweeping racial and religious differences are riddled with complications.

On Friday afternoons in Khartoum I would walk down the river to the Al-Mogran park at the peninsula at the edge of the city, a meeting point where families picnicked and children played on swings. From the top of the creaking Ferris wheel, you can see the two Niles mingle. The Blue Nile, really coloured brown from soil washed down from the Ethiopian highlands, swirls into the White Nile, which has already come on the long journey from Tanzania, Rwanda and Uganda, and then through the South. Blue and White meld together as they flow north towards Egypt into the world's longest river. Romantics call the slow entwinement the 'longest kiss in history'.

Northerners say the Nile gave Khartoum its name, derived from the Arabic for 'elephant's trunk'. Southerners dismiss that, and say Khartoum is named after a term in Dinka, Nuer and Shilluk for the

143

fork created when a branch splits from a tree, the name used also for a crossroads and a meeting place.[10] In their eyes, the seat of the hated government in the North was an ancient settlement established by those from the South.

In Khartoum, I'd call a contact skilled in sourcing contraband drink. Sometimes it was dubious 'Johnny Walter' or 'Black Liable' whisky that came in plastic sachets like hotel shampoo, with as rough a taste. This time it was a better bottle, Eritrea's finest aniseed 'Zibib' pastis. I gathered friends over, and as the beautiful calls of the mosques' muezzins rose at dusk, we sat on the roof terrace.

As the bottle emptied, we troubled over the difficult questions. What was the war really about? Power and resources? Revenge? Or was it about race? Sudan's name comes from the Arabic for 'Land of the Blacks', but the elite in Khartoum declared themselves to be Arab, not African. Power is held in the hands of an Arab minority while the multi-ethnic nation of more than a hundred languages struggles to survive on the periphery, controlled and governed through violence. The pathological belief that they are born to rule and the others to serve is not open to discussion. '*Abid!*' I have seen men in Khartoum shout across the street to those with darker skin 'Slave!'

In Khartoum, official descriptions label Northerners as the colour *akhdar*, green, viewed as the ideal colour of skin, since it avoids the colour *aswad*, black, with its associations of Africa and a slave past.[11] Yet, ironically, of all Sudanese, it was those in Khartoum who came from the most diverse backgrounds.

'They call us slaves, but those born in the South are the ones who were never captured!' said James Natana. He was a burly Southerner from Equatoria, but had grown up as a refugee in Egypt. 'It is those in the North who are descendants of slaves, because they are the ones born from the women their fathers stole from the South,' he said. 'We share the same blood, the same genes. They call themselves Arabs, but we are all Africans. We are all from this soil, we are all from the Nile waters. Look at the people on the streets here—do they look Arab? No! We are all black. It is not about colour; it is about the state of mind.' He sloshed another round of pastis into the glasses.

Even with the luxury of an airplane, the distance across all Sudan is huge. When journeys are by bone-shaking trucks, the expanses become

[handwritten margin note: How about Northern trips?]

vast. By foot, as many do travel, journeys stretch to weeks and the land becomes colossal. All too often across that gap, the ordinary people of the North and South knew little more about each other than the fear, distrust and suspicion from the propaganda they had been fed. It was not so much that they were different in reality, but that they believed they were different.

North–South identities, concepts based on race, culture and religion, were seen as something distinctive. In reality, people from across the divide shared so much. It always surprised me that when I met the people of North and South outside of Sudan, they had far more in common with each other than the foreigners around. It was sometimes baffling; centuries of war, but at peace talks in Ethiopia the enemies chatted like old friends.

So what distorted these relations into war? From stories of the old fighters in Juba, it seemed clear it was about their treatment at the hands of Northern officials: the festering hatred that burst from being treated as inferior, having opportunities blocked, and the gross disparity in development and wealth. In the South, civilians and rebels were lumped together based not on politics, but their identity. The terms of national sovereignty were determined by a people far away; Southerners were excluded from what the leaders insisted was the definition of being Sudanese. Culture and beliefs, even languages, were suppressed.

For the outside world, news reports framed it as a war between an Arab Muslim North and a black African South who were Christian or followed traditional religions. Did religion also drive the war?

'Nonsense, they'd have killed us whatever we believed,' said Musa Kuku, another student, whose ancestral home lay in the Nuba Mountains, the rebel stronghold along the North–South border, where Muslims and Christians fought side-by-side against Khartoum. 'Those in Khartoum pray five times a day not because they are good Muslims, but because they think that makes them more Arab,' Kuku said.

The Islamist government weren't fussy who fought for them after all, Kuku pointed out. Since Uganda backed the SPLA, Khartoum backed the Ugandan rebels of Joseph Kony and his Lord's Resistance Army, the LRA. Kony was guilty of murder and mutilation, but the warlord also boasted his army was a Christian one that followed Biblical teachings. He even had the Ten Commandments embroidered onto his army's crest. Yet the fundamentalists in Khartoum were happy to bankroll their mayhem, whatever Kony did or believed.

'It is about power, and about control,' Natana added. 'They think they are born to rule, that the government and state is theirs to command. You survive if you know your place. Any challenge, and you're dead.'

Natana poured another drink. Then he launched into a summary of Sudan's 'Black Book', the banned revolutionary tract written in 2000 by opposition activists from Darfur, the France-sized region in the west. Darfuris are Muslim, but those in Khartoum looked down on their African roots. The book set out the grossly disproportionate power and wealth held by the select groups based along the Nile who brag of Arab ancestry. The Arab people made up five percent of the population, but since Sudan's independence in 1956, had taken 80 percent of key posts. [12]

As night fell, we went inside. Leafing through the bookcase, Natana pulled out a thick volume by Francis Deng, once the UN Advisor for the Prevention of Genocide. A professor in the US, Deng was born in Abyei, the grassland border zone that both North and South claim as theirs.

Natana read a passage on how the North's pride as an Arab people meant they had discarded their African identity. 'For them, religion is a smokescreen for a policy of racial domination, and the price of an African-based national unity is too high,' Deng wrote. 'The southern Sudanese too, are proud of their race—which has survived recurrent Arab invasions for slaves—and contemptuous of a race they consider morally depraved and bent on dominating, subjugating and humiliating the black race. They would rather take the northern Sudanese for what they claim to be—Arabs. The fact that these Arabs deny their visible black African genetic origins is all the more reason to despise them as renegades.' [13]

Natana snapped the book shut with a puff of dust left by sandstorms that had covered the city a few days before. He shook the bottle upside down to get the last drops. 'Let's go out,' he said.

We squeezed into a motor rickshaw and lurched through Khartoum. It was Thursday night, the start of the weekend in the North. We headed to Papa Costas, about the closest Khartoum got to a nightclub. Beneath the palm fronds in the courtyard we ordered a lime juice, and listened to the echo of pre-Sharia days. The live music that had been suppressed for years was making a discreet return.

'On a dark desert highway, cool wind in my hair,' sang Ali Doka from the veteran Blue Stars band, belting out an eclectic blend of North African hits, jazz covers and reggae. The seated crowd—families, couples and friends—watched as Doka clutched the microphone and crooned The Eagles. Some watching joined in by clapping along. 'I was thinking to myself, this could be heaven or this could be hell,' he sang.

* * *

In 1992, Khartoum renewed the call for jihad, railing against all who opposed the Islamists' rule. Non-Muslim fighters were branded infidels, foreign forces were 'Zionists and Crusaders', and Muslim rebels were apostates. Declaring them all enemies was useful when the overall aim was to take their land. Soldiers had a free hand to kill and raid as they wished. It was not about conversion, for that would have prevented the further exploitation of the South. It was about conquest. 'Their lot is to suffer torture in hell for eternity,' the *fatwa* read.[14] A year later, Washington put Sudan on its list of state sponsors of terrorism.

Khartoum needed men to fight so that the children of the privileged did not have to, and the language of jihad was a potent recruiting tool. For peasant farmers scratching a living from arid scrub, paradise had a certain appeal. It was also useful to divert attention from the basic economic failures and political grievances that drove the conflict from the beginning.

Declaring jihad and casting the war as a religious duty won Khartoum support from other Muslim nations. Still today, a few hours southwest of Juba, people can show you the bleached bones of the 'foreign Arabs' scattered around the rocky hill they call Jebel Iraqi, some of the 200 paratroopers from Baghdad they say died there.[15]

Declaring jihad also brought trouble. On a quiet Thursday afternoon, I crossed the Blue Nile to Khartoum North, weaving down the dusty streets until I arrived at what looked like a building site, with piles of bricks and twisted metal reinforcement bars sticking out of concrete slabs. The Al-Shifa pharmaceutical factory had been left untouched ever since US cruise missiles had smashed into its roof in 1998, days after Islamist bombers attacked the US embassies in Kenya and Tanzania, killing over 200 people.

Washington said the Khartoum factory produced nerve gas, but offered scant evidence for this.[16] Khartoum said it destroyed its ability to produce paracetamol and other basic drugs, resulting in the subsequent deaths of tens of thousands. Bored guards offered plastic medicine bottles from the wreckage as evidence. On a crumbling brick wall, someone had scrawled a message in English. 'Down USA', it read.

* * *

The history of US involvement in Sudan is a short one, but important.

The first time the Stars and Stripes fluttered in South Sudan was in the 1860s, on the back of a slave ship.[17] The next time it flew was when an ex-president came to kill animals.

'A wilderness of savage men and savage beasts,' wrote Theodore Roosevelt, the 26th president of the United States, who in 1910 visited on an East African hunting trip. 'Swamps where the slime oozes and bubbles and festers in the steaming heat.' Even as a retired president, Roosevelt is the most senior American to have spent extended time in the Sudans. Photographs show a portly man grinning in pith helmet and puttees beneath the US flag, displaying pride in the number of animals he had slaughtered. His team massacred twenty rhinos—now likely extinct in South Sudan—as well as two dozen elephant and lion across East Africa. One of Roosevelt's hunting bases retains its name today, 'Rhino Camp' in Uganda, now home to the mass exodus of South Sudanese refugees who fled civil war in 2013.[18] 'Sunrise and sunset were beautiful over the endless, melancholy stretches of water reeds,' Roosevelt wrote, as his steamer nosed through the Sudd to Khartoum, quaffing champagne because the water gave him dysentery. 'Now and then we passed native villages, the tall, lean men and women stark naked, and their bodies daubed with mud, grease and ashes.'[19]

After Roosevelt's shooting spree, Sudan sank back into Washington's foreign policy obscurity. The US became involved again ahead of Sudan's independence in 1956, when pressure mounted to placate Egypt's demand for North–South unity, to ensure critical access to the Suez Canal. The US ambassador, Jefferson Caffrey, was incredulous at British officers' concerns for the South when they left. He told the top British bureaucrat in Khartoum, Sir James Robertson, that unity must be pushed through even at the price of selling the Sudan'. With a quiet fury,

Robertson recalled the conversations with US diplomats. 'It was obvious that he, like many of the US citizens who had come to the Sudan, could not appreciate our concern for what one of them described as "10 million bloody niggers,"' Robertson wrote in disgust.[20]

Washington soon saw Sudan's strategic importance, fearful of Soviet influence and then Libya's Gadhafi. It would take time for the CIA to get up to speed. A year after Sudan's independence, spies warned of the dire lack of assets on the ground.[21] By 1963, the CIA had compiled a 150-page Sudan handbook for guerrilla warfare, but it reveals a troublesome dearth of knowledge. For the South, the handy tips it offers agents included warnings against hungry lions, ferocious crocodiles ('particularly bad along the Nile') and witchdoctors ('a thriving business in charms').[22]

For the next two decades, Washington backed the government. It supported Khartoum during the Anya-Nya war. Then there was the matter of oil, and US giant Chevron made significant investments. When war returned in 1983, the Libyan and Soviet bloc-backed SPLA found no favour in Washington. The US provided Khartoum with weapons instead.

Yet by the early 1990s, politics shifted. The Soviet Union had collapsed, and Khartoum had backed both militant Islam and Saddam Hussein in the First Gulf War. The SPLA now battled a government that hated the US, and the rebels found a more sympathetic ear in Washington.

Garang toned down his Marxist rhetoric, brushed over the murderous excesses of his rebellion, and charmed those eager to believe in a better future for Sudan. The SPLA spoke of the hope of peace, development and equality—and of religion. Describing the suffering of an oppressed Southern Christian minority suffering resurgent slavery from the Islamist North was potent stuff. It won influential backers in the US.

On the left, the largely Democrat-supporting Congressional Black Caucus pushed the crisis in the South to the highest levels of politics. On this one issue, they found a common ally in traditional rivals, for both sides of the political divide became supporters of the South. On the right, evangelical Christians enraged by the persecution of fellow believers also became vocal critics of Khartoum. They were a vital support base of the Republicans.

Key among South Sudan's backers were a tiny team of Washington's 'wonks', an unlikely squad of academics, aid workers and activists.[23] The self-appointed Friends of South Sudan had influential friends, and the group, which included Garang's old college friend Brian D'Silva, helped marshal support in Washington. The gang of half a dozen included English lecturer Eric Reeves—specialties: Byron, Milton and war in Sudan—as well as US State Department staffer and activist John Prendergast. The South, they thought, was a place where they could influence US policy to help end suffering. They used their professional skills to champion supporters in Congress, but it was a crusade born from personal passion. They lionised Garang, wooed by the potent combination of the cause and his personal charisma, the carnage of his campaigns overshadowed by the utter horror of Khartoum's attacks.

Slowly, they opened the doors of power to listen to their plan of forging a new nation. They would have a profound influence, becoming a powerful force to push South Sudan to the top of the agenda.

* * *

The men in suits needed a frontman for the cause.

The American Anti-Slavery Group, a coalition of abolition activists, encouraged Francis Bok, ex-slave turned refugee and now US citizen, to speak out. Bok, who had spent his childhood looking after cattle for his 'master' before escaping, told his powerful testimony to the US Senate. 'I told them how they have beaten me and treated me like an animal,' said Bok. 'I called on the American people, especially my African-American brothers and sisters, to stand up and help my people.'[24]

One other man also stood out and drew the crowds. Dinka cattle herder turned basketball legend Manute Bol broke the record for the tallest player ever in the NBA, standing at 7 foot 7 inches, or 2.31 metres. He was talent-spotted from obscurity and pushed into the big league.

The outside world remembers him for his towering performances on court, an iconic shot blocker. 'My bad,' was his catchphrase, for with his freestyle English and scrappy play, Manute made the saying famous as his own unique apology.[25] At times he was seen as an exotic figure of fun, taking part in celebrity boxing, horse riding and ice hockey matches. US media made much of the fact he was the only NBA player to have speared a lion. He promoted fried chicken. 'Nothing but legs' was the advertising slogan.[26]

Manute brushed it off; what mattered to him was the publicity that could help his people. He used his fame to straddle the opposite worlds of US celebrity and South Sudan's suffering, and bring the world's attention to the pain of a far-away war. He was not a sophisticated campaigner, but he could command audiences that the wonks, suits and spooks could only dream of. He made the world sit up and take notice.

'I made a lot of money,' he said. 'I feel I have to give this back to my people.' He poured the millions from NBA earnings and endorsements into supporting his homeland until he was broke. He spent his cash on food aid shipments for the South, and became a key backer of the SPLA, paying for their Washington office and an expensive lobbyist. There were more direct donations too. Manute once boasted of buying two tanks for the SPLA, and estimated spending over $3.5 million on the rebels.[27] When Garang came to Washington, Manute planned to hire a limousine to make sure he impressed when he arrived at Capitol Hill. The wonks who had wrangled Garang the meetings realised it would give the wrong message for a bush guerrilla looking for funding, and swapped it for a beaten-up banger.

For Manute, the struggle was personal. 'Over 250 members of my family were killed,' Manute told me, in the slow Kansas drawl of his adopted home. Manute returned to South Sudan to offer support in the run-up to the independence referendum, building schools and working for reconciliation.

'The government came with weapons and ammunition to wipe us out,' Manute said, describing how his hometown of Turalei was left in ruins. His long arm stretched out to hand me a Red Horse beer as we sat outside his house in Juba, and he told me of the wars that had ravaged the villages when he was growing up. 'I had to do what I could,' Manute said. 'And what I could do was to speak out about what the government in Khartoum was doing, and tell the people in the United States about that. Back then, there weren't too many of us from Sudan able to say what was happening. People didn't believe me at first, but in the end, they listened. I told them, Garang is not Communist. He is only getting support from them because no one else is helping. So that is what I did.'

* * *

In the dark waters of the Aswa river, the deadly tangle of glinting barbs flickered. It was, quite literally, the rebels' last line of defence: a home-made aquatic barbed wire barricade made of 15,000 fishing hooks, swirling like knives and tied on long lines to snare the unwary. Almost out of bullets, dug into fox holes and trenches to shelter from daily artillery and aircraft bombings, it was a thin line of protection to stop an assault across the river. By 1994, the rebels had been driven so far south that the frontline was within sight of Uganda. If the river was crossed, the SPLA would be over.

'It was the last stand,' said Dan Eiffe, an Irish missionary, who had diverted the hooks from an aid agency come to help feed the exodus of refugees. 'The SPLA had next to nothing, and were running out of bullets to defend, let alone attack.' Eiffe and comrades feared the SPLA in 1994 were on the verge of a defeat that would end what they saw as a rightful cause. 'It reminded me in many ways of an Irish struggle, people fighting for liberty and against oppression,' Eiffe said, a round-bellied man with grey hair. 'I'd been in South Africa at the worst of apartheid. That was a tea party in comparison to the situation in South Sudan. It was ethnic cleansing. It was genocide. The bottom line is, the government wanted the land without the people.'

A Catholic priest posted to government-held Juba, Eiffe had fallen in love with a Dinka woman, married her, and then all but joined the SPLA. The soldiers called him Commander Dan. As the memories of the war rushed back, his soft Irish lilt hardened, and his voice trembled with anger. 'We were there on the ground to fight, to struggle with them,' he said. 'We were bombed, every day. I'm a Catholic priest, so forgive my language, but do you know what it was like to be bombed every fucking day on the ground? Do you? Do you?'

After the 1991 loss of bases in Ethiopia and amid devastating internal fighting, the rebels lost almost all of their territory. They had been pushed ever southwards, nearly out of Sudan itself. In the North, SPLA rebels clung on in the caves of the Nuba Mountains. In the far south, Khartoum threw everything they had to crush them, supported by the men of Riek Machar. The Aswa river was the frontline. 'That was all there was between them and being pushed out of the country,' said Eiffe.

He fought as he could—by helping turn the tide of propaganda in favour of the SPLA. 'It was a cliché of a forgotten war. I organised dozens of trips for journalists to go in and see people dying,' Eiffe said, who became effectively a spokesman for the rebels. 'I told the SPLA this: you've been doing this fighting for 15 years, and before in the first war, another 20 years. So now you need to do something different to get the world's attention.'

It wasn't only the media that Eiffe arranged. He was frustrated at the UN's enormous Operation Lifeline Sudan, then the world's largest-ever humanitarian operation, but which was hamstrung by having to get permission from Khartoum. Strict rules meant they could supply aid only to areas Khartoum allowed, which meant feeding one area at the expense of the government's enemies.

Eiffe worked for the left-wing solidarity group Norwegian People's Aid, NPA, who ran frontline hospitals for the wounded rebels. In their eyes, UN rules politicised the aid and prolonged the misery by keeping people alive but providing no solution. 'The will for peace, in the interpretation of NPA, could only come if either a "hurting stalemate" is experienced by both sides, or a decisive victory is achieved by one,' Norway's Foreign Ministry wrote.[28] So NPA and friends operated outside UN control, helping channel aid from the US and other supporters keen to help the South. 'We ignored the rules,' Eiffe said. 'We could get the pilots and the planes to go to any areas.'

Some said they took it one step further. NPA as an organisation is adamant it never provided military support, but maverick aid workers crossed the line to actively support the SPLA's cause.[29] So NPA got a new nickname: Norwegian People's Army.

Bush pilots packed small planes—one rickety British aircraft was once reportedly part of the royal fleet that flew the Queen—and brought in ammunition, guns and medicine. The small planes snuck in, bouncing down on bumpy fields cleared of rocks by hand, swiftly unloading, then roaring off before Khartoum's bombers could attack. In the besieged Nuba Mountains, it kept the people alive. Cargo manifests were disguised; long boxes of rifles were called 'cut flowers', metal tins of bullets were 'sardines' or 'typewriter parts', and rockets were labelled 'parts for construction'.[30] Trucks crept through on remote tracks supplied through Eritrea, Congo and Uganda. Western security forces were deeply involved.

Some willing to take the risk made hefty profits. Yet this was not the champagne world of mercenary arms dealers earning millions. For many, they did the dangerous and difficult work because they truly believed in the struggle.

'We did it because we supported what the SPLA were fighting for,' one ex-smuggler told me. 'The people had to be able to fight for change.' He had made no fortune in the two decades he had worked in South Sudan. We shared beers in a simple, thatch-hut bar in Juba underneath a slow-moving fan that only served to push the sweaty air around. He and his old war friends still called themselves by their radio call signs from the war. The heady mix of adrenaline, danger, and a passionate sense of a cause had a powerful hold. 'If we'd only supplied food for people to survive but nothing to protect them from being killed, what would have been the point? Why give people bandages to heal the wounds of the bombs, but nothing to stop the bombers?' he said. 'It would be like watching someone beat a man to death and not stopping it, only offering water between the punches.'

Eiffe, the former priest, believes it helped turn the tide of war. 'I advocated for military support,' he said. 'When they needed it, I got people to say "Yes, we'll support them."' Sneaking out from the front-line, he carried a list from Garang to Ugandan President Yoweri Museveni that detailed the support he needed. 'The battle in the making may most likely be the last one the SPLA will be able to fight,' Eiffe told Museveni. 'What is in the making is a terrible massacre.'[31]

Museveni took action. Ugandan tanks and weapons surged north, opening up a barrage of fire over the river into Sudan and driving Khartoum's soldiers back in a messy retreat. The SPLA crossed the water and chased the forces north.

* * *

Slowly, the SPLA pushed back. By 1995, Khartoum's offensives were running out of steam, and the rebels seized key towns. In the SPLA's 'Liberated Areas', the nascent administration of an independent government began to form.

Washington sent help. It provided key military support for three SPLA allies—Eritrea, Ethiopia and Uganda—who then shipped weapons to the rebels. Ethiopia, having fallen out with Khartoum again, sent in planeload after planeload of supplies. Eritrea used the logistical skills and expert guerrilla tactics developed in its 30-year war of independence to provide arms and training. It also supported a separate front in the North, backing rebels in north-eastern Sudan. Eritreans, better suited to squeezing into tanks than the towering South Sudanese, helped as drivers and gunners.[32]

Uganda offered rearguard bases, sending troops across to fight with the SPLA. In revenge, Sudan supported the Ugandan LRA rebels of Joseph Kony, who had slaughtered more than 100,000 people in years of war. They had also kidnapped more than 60,000 children, taking boys to fight and girls to rape. Their calling card was to leave a few behind alive, hacking off hands until they were useless stumps, or slicing away the lips so the teeth were bared.

In 1997, US Secretary of State Madeleine Albright visited Gulu in northern Uganda, the epicentre of LRA violence. She cradled a month-old girl called Charity, whose parents had been murdered by the LRA. 'You are the future of Africa,' she told the orphaned schoolchildren. 'You are God's gift to the world, and we will do what we can to help you.'[33] Sanctions against Khartoum were increased, with Sudan accused of terrorism, religious persecution and human rights abuses. Military support grew.

Albright also met with Garang, the most official high-level contact so far between Washington and the SPLA. 'It appeared intended to send a message to the Sudan's Islamic Government that America supports the rebel's efforts to establish democracy,' the *New York Times* wrote, noting that the US had by then provided 'about $20 million in military aid other than weapons to Eritrea, Ethiopia and Uganda, all of which in turn supply the rebels with arms'.[34]

The SPLA was strengthened, but hope of a decisive victory remained a dream. The new guns pushed the war to a painful deadlock, but Khartoum would not buckle.

* * *

Then, the airplanes smashed into the Twin Towers on 9/11. 'Every nation in every region now has a decision to make,' President George W. Bush said days later. 'Either you are with us or you are with the terrorists.'[35] Bin Laden had left Khartoum in 1996 for Afghanistan, but his former hosts in Khartoum were deeply nervous. If help from Khartoum was not forthcoming, CIA officers told their Sudanese counterparts exactly 'what could be taken out' in an afternoon of air-strikes.[36] The first pipeline from the South to the Red Sea had opened only two years earlier, a gigantic route the distance of London to Rome. Oil was now the core of the economy.

'If we are ever going to reach a solution, we will find it in the smoke that is coming out of this building,' veteran SPLA commander Lual Diing said as he watched the news reports.[37] Sudan tried to show that it wanted to cooperate. They had, in the past, given intelligence snippets to improve relations but revealed nothing ground breaking. After 9/11, they opened their files on old comrades. Spies said it was 'A+' information. By late 2001, the CIA's Khartoum station was back in business, and Britain's MI6 boosted its presence.[38]

Bashir, anxious in his presidential palace with the economy failing and growing splits in the military, was now treading on dangerous ground, both at home and abroad. He needed to shore up his position. Internationally, he wanted to be seen to act, even if, in reality, he wanted nothing to change. He gambled on the idea that being seen to broker peace with the South would allow him to stay in power. Bashir ordered his deputy Ali Osman Taha to open negotiations with Garang. On paper, it would be harder to find two men more different.

Taha, a studious, quiet and conservative Islamist, had helped Bashir take power in the 1989 coup. Garang, the charismatic guerrilla from the bush who combined academic policy with popular rhetoric, had long been his arch enemy. The hatred of decades could not disappear overnight. Yet, as the wider politics shifted, the two men looked for common ground. 'We had both had a rebellious past,' Taha said. 'We realised that both of us had resorted to arms in support of our political aims. So there were a lot of similarities between us.'[39]

The pressure was intense. Bush said finding peace in Sudan was his top Africa priority, calling Bashir almost a dozen times over the negotiations.[40] A year after 9/11, he signed the Sudan Peace Act. It offered a stark warning to Khartoum. 'The Act is designed to help address the evils inflicted on the people of Sudan by their government—including senseless suffering, use of emergency food relief as a weapon of war, and the practice of slavery—and to press the parties, and in particular the Sudanese Government, to complete in good faith the negotiations to end the war,' Bush said.[41]

The abolitionist Francis Bok was there to witness the signing, the former Dinka cattle herder standing out tall from the crowds in the White House. 'You're the first president in 150 years to meet with a former slave,' Bok said as he shook hands with the president, thanking him for bringing hope to the 'boys and girls still in slavery' in Sudan. 'You're so tall,' Bush replied, according to Bok. 'Look at me, and look at you.'[42]

Building trust took years. Past peace efforts had failed before. International backing was given by the US, Britain and Norway, a grouping called 'The Troika', but the mediator was an ex-security chief from Kenya, General Lazaro Sumbeiywo. Key was Sumbeiywo's use of 'back channels' to pass messages. That helped the sides move slowly closer towards each other before the rivals met face to face—the US and Norwegians for the SPLA, and the Egyptians to talk to Khartoum.

Sumbeiywo first brought the parties together in Kenya in 2002. 'You must be careful, for those at the talks can tell you what you want to hear, or what they want,' Sumbeiywo said. 'They don't tell you what the people on the ground want—or need.'

Meanwhile, year after year, war in Sudan continued. In the South, there was optimism, with Riek Machar returning to the SPLA in 2002, breaking his deal with Khartoum. The anger, distrust and bitterness remained, bubbling beneath the surface. For now, however, Machar's Nuer troops—and with them the control of key oilfields—were back with the SPLA and Garang. On the ground, church leaders brought people together for local deals. The Church helped to bridge the hatreds. Peace was needed within the South as much as it was with the North.

As the talks dragged on, Khartoum began fighting another war in the North, in the vast lands of Darfur. Rebels there had similar grievances of marginalisation and theft of their land by government militia. The war added to the pressure.

Painfully slowly, the two sides came closer. There were multiple sticking points: oil, resources, power and security, as well as the biggest of all—possible independence for the South. Rounds of talks were held in the Kenyan lakeside resort of Naivasha, a couple of hours drive north of Nairobi, where giraffe, hippo and antelope wander through the manicured lawns of luxury lodges. The brinkmanship was intense. At times, both sides stormed out and packed their bags to leave, before coming back at the last minute. Sumbeiywo submitted one peace suggestion in 2003. 'Drink it and go to hell!' Bashir told him.

Yet piece by piece, deals were made. A unity government in Khartoum was agreed, with a semi-autonomous regional government in Juba to run the South. In terms of religion, Islamic sharia law would apply in the North, but not in the South. Militarily, the South would keep its army, unlike in the 1972 deal that ended the last war. The SPLA would pull out of land in the North and, in turn, tens of thousands of government troops would leave the South. Special army units combining the old enemies would be formed in flashpoint areas along the border and in key towns. It was hoped the 'Joint Integrated Units' would form the nucleus of a new army, protecting a peaceful, unified Sudan. Economically, an oil deal was agreed. More than three-quarters of all Sudan's reserves were in the South, but revenues from oil from the South would be split equally between each side. The South would get more than a billion dollars a year for its budget.

Millions had died over decades of war. The deal was given a grand title befitting its importance: the Comprehensive Peace Agreement, or CPA.

* * *

Cynics, of course, could point to plenty of problems. For one thing, the Comprehensive Peace Agreement was not comprehensive. It did not include wars in Darfur and the East, and was, in effect, a deal between Bashir and Garang. 'Comprehensive, in my understanding, would be the whole of Sudan,' Sumbeiywo said. 'That was never on the table: the government would not allow it. Every time I tried to raise it they said, "Oh, you want to come and resolve all our conflicts?"'

The CPA was certainly an agreement, but one made under intense international arm-twisting. 'This peace agreement was reached, not necessarily because the parties wanted to, but because both parties were forced to,' Garang said during the talks. 'We negotiated an agreement because we were forced to by a lot of pressures. The cost of continuing the war was felt by both sides to be much higher than the cost of stopping the war.'[43]

As for peace—the P of the CPA—it was, in the end, only an expression of hope that the piece of paper would lead to that. The challenge would come when the hard negotiated details were implemented.

But the deal had a fundamental clause. 'The people of South Sudan have the right to self-determination,' it read. After a six-year gap to show that unity was an attractive option, the South would choose if they wanted to forge a new nation of their own.

Militarily, neither side could claim to have been the victor in the war. Yet now there were fixed steps towards the chance of unprecedented political change. In that, the South had won.

* * *

On 9 January 2005, the CPA was signed. 'I and those who joined me in the bush and fought for more than 20 years have brought to you the CPA on a golden plate,' Garang said. 'Our mission is accomplished. It is now your turn.' The war was over; it had been a 21-year conflict that, since 1983, had left some two million people dead, triple the number killed in the American Civil War. The US Committee for Refugees said it was the largest number of civilians killed in any conflict since World War Two.

Garang was triumphant, and six months later, he flew to Khartoum. The rebel chief was now Vice President of Sudan. Crowds went wild. There was hope. There was a possibility of peace. There was the dream of a New Sudan.

* * *

Days later, he was dead. He had been in Uganda meeting Museveni, who had lent him a helicopter to fly home. On 30 July 2005, flying towards Garang's bush base at New Site, the Mi-172 Soviet-built chopper smashed into rugged mountains just after crossing over the Ugandan border into South Sudan.

'There were clouds,' said Brigadier-General Deng Dau Deng, an aide of Garang. 'Not really rain, but drizzling.' At 17:10, far later than expected, they were called to say the helicopter was taking off in Uganda. The 90-minute flight was expected to land around nightfall. It was flown by one of Uganda's most experienced air force colonels, a personal pilot of Museveni. 'They called to say: "We are leaving now,"' said Deng, who went to the dirt airstrip to welcome the helicopter with Garang's wife, Rebecca Nyandeng. 'Madame Rebecca said, "No, no, no! Why are you leaving this late?"'

The charred wreckage was found the next afternoon, a few minutes short of its destination. All had been killed. News of the crash sparked rioting across Sudan, and scores were killed. The last time Garang had been in Juba was before the war began; this time he entered in a coffin.

Rebecca Nyandeng later said her husband was assassinated, although she has never said who she believes is to blame.[44] Later, a joint Sudanese-Ugandan investigation, carried out with help from US, Russian and Kenyan aviation experts, ruled out foul play. It blamed a combination of pilot error, impending darkness, and poor weather, noting also shortcomings in Uganda's military aircraft in general.[45] Diplomats and security experts say the crash was most likely an accident. Conspiracy theories still swirl.

Standing at his grave in Juba, covered in dusty artificial flowers, I looked at Garang's framed photograph. An SPLA guard, cradling a gun in her arms, watched me warily as I bent down to read the title of the portrait. 'Man of vision,' it read. 'Freedom Fighter. Hero. Icon.' With Garang, so much more than just the man had died.

10

THE LAND OF KUSH

'Violence can destroy power; it is utterly incapable of creating it.'

Hannah Arendt.[1]

Twisting my head to stare out of the grubby airplane porthole, I looked onto a different world of green hills covered with wisps of cloud. Tiny villages appeared in small clearings of forest. Thin, red and twisting pathways connected each to each like capillaries on a breathing body. Then the land grew drier, the villages fewer, and the plains became yellow, dry savannah. It was 2006, and I was flying to Juba. Since conversation wasn't possible, I had time to think, or at least try to, as the thudding judder of the propellers vibrated the metal panels beneath our feet. As the plane tilted, we slid forward towards the jumbled bags and boxes stashed at the front. Two crates of Nile Special beer took pride of place.

Seen from up high, the land seemed endless. I stared at the sweeping, meandering waters below, where wisps of smoke rose from a fishing camp on an island in the swamp. Terrible things had been done here, and there would be no quick fix. So long at war had divided people, so the need for reconciliation was acute. I opened my notebook, and asked myself a question. If nationalism is such a powerful force that people will die for their country, what makes a state?

Nations are human creations. First, I wrote, there were the borders, the frontiers that made it a separate land. Then, there were the obvious emblems: a flag, national anthem, football teams, a coat of arms, currency and passports too. Yet they were the trappings of state, for symbols do not make a country alone. There were the institutions: a government, judiciary, police and an army, the laws and taxes they impose, and the services they should provide. Then there were more intangible elements: culture and common identity, a shared history. But what about language? How did ethnicity fit in? I added question marks after those. Then I scribbled it all out.

For almost every attribute, I could think of an exception. 'War made the state, and the state makes war,' I remembered from a lecture long ago.[2] Yet saying what a nation does is not the same as defining what it is. Nations can feel ancient and eternal, but, beneath the foundation myths, most are very modern constructs. Academics call them imagined communities—social creations that conjure up a collective sense of comradeship. Yet they are dreams so potent that people will sacrifice everything for them.[3]

What made the distinction between 'us' and 'them'? I thought of Britain, where I was from. We'd been state-building since the Romans left, but I still couldn't explain what made our many countries one nation.

What South Sudan faced was very different: to not only define their nation, but then construct it too. Amid their many identities and languages, they were proud to share that of *Junubin*, 'Southerners' in Arabic. The problem was, what did that mean? It was an identity fed by centuries of pain and shared suffering. The bond was based more on what South Sudan was not—its enemies—than what it was, its people. 'Not Arab' was useful for recruitment in the liberation war, but it was a thin and dangerous bond to unite a new nation. For South Sudan, its story was one of war, and of being a suffering victim. I thought gloomily of the old maxim, that the bullied become bullies. Those who see themselves as victims become, in time, the victimisers of others. It was a poisonous cycle of abuse.

The sense we have of ourselves is fragile, built up like layers of an onion. At the heart is our family; then, the nearest neighbours, the wider community; moving out to a sense of a people based on language, life and shared experiences. Usually, the final layers that embrace the whole is a sense of nationalism, of belonging as a country. For South Sudan, that outside skin was paper-thin. People looked to the community directly surrounding them for support, security and safety. When the worst of times come, the layers are shed from the outside first. What remains at the heart is that closest to us, and in South Sudan, that peeled open to some 70 ethnic groups.

My stomach sank as the plane banked sharply over the shining silver waters of the White Nile. The bush gave way to streets of rusted brown tin roofs. Roaring down, we bounced hard on the rutted airstrip, skidded and swayed, and thankfully stopped. The passengers burst into applause. Flying in these clunking Cold War antiques was a risky business, and there had been recent fireball crashes. I felt sick with every take-off and touch-down. I turned to my neighbour, who clapped his hands with a broad smile. 'You were nervous about landing, like me?' I asked. 'No,' he replied. 'I'm happy to be home.' He was bursting with pride, hope and happiness to be back in his fledgling nation to be. A woman sang a high-pitched song of joy. 'Welcome to the Free South,' he said, shaking my hand. 'Welcome to South Sudan.'

* * *

As I stepped out of the plane door, the smothering heat felt like wet blankets smacking my face. Chest-high grass lined the edge of Juba airport, with a rusting fighter jet poking out of the swamplands to the side. Juba was now the seat of the Government of Southern Sudan, and the rule of Khartoum seemed far away. Still, South Sudan faced multiple problems of being almost independent, but not quite yet a country. I pulled out a yellow cardboard pass with my photo stapled to it, the South's own authorisation to bypass difficult visa requirements from Khartoum. A unity government had been forged after the 2005 peace deal, but the ex-rebels ran matters here.

Juba had been the prize the SPLA had dreamed of capturing through the long years of war. It had been under siege for two decades. The SPLA had once fought deep into the city, but pulled out in bloody retreat before they could capture it. Now, during peace, it was in their control at last. Juba was the main city in the South, and it was falling apart at the seams. 'A city repeatedly raped by zombies and forgotten by time,' one South Sudanese writer described his capital. 'Welcome to Juba, the village city of heat, filth, shit, booze, grub and raw sex.'[4]

In other countries I'd been to, where they had toppled the government to take power, rebels had inherited the infrastructure and stepped into the offices to run the state from the departing administration. The buildings might have been ruined by war, but it was somewhere to begin. South Sudan did not even have that. It was starting from scratch, for Juba would be a new capital entirely. Diplomats arriving from sprawling Khartoum with its high-rise buildings and wide roads wandered the dirt tracks in shock. It was hard to imagine two towns so different within the same land.

Almost everything had decayed and collapsed. Juba was better off than many rural areas that saw the heaviest fighting, but it lacked the most basic of infrastructure. Much of the town was thatch huts, or low bungalows with tin roofs rusted through. People lived in the ruins of houses, stringing up plastic sheeting as a makeshift roof, cooking on open fires on the verandas. Diplomats lived under canvas, with one tent serving as the consulate, another for their bed. There was no sewage system, nor any piped water. Trucks pumped it from the muddy banks of the Nile. The water in your bucket shower was brown, even before you'd washed. The only electricity was from private generators. At dusk, as the mosquitos came out with fierce whines and the call to prayer sang out from the mosques, a steady thumping beat of engines rose over the town. The old ceiling fans creaked into action, scattering dust.

Imports were flown in at grossly inflated prices, for the road south to Uganda was in ruins. The umbilical cord for trade was a narrow track with its bridges collapsed and landmines hidden along the route. So the legions of aid workers were a captive market, and the businessmen made a killing. You could pay considerably more for a single bed in a converted shipping container with rattling air conditioning than you could for a luxury safari camp or a business hotel in neighbouring Kenya. A soggy pizza was double the cost of that in a decent London restaurant.

Even getting a mobile telephone line was hard, as the limited masts groaned with too many calls, and companies had run out of sim cards. The Southern government had no country code of its own; they didn't want to use that of Khartoum for fear of having their conversations listened to. As a result, a phone operator piggybacked on the country code of Uganda, meaning that calls to Khartoum became international— although the two systems rarely connected. If you had cash, you had separate phones for different lines. If you really had money, you carried a bulky satellite phone. With several phones jingling in their multi-pocket vests, UN workers sounded like Christmas decorations.

Sickness was rife, for extreme poverty combined with humid weather and enormous swamps created the perfect greenhouse for disease. Aid workers said one in every seven children died before the age of five. Malaria from the bites of mosquitoes, malnutrition and diarrhoea were the main killers, but there was a whole range more. The World Health Organization had a global list of neglected tropical diseases it wanted tackled, from flesh eating parasites to deadly viruses. The South hosted the entire list except one, more than any other nation.[5] Some seemed the sort so long eliminated that you read about them only in explorers' accounts: leprosy, sleeping sickness that sent you into a coma, the deadly kala azar fever, Ebola, bilharzia, blinding trachoma and biting blackflies that inserted blindness-causing worms. The South was even one of the last major strongholds of the terrible guinea worm—named in the Bible as the 'fiery serpent'—arm-length parasites that burrow out after a year feasting inside. In a land without a functioning healthcare system, there was a seemingly boundless collection of ways to die.

* * *

I liberated my bag from the chaos of the decaying arrivals hall, a mosquito-infested oven of sweat. A chalk cross marked on the bag by a tired soldier served as a security check, and I walked out into the blazing sun. There were a dozen army pickup trucks, but the rest of the car park was full of a fleet of white Land Cruisers. All bore the emblems of the UN or aid agencies that promised the world: hope, change, peace and development. Others offered food, water, health, or another governance, and a couple, religion. It looked like a competition about who could give the most.

I had no lift. There were barely any motorbike taxis for the first couple of years after the war, and the big cars offering lifts demanded fistfuls of dollars for just a short ride. I put my bag on my back, and started walking. On the single stretch of potholed road leading out from the sleepy centre of town, I reached the roundabout, where a colonial-era stone pillar covered in long grass commemorated the names of European explorers who had passed this way a century before. It stood at an angle, as though a truck had smashed into it. It gave directions to long since vanished destinations: the aerodrome, Juba Wharf, the Belgian Congo.

An elderly gentlemen stopped his creaking bicycle, and asked if I wanted a ride. I sat astride the bike's luggage rack. We sped down the hill past the hospital, clinging on as we swerved around the sleepy goats outside the cathedral. We parted at the ruined cinema. I walked on towards a tent pitched in the shade of the banana trees, on the banks of the wide river. At night, the stars shimmered like fireflies.

* * *

It was 2006, not yet a year since Garang had died. People were still in shock. There were terrors it would restart war. Many feared the crash had been an assassination and that Khartoum might scrap the peace deal. Yet peace had held and Khartoum had kept, for the main part, its side of the bargain. Garang's deputy Salva Kiir, a battle-hardened general from the Dinka cattle herding lands of Bahr el Ghazal, had taken over. He was a man more used to fighting than diplomacy, an apparently reluctant president who sorely lacked the charisma of Garang. He had fought in the Anya-Nya war, then served as a military intelligence officer in the years of peace. He returned to fight as a founding member of the SPLA in 1983, sneaking off from his post in Malakal with three dozen men shortly after the battles in Bor.[6]

With Garang's death, the vision of one unified 'New Sudan' faded too, for Kiir was known to back independence. His focus was to ensure the referendum set for January 2011 would go ahead on time, fearful that any delay could see it scrapped. Until then, the government in Juba had committed itself to 'make unity attractive'. Under the peace deal, Kiir could not campaign for separation openly. He was still both president of the South and Vice President of all Sudan. It would leave the South in a strange limbo between war and peace, independence and unity.

Kiir was close to the US, keen to ensure he had the backers to provide material support to protect the South. President George W. Bush gave him a black cowboy hat when he visited Washington in 2006. Kiir came from cattle country too, liked the style, and never took it off. Bush also supported him in strengthening the SPLA, for that was seen as the most important guarantee that Khartoum would keep its promises. Bush's Special Envoy to Sudan, Andrew Natsios, said a third of his work was devoted to a multi-million-dollar support programme for the SPLA.[7]

It may have been peace, but the men who won the war would dictate the future. Kiir poured the government budget into the military. It was rearmament on a grand scale. The sheer size of it became clear when just one shipment was made public after Somali pirates seized a cargo ship packed with weapons, including 33 battle tanks for the South.[8]

The ex-rebel generals had switched to dark suits now they were in power, but they remained military men. The old rebel SPLA was now the official army of the South, and its political wing, the Sudan People's Liberation Movement, or SPLM, was the ruling party. In practice, the generals stayed in charge. Foreigners were busy scrambling to provide services for the people, and that left the old soldiers able to concentrate on what mattered to them—guaranteeing that the army was strong enough to secure the referendum on independence, and to have the result respected. So they spent the cash on what they knew best. They expanded the army and bought more guns.

While a state must hold the monopoly on power, force alone does not make a state.

* * *

'You have to understand what we face,' said Mary Poni. 'We fear the war will return.' She had fought for the SPLA, carrying ammunition to the soldiers and treating the wounded on the frontline. Later she fled to Uganda with her three children. Poni, who had returned to Juba to look for other family members scattered in the war, sat with me in the shade of a bulging baobab tree. She was looking for customers to sell her bag of mobile phones. Like so many Southern women, she was strong, determined and vital to keeping her family alive. The generals were the ones who took power and got the cash, but it was women like Poni who found food for the table. So much of the South's survival in the darkest of days depended upon women like her. 'The choice it is not between a free South and a united Sudan,' she said. 'What we face is a choice between a future of peace and a future of war. If we remain as one country, then we go back to fight.'

* * *

I clambered along the banks of the river, where the weeds had long since taken over the old port. A few boys kicked a football made of plastic bags wrapped with string, using the rusted cranes that once unloaded goods from the boats as goalposts. We were a short distance upstream from the old slave market of Gondokoro. Small canoes had hacked their way through the tangled rushes, but there were no big barges here now. Only the smell of drying fish drifted past.

The government had great plans: an $80 million complex proposed by a Kuwaiti company for a freight and passenger port, a fishing facility and a 450-bed hotel. I went to see the architect's model. It was a short walk along a mud track—a four-lane highway, according to the plans—but it was already gathering dust in the crumbling colonial-era Juba Hotel. Dreams sometimes far outstripped reality.

'There is so much opportunity,' said Hadi Diab from the SPLM's investment committee. He spoke excitedly of new oil pipelines, of smooth roads crossing the country, and railways to the Kenyan coast. Leaders did not want a landlocked South Sudan to be dependent on Khartoum. 'There is a lot of money, but there are so many basic needs for it to be spent on first,' he said.

I headed to the university. 'First Southern Sudan Trade Fair and Reconstruction Exhibition, August 2006,' the banner outside read. It sounded so grand. Inside, I stood in the half-empty hall, with its grimy floors and broken windows. The investors were mainly from Uganda and Kenya, and were selling building materials, electricity generators and solar panels. Some were asleep in the heat after lunch, but they were not missing much, for there were more sellers than buyers. 'They need everything, because they are starting with nothing,' said Kenyan salesman Henry Kobia. 'But that also means it is so tough to work here. It's hard when you don't have the basics for business. The people are used to fighting, not building.'

I was given a T-shirt promoting the fair, with the crest of the Government of South Sudan and logos of the organisers. On the back was Bread of Life Africa, a US-backed evangelical missionary group, while on the front, in pride of place, was DynCorp International. The US security contractor had made its millions supporting the US invasion of Afghanistan five years earlier. They'd also made big money in Baghdad, and now they were in Juba too. Once again, they were helping forge a nation. This time their main job was training of the SPLA, equipping them with new transport vehicles and building a new army headquarters.[9]

1. Freedom won: February 2011 celebrations in Juba after independence referendum results are confirmed. © Peter Martell

2. Wrestlers in a competition held to promote peace in Juba in 2016. © Peter Martell

3. 'Liberation of slaves after the capture of the slave boats.' Illustration from Sir Samuel Baker's *Ismaila, the Expedition to Central Africa for the Suppression of the Slave Trade*, 1874.

4. Plant a flag: Major Jean-Baptiste Marchand led Senegalese soldiers carrying a collapsible boat on a two-year trek from the Atlantic to the White Nile, claiming it for France. Illustration from *Le Petit Journal*, 1899.

5. Bog Barons: Ted Nightingale, last British Governor of Equatoria, out on patrol. Photograph courtesy of the Nightingale family.

6. Horsemen from the North: Baggara Arab riders in 1939. Photograph by Ted Nightingale, courtesy of the Nightingale family.

7. Peace dreams: 1970s tourism poster, held by archivist Youssef Onyalla. © Peter Martell

8. Major Kerubino Kuanyin Bol with the elephant ivory he sold to buy guns to start a new war in 1983. Photograph courtesy of Oswald Iten.

9. Major-General Paul Garang Deng, who fired the first shots of war in 1983.
© Peter Martell

10. Rebel army: SPLA recruits in Ethiopia in 1984. Photograph courtesy of SPLA/ Till Lincke.

11. Top chiefs: SPLA commanders in 1984. From left to right; William Nyuon Bany, John Garang, Kerubino Kuanyin Bol and Salva Kiir. Photograph courtesy of SPLA/Till Lincke.

12. Ready for a new rebellion: SPLA fighters, 1984. Photograph courtesy Till Lincke.

13. Red beret of revolution: John Garang in 1984. Photograph courtesy of SPLA/Till Lincke.

14. Mundari cattle herder outside Juba, 2009. Cow urine gives the hair the colour. © Peter Martell

15. Referendum Day: Women queue to vote at Garang's grave at dawn on 9 January 2011. © Peter Martell

16. A waving President Salva Kiir rides on the back of a pickup through the streets of Juba in 2010, alongside then Vice-President Riek Machar. © Peter Martell

17. A malnourished baby is weighed at a clinic in Jonglei. © Peter Martell

Army, America, and God: three big forces that would dominate in the following years. 'Peace through Development', the T-shirt slogan read.

* * *

Everything was a challenge. The land was awash with guns and desperate people trying to survive. The lush lands where farmers should have had fields of crops were empty, and over a million people depended on UN food aid to survive. Drive a short distance outside Juba, and the troubles turned deadly.

If the war with Khartoum was over, the long legacy remained in the rebels it had left behind. The Khartoum-backed Lord's Resistance Army gunmen once lived in Juba when under Northern control.[10] Now the LRA attacked villages on the very edge of the city. The Ugandan fighters had been forced out of their homeland, but now controlled a jungle realm that stretched far across the South, reaching into the depths of Congo, and extending to the Central African Republic. The expert guerrillas operated in small units, raiding villages for recruits, taking the boys as soldiers and the girls as sex slaves. In a land all too used to war, the LRA's dreadlocked men had a reputation for outstanding brutality.

I went to meet them. I cadged a lift with SPLA troops heading deep into Eastern Equatoria, delivering sacks of rice and beans as a goodwill gesture to the rebels, who were meant to be gathering as part of peace talks. The dirt track faded into an ever-tapering path through the scrubland and thorny forest. Our convoy was the first to go in, and the men were terrified.

We lost the track soon after leaving the last big village of Magwi. One shouting soldier insisted we should head to the low hills on the right, the gunner on the rooftop shouted straight on, and the driver just revved the engine, charging forward in meandering lines to wherever he could take the truck. Exhausted, hungry and thirsty, we clung to the sides of the rollercoaster lorry for hours, standing in the back and staring out the bush that stretched to the far horizon. Only the shadows cast by the high clouds seemed to move across the rolling hills. Palm fronds smacked the trucks hour after hour. I told the gunner I felt seasick; he told me I was lucky to have seen the sea. We crossed a wasteland of burnt-out tanks and shattered buildings, a once grand but

169

now crumbling brick church swallowed by creepers, the visible walls pitted with sprays of bullet scars. The long grass was higher than the machine-gunners who stood in the beds of their pick-up trucks. No vehicle had apparently been down this route for years, and I asked if there were landmines here. 'Many,' the soldier next to me replied, sucking noisily on a stub of cigarette, before flicking it into the grass.

Even the rugged pickup trucks were trailing after us. Usually the favoured vehicle of choice for rebel fighters, they were now limping along, and soldiers used winches to haul them up over the worst of the rocky ridges. The snarling engines of the Soviet-built five-tonne trucks of the SPLA crashed their way through ahead. We peered out together at another empty village, abandoned years before. All that remained were the crumbling, circular mud walls. With papaya trees sprouting from inside them, they appeared bizarre plant pots. Under the shade of trees, we found worn grain grinding stones for flour, but no other signs of the family who once lived here.

Sun-blasted and broken, we finally reached Owiny-Kibul, the old Anya-Nya rebel headquarters of the 1960s. We found the scattered huts of the village half empty. The residents were terrified. 'We suffered so much from them,' resident Charles Anone told me, an elderly man in a ragged shirt. 'They attacked us, took children and stole the crops. They are coming, and we are scared.'

We spent the night under the twisted tangle of trees, huddling close to the thick smoke of wet wood fire doused in diesel in a vain effort to keep the whining mosquito clouds away. The SPLA commander of the convoy, Major-General Wilson Deng, kept our spirits up by telling stories of what the LRA had done, as pots of beans boiled in the coals of the fire for supper. 'They killed a lot of people in this region,' Deng said. 'Then they forced survivors to cook and eat the flesh of the dead relatives.' At night I lay scared, my body touching the inside of my tent. I had bought it for a music festival in England, and it felt thin protection. In the darkness, I hoped the sentries were as awake as I was. That time, thankfully, we did not find the LRA.

A little later, there was another mission westwards to the Congo border. Again, we clung onto trucks as they smashed their way through the bush. Where the tracks were wet, the pickups were sucked into mud swamps. Where the tracks were dry, the soldiers drove at such speed that they nearly rolled the vehicle. Our bags, the metal spring bed brought as a peace offering for Kony, and the Reuters reporter were all sent flying.

That time, we did meet the fighters. LRA soldiers emerged warily out of the bush in faded camouflage jackets. Most carried AK-47 rifles with fixed bayonets, but one of our guards brandished a fearsome Galil assault rifle with specialised scope. It was likely taken from the dead body of one of eight Guatemalan commandos in the UN force who had been killed in a botched raid on the LRA months earlier in 2006. Reputations were terrifying, yet in person, the LRA just appeared wretched boys, made to inflict the horrors they had suffered on new generations. After a couple of days, we were playing Reporters versus Rebels with a half-deflated football and trees as goalposts. We let them win, of course.

After a few days waiting, the rebels led us on tight paths twisting deep into the jungle to meet their leaders. We sat in an awkward circle in front of the LRA's number two and three—Vincent Otti and Okot Odhiambo. Both were wanted by the International Criminal Court to stand trial for war crimes, with a dozen charges from murder to rape, enslavement and forcing children to fight. I thought of their victims I had met: the gentleman who could not drink without fumbling because he had stumps for hands; the lady who told her story from bared teeth because her lips had been cut off. Odhiambo was silent and held my gaze, but Otti seemed more like a scary schoolteacher than a fearsome killer. 'My message is for hope, that peace should come,' Otti said. 'We are fighting to go home.'

A year later, on the orders of his chief Joseph Kony, Otti was dragged against a tree and shot. His corpse was left for days as a warning. The LRA ruler had carved out a personal fiefdom and was not ready to end his war. In December 2008, Ugandan jets bombarded the LRA's jungle hideouts, and the rebels scattered. Later, the US sent in dozens of Special Operations forces to help hunt them down. Kony vanished into the forest.[11]

* * *

'I'm doing the Lord's work,' said Sam Childers, a bear-like missionary with a bushy walrus moustache and giant arms covered in tattoos, who

171

called himself the 'Machine Gun Preacher'. Childers, a former biker and drug dealer from the US with a love of heavy weaponry, had come Rambo-style on a mission from God to kill LRA rebels. I met him on a porch outside a grubby bar near the Ugandan border at Nimule, where he ran a simple orphanage. 'You can't make peace with the devil,' Childers said gruffly, pistol in a holster on his belt, scratching the hairy belly that protruded from his shirt. His stories of vigilante humanitarianism were full of burning villages, whizzing bullets and crackling gunfire—a one-man African crusade of Bibles, bikes and big guns. 'Kony is from Satan,' he said. 'And I'm going to get him.' Hollywood loved him, and made a film.[12] South Sudan's army, who Childers said he was working with, called it all lies.

There has been a long line of foreigners who have come to Sudan. Some came out of genuine concern for what they saw as a righteous cause. Others came to find their fortune, or themselves. Even Adolf Hitler's cinematographer Leni Riefenstahl, who filmed propaganda of the Nuremberg rally, once came. She sought to escape censure for earlier Nazi ardour by 'discovering' the people of the Nuba Mountains. Her meticulously composed photographs staged in mud hut studios detailed muscled wrestlers, bodies decorated with swirling ash. Critics said her work echoed the same utopian aesthetic of physical perfection, but this time eulogising a romantic primitivism of a people 'untouched' by civilisation.[13] She was like so many other foreigners looking to fill a hole they could not fix in themselves at home, an invasion of white saviour warriors seeking personal salvation in what they saw as a Wild West frontier land.

Now, a new round of foreigners arrived: gangs of aid workers, spies, fat-necked ex-soldiers offering security training and more, journalists, diplomats, gold miners, cowboy businessmen, celebrities, preachers and policy wonks. Some did good, others did not. Too often, the best intentions perished in the dust.

During slow days in Juba spent trying to cool under the clunking fans of thatch roof bars beside the river, I'd watch these characters drifting in. I'd rank them into the old list of conflict zone stereotypes: missionaries, mercenaries and misfits. One mosquito-filled dusk, I was beckoned over by the only other man in Juba's Afex bar. He was a sil-ver-haired American wearing a sharp cut blazer and gold signet ring. He exuded authority and a patrician sense of power; this was no UN advisor. He bought me a beer, and we stared at the sunset over the Nile. I had just returned from Jonglei, where cattle raiders had carried out a string of deadly massacres with military precision. Many blamed old enemies in Khartoum for supplying guns and ammunition. The American was interested in what I had seen.

As we talked, an ex-US soldier who provided security advice to aid agencies walked past, stopped and snapped a salute. Later I asked quietly who the old man in the bar had been. He was Robert 'Bud' McFarlane: a Cold War icon, Ronald Reagan's National Security Advisor, a former Marine Corps colonel and Vietnam veteran, convicted for a key role in the 1985 Iran-Contra affair, when guns were sold to Tehran to support right-wing guerrillas in Nicaragua. Now he was in Sudan on a murky mission, reportedly advising Khartoum how to burnish a reputation tarred by accusations of genocide and terrorism. Juba attracted such people.

* * *

Hollywood came to South Sudan and, as in other films they made of Africa, they told a story in the simple terms of absolutes—Khartoum the evil oppressors, the South as the underdog good guys. George Clooney led the charge, working with a Washington-based campaign group called the Enough Project—believers in the moral cause of South Sudan. He poured hundreds of thousands of dollars into activism to ensure the referendum took place on time. If he could help, he would. He paid for satellites to monitor the North–South border, to photograph troops' movements and warn of potential war. In person, he was perceptive and well-informed, better than many in understanding the complex mess of politics.

Still, the media were swayed by his chiselled looks and over-focused their attention on him, amplifying his role and that of America far beyond reality. Too often the journalists' stories were ones where Washington was creating a country. While international support was critical in ensuring the referendum on independence, claiming that Washington, or any other nation, made South Sudan was grossly insulting to the millions who fought and died. The US appeared only at the very end, helping the final stage of a very long journey, posing as knights on white chargers to claim the limelight. The focus should have been on how the creation of that country was actually going.

Many foreigners were deeply cynical about the independence proj-ect, but since they were part of the system, it was difficult to criticise. It was their job to ensure that the new nation would flourish; if that wasn't going well, it reflected on them. For UN staff, hefty pay packets meant a reluctance to rock the boat. The gigantic UN compound city of shipping containers was the mission's single biggest construction. Inside the razor wire walls, there was not much to do outside work except drink. The thatch-hut bars were not as glamorous as other post-ings, but the parties were wilder. People danced in the dust and tried to forget where they worked.

* * *

After the decades of suffering, people wanted to help. For the US, after defeat in Somalia in 1993 and the world's failure of the Rwandan geno-cide in 1994, here was a land that offered a chance to assuage guilt and right other wrongs done in Africa. A billion dollars a year poured in as international aid, while the UN peacekeeping mission cost the same again. In a city without banks, much came in suitcases bulging with cash.

Outsiders were welcomed—and they came in their hordes. This was no Baghdad, where the old regime stalked the shadows in revenge. Soon there would be traffic jams of four-wheel drives on the streets of Juba. The fresh-faced graduates came crammed with knowledge of what had gone wrong in the past, from the pernicious legacy of colo-nialism to short-sighted aid policies of the 1980s. They came to solve the future with thick plans for conflict resolution and nation building. The world had a chance to get this one right, at last.

Other nations had been created; the end of the Soviet Union and the collapse of Yugoslavia saw new states emerge on the ghosts of old. Then there were those who had the country restored—Eritrea in 1993 and East Timor in 2002, based on old colonial borders. People pointed to Kosovo as an example of another created country, but even that had a history of self-autonomy, and was 56 times smaller than the South.

None was quite like the experiment of South Sudan. There was no history of self-governance as a country, and no old national institutions to revive. The South was about the size of Afghanistan and, like that war-smashed state, it too needed rebuilding. Other lands offered the promise of national restoration in a return to the mythical better times of old. As a nation, however, South Sudan's very existence had to be built from scratch.

'We're flying the airplane while we're building it,' one expert on governance told me with excitement. For deskbound bureaucrats, it was exhilarating work. So much needed to be done that few ever stopped to ask the people what they wanted and needed. In the long history of the South, it has so often been the way.

The scale of the challenge in the South was beyond what almost anyone had experienced. After decades of fighting destroyed schools, four-fifths could not read or write, while knowledge of the skills of modern bureaucracy—computers, typing, and financial spreadsheets—was even worse.[14] The techniques for surviving war did not build a nation. The handful of trained civil servants were those who had spent the war in the North, but they knew Arabic and were now sidelined in a system dominated by English.

During the war years in the 1980s and 1990s, the legions of charities—non-governmental organisations, or NGOs, in aid worker jargon—provided public services in the absence of government. 'Is New Sudan actually the first NGO-istan?' one academic wrote in the war.[15]

Times had changed, for now there was a government to serve the people. Except rather than supporting, the NGO army took over. Foreign experts helped build up the trappings of the operations of a state, creating fragile bubbles of stability that provided a veneer of functioning institutions. They provided sticking plaster technical solutions to problems which were, at heart, deeply political. Many foreigners soon grew frustrated at the slow pace of Southerners in learning new skills. Teaching the ex-rebel turned government officials how to use a laptop and create budget tables took time. With so much suffering outside the air-conditioned offices, it seemed right to step in rather than wait. In the end, that undermined the very legitimacy of the government they had come to help.

Most aid workers would be there for two years, perhaps three if they pushed it, and they wanted to see change while they were there. They had come to build a country, end a war and save a people.

* * *

While South Sudan was broken, it was very far from broke. Soon it had its own ready source of cash, a pipeline of dollars paid as part of the peace agreement from the oil pumped from its fields. In the first year, $700 million flowed from its share of the oil. A year later, that rose to $1.3 billion, and between 2006 and 2009, income from oil revenue averaged $2.1 billion, a total of some $12 billion by independence in 2011. The government had almost no other outside income for itself—oil provided 98 percent of revenues—making South Sudan the most oil dependent land in the world.[16] For a nation with nothing, it was serious cash.

By 2009, Juba's oil revenues were five times the level of donor aid. The demands were huge, but so was the potential of public funds to spend on services for the people. In terms of potential public expenditure, it was in a far better situation that its neighbours; gross domestic product per capita was more than double that of East Africa's economic hub Kenya, and triple that of Uganda. The vast majority saw none of that cash and lived off the smallest of amounts, well under a dollar a day, but the billions in oil cash and hundreds of millions in foreign aid could transform the land. South Sudan, not yet a nation, also had no debt. There was dire poverty, but it was not poor.[17]

* * *

President Omar al-Bashir danced, punched the air in delight with his walking stick and shouted 'God is Great' in his first public appearance as a war crimes suspect. Hours after being named by the International Criminal Court prosecutor for counts of alleged genocide, I watched Bashir dance a jig with hardly a care in the world. 'My faith is in my homeland, what makes me stand proud and say, I am Sudanese, I am African,' sang pop star Jamal Mustafa, as Bashir clicked his fingers and grooved to the beat. 'This is the land of good people, a country full of untapped resources.'[18]

It was July 2008 and I was in Khartoum. Bashir had been named as the ringleader of the slaughter in Darfur, where tens of thousands of people had been massacred and hundreds of thousands more were dead from starvation and disease. The man now dancing in flowing white robes like a genial grandfather stood accused of ordering those attacks. Bashir's soldiers fought alongside militia fighters, the much-feared Janjaweed, a name derived from 'devils on horseback'. Government soldiers kicked out crude barrel bombs from the back doors of cargo planes. Then the Janjaweed with government weapons would ride in on camels, horses or pickup trucks with machine guns, slaughtering survivors, gang raping and burning. They drove out the Fur, Masalit and Zaghawa peoples to seize their farmland; they were Muslim, but Khartoum deemed them 'African', not 'Arab'. Millions fled into squalid UN camps of dust and plastic shelters. For those watching from the South, it was horribly familiar.

The crowd around me encouraged me to dance. I watched as Bashir waved to the 500-strong crowd from the high podium in the Chinese-built Friendship Hall. His face beamed a wide grin as his people roared their support. 'Mr. President, they will never touch you!' shouted one official. *'Allahu akhbar!'* Bashir cried back.

I slipped outside into the gardens on the banks of the Nile, where a feast was being prepared. The smell of roasted meat drifted through the palm trees. I could understand why the South was hell-bent on separation.

* * *

Salva Kiir preached in the St. Theresa Catholic Cathedral in Juba. Kiir— or Salva as many called him, from his baptismal name Salvatore— appeared almost shy in front of the packed congregation, though perhaps that was only because he seemed oddly naked without his cowboy hat. Church was about the only place he appeared bareheaded.

'You want to vote for unity, so that you will become second class in your own country?' Kiir asked, raising his hands to quiet the congregation who bent forward in their pews. 'That is your choice.' While his speeches were slow and ponderous, Kiir could work a crowd. They hung on his words waiting for the next line. 'If you would want to vote for independence, so that you are a free person in your independent state…?' his voice boomed out. 'That will be your own choice.'[19] There was rapturous applause. The referendum was all that mattered. It was the pursuit of separation at all costs, and became the focus of all government efforts.

One midnight in ~~January 2010~~, my phone rang. I was told to wake and come urgently, so I zoomed through the checkpoints across town on my bike. The first multi-party elections in Sudan for over two decades were approaching, and the SPLM had finally selected their candidates.

The leaders had been meeting in a Thai restaurant, about the swankiest that Juba got, and a handful of journalists waited outside for them to emerge and announce the candidate. The man selected would challenge Omar al-Bashir to be president of all Sudan. If Garang had been alive, there was little doubt he would have run. In a free election, could Garang have won? Would he have become president of a New Sudan, changing the old regime to lead a united nation in peace? Perhaps, but Garang was dead.

As the men in suits came out of the meeting, I watched bleary-eyed as they pushed forward the man chosen to challenge Bashir to be national president. It was not Kiir.

Instead, it was the smiling Yassir Arman, an SPLM stalwart from the North. Yassir shook my hand. He looked exhausted, but spoke defiantly. 'It is part of the struggle that we have been doing for the last 27 years,' Yassir told me, portraying it as part of the long battle since the SPLA began the fight in 1983. 'I am confident that the SPLM can win.' Few, if any, rated his chances.

Instead, Kiir would run only for polls for the president of the semi-autonomous South, a vote he knew he would win hands down. He was a man with a different dream—to be president of his own nation. He positioned himself to lead the people into the referendum and head to the 'promised land' of freedom. Those in the North who had supported the SPLA in the Nuba Mountains and Blue Nile, the old rebels in the East and those in the West who fought in Darfur, had their hopes dashed.

I drove home, editing the story in the courtyard by the light of a paraffin lamp and the moon. It felt like a watershed moment. The country was unravelling. At dawn, the story was broadcast out on the crackly radios tuned to the BBC. Independence for the South was coming.

* * *

It sounded like the tin roof of the giant hall might burst off. Singer after singer took to the stage to perform their attempt, and at the end of each song, the room erupted. The people stamped their feet and clapped their hands. Some wept, others cheered as loud as they could. A new state needed a national identity, and this was a talent show with a twist. It was 2010 in the cultural centre in Juba, and they were making a national anthem.[20]

A singer in a tight, white, flared suit leapt onto the stage, belting out furiously fast beats, the lyrics squeezed uncomfortably into a rejigged pop song. 'Beautiful woman' had been awkwardly replaced with 'black warriors'. Musicians wanted something different from the old military march of Sudan, but no one had any experience of writing a national anthem. So they recast their love songs to fit new lyrics.

'I have had to tell them politely; it is wonderful you love your girl-friend,' Joseph Abuk told me with a grin, chief of the technical com-mittee for the new anthem. 'But it is just not the right kind of tune for an anthem.' The speakers popped, then launched into wailing feedback, and the audience threw their hands over their ears. Abuk, a poet and playwright with an infectious laugh and a love of Shakespeare, had already gathered dozens of poets together for a week beside the river to write the lyrics. 'We wrote about both the struggle for so many years, but also about the future too,' Abuk said. 'We want to be ready for when we become a free nation.'

Rounds of competition whittled down dozens of entries to a final three tunes. As a singer blasted out funk from a synthesiser, I read the lyrics of the old anthem of Khartoum. 'We are the soldiers of God,' it ran. 'Glory, we buy with the highest price this land.' I could see why the South wanted a different tune. 'Land of great abundance, uphold us united in peace and harmony,' the new lyrics ran. 'Let us stand up in silence and respect, saluting our martyrs whose blood cemented our national foundation.'

The anthem wasn't the only thing to be chosen. There was also debate on what the country was to be called. A new nation could do with a new name and identity, some argued. There was talk of choosing Garang's name of New Sudan, or the Anya-Nya rebel title of Nile Republic. Others suggested Azania—an ancient Greek name for a region of Africa—and even Juwama, combining the first letters of the main towns, Juba, Wau and Malakal. Some said it should be simply *Junub*, 'South' in Arabic. A few of the more belligerent writers pointed out that Sudan came from the name, 'Land of the Blacks'. So they said it should be the South who kept the name Sudan—and the North who came up with a new name. Cooler heads warned of the confusion that would arise if that resulted in two nations called Sudan.

Others suggested Kush, the ancient kingdom of the Black Pharaohs. In the dreams of the South, they were their ancestors. It had inspired the anthem writers too, who had titled early drafts 'The Land of Kush'. Yet Kush, when given to babies as a name, also meant 'unknown', and was used by parents who had lost previous children in infancy, when they were uncertain if the new-born would survive.[21] It seemed an ominous choice.

Excitement at the future pushed most fears to the side. As the anthem competition narrowed down to its finalist, the old commanders came to celebrate. 'This is about the spirit of the people of Southern Sudan, who have never accepted to be enslaved without resistance,' said SPLM Secretary-General Pagan Amum, in front of the crowd. 'Southerners are united by a common aspiration to be free.' Amum, along with other old generals, became so overwhelmed by the music that they left their seats to dance in front of the stage. They shuffled a jig, punching clenched fists in the air. Writing an anthem was not simply creating a song. It was about bringing the people in step, together.

Then a choir dressed in neat white shirts took to the stage, students and teachers at the University of Juba. They stood proud with their hands on their hearts, and the audience hushed in anticipation. Their uplifting choral version finished with a flourish of trumpets, and the crowds went wild. It hardly needed the judges to confirm that this was the winning tune.

'I feel like we are ready to build our country,' said musician Mido Samuel, who helped compose the music. 'Having a national anthem means I am declaring to everybody: "I am now free."'

11

A LOOTER CONTINUER

'In a world of roving banditry there is little or no incentive for anyone to produce or accumulate anything.'

Mancur Olson[1]

Thick lines of sweat ran down the face of Peter Gatwech, as he clutched the dressing around the bullet hole in his stomach. The edge was soaked red with blood. 'I was hit by the guns of the soldiers,' said the 24-year-old cattle keeper. Gatwech, marked by the deep bands of scars that wrapped around his head, the initiation cuts of a Nuer man, lay on a thin hospital bed. His chest heaved with bony ribs as he told of how he and hundreds of comrades had ambushed a river convoy of 30 barges carrying UN aid to stop food reaching enemies upstream. As the barges chugged up the slow Sobat river, a snaking tributary of the White Nile in the east, they had let loose with all they had. They had fired volleys of rocket-propelled grenades, then AK-47s.

'They were sending supplies upriver, and we had to stop them,' he said, his voice trembling as he turned in pain. They had killed around 40 of the 150-strong military escort, sunk three barges and looted grain. The soldiers had fought back, raking the river bank with rifles and machine guns, ripping apart the attackers. The gunmen fled, so the soldiers took revenge on villages along the bank. They set fire to the huts. The blackened circles that once were homes could be seen still smoking from the air when I flew in.

Dozens of badly wounded were brought to here to the hospital in the small riverside town of Nasir run by Doctors Without Borders, MSF. The simple brick ward stank of hot blood and bleach. The floor was scrubbed clean, but something was rotting. At the other end of the ward, a man was upright in his bed, staring into the middle distance. His head was wrapped in a bandage, plugging a hole in his skull. A rocket fired by his own side across the river had ricocheted off a barge and into his forehead. I asked a nurse what his chances were. She shook her head.

Violence in the South was a 'humanitarian perfect storm', the UN said, with numbers being killed surpassing the war in Darfur.[2] Gunmen would attack before dawn, moving in organised military formation. They were well planned and coordinated attacks. Women were raped then shot. Children were speared. The South was meant to be preparing for the referendum on independence. Instead, they were killing themselves.

These battles were between rival clans of the Nuer, but there was just as intense bloodshed between different groups elsewhere. Gatwech, from the Jikany branch of the Nuer, had attacked the barges to stop the food they were carrying going upstream to their enemies, the Lou Nuer. The Jikany accused the Lou of an attack the month before in a village when gunmen had shot, speared or beaten to death over 70 people.

Those who survived that attack at Torkech had dragged themselves to the hospital at Nasir too, their guts hanging out. Surgeons had removed bullets from 55 people, all but three of them women and children. The youngest was a two-month-old baby. 'They surrounded the village when we were asleep,' said Nyakem Jok, a teenage girl from Torkech, her leg stretched out with a weights and a pulley system to mend bones smashed by bullets. 'They started firing from all sides.'

Months later, I went to the town of Akobo to see the Lou Nuer. Without the food stolen or sunk in the river ambush, they were now starving. The people were also reeling from a massacre; gunmen from the Murle people had overrun a fishing village, opening fire from all sides, then moved in with spears to kill the wounded. At least 185 people died, mainly women and children. The wounded fled to the river to hide. Those who drowned floated downstream. 'They shot me in the leg as I ran towards the river,' said 12-year-old Namach Duk.

'Then they stabbed me in the back with a spear and left me for dead.' She turned to show me a raw, jagged hole. The barbed spear blade had torn out a hunk of flesh. [3]

The Murle said their massacre was in response to an attack against them. They had been armed by Khartoum during the war to fight the SPLA, and had been attacked by almost every group around. People accused them of stealing children.

Revenge followed revenge. Everyone blamed someone else for starting it.   *I get - it that probably was someone else, just not them blamed.*

* * *

The violence was on a scale and intensity that went far beyond cattle raids grown out of control. This was not like the fighting of past ages. Generations at war had broken society, shattered old rules, and left behind enough guns so that even local militia forces could take on an army. Government disarmament campaigns were savage; military campaigns took guns away by force from one area, only to put them in the hands of others seen as loyal to the government. It left groups grossly vulnerable to their rivals, and so they set out to rearm and then raid. Old scores were settled. Hatred intensified.

There were efforts to resurrect traditional systems of authority. Chiefs were summoned to grand meetings, so that communities could talk through their problems. 'By coming together as chiefs we can help our people live in peace with each other,' Madelena Tito, paramount chief of Eastern Equatoria, told me at a council of leaders. Tito, the only top chief who was a woman, looked across a hall packed with chatting grey-haired men dressed in colonial-era style peaked caps and khaki dress. 'We have a chance for a peaceful South,' she said. 'We must not let it go to waste.'

Yet the power of the old chiefs was fading fast. It was too little, too late. The young men with weapons were the new commanders, and they had tasted power with the free-fire switch of their guns. They no longer listened to the wiser warnings of experience.

* * *

In Nasir, I sat on the hospital's crumbling brick steps alongside an elderly lady, Nyawech Ruc. She had paddled her family in a narrow wooden canoe across the river to the shore by the hospital, bringing her feverous granddaughter whose limbs shook from malaria. When the doctor unwrapped the cloths around the toddler, her belly was extended from malnutrition. The child's parents had been killed in fighting in the past year, and Nyawech now looked after her alone. She would stay in the hospital for as long as it took for the girl to get better, finding what shelter she could for herself. We shared a bag of nuts, and looked out towards the river together.

A flock of white ibis circled overhead, calling as they headed to roost. Juba was so far away that only the toughest of trucks could make it through. Most things unloaded from the boats onto the river banks were from Ethiopia. The river was the only practical route here.

Nasir was hardly unusual. There were towns like it all across the South, where the problem was not that central government was dysfunctional, but rather, that it was entirely absent. Without a government social welfare system or national security forces they could trust, they looked to their own people for self-protection. The notion of the 'tribe' was not some ancient drive of primordial passion, but rather a necessary modern response of community defence and survival.

Foreign aid agencies and the Church were often about the only outside help people had, and they were worn out from just coping with the immediate impact of disaster after disaster. It felt like the charities were casting coins into a deep wishing well, a flash of silver hope sinking to the depths.

The UN peacekeeping mission, one of the world's largest, was no better. A handful of UN soldiers scattered across enormous distances, dependent for travelling on helicopters they often didn't have, were but a spit in the Nile.[4] Massive efforts were made at eye-wateringly high costs, but much of those funds were spent keeping soldiers alive and supplied in far flung forts, where they could do little more than watch and report back what they had seen from the gun turrets of their patrol vehicles. Sometimes they rang the alarm bell, occasionally they deterred attacks. They did not offer a solution, only the troublesome illusion that things could be controlled. Peacekeepers, after all, need a peace to keep.

German surgeon Sebastian Lawrenz sat down beside me, utterly exhausted. In the last attack here, over three dozen wounded arrived within hours at the hospital. 'It is too many injured for the basic setting we have,' he said. 'Far too much. Even for a big Western hospital, that amount coming in is a huge amount.'

Lawrenz and the medics worked around the clock, but they struggled with such overwhelming needs. Sometimes they used ketamine as an anaesthetic for surgery, a drug which put patients into a trance. The doctors said that as they cut the bullets out, the herders sang haunting songs in their sleep of the beauty of their cows.

The old hospital was a former Presbyterian mission station. Riek Machar had used it as a base when he declared his coup two decades earlier, and burned tanks still lay scattered on the edge of town. Children used the barrel of one as a gymnastics bar.

British anthropologist Evans-Pritchard had also stayed here for his research in the 1930s. There was a battered copy of his book in the MSF dining room. As dusk fell, we retreated behind the wire-meshed veranda away from the whining mosquitos. I reread his descriptions of Nuer society as 'ordered anarchy' by the soft yellow light of a hurricane lamp.

'The Nuer is a product of a hard and egalitarian upbringing, is deeply democratic and is easily roused to violence,' he wrote. Someone had underlined the passages heavily in pencil. 'As Nuer are very prone to fighting, people are frequently killed,' he added. 'Indeed, it is rare that one sees a senior man who does not show marks of club or spear.'[5]

I thought of diplomats in Juba who despaired of the South, but who were keen to downplay the violence as 'tribal'. They pointed to such passages of fighting decades before. It made the killings sound ancient and intractable. Country maps made by the UN divided the land like a rainbow patchwork blanket, with dozens of colours each marking a different people with clear-cut borders, like a land of many nations. Viewed as 'tribalism', how could it be solved when it always had been so?

This was superficial shorthand to rationalise the slaughter without actually explaining it. It was far easier than addressing the horrible reality; while people looked to their community because the government offered no support, the violence here was fuelled by all-or-nothing political races for power in Juba. People in places like Nasir had the barest minimum to survive. They were places barely touched by money. Their leaders, however, had access to a ready flow of dollars. The businessmen of war used their people on the ground to carve out their powerbase.[6] How does an illiterate population vote? Is Democracy possible?

185

After elections in 2010, fighting grew worse. Kiir had won the presidency of the South by a landslide, but elections for governor posts were marred by claims of rigging. Commanders who had not been selected to represent the ruling SPLM—in other words, to win the seat—took to the bush as renegade generals and raised armies to maraud and plunder. The politics of power in Juba were fought on remote battlefields. 'Politicians put their hand into these conflicts,' army chief James Hoth said despondently. 'Here in Juba, because someone wants to be minister, sometimes they throw a war to their clan.' This violence was the visible flipside of filthy, faraway politics.

* * *

In Juba, the government accused Khartoum of sending in planeloads of arms, continuing its long policy of divide and rule. In the war, Khartoum had exploited local rivalries by creating proxy militia armies. So much of the war against Khartoum had been fought in the South, by Southerners against Southerners. Now there were new reports of sinister planes dropping weapons. 'These tribal clashes are designed by the enemies of peace,' Kiir told parliament.[7] Khartoum denied it, but at least some reports were credible. It stoked fear that Khartoum wanted to foment war to force an end to the peace deal and scrap the independence referendum.

For the South, the guns only added fuel to an existing fire. Yet it was also a telling sign that things in Khartoum had not changed. After all, in the North, the misery of Khartoum's war in Darfur raged on. My old Darfuri friends spoke of how the war there was worsening, despite every promise of peace. I knew them from Eritrea, when they were rebels in exile plotting war, and I was a reporter based in the country ranked worst in the world for press freedom. We'd all had plenty of time to spend long afternoons drinking and playing cards together. Some had since returned to Darfur to fight, and they called on scratchy satellite phones shouting out details of air strikes and burning villages. Their leaders came to Juba with warnings not to trust Khartoum.

'They don't respect any agreement,' Minni Minnawi told me. 'I know that now. They drive us into rebellion.' The cowboy-boot-loving rebel chief with a boyish smile and film-star moustache had joined the Khartoum government as a presidential advisor to Bashir in a bid for peace. Believing government promises, he had laid down his arms and brought in his Sudan Liberation Army rebel faction with their fighting pickups bristling with machine guns. His comrades had decried him as a sell-out. Sitting in a Juba hotel in late 2010, he told me he was returning to war because his men had been bombed and killed. 'There will be no change in Khartoum,' Minnawi said, throwing his hands into the air in despair. 'The people of South Sudan will choose the separation. Why would they not? Until then, I fear Khartoum will try and stop them.'

* * *

Kiir wanted to win over those whom Khartoum might support. There were dozens of militia armies that had not been part of the 2005 peace deal. The 'Big Tent' policy to create a more unified South included pardoning rebels and buying up old rivals to secure their loyalties. With control of the petrodollar pipeline, Kiir could afford to be generous and outbid Khartoum. Suitcases of cash, plus the lucrative perks that came with the promotion to general, smoothed the way for those who had hated Garang to reconcile with Kiir. Old enemy Riek Machar, who had rejoined the SPLA, was now Vice President of the South. As long as the cash kept flowing Kiir could stay in control, but the demands continually expanded from an ever-increasing circle of paid loyalists. Their support only lasted as long as the next payment. It was a dangerous policy, because it now paid to rebel. Those who challenged the government, after battles, massacre and murder, found themselves rewarded.

It swelled the massed ranks of the SPLA, a bush rebel force trying to turn into a regular, national, standing army. Some of the rivals Kiir bought off, such as the Nuer forces once backed by Khartoum to control oil fields, were as big as the SPLA themselves. Their leader, Paulino Matip, became deputy SPLA commander. Buying that sort of loyalty carries a hefty price tag.

So from some 40,000 SPLA soldiers when peace was signed, the army would grow to well over 200,000 by independence in 2011. Another 90,000 men were posted as police, prison and armed wildlife officers, acting as a reserve army.[8] In peace, the army was meant to shrink. In South Sudan, it grew fivefold. Soon there would be over 700 generals—more than the US—producing a higher ratio of generals to soldiers than any other army in the world.[9] They commanded units organised along ethnic lines, creating an army of uneasy factions that were one force only on paper. Soldiers owed their loyalties to their commanders, and those generals obeyed Juba for a price. Top posts were handed out to leaders from across the South, but the muscle and influence in the army and government remained with Dinka officers. With that came the flow of contracts and cash. A 'Dink-ocracy', some called it.

Peace is not simply the absence of war. Kiir was president and headed the system, but he did not control it. Academics described Kiir as a feudal lord, distributing money and positions based on the strength of the men the leaders could muster. As I contemplated the nature of his government, and watched him stare out from beneath his black Stetson hat, it was not the image of a medieval knight that came to me, but Michael Corleone of *The Godfather* muttering: 'Keep your friends close, but your enemies closer.'

* * *

National liberation and individual freedom are two different things, and turning a guerrilla movement into a government was never going to be easy. For the elite, it was not a problem of education; the majority of people were illiterate, but the top echelon of government was stuffed with doctorates. The problem was that, for many, the only point of comparison they had for government was what they had experienced from Khartoum, and that provided no example of why institutions matter and must be protected. Core principles, such as the freedom of the press and the independence of the judiciary, seemed paper concepts.

As Juba focused on the fear of a new war with the North, they brushed over the violence within. The poisonous seeds of a far longer conflict were growing between the people of the South.

The old battle with Khartoum had been, at its heart, not about race or religion. They had fuelled the rhetoric, but it was not why the ordinary people fought. Nor was it, in the end, about oil. That had paid for the war, but it was not the cause. It was about the monstrous marginalisation of a people who saw the nation's resources gobbled up by a ruthless elite. The 2005 peace deal was hoped to end Khartoum's predations. It did not, however, change the system. It only swapped the rulers. The new masters in Juba had learned from the worst. By purchasing support, they too exploited resources for their own self-serving pursuit of power. The generals followed in the steps of those they had ousted.

* * *

The next plane out of Nasir was in a week. Meanwhile, I squeezed into the back of a pickup for an outreach clinic. We bumped across the wide green plains dotted with herds of cattle to a small camp on a ridge, overlooking a wide pool. The men were fishing with spears in the marshy shallows. The children ran from the thatch huts to welcome us. They posed for the camera with arms held above their heads, each mimicking the special sweep of the horns of their beloved bull. The smaller ones carried toy cows moulded from sun-baked mud, identical to those Evans-Pritchard had depicted in meticulous pen and ink drawings 70 years before. Yet children now also made other models. The younger boys carried mud airplanes. Older boys, aged six or seven, had made something extra. They had fashioned themselves miniature AK-47 rifles.

* * *

To get back home, I squeezed on an MSF flight via the northern Kenyan town of Lokichoggio, the old aid logistics hub of the war years. It was strangely quiet. The swimming pool I dived into was covered in leaves, and the hotel bar was empty. Ragged plastic bags, snared in the acacia tree thorns, rustled in the hot wind. They were almost pretty from a distance, like desert flowers. The days when near constant streams of aid agency aircraft roared out of Loki into the famine zones were over, for now at least.

When I landed at Juba airport, my motorbike was still under the palm tree where I had left it, a little grubbier after a week away. As I swung out of the airport, a line of speeding four-wheel drives screeched in front of me. They straddled the centre of the road, forcing me to swerve into the thick grass. The lead car was a giant black Hummer, an ostentatious American gas-guzzling beast. The rest of the long line were fancy Toyota Land Cruisers. Men in dark suits with guns peered out, as the long convoy bounced away down the dirt track roads, honking horns and scattering the traffic. The Hummer alone was the price-tag of the president's official annual salary.

Juba was transforming. The village-capital had become a city, albeit one mainly of tin-roof huts that stretched far out into the once green bush. It had doubled, then trebled in size, and continued to grow further. The holes in the road that once swallowed a car outside my house had been filled in. Building sites popped up across town. There were even 10-storey towers, and hotels with swimming pools. It seemed like a different land from the South Sudan in the countryside outside. In the city, the people looked healthier; it was no longer so common to see the waxy skin of starvation pulled tight across cheekbones. Ragged clothes were replaced with colourful fabric.

For generations, the people only knew poverty. Now there was cash, and lots of it. If you could access the gravy train, the good times rolled. Cash from oil pumped from the soil seemed like it was free, and it looked like the party would never end.

* * *

Much was, quite simply, stolen. In 2005, the SPLM Secretariat of Finance managed a budget of some $100,000. A year later, after the peace deal was signed and oil revenues flowed, it had been renamed the Ministry of Finance and now managed over $1.5 billion. The cash was gobbled away in wholesale looting on a grand scale. In a government where finance officers drew up budgets by hand with pen and notepads, there was no paper trail for the missing fortune meant to build the hopes of people into a country. Large chunks of cash were taken without complicated schemes to cover fraud. Government tenders were often single sourced and the shell companies of ministers supplied the quote. The payments made were sometimes dozens of times higher than the market price—and the goods were often not delivered anyway. It was robbery in plain sight, for the feast was clear to see. 'The eating chiefs indulged their appetites and celebrated the dawn of peace in grand style,' wrote poet Victor Lugala, in his book, *Vomiting Stolen Food*. 'They gorged themselves and belched like volcanoes, as if to taunt those who didn't participate in the armed struggle: *where were you when we were fighting?*'[10]

Corruption became the culture of governance. The thieves lived up to every stereotype: Swiss watches worth tens of thousands of dollars; Porsche cars that got stuck in potholes; expensive whisky bought in bottles for the whole bar. The more conspicuous the spending the better, for it showed your people that you were in charge. Some was brazenly stuffed in suitcases and flown abroad; one finance minister was seen on his last day in office leaving the VIP section of the airport with seven briefcases.[11] It was not only oil revenues that were taken. International donors opened a grandly titled 'capacity building trust fund', to help set up a government, but that was plundered too; $60 million was taken, with no investigations made.[12]

Hundreds of millions of dollars were thieved in the grain or *durra* scandal. Over $2 billion was earmarked for the building of silos to store strategic reserves against famine.[13] The money was just taken. The big men, quite literally, stole the food from the mouths of the starving.

* * *

The revenues rolled in; over $150 million a month came from oil, but even that was not enough to pay the teachers.[14] There had been policies to develop agriculture, and turn the five percent of arable land under cultivation into large-scale farms to feed the nation. Yet South Sudan remained a land with more cows than people, fiercely guarded by herders who did not eat or sell their herds.[15] Outside the oil fields and telecoms, the single biggest commercial investment was a foreign brewery, a South African-built factory on the outskirts of Juba.

In the afternoon in government ministries, you could hammer on several doors before finding someone to talk to, and usually the answer was to return in the morning. It was a reward for those who had fought the war, providing jobs as a way to keep the peace. It did nothing, however, for the creation of a nation. Much was wasted on paying the salaries of a bloated civil service and army. Ministry budgets were sometimes spent three times over. One ministry tripled its salary expenditure every month for four months straight, with no explanation.[16] Many names on government payrolls did not exist, but someone always pocketed the salaries. They even had a name: 'ghost workers'.

Orders were made for a web of wide and smooth highways to improve trade, cut costs, encourage business and boost security. In Juba, tarred roads were built to ensure the elite could drive their expensive cars, but outside the city, the plans never materialised. The cash was paid for tarmac, but only bulldozed dirt tracks were built. The massive difference was pocketed. The roads, washed away within a couple of rainy seasons back into a rutted morass, cost a jaw-dropping million dollars per kilometre to build. The tarmacked highway to Uganda, the most basic transport link for the landlocked country, was only constructed with direct US aid cash after independence. The UN boss called the government official in charge the 'Minister of No Roads'.[17]

Instead, there were far-fetched dreams—a whole new capital, no less. Leaders wanted to move Juba to the geographic centre of the country, a patch of swampy scrub called Ramciel. I'd marvelled at the architect's model, at the back of the room where Kiir headed the Council of Ministers. The city was to be carved out of the wilds, with enormous housing estates, rings of motorways and high-rise tower blocks. The presidential palace looked like the architect had copied Washington's White House, then tripled it in size.

The new capital was not even the most outlandish proposal—that was the trippy plan to develop the ten state capitals into animal and fruit shapes. Juba was to be redesigned in the shape of a rhinoceros, with the president's office situated in the eye, and the police headquarters in its ear. The town of Yambio was to be a pineapple, while the town of Wau was unveiled as a giraffe. The elongated plan put the army barracks out of town in the giraffe's head, and the sewage works in its bottom.

Sympathisers said it was less about reality, but rather the enthusiasm of a people suppressed for decades, who now enjoyed the hope of planning their own future and country.

Critics said it showed the absolute disconnect of a leadership who saw billions of petrodollars as their personal property.

* * *

Money was the glue the leadership used to bring people into government, for the payments paid for a tenuous peace. It funded the strongmen to extend their grip on power. Men like Paul Malong, later becoming army chief, married as many as 88 wives, using the alliances to create family ties, building alliances and loyalties that spread far and deep.[18] 'Make love not war,' one diplomat called the strategy. 'Money for nothing and the chicks for free.' For those with ill-gotten gains, shelling out vast sums for the bride-price also meant cash was astutely stashed away in near untouchable giant herds of cattle, managed through the new family ties. It was an almost untraceable means to launder cash, safer than any offshore bank account.

Huge tracts of land, an area bigger than Rwanda, were handed over to foreigners under intensely dubious circumstances. The men who signed the contracts over to foreigners had no rights to the land themselves, but they had the guns to scare off critics. In the oil fields of Unity, an ex-Wall Street banker snapped up a lease on vast grasslands, while in the wilds of Jonglei, an Emirati company staked a claim to a wilderness where many feared trophy hunters would fly in to kill the big game that had survived the war. The land the people had fought for was sold off for cash.[19]

'Paytriotism and bribalism,' activist John Penn de Ngong called it, a sharp-tongued poet critical of the heavily militarised aristocracy and their system of patronage. 'We are a generation of degeneration,' he wrote. 'Sons of a gun, only taught songs of a gun.' The big men at the top were feathering their own nest. 'Commanders-in-Thief,' Ngong called them, twisting the old liberation slogan: '*a luta continua*,' the struggle continues. 'A looter continuer,' Ngong wrote instead.

People grew cynical of the rhetoric of the government when they could see the stark reality. With bleak irony, people used 'liberation' as slang for theft, a phrase for how the leaders would 'liberate' what they wanted: cash, land resources, even the women they desired.[20]

Graft went to the highest of levels, but Kiir still appeared surprised, writing a begging appeal to 75 top officials for the return of $4 billion. 'People in South Sudan are suffering, and yet some government officials simply care about themselves,' Kiir pleaded. According to the government's own loose figures, a third of oil revenues were stolen by the time of independence.[21] Diplomats said even more was missing. 'We fought for freedom, justice and equality,' Kiir said. 'Many of our friends died to achieve these objectives. Yet, once we got to power, we forgot what we fought for and began to enrich ourselves at the expense of our people.'[22]

Leaders lost their moral authority. It was both practical and symbolic; in thieving from the state, they stole the funds needed to build the nation. More dangerously, they showed they did not care about the concept of the country, their parade of stolen cash offering the clearest illustration that talk of national identity was but a smokescreen for personal profit.

193

They appeared unconcerned that this was undermining the very foundations of their power. Whatever the dream of freedom meant to the people, it was clear the men in charge offered no solution.[23]

* * *

Sitting by the banks of the Nile over a sunset beer, a grizzled diplomat friend handed me his binoculars. He was a passionate bird watcher, and pointed to a tree. Perched proudly on its branch was a regal African fish eagle, with dazzling white head and deep brown plumage on its body. Through the glasses, I could see it opening its yellow beak to make its eerie, echoing call. The eagle was the centre of the South's new coat of arms. 'It's a kleptoparasite, did you know?' the diplomat said. 'They're pirates. They steal fish from other birds.' He took a hefty gulp of whisky. 'They've only gone and chosen a thief as a national symbol,' he said.

The government had limited time to prove they could build a county and lead the land away from war. Instead, they showed the people that if you wanted a chance of better future, then you must grab what you can for yourself, and drive off others with violence. 'No one likes to eat the scraps of a feast,' a Juba proverb printed in a newspaper read. 'Everyone likes to sit at the table.'

Diplomats grumbled, but the talk was of democracy and development—not of challenging the key structures of power. The blatant theft of a country's future was not their responsibility, but it was their shameful moral failure that the international community ignored it and enabled the rot to fester. South Sudan's future was squandered, and too many stood by and watched it happen. It was not as if the consequences were unknown; too many past freedom fighters had turned their liberation movements into one-party states raping national resources for the exclusive benefit of the elite. It is a path that leads to state collapse.

What South Sudan's leaders did was impressive, for they managed to achieve in a mere matter of years what others had taken decades to do. They supercharged the process to build a system as corrupt and exploitative as anything ever experienced before.

For the USA, the key nation driving the push towards the referendum, it was thought better to keep quiet about the deep flaws in government than seek risky change that could jeopardise the chance of a vote for a new nation. If the government was seen as not ready to rule, Khartoum could use that as a reason to stall. In the US, key backers were the power-ful Evangelical Right, who saw independence as part of a far wider battle against Islamist extremists. Many in Washington identified personally with the cause of the South, blinding them to the faults of a government whose abuse of power was so very far from the rhetoric for the fight for freedom they espoused.

'Pre-independence euphoria and unchecked optimism became the prevailing context for decisions,' said Scott Gration, US Special Envoy to the Sudans, who called for 'tough love' to rein in the astonishing greed of the leaders. 'Without proper buttressing, I believed South Sudan would self-destruct.' The blunt-talking air force general grumbled that his was a 'lonely voice', dismissed as being too pro-Khartoum.

'My warnings were unwanted and unheeded,' Gration said. 'My colleagues in Washington, the US church leaders moved by the number of Christians killed, and the advocacy groups that blamed Khartoum for the years of suffering, all bristled when I advised against coddling the fledgling government too much. Many still viewed southern Sudanese as "victims" and themselves as the "saviours".'[24]

Juba learned early on that someone always came to bail them out. Donors kept supplying the cash to fund the services government should have supplied. Even when global oil prices slumped in 2009, meaning the government revenue dropped by over a third, that didn't stop the party. Kiir's men were shrewd; the international community had an enormous tolerance for the most wayward of behaviour. It might wave big sticks, but it never acted. Red lines were crossed, of human rights abuses and extreme corruption, but Juba's commanders basked in the reputation as liberators. They could literally get away with murder, and they knew it.

* * *

While the men at the top were busy stealing, the ordinary people were trying to build a nation. Jamba Besta had planned to be a secretary now that the war was over. Instead, she led me down a thin alley through the head-high grass. The track was lined by red triangle markers with skulls on. Sweat ran down the inside of my plastic visor as I walked in the heavy protective jacket like a sack of potatoes. The pregnant mother headed an all-female team of de-miners, removing dangerous explosives in the baking heat. As many as two million landmines were laid by both sides, hand-sized bombs that could blast your legs into your stomach in an instant.[25]

'My family were worried I was sacrificing myself to die,' Besta said. 'But this is our land, and if we can't walk on it, then what value is that?' She pointed to a tall mango tree, dripping with fruit and a shady place to rest. 'That is exactly the place there could be landmines,' she said. 'They knew people would want to sit under it.'

I had driven south from Juba for an hour into the long elephant grass at Bungu, down the old rebel supply route from Uganda. The two de-mining teams here were all women. 'The community want to use the land to rebuild the school,' said de-miner Tabu Monica Festo. High pitch squeaks from the hand-held detector revealed a potential explosive beneath the ground. Kneeling on the ground, she gently placed a plastic marker above. She would use water to soften the hard-baked earth, then gently probe the ground to dig the landmine out. 'This is our home,' she said. 'We are cleaning it of the war, so we can all come back to live.'

* * *

The fat generals who rested behind giant mahogany desks in Juba could do so only because of the bloody efforts of others.

Alual Koch was 13 when she learnt to kill with a gun. Now 36, she recounted how she carried ammunition and treated the wounded on the frontlines in the war. She would leave carrying out the wounded, or dragging the dead. The young widow wiped away tears when recounting trying to support her family. 'We are suffering very much,' Koch told me in Bor, where she worked as a prison warder. Her salary was barely enough to cover the needs of her immediate family, but it was often simply not paid. It had to support the 29 relatives and children of her dead fighter husband. 'It is too hard,' Koch told me. 'I must take the children out to the countryside, so they can try to cultivate the fields for food.'

The old veterans were soon forgotten. Women were among the first to be demobilised from the army, along with the elderly and the wounded. 'It is time to do something that is not war,' said Captain Corline Timon Lohure. Her son clung to her leg as she waited for her demobilisation papers. She was provided with a small cash pay-out, a bag of grain and basic farming tools, then let go. The mother of four, who had fought in Eastern Equatoria, was the first female soldier to return to civilian life in a UN-backed programme. I watched her marching proudly, her hair neatly tucked away under her military cap by a red floral bandana. She stood to attention with her rifle for a final time, saluted, and handed the gun in. In return, she got a discharge certificate. 'I will go home,' she said. 'I will bring my children up in peace.'

So much was sacrificed to achieve a dream the government were busy squandering.

* * *

Independence meant so much. There was hope—perhaps too much hope at times.

Sitting on the sidelines of a dusty football pitch, I watched the new national team of South Sudan train at Juba university. The ball swerved wildly as it clipped rocks, while the goalkeeper shared the net with hungry goats who took little notice of the game. The shirts with 'South Sudan' ironed onto the back were worn with pride, even if the letters on some were already peeling off. Like the new land, the squad contained a boiling pot of languages: Dinka and Nuer, Bari and Shilluk, Arabic from those who had come back from Khartoum, English from those who grew up south in Uganda, and Swahili from those who came from Kenya. 'To see the flag raised over the stadium, that will be a historic moment,' said Rudolf Andrea, secretary of the South Sudan Football Association. 'It is what we are waiting for.'

* * *

The people were coming home. They came down from the north, squeezed on barges, sleeping in every space of the flat roof boats on a journey that could take weeks. They came by bus up from the south from Kenya and Uganda, and trekked in from Ethiopia and Congo. Juba's quiet tracks became bustling, crowded roads. It was a movement of people on a staggering scale. Four million had fled the war, and more than half that had returned since the peace deal in 2005. Still more came.

Day after day I went to Juba river port, watching the lines of barges waiting to unload. Their decks were so crowded with passengers I sometimes feared the grumbling engines would sink. People carried all they owned in their hands: battered cooking pots, rolls of mattress, goats and chicken. Shelters of plastic and cloth sheets propped up on sticks sprung up around town. Every tree down by the river port had a family living beneath it, a grey mosquito net strung up under a branch. 'Facilities are very bad,' said Martin Leek, a volunteer teacher in an open-air school by the port, teaching forty children the days of the week in English. 'But it is better to do this than to sit and do nothing.'

Expectations were sky-high, and the needs were endless. A water borehole would be dug, but in the space of days the number using it would exceed capacity. 'We are coming back to nothing,' said Hope Apolo, carrying a baby on her back wrapped in a bright print cloth, and a crying toddler in her arms. She had come from the North. She had made ends meet in the sand blown camps outside Khartoum by brewing moonshine palm wine, and had been arrested several times. 'Living in Khartoum was not easy, because we were not treated as real citizens,' she said. 'We were not free.' Now she was going home to green farmland in the west for the first time in almost 20 years. 'We did have electricity in Khartoum though,' she added. 'It is going to be hard to be back.'

* * *

They jetted in from the US, Europe and Australia too, wearing baseball caps and appearing a little lost. So much had changed. Even the famous came home. Luol Deng, favourite basketball player of Barack Obama for his skills with the Chicago Bulls, returned to show his support. The towering man, confident on screen and court, appeared overwhelmed at the return to a land he fled as a refugee aged five.

Perhaps he was aware that his story of running from war was nothing unusual here. UN officials had brought him back as an ambassador to highlight their work, and he went to meet children at a school in Juba. The British Olympian was humble and quiet. 'I feel home again,' he said. 'I'm not a refugee anymore.' As he spoke, rain drops began to fall, and UN officers handed him an umbrella for shelter. Luol handed each umbrella he got to the children he spoke to, and the officials scrambled for more. 'Maybe you will be the president of this country, and you are going to lead us,' he told the children. 'We're going to have a great country.'

Rain drops smattered down onto the parched ground, then grew harder. We ran as the clouds opened to find shelter. The powerful, earthy, warm scent of rain on sun-baked soil rose up. 'That smell,' he said softly, shaking his head. 'Man, I've not smelt it since I was a kid.' Drops of rain ran down his cheek.

* * *

Even those who had been taken to Cuba came back. 'We said it is now time to return because there is peace,' said Okony Simon Mori, who had left along with 600 children in 1985 on a Russian troop ship from the Red Sea, to take up Fidel Castro's offer of education. The first batch of trainees Cuba had sent back were decimated in the war, so later rounds of students found other nations to live in. Two decades later, after so much longer than anyone could have imagined, eventually they returned with the skills they'd been taught to build their nation. The Cuban Jubans, people called them.

'We came back to put in a basic health structure, because even that was missing,' said Mori, an orthopaedic surgeon who helped with the huge numbers of war wounded with missing limbs. 'Everything was destroyed.' Mori, like many others, had earlier left Cuba for Canada, but the medical certificates were not recognised there, so they had to find what work they could. For a people who revered cattle, some ended with the worst job possible: butchery on the soulless floor of a slaughterhouse.

They were glad to be back in South Sudan, even if they remembered their Caribbean upbringing with nostalgia. They would meet at De Havana, a thatch-hut bar in the heart of Juba pumping out salsa beats full of Latino dance, full of the scent of roast pork and beans, where they could speak Spanish, drink rum and coke, and remember the days of parties on golden beaches. 'Sometimes I miss Cuba,' Mori said. 'But it is true what they say; east or west, home is best—and that is here in South Sudan.'

The Cubans, who came from across the South, had been brought up alongside the children of other African revolutionaries. It meant they never got that same sharp sense of ethnic identity that others had. 'I was only ever told, "You are South Sudanese,"' said Achol Jok Mach. 'It was only much later I learned I was Dinka.' When she arrived in Juba airport, she was overwhelmed. 'It is one thing to say "my country" and point to a place on a map,' she said. 'But to actually be in your own nation? It is a feeling that you cannot really describe. When I landed in South Sudan, the first thing I did was bend down and touch the soil.'

* * *

Valentino Achak Deng was bursting with enthusiasm. Over the plastic table in the tent compound we both stayed in, he spread out bundles of papers. Organising metal roofing sheets and cement in one of the most far flung towns in the land was a logistical headache, but his passion was catching. Valentino, a soft-spoken man with a neat moustache and studious reading glasses, had returned from his refugee life in the US to come back and build a school. 'I came back as soon as I could,' he said. 'I came to invest in education, so I could improve the lives of the young ones. I will build a school for children from all parts of South Sudan.'

Valentino was one of over 3,000 teenage boys who won a refugee resettlement ticket to the US in 2001, discovering the strange new world of hot and cold running water, microwaves, busy motorways and ice cream in the urban sprawl of Atlanta. 'They called us the Lost Boys,' said Valentino. 'Yet it was those who stayed were the lost ones, because they did not get any education. I ran from this country, but got advantages abroad.'[26]

He fled South Sudan in war. 'We were an exodus,' said Valentino, describing how as a young boy he fled the raids of the Khartoum-backed horsemen, who destroyed his village of Marial Bai in Bahr el Ghazal in 1987. 'Everyone left. Every day we would walk, without shoes, with no food. We did not know where the sun would rise when we woke up, or where we would be when the night would find us.' Thousands of children sought safety, sneaking through malarial-infested swamps and braving crocodiles by swimming across the wide rivers. Many of his friends died. Those who survived made it exhausted across the border to Ethiopia, hoping to find family and school. Instead, they became the Red Army, the children's battalion of the SPLA who carried guns as long as they were tall. In time, the children escaped again, many to the northern Kenyan desert refugee camp of Kakuma—a tough shack city, but one where they no longer had to kill.

Outside South Sudan, the extraordinary tales of the Lost Boys were shocking. Valentino's story of survival had been turned into the bestselling book *What is the What*, written after he met American author Dave Eggers.[27] Back home in the South, what was alarming was how ordinary such stories were. They were nightmares so many could tell.

Yet if Valentino's life had been a story of suffering, that was only half the tale, for the story of his life today offered the hope of a happier ending. There was a sequel, and this was it. He was using the proceeds from the book to fund the school in his village. Too many schools in the South after the war were roofless walls. Over a million children were enrolled in school, but with one teacher for every thousand children, less than two percent completed primary education. Secondary education was even rarer. Valentino would create something that was unique in the South: one of the best equipped secondary schools in the country for boys and girls, complete with science laboratories and a school farm to teach sustainable agriculture. He built dormitories too, so that students could come from all across the South, to build a sense of national identity among the many peoples and languages, and not one based on ethnicity. They lived alongside each other not as separate tribes, but as South Sudanese.

'Before, in the war, when I was young, we did not have the knowledge. All across the country there were not enough schools to teach us how to build our country,' Valentino said. 'If we had had education, we could have done something more to help. We could have looked for a solution that wasn't only war.'

The boys were now men, and they were lost no more.

* * *

The referendum was approaching. A little out of Juba, I met with Joseph Wani Cirillo. He was a kind man, chuckling as he told me stories while hobbling around the small clinic he ran in the leper colony at Luri-Rokwe. He handed out pills to a young girl, who held a long stick to lead her blind mother. Cirillo, a nurse, had looked after dozens of people afflicted with leprosy for decades. During the years of war, when Juba was besieged and drugs ran out, he felt his fingers becoming numb. After years of close contact, he had become infected himself. Had he escaped to find medicine, he could have stopped the infection—but he chose to stay. 'They are my friends,' the nurse said. 'I couldn't leave them, because then they would have had no one.' In time, he had lost his right foot and several fingers on both hands. Now with treatment, leprosy was stopped, but the missing flesh could not be replaced. He did not dwell on his condition, however. It was the upcoming vote that was on his mind. 'We will have a country,' he said. 'We will vote for freedom in the referendum.' Excitement was intense. 'I will vote with this,' he said, holding up his twisted stump of his finger. His smile went right across his laughing face.

* * *

Dawn broke on 9 January 2011 with a fierce, red sun. I watched the light rise over the grave of John Garang. Against the expectations of many cynics, referendum day had arrived, on time and without all-out war. Driving through town as the light crept through the trees, I passed patient queues already deep and long, waiting for a chance to vote. Men stood in one line, women in another. One lady held a small radio. 'Make your decision in a peaceful manner as we end the long journey,' Kiir said, broadcast on the radio. Tens of thousands stood in the snaking lines. Posters were plastered on the wall, with two hands breaking free from chains. 'UNITY BY FORCE IS SLAVERY,' it read.

'It was so important to me I could not sleep,' said Yar Mayon, her baby strapped in a cloth on her back as she stood in line. She had grown up in refugee camps in Ethiopia and Kenya, and I asked her how she would vote. She smiled, and held her hand up waving with the palm flat, the symbol on the ballot for independence. Unity was two shaking hands. 'I came here early morning because I wanted to show just how much I wanted to vote,' she said. 'This is for a new country. We are voting for peace.'

They queued to vote across the world, from Kenya to Australia, to Britain, Egypt and the US, all the places the Southerners had scattered to. In North Sudan, all those who laid claim to ancestry of the South could vote too.

George Clooney had been swept up within the vast crowds in Juba. Hollywood seemed a long way away. 'It's a great day for the world, watching a country get its freedom for the first time,' he told me. 'They've been walking this walk for a long, long time.' He was surrounded by foreign reporters, but none of the Southerners queueing seemed to give him a passing glance. They had more important things on their minds.

Kiir was the first to cast his ballot. Cheers broke out as he pushed the paper into the box in front of the crowd. Women wailed in ululation. Drum beats were thumped out. Men wrapped in fake leopard skins danced. 'Freedom!' someone shouted. 'Separation!'

* * *

When the voting ended after a week, the counting began. At dusk, I walked up to the polling centre in a school near my house in Hai Malakal. I crept into the back of a packed room. For a while, the only sound was the hissing of a pair of pressurised paraffin lamps, lighting the piles of ballot papers emptied onto the desk. All eyes were on the table. The returning officer picked up a folded ballot, and opened the paper. 'Secession,' she said, handing it to be checked, while she moved on to the next. 'Secession. Secession. Secession.' The scene looked like a religious painting, the people crowded around a priest at the altar lit up by the warm lamplight. Goosebumps ran up my arms. After half an hour, the official pulled out a ballot. 'Unity,' she said. The room looked up, as if the trance had been broken. Then the next paper was opened. 'Secession,' she said. I could feel those squeezed in tight around me at the back of the classroom sigh with relief. 'Secession. Secession. Secession,' she continued.

I slipped out the classroom, and walked home down the sandy street by the light of the moon. I had just witnessed something magical. My heart was pounding, and I felt like crying.

* * *

Nearly a month later, I was back at Garang's mausoleum. Crackling speakers and an outdoor cinema had been rigged up, screening live the results being read out in Khartoum. We craned our heads forward to hear the historic words. The atmosphere was electric. The sun set, and the final figures were confirmed: 98.83 percent had voted for a new nation. A total of 3,792,518 had voted to split. Only 44,888, one percent, chose unity. 'South Sudan has chosen secession,' President Bashir said in Khartoum, as he accepted the results. 'We are committed to good relations based on cooperation.'

The crowd went wild. Those at the front leapt up, waving flags and cheering. Those at the back, hearing the shouts of delight, began to dance. 'I am free today,' said Abiong Nyok, a housewife, waving a South Sudan flag. 'Now I am a first class citizen in my own country.' South Sudan had achieved what many had said was simply the impossible: to hold a peaceful, credible referendum for independence, and to have that decision recognised by the government in Khartoum. We skipped in a circle to the music. As dark fell, people lit candles, to celebrate the 'birthday' of the new land. 'This is what happens when you oppress and marginalise a people for over 50 years,' said Puok Dhieu, a veteran soldier taking my hand to dance. 'One day those people will rise up and say: "It is enough."'

* * *

South Sudan hurtled towards separation, but divorce involves more than the paperwork of changing a name. The details of how North and South would divide needed to be hammered out. An oil deal was needed for transport fees of crude pumped from the South through the only pipeline that ran North to the Red Sea. The North was facing an economic nightmare, for not only was Africa's biggest nation about to shrink by ceding a quarter of its land when the South split, but Juba would be taking more than three-quarters of total oil production from the old united Sudan, roughly 350,000 barrels a day.

A new currency was needed, as well as passports, international telephone codes, a constitution, and laws. There was the issue of citizens on either side of the border. Aid workers were preparing for terrible scenarios, with many fearing half a million Southerners still living in the North could be forcibly expelled. The undefined frontier weaving through oil fields was contested—and heavily militarised. The threat of a return to North–South war was all too real. Abyei, the Lebanon-sized border region claimed by both sides, was already in flames after Khartoum sent troops in to seize it. In the old rebel zones of the Nuba Mountains and Blue Nile in the North, there was terror about what would happen. They had been key fighters in the war with the SPLA, but now the South was splitting, they were being abandoned on the wrong side of the border.

A month before the South's independence, Khartoum moved to crack down on the old rebels of the Nuba Moutains, beginning in the town of Kadugli. 'The bodies were just lying in the streets,' one Nuba man told me. He had escaped the street-by-street massacre only because his neighbour, who had been called to join a government militia to fight, had warned him of what was to come. 'My neighbour had got clear instructions,' he said. 'They were told: "Just sweep away the rubbish. If you see a Nuba, just clean it up."'

There were those who said independence was coming too fast. For those who had spent their lives in war, it couldn't come soon enough.

* * *

The balloons fluttered red, white and blue. The smell of sizzling burgers and hot dogs drifted across the yard to the sound of a jazz brass band. Inside the fortified walls of the US Consulate in Juba, it was the Fourth of July party. The diplomats in suits mopped their brows in the steamy heat of what would soon be the world's newest capital. It was 235 years since the US Declaration of Independence from Britain, and five days before South Sudan became a new nation.

The guest of honour took to the stage, and the crowd watched as the man who helped launch Africa's longest war with a machete half a century before tapped the microphone for attention. General Joseph Lagu, the old Anya-Nya chief, raised his fist into the air. 'My fellow Southern Sudanese have been marching to their freedom for over fifty years,' he told the crowd. 'Our promised land is South Sudan!' He paused, and I thought that the speech was over, but the 80-year-old ex-rebel had also composed a song. He cleared his throat, and with a little shuffling dance, burst out singing. 'To freedom, to freedom,' he sang, his voice proud and clear. 'To freedom happily marching, we go!'

Amid the slogans, it was still not clear what freedom would mean. On the most basic level, it was the hope for an end to war, to build a better life in peace. Yet what the new nation to be was to look like was a far harder question. Who would decide what that longed-for freedom would mean in reality?

Lagu's faith was inspiring, but as he stepped off the stage, I asked him if he believed South Sudan would grow into a viable state. The long battle to reach independence marked only the very starting line for the land. On paper, there was every reason to be gloomy, yet this was a land where hope often overcomes all apparent practical logic. Lagu's

205

hands left his walking stick and clutched mine with a firm grip. 'First raise a flag,' he said. 'Then we make the country.'

* * *

Five days later, on 9 July 2011, South Sudan became the world's 193rd nation. When the giant flag was raised, there was a wave of sound, a roar of a people cheering for freedom. Tens of thousands dancing into the square wailed in joy. Around me in the ecstatic crowd, under the intense, burning sun, men and women were crying.

'After so much struggle by the people of South Sudan, the United States of America welcomes the birth of a new nation,' President Barack Obama said, as he sent a message to recognise the new nation. 'Today is a reminder that after the darkness of war, the light of a new dawn is possible.'[28] People kissed the ground. There was a hysteria of happiness, an electric beat of exhilaration quite unlike anything I have felt anywhere, nor expect to again.

'It is a day which will be forever engraved in our hearts,' Kiir told the crowd. 'The independence we celebrate today transfers the responsibility for our destiny to our hands.' Bashir, his old enemy, stood next to Kiir. He was the first to congratulate and recognise the South. 'Its success will be our success,' he said.

Yet amid the celebrations, there were also warnings. 'Our detractors have already written us off, even before the proclamation of our independence,' Kiir told the crowds. 'They say we will slip in to civil war as soon as our flag is hoisted. They justify that by arguing that we are incapable of resolving our problems through dialogue. They charge that we are quick to revert to violence. They claim that our concept of democracy and freedom is faulty. It is incumbent upon us to prove them all wrong.'

12

THE BROWN CATERPILLARS

'If a dog bites you and you don't bite him back, it will say that you have no teeth.'

Sudanese proverb

There was a low rumble like thunder, but the sky was clear. I squinted against the fierce sun into the distance. Booming explosions echoed again across the river. There was a roar of a fighter jet, now much closer, and a thick plume of black smoke rose on the horizon. The town of Bor was burning.

It was January 2014, two weeks after fighting had erupted in Juba and split the army. The killings spiralled into a war and spread north to Bor. The town had been captured by the massed forces of the White Army, gangs of Nuer militias raised in revenge for their relatives killed in Juba and to protect their families from attack. They stormed in, screaming war cries, smeared in white ash and with red rags wrapped around their heads as uniform. Many charged with only spears and machetes, overcoming the better-armed government soldiers in their trenches only by sheer numbers and the intense ferocity of the assault.

Thousands were killed in the most barbarous of ways. Women in the hospital were raped and then killed in their beds, the men and children bludgeoned and shot where they had crawled to escape. Teenage gunmen opened fire on women sheltering inside a church. People escaping were machine-gunned in the swamps. Disabled veterans, heroes of the freedom war, were shot as they struggled to escape on their wheelchairs.[1]

The government soon took Bor back in a counter-attack, then lost it again. Each battle brought a new wave of destruction, and the town was reduced to rubble. Government soldiers were now fighting their way towards the town again, but this time backed by Ugandan helicopter gunships, jets and tanks. Cluster bombs targeted the massed rebels on the ground, scattering explosions that devastated in wide killing arcs.[2]

UN peacekeepers waited. Days before, a UN base in the Jonglei outpost of Akobo had been attacked by 2,000 gunmen, the defences swiftly breached and gates torn open. Two Indian peacekeepers had been killed and one shot in the chest, while the forty others surrendered. More than twenty civilians sheltering inside were dragged out, mainly young Dinka men, some working for an aid agency. The gunmen celebrated as they shot or beat them to death. 'They were dancing, shouting that they have killed all the Dinka,' one survivor said.[3]

Fearing a massacre of their own men, the UN scrambled to pull troops out of forts too isolated to defend. The next day, two UN helicopters evacuating forty peacekeepers at a base in Yuai were shot at, with one crash landing. In Bor, the UN soldiers watched the devastation from their camp. The base was now sheltering up to 17,000 civilians. Gunmen encircled the wire, waiting to attack. Terrified peacekeepers dug the trenches deeper and built the sandbag emplacements higher.[4]

* * *

We watched those fleeing Bor arrive at dawn, squeezed onto barges that slipped across the river and the frontline. Over 100,000 civilians escaped west across the Nile, crammed onto narrow metal boats that nosed their way through a network of swampy channels. They reached the once-tiny fishing village of Mingkaman, a night's journey though the marsh. Children led the elderly out of the boats, as relays of people waded out into the river to carry babies and luggage to shore on their shoulders.

'We came through the night to avoid being seen,' said boat captain Kulang Mayen, a rangy soldier dressed in mismatched green fatigues and cloth cap. 'We go every night to pick those running from the fighting.' Some had spent days hiding out in the bush, or on the dozens of islands out in the Nile. 'They had a machine gun raised up, and they fired and fired and fired as we swam,' said Gabriel Bol, a cattle herder, wearing a tattered T-shirt promoting the use of latrines gifted by the UN. 'The bullets were hitting the water, but we knew we could not stop or they'd shoot us.' They carried what they could—a battered cooking pot, a plastic sack of clothes or a blanket—but most fled empty handed. Many sat exhausted where they collapsed in the dust. Children slept, wrapped in colourful cloths on the backs of their mothers. The cooking smoke from thousands of small fires lit by those living out under the trees curled into the sky. 'They killed my wife, my three daughters, my cows,' said Bol. 'Now I will go back and kill theirs.'

A weary nurse from Doctors Without Borders helped people off the boat. I spent hours writing dark lists in my notebook, as a miserable line of survivors made their way onto dry land. 'Elderly lady, shot in leg,' I noted. 'Soldier with belly wound on stretcher. Rotting stench, strangely sweet.' In the two days we'd been at the port, there were already some thirty with bullet wounds offloaded and taken to a newly set up clinic. Philip Deng, a 20-year-old student, paced up and down searching the shore, slipping in the sucking mud in the impractical black leather shoes he was wearing when he ran. He was searching for his family, who he had lost in the chaos of the fighting. 'Their phones have been off ever since,' he said. 'I hope they are like me, alive and well, but searching.' His faced was creased with worry.

Going the other way were government soldiers, heading back to counterattack. One lifted his rifle and let loose a crackle of gunfire over the river towards Bor to raise morale. Instead, it sent ripples of panic amongst the already traumatised families.

A photographer and I went down to the boats now carrying only government soldiers, and threw our flak jackets and helmets inside, along with all the supplies we could muster: a box of bottles of water from an aid agency, and a bag of dry flat bread. We sat on wooden slats of the decking, ready to cross on the afternoon mission to Bor, or as close as we could get.

'We finished the war with the Arabs and made our new nation,' soldier Jacob Achek told me. Most of his battalion had mutinied to join the rebels, but he had stayed loyal to the government. I asked him what the war was about, but he returned the question. 'Why are they fighting?' he said. 'You'll have to ask the politicians for that answer. Perhaps they might know.'

Everything was supposed to have been different. Freedom had been won, and South Sudan was a country. No one, however, knew exactly what creating a new nation really meant. Two years later, the people were ripping themselves apart.

* * *

Independence was only the beginning. As the rallying cry of freedom faded, they had to find other reasons to pull together. Splitting from Sudan was meant to make things better, but the signs were not positive. The South was already fighting amongst itself; in the six months running up to independence at least 2,300 people had been killed in hundreds of cattle raids and revenge attacks in the South, forcing over a quarter of a million people to flee. Meanwhile, a thousand people every day returned home to the South by bus, boat, plane and on foot. Most arrived with nothing, a flood of people that was an epic logistical feat to cope with in itself. There were little or no services awaiting them.

After the parties, the government now had to fulfil the promises. Inside the high walls of the UN compound, independence celebrations were muted. Lise Grande, the UN's aid chief in South Sudan, understood the task ahead. 'The scope and complexity of the capacity building task in Southern Sudan is almost unimaginable,' the American warned, days after independence. 'South Sudan represents the single largest state building challenge of our generation.'

She handed out to journalists a document called 'Scary Statistics' detailing the challenges. The list was long: one out of every seven children dies before their fifth birthday; half of children fail to complete primary school; less than a third of people are literate; only a fifth can access a health facility. Life was especially hard for women; almost a fifth of girls would be married off before they reached the age of 15. Often, they were treated as property to be exchanged for cattle in a wedding dowry. One in fifty women died in childbirth, a rate far beyond anywhere else.

'Trends are moving in the wrong direction,' Grande's office wrote in a cold-eyed paper, charting the next two years ahead. 'Tensions are rising along the border, clashes between the SPLA and renegade militia and counter-insurgency campaigns are continuing, and inter-communal violence has intensified.' Things had to move swiftly to show that peace was better than war. There wasn't much time to make a difference. 'Three-quarters of all post-conflict countries returned to conflict after five to seven years,' the paper noted.

History holds a glimpse of the future, for the story of other nations offered warnings for the South. New states face tough beginnings. Firstly, they must create the nation by defeating external enemies. Secondly, they must fight an internal battle over who will control it.[5] For South Sudan, that would mean first a war with the North. Then it would be a war with itself.

* * *

One key problem was the absence of a map. In Juba, so many official documents had been lost that the records of the borders had vanished. They had rotted away or been munched by decades of termites.

The border itself was not demarcated, and war still raged along the frontier in the old SPLA rebel areas now in the North, the Nuba Mountains and Blue Nile. North and South traded accusations; each backed rebels fighting the other. The border oil zone of Abyei claimed by both sides had been overrun by Northern soldiers. It added poison to the pot, for elders of the Dinka clan from Abyei held powerful posts in the South's government and army. The loss of the land would be cause for revenge.

About a third of the frontier between North and South—the distance from Britain to Russia—was contested. There were half a dozen key flashpoints, many around oil fields.

So the two sides went searching, scouring archives for papers that might help demarcate the border. People wanted to know how the boundary stood at independence in 1956. Teams were even sent in desperation to Durham University, where many old British officers had stored their papers. In Durham library's centuries-old hallways, in the shadow of the ancient cathedral, library archivist Jane Hogan made thousands of copies of maps and records for government delegations from both Juba and Khartoum, as well as the US State Department, London's Foreign Office, multiple oil companies and more. 'Everyone had this idea that on the last day when the British left, they produced a map showing the boundary between North and South,' said Hogan. 'That is just a total fantasy.' When the British quit, they left in haste.

There was neither need nor time to map an internal border of a land they were leaving.

Still, as they searched through the long lines of leather bound books, the Sudanese from both North and South would be diverted. So far from home, the differences of borders no longer mattered. Chatting and laughing, they would take a break from the map quest to scan through the database of tens of thousands of black and white photographs from Sudan. Border wars were forgotten, as the librarians pleaded with them to quieten their excited voices. 'I think every Sudanese I've seen sit in front of that computer screen has eventually come across some relation,' Hogan said. 'It's like a family album.'

* * *

Along the border, the slow convoy of four-wheel drives and troop lorries pulling water tankers pushed through dry scrub. It kicked up plumes of fine dust, like smoke rising high into the air. Sweat stung our eyes. Back in South Sudan, I had joined a UN patrol, weaving from village to village through the northern area of Unity. We trundled along the edge of the oil fields from the base in Bentiu, to Mayom, Abiemnom and the edge of Abyei, through small scattered hut villages few had heard of. The patrol monitored areas where there had been clashes between Misseriya horsemen, coming from the North, and Southern troops. I met SPLA troops oozing blood from gunshot wounds to their legs, lying on filthy beds in a clinic with broken windows. They boasted of killing several enemies.

On maps, borders seem so clear. Thick red lines mark us from them. On the ground, the reality blurs, and the divisions seems arbitrary. It was all one, long dusty haze of yellowed thorn bush broken by occasional stretches of dry grass, the horizon shimmering in the heat. We were on the edge of one of the most lucrative oil fields, and we'd been stopped by SPLA troops who blockaded the track with foxholes. In Arabic, they called the field 'Heglig', the name of the desert palm tree still scattered around. It produces thin but just about edible dates. In the South, they called it 'Panthou', the Dinka name for the same tree. The exact location was disputed, for colonial maps loosely referred to a 'clump of heglig'.[6] The thick crayon lines on the maps alone might translate to a walk of several hours on the ground. Noting locations of a small wood might have been a useful waymark for a weary officer far out on trek. It was not, however, much basis for an international frontier to divide oil fields between two nations emerging from so long at war.

Through the trees two young men emerged, dressed in blue flowing tops, with leather amulets containing Koranic passages for protection draped around their necks, and thin blue tattoos across their cheeks. They were Fulani, nomadic cattle herders, who wander with their animals across Africa from west to east. Frontiers meant little to them. A UN officer, a burly lieutenant commander from the New Zealand navy, stopped to ask them where they had come from, and if there were soldiers around. They were nervous to talk, but sold us a fat sheep for supper, then wandered off back towards the border.

Towards dusk, the Indian soldiers rolled out a perimeter of barbed wire and hoisted a UN blue flag up a pole. Those not on duty set up makeshift stumps using a plastic chair for a game of tip-and-run cricket. Children came and watched, laughing at the generously-sized German colonel learning to bowl. As the smell of sizzling lamb and spices drifted out from the mess tent, I strung a mosquito net up beneath a tree.

* * *

An oil agreement was needed. Before independence, the oil was split equally between Juba and Khartoum. After July 2011, South Sudan got all the income from the oil pumped from its lands, more than three-quarters of what was once Sudan's total production. But with no refineries, and all the pipelines heading north, they needed a deal. For the first six months, the South exported oil without paying. Then Khartoum began to sell the oil itself to pay pumping fees. Juba said it was theft, claiming over six million barrels, or $815 million worth of crude oil, had been taken. By January 2012, anger escalated to fury.

Talks in Ethiopia went nowhere. Kiir, staying with his team in the Sheraton Hotel in sumptuous suites with marble baths reportedly costing $30,000 a night, refused to sign a deal.[7] Juba used their only card to threaten with: shutting down the oil entirely. No one took it seriously, because the consequences were simply too great. After all, South Sudan's economy was the most oil dependent in the world, providing some 97 percent of the budget. Who would be reckless enough to shut

213

down a pipeline that provided the near totality of government revenue? It would be an act of spectacular self-sabotage.

'We will all be in the dark,' one senior politician told me, when I called again to check it was not merely a bluff. 'But we have been in the dark for far longer, and are used to it. We can survive with a candle.' Juba banked on Khartoum collapsing first without its share of the oil cash.

So Juba turned off the oil. 'South Sudan has set off its economic doomsday machine,' said Alex de Waal, the advisor to the African Union-led talks. 'It seems a suicidal step,'[8] It produced panic. 'Neither the president nor senior ministers present in the meeting were aware of the economic implications of the shutdown,' a leaked World Bank briefing note read, warning that it had 'never seen a situation as dramatic as the one faced by South Sudan.'[9] It was not a matter of damaging financial growth, but of killing the very economy itself. In one blow, it cut 80 percent of gross domestic product. Journalists gave a more succinct summary. 'World Bank to South Sudan: Are you out of your freaking mind?!' one headline read.[10]

Instead, ministers spoke of grand plans to build South Sudan's own pipeline east to Djibouti via Ethiopia, or south to Kenya—about the distance from London to Rome.[11] Until that multi-billion scheme could be built, funded by loans that no one had details about, they would be taking the crude out on trucks.

It was delusional. The only roads were mud tracks at best, key oil fields were on the wrong side of one of the world's biggest swamps, and if they crossed that, the only bridge across the Nile was in Juba, at the opposite end of the country. All that assumed the plundering gunmen wouldn't stop the convoys. Oil tankers didn't have a hope.

* * *

By late March 2012, Juba broke the stalemate in the manner it knew best: war. Kiir sent in SPLA soldiers to the oil fields of Heglig, seizing the drilling and pumping stations, and forcing Northern troops to flee. Eight months since the independence designed to bring peace, North and South were back fighting again. Bashir called for jihad and a 'final lesson by force'. Sudan sent aircraft on bombing missions, and the SPLA dug down thin trenches, from where they crouched, firing wildly at the planes.

Yet while Juba was ready for attack from Sudan, it was shocked by the response from those it saw as friends abroad. The violence sparked massive condemnation—including fury from China, Malaysia and India, the countries operating the main oil companies. The UN Security Council unanimously backed a resolution threatening sanctions if the fighting did not stop. The liberation leaders were bewildered at the heavy criticism for the violence; no longer were they the darlings of the West. The SPLA pulled out after a month, leaving rotting corpses in the damaged oil pumping stations.

In August, US Secretary of State Hillary Clinton flew to Juba to try to break the deadlock. 'Behind all the arguments about pricing and refining was a simple human reality,' she wrote. 'These battle-scarred freedom fighters couldn't bring themselves to move beyond the horrors of the past.'[12]

Still, the top leaders were insulated. They had sold their country for glitzy houses, and salted enough away to live in luxury for life. Their families enjoyed private schools and hospitals abroad. I'd watch the leaders' children laugh and dance with painfully expensive whisky bottles in their hands at poolside rooftop bars in Kenya's capital Nairobi, far from the troubles at home.

The government also took out colossal loans against future oil production. Since they were desperate, the loans were made at appalling rates. As the screw tightened, the leaders scrambled to take ever bigger slices of the pie, grabbing what they could when the going was still good. The greed got worse, not better.

Inside the South, it was a different matter. With funding for education and health gone, the death rate for children under five was expected to double. The most basic of services survived only because foreign aid agencies funded or supplied them. More than half of food came as imports, and that hit even those who appeared to live outside the cash economy. As always, the poorest suffered the most.

In the long run, it was a disaster for Kiir. Buying loyalty lasts for as long as you can afford it, but when the money ran out, old enemies resurfaced. He could no longer splash the cash with patronage dollar briefcases of support. Yet the men with armies still needed to be paid. Old rebel turned Vice President Riek Machar made clear he would challenge Kiir in the elections due in 2015 for the presidency. It shook the leadership, and they grew increasingly paranoid. The ruling party and military were one and the same, so political challengers threatened the army too.

* * *

'Is this the South Sudan we fought for?' the banner read, raised at the memorial service for Diing Chan Awuol, a prominent political commentator. Awuol, using the pen name Isaiah Abraham, was a veteran officer from the Dinka grasslands of Twic who had served in Kiir's old battalion. Retrained as a pastor, he felt confident enough to shrug off anonymous phone calls warning him to stop writing. His opinion pieces suggested Kiir would not win an election. In December 2012, he was shot in the face on his own doorstep. The murderers were never caught, and no one seemed eager to find them. The government rejected FBI assistance.[13] They did not want US agents asking questions about who was responsible.

Criticism is often the hardest to hear from those closest to you. The old rebel chiefs had learned their leadership in war, and did not know how to handle civilian governance. Those who spoke out had their loyalties challenged. First in the firing line were journalists and human rights activists. Many got death threats, and taking Awuol's killing as a warning, they slipped out of the country.

Power bases in South Sudan rest on ethnicity, but there is no majority group and none offer monolithic support. The multiple clans of the Dinka are the largest, making up around a third of the population. The many Nuer groups come next, totalling about half that.[14] The South is so diverse, and all are so heavily armed, that only the toughest of tyrants could hope to lead a dictatorship dependent on the support of one group alone—and would need significant cash to do so. Even then, it would be a fragile rule unlikely to last long.

Kiir, however, was unsure how far he could even rely on Dinka backing. Support from his homeland in Bahr el Ghazal was strong, but some from the Dinka lands in Jonglei viewed Kiir with suspicion. Powerful Dinka party stalwarts once loyal to Garang did not have the same allegiance to him. Since Kiir lacked the cash to pay them off, they wanted to take it themselves. Threatened on all sides and backed into a corner, Kiir gathered the forces he could to protect him.

By September 2012, the governments of Khartoum and Juba were dragged to talks again. 'Whether you're in a marriage, business partnership, or in a trade association,' Ugandan President Yoweri Museveni advised helpfully, 'you can't be successful if your partner is dead.'[15] Reluctantly, Kiir realised he needed Khartoum, and capitulated to a deal. After all the suffering and fighting, the terms were worse than those offered originally. The oil pumps finally resumed in April 2013. This crisis was over, but it had set in motion one even more deadly.[16]

* * *

Three months later, the purge commenced. On 23 July 2013, the decrees were read out after dark over Radio Juba, the government-run station. I listened to the crackling broadcast, terrified at what it would mean. Kiir dismissed almost the entire government. Along with 54 ministers and their deputies, an order against Riek Machar was read, relieving the Vice President of his duties with immediate effect.

I expected chaos. First thing next morning, I called everyone I knew in Juba. Soldiers patrolled the streets, with a heavy presence around the presidential palace and parliament. 'This is only routine work,' army spokesman Colonel Philip Aguer told me multiple times. 'They are being deployed to protect the ministries.' I was doubtful of his reassurances.

Despite this, Juba remained calm, on the surface anyway. Many of the ministers were reshuffled and reinstated, but Machar remained out in the cold. Still, it was clear that something was brewing. In the atmosphere of fear and mistrust, both sides prepared for the worst. It would become a self-fulfilling prophecy. As always, it was the people who suffered.

'What is happening to the ordinary people in this country under the weight of this mix of poor governance, inflation at 50 percent and rising, skyrocketing food prices, economic inequality, waning pride in the nation and subsequent ethnic warfare?' former government minister and academic Jok Madut Jok wrote at the beginning of December 2013, warning that an incompetent leadership had corroded the foundations of the state before construction had even began. Austerity measures of the oil shutdown were over, but the economy struggled to service the crippling levels of debt run up through shady loans of reportedly over a billion dollars. Oil revenues were back online but salaries of civil servants were still unpaid. 'Such is the stuff with which civil unrests, protests, and even outright revolutions are made of,' Jok added. 'The political leadership of South Sudan should not play with fire.'[17]

Princeton Lyman, a former US Special Envoy to the Sudans, was clear that the peace was fast unravelling. He was frustrated Kiir had ignored calls for internal party talks in favour of strong-arm tactics to show his power, provoking a crisis through mass dismissals.[18] 'If Machar took his cause to the bush and revived his militia, the country's unity would be shaken,' Lyman warned.

The next day, Machar threw down the gauntlet to Kiir.

* * *

Riek Machar looked almost cheerful, as though it was all one big joke. 'General Salva Kiir is driving our beloved Republic of South Sudan into chaos,' Machar said on 6 December, speaking at a press conference in Juba alongside other disgruntled politicians, including Rebecca Nyandeng, Garang's widow. 'It is likely to plunge the party and the country into the abyss.'

He accused Kiir of 'dictatorial' tendencies and of recruiting 'a personal army'. Perhaps Machar hoped for the hand of reconciliation and a return to power, but he knew that it was a dangerous gamble. 'Is it crisis of visions, or crisis of personalities?' Machar said of Kiir. 'It is both.'

The Presidential Guard were known as the Tiger Battalion, after Kiir's old rebel codename. The Tigers flanked Kiir when he drove at high speed through town, draped in ammunition belts, hanging off pickups. Cars swerved into ditches to avoid the convoy. They had a fearsome reputation, easily identifiable from their striped camouflaged fatigues, topped by red berets with snarling tiger cap badges. They were well equipped, often carrying Israeli Galil assault rifles, not the battered decades-old AK-47s of the regular soldier. 'The Tiger has taken out his claws and is ready to crush their faces,' Kiir reportedly told a rally in his Dinka homeland of Bahr el Ghazal after sacking Machar. 'Blood will flow.'[19]

After years spent integrating ex-rebel forces into the military to build peace, the largest portion of the army were Nuer.[20] Kiir wanted men he could trust to protect him, so he had also given orders for an extra force to be enlisted. Batches of young men were recruited from his homeland and given weapons training, becoming a secretive Dinka militia force Kiir could command directly outside the hierarchy of the army. It was one that he could raise, arm, train, equip and order directly, without scrutiny. Estimates of its size range from a few thousand to as many as 15,000 fighters.

People called them the 'Mathiang Anyoor', a type of poisonous hairy worm with a fearsome sting, or the 'Brown Caterpillars'. I had seen the militia marching in snaking lines with their massed army boots stomping like the black feet of an insect. In Dinka they called themselves *Dot Ke Beny*, or 'Rescue the President'.[21]

Machar's challenge was exactly what they had trained for.

* * *

It took a week to explode. Machar made his press conference on a Friday. Kiir meanwhile headed to South Africa to attend the memorial service for Nelson Mandela. While he was gone he gave two orders. The first: that flags nationwide be put at half-mast for three days of official mourning for Mandela, a president who more than any other preached forgiveness. The second: for his men to be deployed on the streets.

Officially, it was presented as a clean-up exercise, Kiir's men sweeping the swirling dust on the rubbish-strewn roads of Juba. The idea that an elite presidential force of proud Dinka warriors might be diverted to help out as street cleaners in the midst of a crisis would be laughable, if the other option were not so disturbing. Ugandan Professor Mahmood Mamdani, seconded from Columbia University to be an investigator for the African Union Commission of Inquiry into the crisis, said the lowly litter picking was a ruse to conceal a far darker purpose. 'The cleaning,' Mamdani wrote, was 'a pretext for Kiir's loyalists to identify and demarcate areas in Juba that would be targeted when the massacres began.'[22]

* * *

On Saturday, 14 December, the SPLM's top leadership committee met. Kiir's opening speech recounted the sacrifices of the long struggle for independence. He spoke of those who 'joined the enemy' and the violence of 1991 when Machar challenged Garang and the South turned upon itself. Like a headmaster before an assembly, he stared around the meeting hall addressing those who defied his rule.

'In the light of recent developments, in which some of our comrades have come out to challenge my executive decisions, I must warn that this behaviour is tantamount to indiscipline, which will take us back to the days of the 1991 split,' Kiir said. 'We all know where that split took us from that time. This could jeopardise the unity and the independence of our country. My dear comrades, I am not prepared to allow this to happen again.'

The threat was clear. Machar, sitting deep in wide armchair, did not applaud with the rest. He stared back grimly. 'Allow me to say this,' Kiir said, concluding his speech. 'Since I decided to take up arms in the 1960s, I have never betrayed the cause of my people.' As he concluded, blaring trumpets from the presidential band played a military march. As the music wound down, a woman wrapped in the South Sudan flag stood and sang from the audience, her eyes closed and arms waving. She sang an old Dinka war ballad, singing of how it is better to take up arms to fight than to be humiliated.

Kiir initially waved for her to stop. Then as the crowd clapped along, he grinned and joined in.

* * *

The next day, Sunday 15 December, Machar and other keys members boycotted the meeting. At dusk, as the sun hung low in the sky and the Sunday church bells rang for evensong, someone fired a stream of bullets into the air close to the SPLM meeting. People were on edge, and fear grew. Three hours after dark, more gunfire was heard. This time, it continued, echoing out of Juba's Giada Barracks, Khartoum's old torture centre known as the White House, and now home to the Tiger Battalion.

Each side blamed the other. The government claimed it was a coup bid by Nuer soldiers loyal to Machar, and that battles started when Nuer soldiers tried to break into the armoury to grab guns. Machar said the opposite, that Dinka officers moved to massacre Nuer troops, and the shooting was a signal for battles to begin elsewhere.

Whoever fired the shot, it was the spark that started a war.[23]

Fighting raged for hours. Nuer troops in the barracks were defeated, but the shooting spread. UN chief Hilde Johnson spoke to ex-deputy defence minister Majak D'Agoot. 'You have no idea what can happen in this country,' D'Agoot told her that night. 'This can set off ethnic violence between the Dinka and the Nuer which can drive us all down. This can become another Rwanda.'[24]

* * *

In the morning, the butchery began. Doors of homes were smashed open, and those inside dragged out into the streets. Nuer men were rounded up. Their hands were tied, and rags wrapped around their heads as blindfolds. If they had the Nuer facial scarring, the horizontal lines across the forehead, they would be taken. If they were unscarred, soldiers screamed at them. 'What is your name?' they shouted in Dinka. 'Where are you from?' The incorrect answer or the wrong language, and they'd be killed. Some were shot in the streets, and their bleeding corpses left in the dust. Others were dragged away. Piles of bodies were taken by truck to mass burial sites, and plumes of smoke rose high from near the army barracks. 'Nuer were being killed like chickens,' one survivor said.[25]

The Mathiang Anyoor were supported by Dinka members of the Tiger Battalion, as well as soldiers and police. In one report, Tiger soldiers rampaged through a district near the river. Around 240 men, all Nuer, were bound and blindfolded. Then they were shot. Their corpses were thrown into the Nile.[26]

In Juba's Gudele district, at least 300 Nuer men, but possibly as many as 450, were rounded up and taken to a low building used by police and army. 'They came house to house to collect and kill,' described one man. He was dragged from his home along with his three brothers, and stuffed with hundreds of others into police cells. They were forced in so tightly, many simply suffocated to death. 'We were so many we could not sit,' he said. 'We had to stand the whole day until the night.' Some tried to explain the killing on the streets as an effect of the heat of battle, but the premeditated rounding up of hundreds was something very different. For with the men in cells, soldiers then went to their officers for instructions of what to do next. The orders were for massacre.[27]

'They started shooting through the windows that were bringing some oxygen,' said a survivor. 'Then they opened the door and started shooting. It was continuous shooting until all fall down. They opened the door, lit a torch; if they saw you breathing they would shoot. If someone starts crying, they would come back and shoot.' To save bullets, soldiers stabbed survivors. When the soldiers thought that all were dead, they left. A handful were somehow still alive, wounded and playing dead under the stinking corpses of their friends. They crawled out through the mass of congealing blood and buzzing flies, and managed to escape.[28]

In the chaos, the exact toll is impossible to know. South Sudan's Red Cross struggled to collect the corpses, but were stopped when they tried to log the details to help identify all those killed. Records were not wanted. Army trucks took over, and the bodies disappeared. Even South Sudan's Human Rights Commission, working under the tight-leash of government scrutiny, said more than 600 people were killed in Juba in the first three days.[29] Other more independent sources suggested figures several times larger.

The army called it lies. 'It is the work of criminals,' army spokesman Philip Aguer said. 'Trust me, Peter. The situation is under control.' He repeated it several times. Listening to him, I wanted to be sick.

Just like Machar & Bor & Massacre to the

* * *

The usual explanation for the war's beginning was a political fight between Kiir and Machar. It erupted into violence, which spiralled into revenge. In that story, the grisly killings were not planned. Blaming the killings on the madness of war was easier to comprehend than the alternative.

Yet this was not a matter of a battle in the barracks that could not be contained. That fight was over long before the break of dawn on the first day. What happened next was different. The killings that took place the next morning were a new wave of violence. 'Witness after witness recounted horror as they watched security forces enter their communities, sometimes in tanks and with heavy weaponry, and round up their relatives and neighbours,' UN human rights investigators wrote. 'In some cases, victims were killed immediately; in others, they were taken to other locations and killed. This pattern spread widely throughout Juba, with similar tactics seen in various neighbourhoods, suggesting organisation and planning.'[30]

This is hard to read.

Minister of Defence Kuol Mayang blamed the 'shadowy' forces of the Kiir's terrifying Brown Caterpillars for leading the massacres. 'It killed most people,' he told the AU. 'It was even more powerful than organised forces. This is a very militarised country.'[31]

222

The African Union Commission of Inquiry, led by Nigerian ex-president Olusegun Obasanjo, found no evidence of government claims of a coup attempt by Machar. 'It was an organised military operation that could not have been successful without concerted efforts from various actors in the military and government circles,' the AU report read, describing the widespread and systematic nature of the attacks. 'The evidence thus suggests that these crimes were committed pursuant to, or in furtherance of, a state policy,' it added.[32]

Yet if Kiir aimed to crush Machar and cower political rivals to cement his grip on power, that did not require the mass roundups and gratuitous killings seen on such a monumental scale. What chilling logic could have made such evil a rational choice? I could only think of one answer. If it was deliberate, done to divide the people and force moderates to pick a side based on ethnicity, to secure support by destroying the middle ground and polarising society, then it worked only too well.[33]

* * *

The UN chief in Juba was Hilde Frafjord Johnson, a Norwegian ex-government minister who led Oslo's efforts in signing the 2005 peace deal. The descent from political arguments to the unravelling of a country so quickly took her also by surprise. She thought leaders on all sides were her long-time friends, and so trusted what they would tell her. They lied.

'We did not see this coming,' Johnson said. 'The speed, the gravity and the scale, I think nobody would have expected that.'[34] Even if there had been the will to drive the white-painted UN tanks into the slaughter, the forces available were incapable of stopping the battle. Some 5,000 UN infantry troops were deployed in remote lands to stop cattle raiding violence, but the only forces in Juba were already busy guarding UN bases. It was one of the world's biggest ever peacekeeping missions, and the entire number of soldiers spare totalled no more than 150 men. War in the capital was not a scenario planned for. 'Our capacity to protect in Juba was close to zero,' Johnson said.[35] Soldiers may be willing to die for their country, but few feel such sacrifice when on deployment for the blue flag of the UN. As the fighting raged, they hunkered down inside their bases.

The war, however, would come to them. Desperate crowds of thousands fled to the only protection they could think of, scrabbling at the wire fences of UN bases to try to break in. A UN police officer from Bosnia, Nedzad Handzic, whose family had been killed in the 1995 Srebrenica massacre, watched the crowds grow and grow. He pleaded with superiors to open the gates. 'I remember thinking, "What happened in Srebrenica must not be repeated here,"' he said.[36] An hour after dawn on Monday, the order was given and the people poured in. The UN did not stop the war, but by taking in the people it did save tens of thousands of lives. 'It was on a scale never seen before in the UN's history,' Johnson said.

[handwritten margin note: What an Orwellian title!]

Minister of Information Michael Makuei dismissed the exodus on state television, claiming it was normal. People were simply leaving Juba to go home to their villages for Christmas, he said.[37]

* * *

When it was not being used as a parking lot for diggers and water tankers, I used to play football on the dusty square. Now it had become home to tens of thousands. The UN base next to Juba airport was crammed full of people in every conceivable space. They sat, despondent and exhausted. If they were lucky, they found thin shade under the trees. Others rigged up a piece of cardboard from the sun, or ragged plastic sheeting as the new roof of their home. There was a stench of dust and urine. Children waded waist deep in a foul-smelling stream, below what looked like a sewage outflow. The sound was a constant chatter of people, but the babies with their mothers were quiet, too exhausted to cry for long. Somewhere, a woman was wailing, keening with a piercing cry that didn't stop.

I was used to the misery of poverty of the South, the wretched normality of interviewing the victims of cattle raids forced from their homes. I was not used to the brutality of bloodshed being meted out on the doorsteps of a town I knew so well, and of seeing old friends amongst them.

'I have lost my wife and children, two girls,' said James Puok, a driver for an aid agency, sitting with his head in his hands. 'When I went to my house, it was smashed into. Everyone had gone. There was blood on the street.' I remembered past times when we had driven out visiting water pumps being installed in school grounds, when he had spoken so proudly of what his new nation could be. Back then, he told me how he wanted his two daughters to go to university. 'I ran here at night to the UN, because I had nowhere else to go,' he said. 'There were bodies lying in the streets I had to run over.' He had heard no news of his family.

It seemed everyone could tell tales of atrocities. 'They dragged us out the houses, shouting at us, and threw us on the ground,' one Nuer man told me, a student who gave his name only as Gatluak, too fearful to be otherwise identified. 'They were young Dinka men, with guns and uniform, and they took my neighbours away.' Gatluak looked up, pointing to his forehead, clear of the fatal identifying horizontal Nuer scars. 'For me, they asked who I was. They kicked me, and smacked me. They pushed a gun in my face shouting in Dinka, but I can speak Anyuak language, so they let me go.' I asked him what had happened to his friends. 'I just ran,' he said. 'There were gunshots behind me.'

A tall man pushed through the crowds towards me, an aide of Riek Machar I knew from happier days. He had thrown away his army fatigues, and was dressed in a shirt and suit trousers. He was furious, spitting with rage. 'They have forced us into this prison,' he said. 'If we go outside, they will kill us. We have nothing here. We can't stay here.' He twisted to walk away in anger, speaking as he turned. 'They will pay,' he said. 'What they have done to us, we will do to them double.'

* * *

Amid the killings, Kiir dressed up. Gone was his dark suit and cowboy hat. Instead, he wore the streaked camouflage uniform of his Tiger Battalion, the men carrying out murder on the streets. His epaulettes were so heavy with gold braid they sagged low off his shoulders.

On Monday afternoon, hours after the shooting commenced, Kiir made a broadcast to the nation. He called Machar the 'prophet of doom' and recalled the violence of the Bor massacre two decades before. 'My government is not, and will not, allow the incidents of 1991 to repeat themselves again,' Kiir said, reading in ponderous tones from his speech. He peered out from his reading glasses beneath his combat cap. 'Long live the unity of our people,' he finished. 'God Bless South Sudan, and you all.'

225

Across the other side of the street from the fortified presidential palace where Kiir was speaking, dozens had sheltered in the large, walled compound of Machar's house, hoping they would be safe. Instead, they were in the firing line. Soldiers hunting Machar could find no sign of him. There were rumours he had sought shelter in an embassy, but, in fact, he escaped hours after fighting began, slipping out of Juba in the darkness and heading north. His wife Angelina said she fled in her slippers and nightdress.[38] A day after Kiir's speech, the assault on Machar's house started. Tanks smashed into the gates.

Soldiers arrested eleven key politicians including ex-ministers and prominent Dinka leaders accused of being part of a plot against Kiir. Many of them were dragged from their beds at night, not captured on the frontlines of war. Even Garang's widow was targeted. 'There was no coup,' Rebecca Nyandeng told the BBC from house arrest. She said Nuer were being killed on the streets, and accused Kiir of using a mutiny in the barracks of his own men as a justification to crack down on rivals. 'He wanted to create it, so that he can catch up with those people he wanted to arrest,' she said.[39]

* * *

The swathe of killings in Juba lasted for three days until 18 December. At that point, the city calmed enough for the UN to emerge in armoured cars on limited patrols. Sweating and swearing diplomats in helmets and flak jackets focused efforts on getting long queues of aid workers out, as foreign military cargo airplanes flew in to evacuate their citizens.

As Juba calmed, the war erupted elsewhere. The speed with which the violence broke out shocked. It soon burst out of any control the government in Juba may have had, and took on a life of its own. It divided the security forces, turning 200,000 soldiers as well as some 100,000 armed police, prison and wildlife officers and other security forces against each other.

Machar, finally picking up his satellite phone, said he was a 'scapegoat' for the violence. His rage was palpable. 'Kiir is killing people like flies,' he said, claiming he was marching on Juba. 'We did not ask for this battle. It was forced upon us.'

In Jonglei, thousands of men had mobilised to form the Nuer militia known as the White Army. They went on the war path for revenge.

Hundreds were killed in Bor, a mainly Dinka town. Others were taken to the river and executed, their bodies washing away into crocodile swamps. One witness said she saw pregnant women have their stomachs cut open. Gunmen even broke into the town's mortuary, and, failing to find anyone alive to kill, fired bullets into corpses.[40] Just as Nuer were hunted house-to-house in Juba, the White Army sought out Dinka to kill.

So many raw babies (handwritten margin note)

* * *

The US Special Operations forces came in three Ospreys, sci-fi like aircraft with hybrid rotors that fly like a plane but land like a helicopter. As they came into land at Bor, on the dirt airstrip beside the UN base, the rotors twisted, throwing up clouds of dust. They had been sent from the US base in Djibouti to swoop in and pull citizens out. One year on since the Libya attack on US diplomats in Benghazi, Washington did not want another disaster. The US had spent billions on the South, but they had no apparent leverage—it took them three days to get Kiir on the phone after fighting broke out.[41]

Bor was under the control of the White Army, but the US came confident with assurances that rebel chiefs had agreed to a rescue mission. Yet these were not gunmen who followed a military chain of command. Once unleashed, the violence was not easily reined in. Machar had influence over the rebels but was not in control, though he claimed responsibility for leading the forces. He craved power, and to keep it, he had to say he led the rebellion. In fact, he merely rode the crest of the waves of revenge, an upsurge of hatred that generated an opposition force in a startlingly short time. Those who came to fight did so to protect their families, not for the squabbling politics of Juba power.[42]

The sheer ferocity of the gunmen shocked the US forces. Perhaps the White Army thought they were Ugandan aircraft coming to attack them, but they never waited to check. 'It just erupted,' said David Shea, a technical sergeant manning a heavy machine gun out the back of the aircraft, who was thrown back by a bullet that smashed into the chest plate of his armoured jacket. 'They lit us up pretty good.'[43] There was a barrage of AK-47 fire, then heavier machine guns and rocket-propelled grenades. Bullets ripped into four people, hitting the team leader in an artery. Shea looked around and saw the aircraft awash in their blood. 'Everybody was laying on the ground,' Shea said. 'In my head, they were all dead.'

Dragging himself up from the floor, Shea grabbed the machine gun, but was unable to fire back, as the gunmen were mingled with the civilians below. 'These guys had embedded themselves inside of the crowd around the compound and they were everywhere—I mean just all over the place,' Shea added. 'It was a full-up ambush.' Muzzle flashes leapt up like fireworks, as medics tried to stem the blood spurting out.

The three Ospreys had been hit by nearly 200 rounds, with fist-sized holes punched into the fuselage, and jet fuel gushed out at speed. Smoke poured from the rotors with multiple systems failing.

The air crews won medals for the most meritorious flight of the year, managing to bring the three aircraft safely to land in Uganda and save the lives of the wounded. One Osprey needed to be refuelled twice in mid-air before it smacked down with its landing gear broken.

They had been a hair's breadth short of another Black Hawk Down disaster, the 1993 downing of two US helicopters in Somalia and the subsequent 'Battle of Mogadishu'. I wondered what Washington would have done if the men had not made it back from the 'Battle of Bor'.

* * *

The killings in the first three days of bloodshed in Juba might have been planned, but the reaction was not. The payback was vicious, and the new rebel forces carried out atrocities as murderous as those meted out to their families. A day after rebellion in Bor, troops in the oil town of Bentiu followed. There, Nuer soldiers turned on Dinka comrades in artillery and tank units, taking their weapons for the new rebel army. Large parts of the town were torched. Malakal soon followed suit. Once again, there were massacres in churches, patients raped then killed in their hospital beds, civilians shot dead, gang rape and torture. The towns were abandoned to the dogs.

There were real fears the rebels could march on Juba. With the army split, Kiir panicked and called in outside help, opening up the government coffers to buy support. From the south came the Ugandan army.[44] The clouds of dust rose high in the air from long convoys of Ugandan troop trucks and tanks coming to Juba. From the north, the

Mad Max mercenary fleets of Darfuri rebels from Sudan arrived with machine guns welded onto the backs of pickups. It was a humiliating show of how weak the government was. Opposition supporters mockingly dubbed Kiir the 'Mayor of Juba'.

The violence was far worse than even the most hard-line generals could have imagined. On Christmas Eve, Kiir made an appeal in a broadcast to the nation. Within a matter of days, the war had gone too fast and too far out of Kiir's hands.

'Fellow citizens of our beloved nation, if we allow the zeal and spirit of tribalism to reign over our country, we will not be able to foresee what will happen to us,' Kiir said. 'It will only lead to one thing, and that is to turn this new nation into chaos.'

13

THE OTHER CITY

'*The dead are invisible, not absent.*'
Saint Augustine of Hippo

One city had been destroyed, but a new one had been born. From the watchtower, looking down into the land inside the long earth embankment, the tent camp at Bentiu stretched far into the distance. The sun was going down over the UN site, crowded with row upon row of plastic sheeting. It was 2015, over a year into the war. The crowds, who at the beginning of the war had hammered at the UN gates, pleading for a temporary camp there until calm returned, had grown.

Peace had not come, and rather than leaving, more people came. The UN called them 'Protection of Civilians' camps, and soon they housed a staggering quarter of a million people in six sites across the South. Bentiu camp was by far the largest, made up almost entirely of Nuer civilians.

Bentiu town looked like a hurricane had ripped through it. It was a wasteland of torched homes, wrecked buildings with twisted tin roofs and burned pickup trucks. It had swapped hands several times. When rebels took it, they massacred hundreds who had taken shelter in the main mosque and hospital, and used the local radio station Bentiu FM to exhort Nuer men to rape Dinka women. There were chilling echoes of the radio broadcasters who goaded on Rwanda's genocide in 1994.

Now the government had taken it back. A herd of cattle wandered down an otherwise empty street, munching weeds that had sprung up outside once neatly kept houses. Several families sheltered inside the ruined shell of a bank, where the thick metal of the strong room door had been ripped out. Bentiu had become a ghost town, where about the only thing moving was a rumbling tank.

A short walk from the ruins was the UN base. Inside its walls, the temporary tent camp had become a crowded, stinking home of some 125,000 terrified people. It was not a refugee camp, where people had fled for safety in a neighbouring nation. They were behind barbed wire in their own land, sheltering inside an anarchic prison from hell, because what was outside was worse. Since the main towns had now been destroyed, the Bentiu camp was so big that it counted as South Sudan's second biggest city. It was beaten in size only by the capital Juba.

* * *

Inside, it was utterly miserable. The UN troops guarding the gates watched for attacks from outside, but patrolled inside using armoured carriers, for they found it hard to stop the young men cooped up inside from joining violent gangs fighting turf wars. Each month there were reports of men hanging themselves.

The camp had not been planned; the area in which people were forced to take shelter alongside the main UN base had previously been uninhabited because it turned into swamps when the rain came. In the early days, a mix of fetid sewage and bog water could rise as high as the waist. Children drowned in the slime. Later, heavy diggers made roads and carved out drainage ditches, but life inside was still a matter of surviving in squalor. In the rains, the road to the camp from Juba became impassable, and the UN had to fly an air bridge of the most basic of supplies to keep the people alive. It took several flights a month just to provide enough soap for everyone.[1]

'If we go out we will be killed,' said Nyakouth Biel, a quietly spoken woman who eked out her meagre rations by running a tea stall. 'I didn't want to come here; we stayed in our homes, and when the soldiers attacked our homes we said, "If death is to take us, let us be together." But they didn't let us, because my husband they shot, and my children they smashed into the ground. They abused the women. They put a gun in my mouth, and hit me with a gun. When I woke, they had left thinking I was killed. Everyone else was dead or gone.'

She had been in the camp for a year, and had no news of her four children who vanished that day. The camps were becoming permanent enclaves, as people built mud walls to replace the plastic tent sheeting, and settled down to making home where they now lived. In the early days, Biel used to find a vantage point to look out over the scrubland outside towards her home, three days walk on the far horizon. 'I would go to look towards the village,' she said. 'Now I stay here in the tea shop. What have I got to go back to? We do not feel safe in here, but it is better than being outside. My family was taken. Our home was burned. Our cattle were stolen.'

* * *

The fratricidal bloodshed destroyed the very fabric of society itself. People fought to protect themselves and their families, not a greater vision of South Sudan. The collapse was quick, because institutions were absent. The normal ties of authority and civilian security to rein in madness—government, police, civil service and the judiciary— were paper thin. If the millions spent by international donors on capacity-building conferences had had any impact, it had vanished like smoke. In times of crisis, the only thing people felt confident in relying on was a gun. War crimes and crimes against humanity were committed by all sides.[2] The little infrastructure that wasn't already broken was soon battered into dust.

The leaders had not learned. Sudan split into two because those excluded from power were driven to take up arms to seize it by force. In that war, the generals now in Juba had been the victors. Now, when they were faced by the disenfranchised pushed out from power, they sought to crush them. The pattern was repeated, until the excluded were left only with violence as a means of taking control. They were seen as irrelevant to the creation of a country. In the end, it was their violence that would define the formation of the nation.[3]

* * *

The violence was gratuitous, degrading and brutal. 'Some of the people who had been gathered were compelled to eat human flesh, while others were forced to drink human blood belonging to a victim who had been slaughtered and his blood collected on a plate,' an African Union report into the war read. I thought I had heard all the unthinkable things there could be. 'I have seen people being forced to eat other humans,' said one witness. 'Soldiers kill one of you and ask the other to eat the dead one.' The reports seemed too extreme to be believed, egregious outliers of the abyss, but stories of cannibalism from different places and multiple sources persisted as the war spread. 'They found me, tied my arms behind my back and forced me at gunpoint to drink blood and eat flesh,' one survivor of a massacre told Amnesty International. 'I was told that if I didn't do this I would be killed.' One woman who fled to Ethiopia said her baby was ripped from her arms and thrown into the fire. Then she was made to eat the flesh.[4]

Reports from human rights investigators and aid agencies piled up. Each time, there was something worse. Forensic experts found the rotting corpses of children, one apparently suffocated with a plastic bag around the head.[5] Children and the elderly were hanged on trees, others rammed into thatch huts, then doused with fuel and set alight. One boy reported how his mother had her eyes gouged out with a spear when she tried to protect her 17-year-old daughter. As she bled, seventeen men raped her, while fourteen more raped her daughter. The father of the family was beheaded, his castrated penis stuffed into his mouth.[6]

Soldiers tore tiny babies from their mother's arms, checking to see if the child was a boy. 'When he grows up he will fight with us, so I have to kill him,' one soldier said, before shooting the boy in front of his mother.[7] Other boys were lined up as though in a school line, then castrated with machetes and left to bleed out. Government troops crushed fleeing civilians with tanks, then reversed to check whether they had killed them.[8]

The government won and lost towns again and again. Packs of dogs owned the streets. They grew wild feeding on the corpses of the dead, and UN peacekeepers had to shoot them. Many of the towns were simply abandoned. People moved deep into the bush for safety. Witnesses said some died of thirst while hiding, preferring that torturous death to risking the killing that faced them at home.[9]

* * *

Diplomats were desperate for anything that might halt the insanity. A ceasefire was agreed in January 2014 with celebrations and handshakes. It was never observed. In May, Kiir and Machar prayed together in Addis Ababa and praised a deal ending war. It was briskly broken. So were the next half a dozen deals and promises for peace. In rounds of talks in the five-star hotels of Addis Ababa, the South earned a reputation for being slow talkers and hard drinkers. The South's old friends, the US, Britain and Norway, as well as the EU, picked up the tab—well over $20 million in the first year alone.[10] The war ground on. Leaders on both sides told the world what it wanted to hear.

Back in South Sudan, the killing continued. Machar's forces sought shadowy arms dealers for their supplies. Documents seized by Spanish police when French-Polish arms dealer Pierre Dadak was arrested at a luxury villa in Ibiza suggested he had been approached by rebels to supply weaponry including 40,000 AK-47 rifles, 30,000 PKM machine-guns and 200,000 ammunition boxes.[11]

The government had far more cash to splash; murky networks brought in an arsenal from China, Egypt, Israel, Uganda and Ukraine. As well as Ugandan army help and rent-a-rebel support of fighters from Sudan's Darfur, the government brought in former US Navy SEAL Erik Prince, founder of the private security company Blackwater.[12] At least three Mi-24 attack helicopters—totalling some $43 million—as well as two L39 fighter jets were purchased. One was flown by a Hungarian pilot, Tibor Czingáli, who used the jets to hunt down rebel units. Czingáli posted pictures on his Facebook page of him grinning and pointing to where rebel bullets had hit the jet.

Chinese arms manufacturer Norinco delivered a shipment in July 2014, including anti-tank guided missiles and grenade launchers, as well as over 95,000 automatic rifles and 20 million rounds of ammunition. That one shopping list alone contained enough bullets to kill every single person in the country twice over, but in case they needed more, powerful Dinka general Paul Malong, Kiir's army chief, investigated the possibility of creating a munitions factory.

The National Security Service armed itself with enough weapons to be an independent army. A deal brokered with a Seychelles-based company in June 2014 saw a contract signed worth $264 million, that included 30 tanks, 50,000 AK-47 rifles and 20 million bullets, as well as anti-aircraft guns, truck-mounted rocket launchers and helicopter missiles. Amphibious tanks were bought to chase enemies deep into swamps that had once been refuges, and river barges were turned into gunboats equipped with anti-aircraft machine guns, able to rake villages whilst spewing chains of fist-sized bullets.[13]

Still, many of the assaults involved little more than massed waves of infantry charging across grassy plains, spraying bullets from guns at their hip. Casualties were heavy, and doctors able to treat the wounded few.

* * *

Rape, the UN said, reached 'epic proportions'. The statistics are staggering; 70 percent of women who had fled inside the UN bases in Juba reported that they had been raped since the war began, according to a UN survey. It also found that three-quarters of those questioned in the camps had been forced to watch someone else be raped.[14]

There were public gang rapes, rape of the very old, and rape of the very young. In one case, ten women were shot in the vagina because they refused sex. Children were forced to watch their mothers gang-raped, then given a gun to kill them. Men and boys were also raped or sexually assaulted, or forced to rape relatives themselves. In one case, a man was forced to lie down to serve as a 'mattress' while a woman was raped on top of him.[15] 'If you look them in the face when they are doing it, they will kill you,' one survivor told UN rights monitors. One mother was raped, then had the arm ripped off her three-month old baby forced into her vagina.[16]

'The war has brought me nightmares,' said one mother, who was made to hold the bleeding testicles chopped off her husband in one hand as she held her new-born baby in the other. In front of her, soldiers gang-raped her 70-year-old mother, then forced her son to do the same. 'It didn't just scare me to death,' she added. 'It forced me to watch my own 12-year-old son have sex with my own mother—otherwise we would all die.'[17]

The UN Special Envoy for sexual violence in conflict, Zainab Bangura, travels the world investigating the most heinous of crimes. Bangura said it was the worst conditions she had ever experienced.[18]

Rape was a tool used for ethnic cleansing, as means of humiliation and of revenge. It was about ensuring that each side could tell the enemy of

236

the horrors they had meted out on their mothers and daughters. There was no possible military rationale; this was about making an entire people the enemy, and of coldly denying them a future. The pain was fuel for the fire of yet more cruelty. 'Perhaps the worst thing is that many now treat sexual violence as a "normal" facet of life for women,' said Yasmin Sooka, who headed the UN Commission on Human Rights for South Sudan.[19] 'We are running out of adjectives to describe the horror.'

As I waited for a helicopter out of Bentiu, a British security officer going on leave told me how I should explain the horror in the stories I was sending. 'Killing for these people is a game,' he said dismissively, snapping his fingers repetitively. 'Life is so cheap here, it means nothing.'

The flippancy of his words filled me with anger. I thought of the mothers sacrificing all to save their babies. No, life was not cheap here, I wanted to shout at him. Survival here was the hardest fought thing in the world.

* * *

In 2016, I returned to Bor, the town I had watched burn at the beginning of the war. Now, largely owing to Ugandan help in the fighting, it was back under government control. The bullet scars in buildings and tin roofs twisted from fire were still there, but the market was operating and there was life on the streets too.

The bodies once rotting on the streets had been bulldozed into giant pits. The concrete covering the mass grave beside the Nile at Saint Andrew's Church contained the bodies of twenty-two women who had been raped and shot after seeking shelter here, as well as those of the priests who tried in vain to protect them. It had already cracked in the heat and there were weeds growing out. Still, at sunset, looking out over the marshland, quiet apart from the white egrets calling as they circled for a place to settle for the night, it felt for a moment as if that violence was in the past.

Except, just a short walk away, civilians sheltering in the UN camp still had to be heavily guarded. Even the peacekeepers manning machine guns on the watchtowers were not enough to deter assault. 'If you are Nuer, come out or else we will come and kill you,' attackers shouted at the 5,000 people trapped inside in April 2014.[20] Watched by the police and army, gunmen broke through the wires, opening fire at the families crowded inside. Under the terrible rationale of collective guilt, they wanted revenge for those who had been killed: your people did this to us, so we will do it you. At least fifty-one people were slaughtered, including an eight-month-old baby, before UN soldiers fought them off.

As for those still left inside, they lived in terror. The UN had since shifted the camp, rebuilding it with thick earth walls and posting tanks along its edge. It protected those inside, but the lines of plastic tents felt more like a prison than ever. Despite it all, I watched as a dozen children used old plastic jerry cans to toboggan down a mud slide they had made on the inside slope of the fortress-like embankment perimeter. Their laughter drifted over the camp.

'My son was born while I have been trapped here,' said Diu Majok, a former local government civil servant from Fangak, dressed in a threadbare black suit. He had been inside the camp for almost two years when I met him, fearing he would be accused as a rebel fighter and killed if he stepped outside.

'I want to go back to my family, but how can I get there? I will die on the way,' he said. 'This is like a jail sentence but with no date for release.' He saw no hope of it ending. His wife, at home in Fangak, was pregnant when he entered the camp, and the son he had never seen was now a toddler aged 18 months. As I lent Majok my satellite phone to send a message home, I asked him the name of his son. 'I have called him Billiu,' he said. 'It means, "people will die".'

* * *

Nearly two years into the war, retired Canadian general Roméo Dallaire came to South Sudan. Tens of thousands of children had been killed, and nearly 20,000 had been recruited as soldiers since the war had begun. Dallaire, the former UN commander during the Rwandan genocide, runs a foundation to end the use of child soldiers. He flew to Jonglei, where he saw 300 battle-hardened veterans released, children little taller than the height of their guns. What he saw worried him deeply, he told the Canadian ambassador Nicholas Coghlan. 'There is a smell here in South Sudan… I just can't get away from it,' Dallaire said. 'It reminds me of Rwanda, before hell broke loose.'[21]

* * *

We carry with us the ghosts of our past, for how we remember makes sense of who we are now. The youngest nation was trying to forge a future, but is a land trapped in ancient trauma. Violence begets violence, and seeds of hate are sown early in the next generation. Memories of inherited suffering are passed down to new generations, then compounded by the pain of new war. The children fled or were taken to fight, so that over two-thirds of the country's children are out of school, the highest proportion in the world.[22] For the young—and census figures suggest over half the people are under 18—the past is retold alongside new stories of pain. Soon the tales of the war against Khartoum will fade, and the unifying story of how the South fought for its freedom will be lost among the day-to-day violence of neighbour against neighbour.

There had been dreams of making a museum and memorial to create a common story of South Sudan that would celebrate diversity, while helping unify nationality into one identity. Designs had been drawn up for a sleek building to be built close to where the first flag was raised at independence in Juba. It was to be a place to mourn, and celebrate the future. The new war meant it was shelved. Instead, the army set up canvas tent barracks where the peace museum was meant to be.

The only memorial the South had was an abandoned graveyard at the base of the rocky hill that overlooks Juba, under the lonely watch of Brigadier-General Daniel Abudhok Apiokuach, the director of the army's historical archives. It took half an hour of banging the metal gate until Apiokuach, a scarred fighter with a grizzled beard, opened it to let me in.

'Without a history, a nation is lost,' said Apiokuach, as he walked me around the walled compound, shuffling through ankle-deep dust around a memorial to the soldiers who died in the helicopter crash with John Garang. He swept his hand through a layer of dry leaves, pushing them from the slab of a grave. Long, yellowing grass grew tall through the concrete, and he pressed past chest-high bushes already grown wild around the base of a statue. We squinted at the figure above, a soldier calling to comrades, his arm raised in a triumphant North Korean pose. Apiokuach asked me to wait before taking photographs so that he could change out of a worn shirt into his general's uniform, then stood to attention proudly. 'If you forget your history, then how do you know where you have come from?' he said. 'Knowing the past is part of understanding who we are.'

The past defined a society. In South Sudan, an entire people was suffering—flashbacks, anxiety, rage and depression. Assessments found that over half of the people suffered post-traumatic stress disorder, the sort of levels found in post-genocide Rwanda or Cambodia, up to five times higher than among US or British combat soldiers returning from Iraq or Afghanistan. In crises, such trauma makes one far more likely to turn to violence to end conflict.[23] There had been no justice, and no healing. The trauma was held inside, moulded only by bitter memories, waiting to explode in anger again. Peace does not come by forgetting the past, but by addressing the problems it caused. South Sudan needs reconciliation to survive.

Apiokuach had gathered a small collection of spears and broken guns from past wars to start an army museum. 'People will see what their ancestors used to fight for their freedom,' he said. 'I just need to get money to build it.' He showed me the other artefacts he had, including ragged photographs of now elderly generals when they were young liberation heroes. 'South Sudanese are killing themselves like nobody's business,' he said mournfully. 'Most have not become good liberators, but rather warlords. They have become thieves. I can say I am the only one who fears God, and that is why I remain poor.' Above his desk he had stuck up a poster with biblical quotes. 'God Will Punish Sudan,' it read.

Apiokuach and I walked back into town together in the sweaty heat, looking for a motorbike taxi for a lift. His car, one perk of being a general, had been stolen. With hyperinflation, his salary was now worth next to nothing, and his shoe heels were worn right down from his long walks. He asked me to give him money for a ride back into town. 'Visitors?' he queried, when I asked who comes to see the memorial. 'No, not often. People are too busy fighting themselves these days.'

* * *

Yet read the news inside South Sudan, and the horror hardly featured. 'The freedom of the press does not mean you work against your country,' Kiir warned journalists, as newspapers were shut down and journalists arrested. 'If anybody among them does not know that this country has killed people, we will demonstrate it one day.' Four days later, when walking home from work, journalist Peter Moi was shot twice in the back and killed.[24]

Veteran journalist Nhial Bol, editor of *The Citizen* newspaper, quit journalism in 2015 amid death threats. A giant of a man with a booming voice, he had regularly been picked up by security forces when he worked in Khartoum as a journalist in the 1990s as an outspoken supporter of the South's freedom. He set up the South's first ever newspaper printing press, an antique machine of pounding pistons, squirting ink the length of a bus, that he would march up and down with wrench in hand to encourage the juddering conveyor belt as the paper rolled off. 'Fighting Corruption and Dictatorship Everyday,' the bold masthead read.

Bol closed his career with an editorial, warning that Kiir and Machar had 'no ability to stop this war'. He likened their fight to that of the conflict between warlords in Mogadishu: 'Kiir and Riek Machar will end up in a situation similar to that of Somalia,' Bol wrote.

Foreign journalists were expelled or banned, so some sneaked across the border from Uganda. Few risked that after American reporter Christopher Allen, embedded with rebels as they battled government forces, was shot multiple times by a large calibre gun. The government called him a 'white rebel', and the army warned others faced a similar fate.

The government's blackout worked. One by one, the voices were silenced. Empty gaps appeared on newspaper pages, where security officers had ordered a story be deleted just before printing, the blank space the only record of a critical report. 'The struggle of the people of South Sudan has been hijacked,' said Alfred Taban, the much-respected editor of the *Juba Monitor*, his voice wobbling as though on the brink of tears. 'Before, we were struggling for our rights as human beings, for the betterment of the people. Then the killing of one another started between each of the tribes. Then I knew things had really gone bad, and that the leaders were not really struggling for the people, but for themselves. It became a struggle for money and power.'

In July 2016, he wrote in an editorial arguing that South Sudan's leaders had 'completely failed'. He too was arrested and his newspaper closed.

* * *

No one knows how many have died, because no one ever counted. Tallying the dead in war is a dangerous and imperfect science, but it is done in other conflicts. In battles in Syria or Iraq, the deaths are largely casualties from bullets or bombs, and killings take place often in urban areas where witnesses can try to record them. In South Sudan, where clashes take place in lonely lands, even big battles can go unremarked. Neither the 14,000-strong UN peacekeeping force nor any other officials kept a tally.

A year into the war, the International Crisis Group, which tracked the fighting as closely as anyone, said its best guess was that at least 50,000 had been killed. Researchers suggest the number of indirect deaths—from starvation caused by aid blockades and, following the targeted destruction of hospitals, deaths resulting from a lack of healthcare—can be 15 times higher than those killed in fighting.[25] If you add those killed as a consequence of war, the numbers skyrocket.

Hospitals were deliberately and systematically targeted. Doctors Without Borders' hospitals and clinics were looted or destroyed, with over two dozen major attacks. Medicine not taken was trashed so as to leave nothing to help the enemy; disease and infections spread. Easily preventable and treatable malaria became the biggest killer, with death rates quadrupling in some areas. Water-borne cholera infected thousands in one of the most protracted, widespread outbreaks the South had suffered, unusually lasting even throughout the dry season.

'Millions of citizens have been displaced, and thousands are sheltering in the bush, resulting in untold deaths from starvation, thirst, exposure, and lack of access to medical care,' UN human rights experts wrote. 'These deaths are a direct and foreseeable result of the conflict, and no less part of the war's casualties than those shot, beheaded, burned in their *tukuls* (huts), or strung up from a tree.'[26]

After four years of fighting, the African Union said as many as 300,000 might have died, but that was a guess too. Some said they feared even more. The total kept on rising.

The only ones who tried to count were a group of South Sudanese civil society activists. The failure to clarify a clear toll dishonoured victims, they said, contributed to South Sudan's suffering staying off the international radar, and enabled impunity for the killers. 'It's a vital step to recognising the collective loss,' said Anyieth D'Awol, who helped set up the Naming The Ones We Lost project to list those killed. 'The lack of justice, accountability and acknowledgement of losses suffered by people has fuelled the conflict.'

The oldest person they recorded killed was 107, the youngest, two weeks old. One by one, they added to the columns of the dead, recording the names and details of those killed. Even then, the thousands of names gathered were but a fraction of those killed. After all, it did not take long for evidence of those killed to rot away. Whole communities, and the memories that went with them, were obliterated.

The visible scars fade fast. There are often not even the concrete ruins that in other war zones act as a shattered memorial of a city that once was there. Here, house walls melt back into mud and thatch roofs rot. Even the rusted hulks of tanks are taken for scrap.

I went to Leer, birthplace of Riek Machar, a town that had been destroyed multiple times in the fighting. When I was there, it was held by men loyal to Machar.

The UN's World Food Programme was airdropping in food. Flying in food is usually prohibitively expensive, but it was the only way to get food into areas cut off by war. The International Committee of the Red Cross had also begun food aid flights; the last time they had resorted to such drastic means was almost two decades before in Afghanistan. I watched as bundles of food tumbled out the back of a cargo plane, tons of grain thumping down so hard the cracked earth seemed to shudder. Above, the screaming engines pulled the plane out of the dive. The town was effectively besieged. Many here came to the town to collect food, but then retreated back out into the swamplands where they could hide and feel safe.

There was little left of the town anyway. Walking near a compound of the Catholic Church, I found a human skull in the dirt, the surface grey. There were no other bones, and it was impossible to know how old it was. There was no one to ask who might have known anything about who died here. For a moment I considered burying it, but then it would disappear, and I didn't know if that was the right thing to do. I stood for some time beside it, but left it lying in the dust.

A few months after I was in Leer, it was attacked again by government forces. The hospital, which had been torched in fighting two years earlier and then rebuilt, was destroyed for a second time. In the church compound near where I'd found the skull, some 60 men and boys were stuffed into an airtight storage container in the baking heat, and the door closed. When it was opened again, the only survivor among the piles of bodies was a boy, small enough to have climbed up onto the corpses to reach enough air to breathe.[27]

* * *

Humanitarian operations in South Sudan became the largest to function inside any single country.[28] The UN calculated the global relative price of food, with a meal-to-income ratio of a plate of simple rice and beans; while in New York the ingredients would be less than one percent of average daily income, in South Sudan, it would be 155 percent.[29] It was the most expensive in the world.

When UN chief Ban Ki-moon returned to Juba, he looked gloomily at a land where so much had been dreamed. 'I was here in 2011 as the flag of the new South Sudan flew high and proudly for the first time of this independent state,' he said. 'I saw in the faces of the people of this country all that the flag represented: the pride, the spirit, the hope. That hope has been betrayed. It has been betrayed by those who put power and profit over people. The people of this land suffered decades of bloody civil war. Yet over the last two years, the nightmare has returned with a vengeance.'[30]

14

THE WAR AMONG OURSELVES

'It is necessary for these sad conditions to be reported, because evil thrives best in quiet, untidy corners.'

Chinua Achebe

The speckled pigeons—the closest South Sudan got to white doves of peace—had been stuck in a box waiting on the hot airstrip for days. When they were finally freed, they had to be hurled high into the air to make them fly. They fluttered briefly past the head of the man stepping out of a white UN jet onto the tarmac, before swiftly escaping. It was April 2016. Two years since he fled for his life, Riek Machar returned to Juba.

'The war was vicious,' said Machar, arriving as part of an internationally-brokered peace deal to place him back in power. 'We have lost a lot of people in it, and we need to bring our people together so that they can unite, reconcile, heal the wounds—the mental wounds that they have.'

Machar was to be Vice President again. The strongest international arm-twisting returned South Sudan to the status quo that existed before the 2013 sacking of Machar had precipitated the war. Except, of course, the situation now was compounded by two years of bloody division and an economy in utter ruins. Machar also brought with him his own force of soldiers. That meant there were now two armies which hated each other in the same city.

Yet with over half a dozen ceasefires already discarded, diplomats wanted a political process to cling to. The war was cast as a battle between two tribes, so it was thought the solution would be to bring the leaders together. Efforts focused on a new power-sharing deal between Kiir and Machar. Even if it was a quick fix, the logic ran, there had to be a start. If fighting could be calmed with the beginnings of a ceasefire, then perhaps a stronger peace could be made. It was given a title as long as its flaws: The Agreement for the Resolution of the Conflict in the Republic of South Sudan.

The problem was, however, that their feud was now only one part of a much wider war; they had become figureheads for a battle they claimed control of but that had escaped their grasp. Just because the big men began the butchery did not mean they could end it. In forcing a deal based on the two men, those not included now had to fight to carve out their slice of the pie. Meanwhile, those who had enjoyed the profits of war did not want to share with their enemies.[1]

Kiir came under increasing pressure from powerful Dinka chiefs, the self-appointed Jieng Council of Elders. They cast themselves as liberators of the nation, and those who challenged them as opposing the country. They bristled with rage at having to capitulate to their enemy through outside intervention. In their eyes, UN peacekeepers were, therefore, not trying to end the conflict. 'The proposal simply confirms the intention of the international community to take over the country,' they wrote, warning it would 'breed a much bitter war'.[2]

A furious Kiir made clear he had been forced to sign. Making Machar his deputy again was a humiliating 'reward for rebellion,' he said, as he set about promptly demolishing the deal's main pillar, a power-sharing formula in which rebels got a share of seats, including the governor posts in the oil states of Upper Nile and Unity.[3] Kiir, claiming to be offering more services to the people, simply scrapped existing government structures by nearly tripling the number of regional states. Critics saw it as social engineering that institutionalised Dinka dominance by redrawing boundaries to divide opposition.

Nothing diplomats could offer or threaten seemed to matter. East African neighbours wielded clout, but that influence was bound up in rival strategic, political, military and financial interests, including control of the Nile waters. There were big profits to be made in war, resources to take, and points to score against regional rivals.

The UN Security Council had imposed sanctions on commanders from both sides, including a travel ban and an assets freeze. They shrugged it off. The fortune that mattered to them was cattle not foreign banks, and they were not looking for a European holiday any time soon. As for Kiir's men, they enjoyed a promotion.

When Machar's advance team arrived, I watched two of the sanctioned men, erstwhile enemies, greet each other at the airport with grins, patting each other on the back in an embrace. There was Kiir's presidential guard commander Marial Chanuong Yol Mangok, accused of leading the slaughter of Nuer civilians in Juba in 2013.[4] He stood shaking hands with fellow generals without, it seemed, a care in the world. He met Machar's military chief Simon Gatwech, accused of massacring Dinka prisoners of war according to UN sanctions orders. His orders, the sanctions note read, had reportedly been brutally direct: 'Kill all of them.'[5] Gatwech stepped out the plane waving a walking stick in the air like a champion.

Yet beyond the surface smiles, the mood was poisonous. I asked a diplomat if they thought the deal would work. 'We have to hope,' he said half-heartedly. 'It's the only option we've got.'

I went to the outskirts of Juba where some of Machar's 1,400 bodyguards were hacking out a base by hand to build thatch huts. An army barracks was within shouting distance, and the two forces watched each other suspiciously. Both sides still seemed committed to a military solution.

Posters erected by Machar's supporters broadcast messages of reconciliation. 'United for peace', one read, with smiling faces of Machar and Kiir. They were ripped down. Machar's return had been delayed for days because the government opposed the number of weapons his protection force could bring. In a country where weapons are the one thing you can get easily, the agreement nearly faltered over two dozen machine guns and a handful of rocket-propelled grenades. The deal was dead before delivery.

Finally, nine months after signing the deal, Machar returned on 26 April 2016. He walked through the crowd to a convoy of cars waiting to take him to meet Kiir and be sworn into office. Dapper black hat on his head and a colourful shirt stretched over his belly, he waved and reached out to those around him like a returning hero. When he clasped my hand, however, it was wet and clammy. Close up, he looked utterly terrified.

An hour later, standing in front of Kiir inside the fortified walls of the presidential palace, Machar was sworn into office. Kiir called Machar his brother. The rivals who had fought and made up, then fought again, made up one more time. 'I have no doubt that his return to Juba today marks the end of the war and the return of peace and stability,' Kiir said, brushing the start of the conflict off as an 'incident'. I watched the two men shake hands, then stand alongside each other on the parade ground with hands on hearts under the flapping flag. A red-coated marching brass band played the national anthem, 'God Bless South Sudan'.

As I walked out of the palace grounds, I passed Machar's abandoned former house. The metal gates were still twisted where the tanks had smashed inside, and riddled with bullet scars. The only resident appeared to be a mangy dog, who had found peace sleeping in the sand of the courtyard.

* * *

Three months after I saw Machar take office, I stood in the presidential palace again. My boots crunched on broken glass and some of the hundreds of bullet casings that lay in thick piles scattered around. If Machar had thought that UN peacekeepers would protect him and the peace deal, he was horribly wrong. Pigeons pecked at pools of blood that had congealed and dried on the concrete. I wondered if any had been the birds released to celebrate peace when Machar arrived weeks before.

I had intended to see the fifth anniversary of independence, but celebrations had been cancelled with economic failure and runaway inflation. The peace deal had all but collapsed—if it had ever worked. Machar was sidelined, a Vice President in name only. Kiir had tried to smooth things over by inviting Machar to be a guest of honour at his daughter's wedding, but otherwise the president and his deputy hardly saw each other. Everyone I spoke to said the war was coming again.

At dusk on 7 July, Machar's men were stopped at a checkpoint in Juba's Gudele district, provoking a shootout that left five government soldiers dead, the latest in a string of shootings between the rival forces. Later that night, government soldiers emptied their guns at two armour-plated US diplomatic cars returning from a curry house, shooting out the tyres. In panic, the embassy scrambled to send out Marines to rescue one car that burst through the road block but later swerved to a stop.[6]

The two leaders met at the presidential palace the next day for a press conference, attempting to calm tensions with broadcast public messages. As the two men talked and the journalists waited, Machar's men parked their pickup trucks alongside Kiir's Tiger guards. Moments later, fighting erupted. Each side blamed the other, but whoever fired first, all piled in.

Journalists lay on the floor as machine guns opened fire around the compound, and rockets ricocheted into the walls. Dozens died in the battle, but Kiir saved Machar, realising that the killing of his peace partner inside his own palace would not look good, however it happened. He physically shielded Machar into a car during a lull in the shooting and ensured that he got out safely—but the battle was far from over.

The next morning, Independence Day, Sunday 9 July, the city was calm. One day later, the heavy thump of helicopter gunships rose over Juba, as Kiir tried to finish the job for good. Fighter jets and attack helicopters flew low over Juba with all guns blazing. Tanks advanced firing shells. As rockets thumped down into his compound, Machar fled on foot.

* * *

A week later, the corpses were still lying swollen on the streets. The stench of rotting bodies drifted across the hospital grounds, as the latest load were piled onto trucks, to join well over 200 already thrown into mass graves. I watched as Red Cross workers peeled off white protective suits and face masks, kicking off thick black rubber boots as they sat dripping sweat in the intense heat, sharing cigarettes after the grim task. Some sat quietly in the shade of a tree, heads between legs, retching at the foul stench.

Soldiers said it was some of the most intense fighting they had seen. 'I have been a soldier since I was a child,' said 50-year-old Richard Bida, a lieutenant. 'I have never experienced a battle like that. It was soldier on soldier, and then soldier on civilian. The dead lined the streets.' Like thousands of others, he had sought shelter in the compound of St. Theresa Catholic Cathedral. Survivors reported stories that had become miserably familiar—gunmen asked what language people spoke before shooting them if they were from a rival people. 'They drove a tank through houses,' said 27-year-old Jacky Lasuba, sitting with her three children outside the church. 'Mine they burned.' One mother of two held her eyes down. The right side of her face was heavily swollen, smashed with a rifle butt by the man who had knocked her to the ground before assaulting her. She cradled her young baby tight to her chest, and sang a church hymn quietly. A nun played with her older daughter.

Uganda, which had officially pulled out troops that had previously in the South as part of the peace deal, sent back in long convoys of army trucks to rescue its citizens. Market traders, investors, taxi drivers, the Ugandans, Kenyans, Ethiopians and Eritreans who underpinned so much of the economy were leaving in their tens of thousands.

A fellow reporter and I found motorbike taxi drivers willing to take us out on the near-empty streets of Juba, with the caveat that they'd turn back when they did not feel safe. On the way to the heavily fortified army headquarters, I passed an unfinished six-storey building, briefly occupied by Machar's troops. Door-sized chunks of concrete had been smashed out of it by explosions, while the tin roofs of nearby houses were punched in by artillery shells.

We motored out through the hot orange dust to Gudele, past the site of the checkpoint where the shooting had started. The market there was reduced to a twisted wreck of smoking metal, and it stank of burned plastic. We turned up the thin side streets, among the maze of mud-walled homes. Doctors Without Borders had pitched a small tent, providing what treatment they could; all those who came in told tales of terror. We pushed on up towards Machar's ruined base.

In the other direction, we passed lines of people dragging bags from the UN's World Food Programme, aid intended to stave off famine. It was looting on an epic scale; a month's worth of food aid for over quarter of million people, or a year's supply for a small army. In the midst of a battle, it was an impressive logistical feat, a large-scale, well organised $20 million heist requiring hundreds of truck trips to steal 4,500 tonnes of food in just two days. Nearby residents said soldiers even brought a truck mounted with a crane to steal the minibus-sized generators that once powered the giant site.

When we passed—we didn't stop as a drunk soldier waved his rifle angrily at the bikes—only the scraps were left. Men hammered at broken trucks for spare parts, while others ripped off electrical wires from an office block. Some of the looters tore down the remaining few sections of thick plastic sheeting that had covered the metal frames of rows of warehouses, now standing like a skeleton's ribcage picked clean of flesh.

We headed out towards the main UN base, in the shadow of the rocky hill that looms over the town called Jebel Kujur, 'the mountain of the witch'. Several people had been killed in fighting around the UN base, including inside the guarded camp sheltering over 27,000 South Sudanese civilians. They included two Chinese peacekeepers, who died when a bomb hit their armoured personal carrier inside the UN walls.[7]

The soldiers were on the roads manning makeshift roadblocks. They scared me, especially the young boys of Kiir's Brown Caterpillars, who could flip from friendliness to extreme violence in moments. So we swung down a side track, skirting around the hulk of the Blue House, headquarters of the feared National Security Service. The Blue House had, in only a couple of years, earned the same chilling reputation as the White House torture centre had done before independence. Internal security operated on their own with terrifying powers, and there were accusations that they operated a dedicated assassination team. They even picked up opposition supporters who had fled to Uganda and Kenya and brought them back for punishment.[8]

People called them 'the unknown gunmen', but when someone disappeared, everyone knew of the black hole they had been taken to. Security chiefs were terrifyingly blunt about who they held. 'Political prisoners,' they called the men inside, without even the thinnest pretence they were criminals. Even when foreigners were arrested, diplomats had no access. Those who went inside vanished. There was no recourse for appeal. Looking back from the crossroads, I could see a couple of soldiers pulling over cars. We drove on fast.

We headed to Terrain Hotel, a favourite of aid workers. It was the place for beers around the pool, where people met for a few hours to banish the sweat and suffering outside. I knew it too had been attacked, and wanted to check the damage. We almost made it. The roads here were empty, but what seemed at first to suggest calm indicated something more sinister. We got within a stone's throw of the turnoff from the main road to the hotel, when a man in dirty combat trousers and a T-shirt ran out and flagged us down. I felt that strange and sudden cold skin prickle of nerves. But the man was waving to warn us to turn back, not stopping us.

'He said the soldiers are still there in the bush,' the motorbike driver said, gesturing at the scrubby trees along the track. 'It is far enough.' He swerved the bike around, revving the engine and speeding back the way we had come, as the sharp gravel flew up.

* * *

The attack at Terrain Camp, one of the worst targeted assaults on aid workers, came to symbolise the inability of the international community to act—even to protect their own. Soldiers stormed in, overpowering guards armed with shotguns. Soldiers used crowbars to prise open doors, or shoot through locks of special safe rooms. Even the strongest of iron doors can be forced open with enough firepower. They were designed to protect people for long enough for help to come. None did.

The hotel was home to several international workers, a place that felt safe given its close proximity to the UN base. The peacekeepers were alerted moments after the attack began. A UN tank could drive there in minutes, for you could run between the two in the time it took to boil a kettle and make a cup of tea.

Troops, several wearing the badges of Kiir's Tiger guards according to survivors, went on the rampage, separating women and dragging them into different rooms. At least five foreign aid workers were gang raped, one by fifteen men. One soldier bit a woman on her face and neck, another rapist sprayed insect repellent into his victim's face while singing. Fighters forced foreigners to stand in a semi-circle, screaming abuse at them, and blaming them for the chaos. 'UN mess our country,' they shouted, accusing them of supporting the rebels, and beating an American man on the ground. 'Tell your embassy how we treated you,' soldiers said, as they pushed him out of the camp.

John Gatluak, a journalist, was dragged out and thrown down in front of them. I had known Gatluak as a quiet, dedicated young father, a man who believed passionately in the risks he ran as a journalist to help his nation. The 32-year-old had run a community radio station in Leer, but that was destroyed by government soldiers, and he escaped by hiding in the swamps for months. He rebuilt the station, but when it was destroyed for a second time he made his way to Juba. He came to Terrain thinking he would be safer surrounded by international colleagues. Instead, he was singled out. 'Nuer!' one soldier shouted, pointing to parallel scars across his forehead. Another soldier raised his rifle and shot him in the head. Then they shot him in the head again, then four more times in the body to make sure.[9]

The attack only ended hours later, when a separate unit of South Sudanese soldiers arrived. Most of the aid workers escaped then, with others too scared to come out from hiding places saved the next day by a private security company. No UN troops came. As Gatluak's body lay in the dust where he had been shot, his widow gave birth to his son.

For the South Sudanese, such killings and rape were daily occurrences, so the horrific attack on Terrain was terrible but nothing new. Nor was it the first attack on aid workers; scores had been killed in the course of the war.[10] Nuns had been shot dead, others raped. Gunmen had even shot down a UN cargo helicopter, murdering three Russian crew members.[11] Most of the aid workers killed had been South Sudanese trying to help their nation.

Yet for the outside world, it was the Terrain attack that exploded the false bubble of a sense of safety. The war had burst through their gates. For foreigners, inured to reports of the violence of Southerner against Southerner, this marked something different. This was no rebel attack on a lonely outpost. This was a luxury poolside restaurant in the capital, the gunmen and rapists were government forces, and UN peacekeepers, who could see the attack unfolding next door, did nothing. It was clear foreigners were no longer seen as separate from the conflict, but part of it. They too now were a target. For many, it was the moment when those who still had hope turned to despair.

* * *

With the facade of peace over, men got back to the business of killing. The slaughter that had calmed in Upper Nile and Jonglei resumed. The army and politicians supplied guns to Dinka cattle herders, creating heavily armed pro-government militia forces who went out raiding. The vast herds of cattle robbed from Nuer lands were a handy, mobile way to stash loot in a country where the domestic currency had collapsed, and external finances stored abroad were at risk of sanctions or seizure. Yet every action has a reaction, and those who had their cows stolen found joining a militia gave them back some sense of identity, respect and means of survival. They were a ready-to-go army.

Dinka herders pushed south along the border with Uganda and Congo, into the lands belonging to the peoples of Equatoria, in order to take the lush grazing lands for their cows. In Equatoria, people now had a reason to fight. Communities looked to protect themselves, and built their own self-defence groups. The military in Equatoria became increasingly a Dinka army of occupation. 'The new slogan which people are now singing is that this army has become a tribal army,' Kiir said, as he threatened to lead operations in Equatoria himself. 'Why is it composed of Dinka? But where will I get people from if the people of Equatoria have refused to join the army, and Riek Machar has rebelled with his Nuer people? Where will I get other nationalities from?'[12]

The old question that had shadowed me for years returned; what makes a country? If it was the flags and symbols of the trappings of state, then all the sides laid claim to them. It was like the old wars of religion, where every army said they were fighting for God. Someone, but perhaps everyone, had to be wrong. If you were fighting for freedom, whose freedom was that? Who had the right to say what made up the nation? If it was the institutions of government, then they had all but collapsed. If the state was the people—their ideas, hopes and pride in their homeland—well, they were fleeing. The dream of South Sudan had become a nightmare.

* * *

Tactics were repeated with grim success: helicopters, tanks and trucks attacked villages, before Dinka forces from the SPLA and the Mathiang Anyoor militia swept in. Reports were common of villages reduced to ashes, and of bodies found with their arms bound, or washed downstream in the rivers. Nothing seemed sacred; churches and mosques were desecrated and used as holding centres for slaughter. Buses with civilians were stopped, the people dragged out and massacred.

Scorched earth attacks were deliberately aimed to clear land and end village life so there was nothing to return to.[13] The brutality was carried out with a callous and systematic cruelty; soldiers hacked children to death, cleared the land by burning village after village, and blockaded food in deliberate, targeted starvation of whole districts. The anger reverberated deep in society, turning to hatred. The UN said at least two-thirds of the country's 12 million people needed aid. Equatoria, once the breadbasket of the country, was a war zone.

'President Salva Kiir and his Dinka leadership clique have tactically and systematically transformed the SPLA into a partisan and tribal army,' wrote the army's logistics chief General Thomas Cirillo, a respected commander from Equatoria, as he launched his own rebellion.[14] 'I can no longer continue to be part of the ongoing destruction of our beloved country by the same army.'

The toxic rivalries of the Juba elite reached down to a local level, where fights were fuelled by decades of marginalisation, fear and poverty. In the towns not burned to the ground, or the UN camps where the rest had fled, people divided according to their ethnicity. It was a war of many sides, not a fight that any single force could win outright.[15] If the war had begun as a political conflict between elites, it had evolved into anarchy, opportunism and revenge. The violence had metastasised, and took on a life of its own.

After the July 2016 battles in Juba, Kiir sent men to the central bank vaults at night, handing over $5 million in cash to army chief Paul Malong to track Machar down and kill him, according to Kiir's own spokesman. Those dollar-stuffed briefcases funded the foreign mercenaries who bombed him from fighter jets as he fled.[16] Machar, however, escaped to Congo. Eventually, he made it to South Africa, where he was placed under effective house arrest.

The last time I spoke to Kiir, standing amid the spent bullets from the battle with Machar in his palace, he looked exhausted. 'I don't want any more bloodshed,' Kiir said. I wanted to believe him, but then I also had reports his helicopters were busy firing rockets and machine guns. Either he was lying, or he had lost control. Perhaps it was both.

Yet without Machar, the war ground on as bad as ever before. As their country burned, leaders in Juba played a complicated game of musical chairs. Leaders on each side swapped sides as fortunes rose and fell. The many clans of the Dinka or Nuer cannot be generalised into a single unit, and they were at times as bitterly divided among themselves as they were against the other group. Individuals went against their people too. There were Nuer in government, and Dinka with the rebels. 'A zero-sum struggle,' the UN Panel of Experts called it; whatever one side wins, the other loses.[17]

Forces fractured. Machar's second-in-command, Nuer leader Taban Deng Gai, saw the opportunity to join the government and replace him as Vice President. Yet as Kiir gained an ally, he lost old ones. He was increasingly isolated, with divisions growing within his core Dinka support. Eventually, Kiir even fell out with Paul Malong, the Dinka strongman who had raised the Mathiang Anyoor forces for him. 'History will judge us harshly,' said Malong in an unusually reflective mood, when the US-sanctioned general responsible for some of the very worst carnage finally launched his bid to topple Kiir too. 'The country has become a failed state.'[18]

* * *

'I don't care what deal they sign in Juba,' said James Koach, a rebel officer, a lanky man with nervous hands that twitched constantly, tapping the trigger of his AK-47. 'The deals are with the government, and where is the government? They mean nothing to us and make no difference here.' We sat under a tree, surrounded by huddled groups of mothers and children, waiting in hope for food. Some had been there for days. As we stared out across the swamps near Leer, he searched through the pockets of his faded green jacket and pouches of a canvas ammunition belt, finally pulling out a cigarette packet. The smoke helped clear the clouds of mosquitoes. He pushed up his Dallas Cowboys baseball cap. 'They took our wives and killed my children. My family has gone, so what do I care if I live or die?' he said, sucking hard on the cigarette. 'They took our cows. You who come from outside don't know what this means. Our cows are everything, because without them how can we survive? They are trying to wipe us out, to remove us from the earth.'

Diplomats said peace was matter of perseverance, continuing dogged efforts to support a formula that had already failed over and over again. Critics said it was madness.

THE WAR AMONG OURSELVES

'*Dum spiro spero*; while I breathe, I hope,' said Festus Mogae, who headed the internationally-backed commission monitoring the peace deal. 'If there is no attempt...' His voice trailed off. Mogae, an ex-president of Botswana now in his late 70s, looked drained at the enormity of the task. He was aware of the failings, but feared the consequences if the process ended entirely. 'We have to continue to do something, because if the international community should say, "we are tired of South Sudan," worse will occur,' he told me. 'Worse will occur.' He sighed as he repeated it, as though to convince himself.

The US proposed an arms embargo to the UN Security Council. Alone, it would not stop the war, for the country was already long awash in guns, but a blockade would limit the flow of heavy weaponry and stop the government's attack helicopters operated by foreign crews. It was one thing diplomats could do.

'Do we just sit on our hands until the government calls off the militias, to stop some of the most systematic sexual violence that we've seen in any conflict in our lifetimes?' said Samantha Power in exasperation, Washington's ambassador to the UN. 'Given the accumulation of warnings, we have lost the right individually and collectively to act surprised in the face of even greater atrocities in South Sudan,' the diplomat said, who once won a Pulitzer Prize for detailing past American failures to prevent genocide. 'None of us can say that we did not see it coming. The question therefore for us is—what will we do?'[19]

Nothing, it seemed, for the proposal was blocked. It would take another year of killing before the US even imposed its own arms ban, and that was largely symbolic. The government could circumvent it with ease.

* * *

In the dry season, when the mud tracks dried and troops could move, fighting grew. When the wet season came, the fighting cooled and the soldiers rested to lick their wounds. At that point, diplomats tried to persuade the sides to keep the peace.

More effective were church leaders, who worked as mediators between the rivals. In the past, they had been crucial in bringing communities together, to strike local deals of peace by people frustrated and exhausted at a war far from their control. The Church was often

257

the only organisation offering any support in terms of health or education in places deemed too dangerous for other aid workers, and the
bishops were about the last left who dared speak out to condemn the
warring forces.

'All they've got is the rainy season and God,' one diplomat said. 'We
don't see a solution soon.'

* * *

The motorbike drivers, standing in a long and snaking line queuing for
fuel, looked up at the storm clouds with a miserable stare. The oil
producing nation had no fuel for itself and the waiting line could sometimes last for days when deliveries were delayed. I ducked into the
maze of tin roof shacks, and found the man I was looking for. He quietly took my hundred-dollar bill, held it briefly to the light to check it
was genuine, then handed over fist-sized bricks of cash to fill a plastic
bag. South Sudan's pound was in freefall, but with hard currency on the
black market you could still buy enough to get what you needed. A
couple of bricks paid for an overpriced plastic bottle of petrol from
another stall, bypassing the long wait for fuel at the station. With that,
I could get a bike to take me back before the rain clouds returned and
turned the tracks to mud.

South Sudan was broke; oil production had slumped, with wells shut
down in fighting. Even the limited oil produced didn't earn much. The
fixed fee paid per barrel to Khartoum for pumping oil on their pipelines to the Red Sea had seemed a good deal when the oil prices were
sky high, but when the market slumped, the transport charge remained
the same. At times, the cash Khartoum took nearly equalled what Juba
itself earned for its oil. In practice, Juba just deferred its payments
down the line, swapping the wealth of the nation for debt to its old
enemies. It was as if the South's great war of independence to control
its own resources had never happened.

The country's great assets were being bled dry. Teak plantations
were logged and looted, while other forests were hacked down so
people could survive by selling charcoal. In past wars, wildlife had
survived—once, there had been hopes that intrepid safari visitors
might return to provide an alternative income. This war was different,
for some of the worst fighting cut across the migration routes of the

animals. Elephants were gunned down for their tusks, while herds of giraffe and antelope were shot with machine guns. It was organised large-scale destruction of herds of animals, with the flesh sold for commercial bush meat.

Even what cash did come in was wasted. The government borrowed several billion dollars at ruinous rates against future oil production. Yet those dollars were not spent on health or education. Government officials who could access the dollars at a fixed government exchange rate swapped them on the black market to rake in gross profit by pocketing the difference, leading to the collapse of the currency. Hyper-inflation soared at times to over 800 percent.[20] People struggled to find food. The hopes for a country had been wasted on a pointless scrabble for power, a winner-takes-all battle where all that is left is destroyed.

* * *

Donors funded the billion-dollar-a-year UN peacekeeping operation and provided hundreds of millions of dollars every year in basic aid, keeping the country continually just a step away from total collapse. However, in taking over government's social and moral responsibilities, the aid industry also helped the elite. It was the cruellest dilemma; cut the aid and hurt those already hit hardest from war, or keep aid flowing and provide a life support for the economy, paying painfully high rents and providing food in the markets. It propped up a government to steal or spend the remaining cash on more war. 'The government has cynically sub-contracted its own responsibility for taking care of its people to the international community,' experts from the UN Commission on Human Rights wrote in a 2018 report. 'Parties remain totally indifferent to the deliberate suffering of the people.'[21]

There were few other suggestions of how to salvage peace. One radical US proposal was to put South Sudan on 'life support' by taking power from the leaders and handing it to an international administration from the UN or the African Union for the next 10 to 15 years. 'Given South Sudan's extreme degree of state failure, temporary external administration is the only remaining path to protect and restore its sovereignty,' the report read, penned by two ex-Washington officials, two of the most senior to have served in Juba, the ex-Special Envoy Princeton Lyman and the former USAID mission director for Sudan

Kate Almquist Knopf. 'While a morally bankrupt and predatory elite will falsely characterise such an initiative as a violation of sovereignty, it is this very elite that has put the country's survival at risk.'[22]

While the authors cited ex-war zone examples such as Kosovo, Cambodia, East Timor or Liberia where the UN had temporarily run the country, it made me think only of the colonial 'Bog Barons', whose proposal six decades before had been exactly that—to govern the South after independence under a UN mandate for twenty years. It felt like international attitudes towards the South had hardly changed at all. Like that proposal, this suggestion was shelved too. It did not make clear why international bureaucrats, whose support for the government had already failed so spectacularly, would do a better job if they were in charge.

In any case, the government was never going to let it happen. Kiir was already blocking UN pressure to send extra peacekeepers to Juba, so the idea that the government would step down and surrender sovereignty without a fight was a fantasy. South Sudan's leaders called it neo-colonialism.

* * *

Famine conjures up images of children dying in the dust. Formally declaring one is rarely done, for it must meet strict international definitions, including malnutrition so severe that two adults or four children starve to death per 10,000 people every day. The last declared had been in Somalia in 2011, a manmade catastrophe where a quarter of a million people died amid extreme drought exacerbated by a war against Al-Qaeda-linked fighters. Back then, I sat watching child after child die in Mogadishu, their ragged breath soft as the beat of a butterfly's wings. Their bodies had collapsed from cholera, and, even with help from doctors, were too weak to save.

In February 2017, I was in South Sudan when famine was declared again. At least 100,000 people were dying from a simple lack of food in the largely Nuer lands of Leer and Mayendit, and a further one million were near starvation, according to the UN.

There was no drought to provide the veneer of an excuse; the government had pushed the people into starvation on the edge of a lush swamp. It was a deliberately engineered catastrophe designed to break the enemy. The cheapest way to attack the men was by killing their children. Food was blocked, aid was stolen, rations were raided, and medicine destroyed. When stores too large to carry away were seized, soldiers slashed bags open to rot in the rain.[23] People fled fighting carrying nothing, and the cattle used as a final lifeline were stolen.

When technical advisors finally gathered data to prove areas met the international definitions of famine, I was in the Dinka town of Bor. In a tin-roof restaurant, eating freshly grilled Nile perch from the nearby river, I watched a report on Al Jazeera that showed painfully thin children crying as nurses in a simple clinic struggled to cope. There was no mention of the famine on state-run television, only looped footage of dancing soldiers celebrating victory. I asked fellow diners what they thought. 'A hungry dog follows its master,' one said.

Conquest, war, death and finally famine; the Four Horsemen of the Apocalypse had all arrived. Then, the UN rang one more terrifying alarm bell—genocide.

* * *

When atrocities in other countries took place, the excuse was made later: 'We did not know.' No such claim can be made for South Sudan. The crimes were all too clear.

'An environment ripe for the commission of mass atrocities,' said UN Special Advisor on Genocide Adama Dieng, recounting the reports of targeted killings, mutilation, and the use of machetes to hack whole families to death. These were people deliberately targeted for who they were, not their politics. No distinction was made between soldiers and civilians, for all were a potential target, even the very youngest. 'There is a strong risk of violence escalating along ethnic lines, with the potential for genocide,' said Dieng. 'I do not say that lightly.'[24]

Degrees of intent, scale and motivation differentiate the categories of killing, murder, massacre, ethnic cleansing and genocide. To name a genocide, one also must prove intent—that the violence was to destroy, in whole or in part, a national, ethnic, racial or religious group.[25] Gathering that evidence in the chaos of war is near impossible. To argue over definitions might seem little more than an academic exercise; the definition did not change the fact that the growing piles of corpses were all still dead. Yet to name is to also acknowledge, and with that comes the moral duty to prevent it. Like counting the numbers of the dead, it matters on grounds of justice. Without accountability for the crimes committed, the end to war rarely brings a lasting peace.

UN rights experts said there was sufficient evidence to show that both government and rebels were deliberately killing civilians and destroying homes on the basis of their ethnic identity, including communities with no armed forces. The violence constituted war crimes and crimes against humanity.[26] It bore almost every hallmark of genocide: mass rape, forced starvation, ethnic divisions, critics silenced, homes systematically destroyed, hate speech and inflammatory rhetoric whipping up violence.[27]

'The stage is being set for a repeat of what happened in Rwanda,' said Yasmin Sooka, the chief of the UN Commission on Human Rights for South Sudan.[28] Satellite photography showed village after village reduced to burned ashes. Such wholesale destruction took time and effort, for setting fire to tens of thousands of well-built homes was no accident in the heat of battle, but the organised excision of people from their land. Soldiers even systematically destroyed wells and water pumps, blowing them up or leaving landmines behind. In one offensive in Upper Nile, 80 percent of water points were reported to have been so destroyed.[29] Even the old trees in the heart of villages, meeting places of the community for generations, were torched. Nothing was left for people to return to.

Outside witnesses were driven away, for observers were blocked and aid workers faced targeted attacks. South Sudan had become one of the most dangerous places in the world to be an aid worker. By mid 2018, one hundred aid workers had been killed since the war began.

'There is already a steady process of ethnic cleansing underway in several areas of South Sudan using starvation, gang rape and the burning of villages; everywhere we went across this country we heard villagers saying they are ready to shed blood to get their land back,' added Sooka. 'Many told us it's already reached a point of no return.'

Insults dehumanised one group to another. Threatening letters were issued to aid agencies and the UN to sack South Sudanese staff who came from the 'wrong' area. The Dinka called the Nuer pigs, parasites, monkeys and rebels. The Nuer corrupted the name the Dinka call themselves, Jieng, to *jiang*, meaning slave. The Equatorians called the Dinka land grabbers or 'unwanted goods'.[30] If the fight was not about tribe to begin with, it was becoming that now.

Amid the litany of horrors, the one that disturbed me most was the quiet-spoken 21-year-old woman I met who had fled to Uganda. She told her story looking down at the dirt on the floor of her hut, rocking slowly on her heels, embracing herself with her arms. She asked not to be named. In early 2017, government soldiers had swept into her sleepy farming village in Equatoria in vehicles, shooting as the people fled. She had been pregnant, so was easy to catch as she ran. 'The soldiers beat my belly with the guns until I lost my baby,' she told me. 'They told me to spread the message that all will be killed if we return.' She had been then allowed to leave, running from her village as the flames rose from the huts.

She had been used as an envoy of the most disturbing violence; this was something more planned than rape and robbery. The gunmen had shown no qualms in murdering others—shooting her would have been much quicker and simpler. Beating her to ensure forced abortion was part of a wider pattern of ethnic cleansing designed to drive people away for generations to come.

As old bush rebels, the leaders knew well it is all but impossible to defeat insurgents entrenched in the civilian population. So, they did what was once done to them: drove those civilians out, and destroyed those who remained. 'One comes to the terrifying conclusion, that if genocide was avoided, it might only have been down to disorganisation,' said one aid worker, who spent time across some of the worst war zones of Equatoria. 'It was not due to a lack of effort.'

The international community expressed concern, but statements on human rights abuses had little impact. Those leading the killings had learned from the past, for the names killed in the decades of atrocities in South Sudan had faded into the earth. Silence favours the powerful—why should this time be any different? In Juba, there were furious denials, with journalists accused of fabrication.

'I'm surprised you came,' Kiir said when he welcomed British aid minister Priti Patel on a visit to Juba in April 2017. 'The media says there's bodies at the airport.'

Days later, after Patel had left to visit refugees who had fled into Uganda, she named the massacres outright genocide.[31] Kiir named 2017 the 'year of peace and prosperity'.

* * *

South Sudan has become the basket case warning for lands wishing to split to become their own nation. In Khartoum, they pointed to the South to excuse their failure, as though it were somehow an ungovernable land where disaster had been inevitable. They were not to blame, Khartoum insisted, ignoring their role in the chaos to criticise Western arrogance for supporting separation when they had predicted collapse.

Washington, once so proud to boast of having 'helped midwife the birth of this new nation', watched its $10-billion-dollar investment go up in flames.[32] There was anger, as if they had been duped. 'South Sudan owes its existence to the United States,' the *Washington Post* wrote. 'South Sudan was supposed to break the sad, familiar African model of petty rivalries, corruption and oppression.'[33] Many were bitter, seeing it as a radical experiment, a miscarriage not a birth. 'South Sudan must rank among the most astounding failures in Africa,' the *New York Times* wrote in an editorial. 'What makes the South Sudan tragedy all the more astounding is that the country was initially hailed as a triumph of American foreign policy.'[34] The collapse provided a sober lesson on the limits of state-building plans. The supporters who had rallied behind the cause of independence now lined up to dismiss it, swift to absolve themselves of any guilt in failing to hold the leaders responsible while they had the chance.

For the chaos of South Sudan was not the result of freedom, but rather the result of how that independence was carried out. If the US was the midwife of a nation, then it was a naive but negligent one, providing money for the latest equipment but failing to check the heartbeat of the patient. The euphoria at claiming to 'birth' a nation led the international community down a dangerous path, where like extravagantly indulgent parents, they poured every resource in without proper care as to how it was spent. International donors turned a blind eye to the faults of the leaders they backed. Cash alone cannot create a country; in fact, given without criticism and oversight, it did the very opposite. Massive international support bolstered leaders unaccountable to the people, who treated the country as their personal fiefdom.

International donors have had their fingers badly burned, and when— cynics say, if—peace comes again, they will not rush in to rebuild as they did when the great war ended in 2005. In 2018 South Sudan was listed as worst in the world in the annual measurement of failed states, beating perennial war zones and pushing Somalia into second place to top the Fragile States Index. Even the butchery of Syria was deemed better.[35]

The world came to fix a land, but ended with a failed state. Yet it should not have been unexpected. It was the pattern seen in new nations before. The external fight for its borders had been won, but it still needed to work out who was in control of the country. Now, South Sudan is in a battle for its very existence.

* * *

Five years into the war, the country was in ruins. The situation had outstripped even the worst of predictions made when the fight began. More than a third of the entire population, some 4.5 million people, had been forced from their homes. Half of those had fled the country as refugees, some even running north back to Sudan, the land they had left only years before, finding the war zone of Darfur a better place to be. '*Malesh Bashir*,' one camp was called, 'Sorry, Bashir.' The numbers driven out were comparable to those who had fled the long war with Khartoum in the 1990s. It was the largest movement of refugees in Africa since the genocide in Rwanda in 1994.

Over a million fled south to Uganda. It attracted little attention outside the region; it was not seen as a problem that had wider political consequences outside of the South. Although the war spills over into the lands of its neighbours, refugees settle in squalid areas, the half-forgotten scrublands of northern Uganda, Kenya, Ethiopia and Sudan. Barely a handful are able to make the trek to knock on Europe's door for shelter.

One of several camps opened by the UN in northern Uganda was called Bidi Bidi. In early 2017, just six months after opening, it was declared full. With some 280,000 residents, the bush city had become the largest refugee camp in the world. The great majority were women and children; a whole new generation of lost boys and girls was being created.

Kiir brushed off the concerns, and spoke instead of holding elections in war, for South Sudan had never held a vote for its leaders since independence. He appeared indifferent to the suffering of the people he claimed to lead. 'The people who ran to Uganda were chased away by social media,' Kiir said in an interview, denying genocide. 'It is a conspiracy against the government.'[36]

Fuck this
dude

265

In April 2018, Kiir said he would not step down from power as part of any peace agreement. 'What is my incentive in bringing peace if it is peace that I will bring and then I step aside?' he said, looking to his old enemy in Khartoum as an example. 'Nobody can do it,' he said, 'Bashir did not do it when we were fighting with him.'[37] *He sort of did in 2005...*

* * *

It was a sleepy hot afternoon, and I shared a plate of rice and beans, laughing as old friends told stories. I'd driven to the outskirts of Juba to Eye Radio, which had been at the heart of the battle in July 2016. Then, soldiers had parked a tank at their gates, but the journalists continued broadcasting for all but the worst few hours, when the thunder of tanks firing shells shook the studio too much, and bullets ripping through the walls forced them to lie on the floor. Dead bodies had been scattered in the grass around the station. The reporters, trapped inside, spent their days calling politicians and generals in a bid to broadcast messages of peace. 'We will stand beside you, we will raise your hands,' the music ran over and over, as they played reggae star Emmanuel Kembe, singing for the unity of the South. 'We're going to the promised land.'

Now the newsroom was chaotic with people finalising reports, as the clock ticked to the next bulletin. It broadcast in eight languages, with its two-dozen staff coming from every corner of South Sudan. At one time, before their repeater stations were damaged in fighting, they broadcast to over a million people. The old fight against Khartoum the reporters called 'the wars of liberation'. The new fight within the South had another name. 'The war among ourselves,' the journalists called it.

The bullet holes in the wall were still visible in the plasterwork. During the fighting, the reporters had kept each other safe. Ayuen Panchol, the news editor, pushed aside his thin dreadlocks and pointed to the V-shaped scars on his forehead that marked him out as a Dinka from Bor. 'My number plates,' he grinned. They had allowed him to negotiate with the soldiers fighting outside, while inside, his friend Koang Pal Chang, the station manager and a Nuer, hid from the battle.

'We really messed up the country,' he said. 'It'll take a long, long time before we can recover.' He looked out towards the UN base, a short walk away, where thousands of the quarter of a million civilians stuck inside barbed wire camps for their own protection lived a life of limbo. Years into the war, there were few signs of them leaving. The plastic shelters were becoming permanent.

'They are building up a reservoir of hate that will take a long time to go. Even for my children, it will take for my daughters' daughters to find this country a better place,' Panchol said. 'If you are growing up here today? There will be bad things to come.'

15

FREEDOM NEXT TIME

'The domestic struggle over who 'owns' a new state does eventually come to an end—on *Taiwan? South Korea?* average, after 60 years.'

Andreas Wimmer[1]

It was still cool in the morning so soon after dawn, and a low mist hung amongst trees at the foot of the rocky hills. Later, the sun would be blazing fierce, but for now, the mothers and children huddled close to a thin fire to boil water and to warm themselves. They had travelled in the night, slipping through narrow footpaths in the wet, high grass, crossing from South Sudan into Uganda at first light. Now, just a few feet across the frontier, they sat on rocks in the dust waiting for the Ugandan border guards at the Madi Opei post to wake and tell them what to do next.

It was December 2017. The big men in suits had flown to Ethiopia and agreed a ceasefire deal, the latest in around a dozen. Like all those before, they broke it within hours.

People voted with their feet. Over two million had already fled South Sudan, but more kept coming every day. Uganda was the biggest destination, with over a million people arriving with little other than the clothes they wore. In the worst times, thousands crossed each day, at other periods, a handful of people snuck through the bush to escape. On this dawn, there was a tired group of about twenty people from the South, almost all women and young children.

'Food,' the tired lady said, looking up when I asked what she needed most, as she cradled her baby asleep in her arms. 'And medicine for my son.' She had run from fighting near her farm, two day's walk across the border into Eastern Equatoria. I asked what she was called, and she pulled out a plastic-covered scrap of blue paper, tatty around the edges. The document, the only identification she had, was her registration card for the 2011 referendum on South Sudan's independence. 'Joyce Otto,' she said, as I handed her card carefully back. She stared towards the border and the homeland she had been forced from. Then, with incredible sadness in her voice, she added one more need. 'We need shelter,' she said. 'We need a safe place to live.'

The group here planned to travel on to find family already settled in the refugee camps of northern Uganda. Bidi Bidi, one of several camps, was home to over a quarter of a million refugees from the South alone. Spread across the vast low woodlands, it took hours to drive across.

The Ugandan government had given each refugee a plot of poor quality scrubland, but it was enough to build a small hut, carve out a patch to plant crops, and start a future. Walking down the winding footpaths through the homesteads, cheeping chicks scattering like balls of fluff in front of my feet, it felt less like a refugee camp of crowded tents, and more like a never-ending village.

'We are building a new life,' said 18-year-old Vicky Akulu, who lived in a one-room hut with her 24-year-old sister. 'I wanted to be teacher, but I don't think I will get the opportunity, so I am farming.'

I sat on the swept floor as she held up her much-prized school uniform, a patched purple skirt, that she had fled in when the gunmen attacked her village of Pajok in April 2017, torching the homes. 'This is all we had,' she said. 'Nothing more.'

The dream of South Sudan soon faded. Those who have left are sceptical of peace, and will not return anytime soon. When the time is ready, if war ends, many will still not go back. They were settling here for the long term. With the great majority of refugees in the camp women and children, many are creating a new society amongst themselves.

'We have learned our lesson,' said Charity Datiro, a tough-built woman, digging weeds out of a patch of potatoes circled around her thatch hut in Bidi Bidi. 'It is not easy here, but we are safe, and we look out for each other.' I watched a young girl lead a blind man with a stick, meandering into the low scrub, kicking up puffs of dust with their feet.

Datiro, who escaped heavy fighting around the town of Yei, abandoning her food stall where she fried eggs rolled into flatbread chapattis, had grown up in northern Uganda during the war with Khartoum. Like her, many here had lived in the Ugandan camps when they ran from the wars of the 1980s and 1990s. They returned to the South with high hopes for the independence of their country. That failed, and now they were back. 'The problem was the fighting there by the men,' Datiro said. 'Women here just want to bring up their children in peace.'

* * *

The war grinds on. In May 2018, I crossed into rebel-held Upper Nile, where the people had set up a parallel bush government of sorts. In the palm-thatch hut market of Udier, as I drank coffee thick with ginger, the stalls refused payment in the Juba government's pounds, taking only Ethiopian and US banknotes. It still took a day to march to the frontline at Pagak, far enough away that the gunshots that shook my tent at night were to scare off roaring lions and not those of battle. At dawn, the only sounds were laughing children chasing cattle as they drove them out into the grasslands to graze.

Still, later in the day, dust drifted high as planes from the Red Cross brought those wounded in fighting to their field hospital. I watched from the shade of a tree at the side of the airstrip as the injured were carried off. Above me, the rebel government, now named the 'Sudan People's Liberation Army—In Opposition', had hammered a tattered banner into the tree trunk. 'You are highly welcome,' it read. 'SPLA-IO VIVA!'

The revolution is dead; long live the revolution.

* * *

The last time I visited the thick-walled fortress headquarters of the SPLA in Juba, the army's flag snapped in the wind from a pole, as dust devils whipped up the stinging sand from the parade ground. 'Victory Is Certain,' the motto on the flag read.

Except in this war, there can be no winner. Those in power will fight it out until they are left in control of the country, but after the final shot is fired, their triumph will be over ruins. Their strength was based on the support of the people, and that has now gone. The country is more ruined, more divided, more destroyed and far more desperate

271

than ever before, even than at the end of the great wars with the old enemy in Khartoum.

'South Sudan is a young country tragically devouring itself,' UN human rights experts wrote in a report to the Security Council, as the war slipped into its fifth year. They submitted a list of forty-one top commanders and politicians for potential prosecution for war crimes and crimes against humanity.[2] There were already over forty armed groups and rebels, more if you counted splinter factions, and the numbers were growing. 'It is clear to me, and I'm sorry to say so, but I've never seen a political elite with so little interest in the well-being of its own people,' UN chief António Guterres said.[3]

* * *

'We fear that our leaders do not know how to make peace,' said Archbishop Paulino Lukudo Loro in Juba's St. Theresa Cathedral, in a joint message from the South's bishops. 'They are military people who see the world through the lens of violence.'

The Church was about the only organisation left who could try to make people see sense. The bishops' message, to mark a day of prayer for peace backed by both the Pope and the Archbishop of Canterbury, was read in the church that Kiir prayed in. But the leaders had long stopped listening to even their own priests.[4]

'They fear peace,' Loro added. 'They are finishing their own people. They have called on their followers of whichever tribe to sacrifice for some gain, but what is the gain? The leaders are afraid to return to the people without anything to show, so they continue this senseless war because they do not know what to do. To continue fighting is easier for them, than to take the risk of making peace. They fear not only international justice. They fear what their own people will do to them when they fail. They have already failed.'

* * *

South Sudan faces the hardest of times ahead. The numbers in need continue to rise. In 2018, the highest ever number needed urgent aid: over seven million people, or two-thirds of the entire country. Despite condemnation of the famine in 2017, things had got worse; there was an increase of 40 percent needing critical aid from the year before. Tens of thousands remained in famine conditions and the government continued to use food blockades as a 'weapon of war.'[5] In June 2018, Kiir met Machar for the first time since chasing him to Congo with fighter jets two years earlier. Diplomatic hopes for peace lay on the two men one more time, and they embraced in an awkward hug in Ethiopia. Then, hosted by Bashir in Khartoum, the two men promised peace, again. Few believe things will be different soon. The vision of freedom remains as far away as ever. Most people are living a quiet catastrophe, surviving each day as an extraordinary win against the odds.

Activists have painted a mural on the streets of Juba. It shows a line of silhouette figures with feet that spread like a tree, and arms wielding axes high above their heads. They are bringing them down to chop the very roots that nourish them. '*Ana Taban*,' the painters have written in Arabic. 'We are tired.' Brother kills brother. Children fight children. Their greatest enemy has become themselves.

* * *

What hope is left? This is a history, not a foretelling of the future. Still, some predications are easy to make. That the war will worsen and hunger will grow. Famine will return, and the threat of genocide remains. People will continue to flee and the refugee camps will increase. There will be new rebel groups as forces fracture—and more killings. The country is broke, but there is still oil, and even when it has gone, the generals will beg, borrow, or steal more funds to buy new guns.

Regional nations will oblige, supporting one side or the other, as they play out their power rivalries by pulling the puppet-strings of leaders in the South for dominance. In return, they will strip out what resources are left. As populations grow and the land dries, Egypt and Sudan will covet the swamps of the Sudd again. As Ethiopia sucks out water from the Blue Nile after damming the flow, the White Nile of the South becomes ever more valuable. When the oil has been pumped out, the water will be next. The great forests of trees will be chopped for timber and charcoal, and the vast herds of wild animals will become a fading memory.

Extra peacekeepers will be promised, and some will come. Charities will call for more cash, and newspapers will talk of 'unspeakable atrocities'. Leaders will meet again, and diplomats will say that the time for words is over, and issue a statement warning of the threat of action. Generals will be sanctioned but, as in times before, they will be promoted not punished. Arms embargos have been issued, but the government will find it little challenge to circumvent them and resupply. The rebels will take the guns from them.

So, there will be a new push for peace, more rebels brought in to negotiations, another deal signed, and it will be broken. There will be talk of justice, and papers calling for holistic approaches and all the community to be involved in peace. Few, if any, will provide specifics as to how all that will be achieved. It is easy to point blame, far harder to find solutions that really work. Things have fallen apart so badly they cannot be simply put back together again. The longer it lasts, the slimmer the chance of peace becomes.

In time, the leadership must change, for all in the end will be accountable to their maker, if not to man. The fear is that the new leaders will be unable to change the course of conflict, and one war will be replaced with another. Commanders in combat rarely make good presidents in peace.

The big deals crumble. The solution for South Sudan can lie only with the South Sudanese themselves. Peace is made between person and person, community and community. It has, in the past, always been the way. The story of strength and survival is that of the ordinary people, not the people at the top. Despite the worst of horrors, people pick themselves up, they survive, and build again. In the face of so much loss, despite everything breaking down, in the midst of utter hell, life goes on. Amid the cruelty and the evil, there is also courage, compassion and love. War cannot destroy everything.

If I have seen a glimmer of hope in documenting the long history of chaos, it is that terrible times have ended before.

* * *

I think so often of how it could have been. Soon after independence in 2011, I packed up my room in Juba after three years there. I'd still return many times to visit, but I said a deeply sad farewell to my friends, to those who had shown such kindness, and to a village that had become a city, then a capital, and for me, a home. As I stuffed a bag, the dog that had adopted me ran in circles chasing geckos. The lizards scattered as I peeled a sun-faded map from the wall of my room. It was covered with pencil crosses and dates, tracking the years of battles I had followed all across the country. Reporters are rarely optimistic, for the nature of news means we seek out the most extreme misery. Yet at the bottom of the map, I read a faded quote I had scrawled there long before, and quite forgotten. It was part of a poem I once heard Seamus Heaney read:

> History says, Don't hope
> On this side of the grave.
> But then, once in a lifetime
> The longed-for tidal wave
> Of justice can rise up
> And hope and history rhyme.

Perhaps I was naive, but hope is not a bad thing. I was privileged to see South Sudan in the best of times, but I have witnessed the horror as well. I knew the challenges ahead. Still, as I recorded a farewell BBC broadcast under the mango tree in my sandy courtyard, I believed the visions of a people for their new nation could become real.

'There are more than enough international experts and advisors in South Sudan telling the country what to do and how to develop; it does not need a reporter to add their voice,' I spoke into my microphone, three days after independence. 'But I do have a dream—and that is to come back to visit South Sudan in years to come and see the change for the better; to watch the growth of a nation, a generation of children living in peace and going to school, under a government and an army that serves the people and is accountable to them.'

Back then, it was easier to be optimistic. Yet I still have that dream. As I write this, in a green garden in Kenya, the dry season approaches in Juba. I think of the heat of those days, the feeling of a parched throat during the long wait for the cool of the rains. I don't doubt that when the grass becomes thin and the cattle grow hungry, the bloody violence that escalates every year will occur again, this year, and in the years to come. Have we seen the worst of the war? Perhaps, but I fear not.

Yet I still have hope. The history of South Sudan has shown that the impossible can be achieved. All does not need to be lost. The struggle continues.

Ride to freedom, my friends.

NOTES

PREFACE

1. UN Security Council, 1 July 2015, Sanctions List, Marial Chanuong Yol Mangok.
2. South Sudan was ranked worst in the Fragile States Index in 2014, the annual report published by US-based Fund for Peace. In 2018, it remained at the bottom.
3. Key theories to understand the South's past rest on the nature of the political economy as a cause of conflict. The rentier political marketplace worked as long as there was cash in the system. Alex de Waal (2014) 'When Kleptocracy Becomes Insolvent: Brute Vauses of the Civil War in South Sudan', *African Affairs*, Vol. 113, No. 452 (1 July 2014). Cherry Leonardi (2013) *Dealing With Government in South Sudan: Histories of Chiefship, Community and State*, Woodbridge: James Currey. Edward Thomas (2015) *South Sudan—A Slow Liberation*, London: Zed.

1. JUST DIVORCED

1. In 2011, South Sudan had the highest maternal mortality rate in the world, at 2,054 per 100,000 live births, according to the UN. Under the Taliban, in 2000, the rate was 1,800 per 100,000 live births.
2. South Sudan Infrastructure Plan, 2012.
3. Three-fifths of main roads are impassable from June to October, the UN calculated in 2014.
4. R.C.R. Whalley (1932) 'Southern Sudan Game and its Habitat', *Sudan Notes and Records*, Vol. XV, Part II, pp. 261–7.
5. Ernest Hemingway (1999) *True at First Light*, New York: Scribner, p. 151.
6. John Ryle (1987) 'A War of Words among the Agar Dinka of Sudan, in' *Domestic Warfare: Essays in honour of Sir Michael Howard*, ed. M. James, Oxford: Eastbury.

7. Census figures estimate the Dinka to make up 35 percent of the people, and the Nuer, 15 percent.

8. A.J. Arkell (1961) *A History of the Sudan to 1821*, Oxford: Oxford University Press, pp. 2–3.

9. Francis M. Deng (1998) 'The Cow and the Thing Called "What": Dinka Cultural Perspectives on Wealth and Poverty', *Journal of International Affairs*, Vol. 52, No. 1 (Fall 1998), pp. 101–129.

10. The Bible, Isaiah, 18:1–2. South Sudanese often prefer American translations which refer to 'a nation tall and smooth, to a people feared near and far, a nation mighty and conquering.'

11. The Bible, Acts, 8:26–40. He is referred to as Ethiopian, then a general term for 'African', and appears to pre-date the conversion of Cornelius the Centurion.

12. The Bible, Genesis, 2:13.

13. There are more pyramids in Sudan than Egypt, but early archaeologists focused excavations on Cairo and Luxor. The Nubians have been eclipsed in popular history. On the Blue Nile, archaeologists have found Kushite remains at Sennar, 180 miles/300 kilometres south of Khartoum, but explorations on the White Nile have barely looked much beyond Khartoum. Derek Welsby, (1996) *The Kingdom of Kush: The Napatan and Meroitic Empires*, London: British Museum, pp. 8–9, William Yewdale Adams (1977) *Nubia, Corridor to Africa*, Princeton: Princeton University Press, pp. 297–315, also Khider Adam Eisa (2002) *Archaeological Discoveries along the East Bank of the White Nile, 1997–2000, Sudan & Nubia*, No. 6, Khartoum: The Sudan Archaeological Research Society, pp. 64–6.

14. The Kushite kingdoms converted to Christianity from around 300–400. An Arab army from Egypt invaded in 641, but was defeated. Arab traders and settlers arrived in following centuries, and by 1500, people slowly converted to Islam. Yusuf Faḍl Ḥasan (1967) 'Main Aspects of the Arab Migration to the Sudan', *Arabica*, Vol. 14, No. 1, pp. 14–31. Anders Breidlid, Avelino Androgo Said and Astrid Kristine Breidlid (2014) *A Concise History of South Sudan*, Kampala: Fountain Publishers, p. 20.

15. A handful of nations declared independence early on: Egypt in 1922, South Africa in 1910 (but true independence not until 1994), and Libya in 1951.

2. THE CATTLE PEN COMMANDERS

1. Rudolf Carl Slatin (1903) *Fire and Sword in the Sudan: A Personal Narrative of Fighting and Serving the Dervishes 1879–1895*, London: E. Arnold, p. 333.

2. According to oral tradition, the Dinka and Nuer left central Sudan for Bahr el Ghazal between 1400 to 1700 in several waves. Breidlid et al. (2014), p. 64.

3. The snow-capped Rwenzori between Uganda and Congo, far south of the map's suggestion, are also dubbed the Mountains of the Moon—a source of the Nile as geographer Ptolemy suggested in the second century AD.

4. Sir Ernest Wallis Budge (1907) *The Egyptian Sudan*, Vol. II, London, p. 172.

5. L. P. Kirwan (1957) 'Rome Beyond The Southern Egyptian Frontier', *The Geographical Journal*, Vol. 123, No. 1, pp. 13–19.

6. Egyptian Pharaoh Ptolemy III (246–222 BC) is said to have established an 'elephant-port' on Sudan's Red Sea coast. Musawwarat es-Sufra, a 3rd century BC site north of Khartoum, contains sculptures of elephants, including a relief showing a king riding one. The Romans and Carthaginians most likely used the now extinct North African elephant for battle—but not exclusively. Contrary to popular belief, African elephants are possible to train; Belgium did so in Congo in the 19th century. Adams (1977), pp. 297–315.

7. The Ottoman viceroy of Egypt, Muhammad Ali, sent the animals as part of his 'giraffe diplomacy'. Heather J. Sharkey (2015) 'La Belle Africaine: The Sudanese Giraffe who went to France', *Canadian Journal of African Studies*, Vol. 49, No. 1, pp. 39–65.

8. Samuel White Baker (1888) *The Albert N'Yanza, Great Basin of the Nile, And Explorations of the Nile Sources*, London: Macmillan, pp. 24.

9. Letter from Ali to Sudan commander, 1823, quoted by Richard Hill (1959) *Egypt in the Sudan, 1820–1881*, Oxford: Oxford University Press, p. 13.

10. Paul Lane and Douglas Johnson (2009) 'The Archaeology and History of Slavery in South Sudan in the Nineteenth Century', in *The Frontiers of the Ottoman World*, ed. A.C.S. Peacock, London: British Academy, p. 515.

11. Ferdinand Werne (1849) *Expedition to Discover the Sources of the White Nile, In the Years 1840–1841*, trans. by Charles William O'Reilly, Volume One, London: Bentley, pp. 163–4.

12. Ibid., pp. 99–102.

13. Slavery in Sudan can be traced back for centuries. A 652 AD treaty between Egypt and the Christian kingdom of Nubia (now north Sudan) set down details of slave payments, possibly as part of a trade deal. Douglas Johnson (2007) *Root Causes of Sudan's Civil Wars*, Woodbridge: James Currey, pp. 2–3.

14. Werne, p. 122.

15. Ibid., pp. 7–8.
16. Richard O. Collins (2008) *A History of Modern Sudan*, Cambridge: Cambridge University Press, p. 16. Italian explorer Romolo Gessi, later appointed as Governor of Bahr el Ghazal, believed numbers were as high as 28,000 a year. Romolo Gessi Pasha (1892) *Seven Years in the Soudan: Being a Record of Explorations, Adventures, and Campaigns Against the Arab Slave Hunters*, London: Samson Low, p. 2.
17. Baker (1888), p. 11.
18. Ibid., pp. 12–14.
19. Salim Wilson (1901) *Jehovah-Nissi: The Life-story of Hatashil-Masha-Kathish, of the Dinka tribe, Soudan*, Birmingham, pp. 27–8.
20. Slatin, pp. 337–9.
21. Baker (1888), pp. 12–14.
22. Baker (1888), p. 234. Baker calls him Commoro.
23. Lane and Johnson (2009), pp. 509–537.
24. Baker (1888), p. 5.
25. Wilhelm Junker (1890) *Travels in Africa During the Years 1875–1878*, London: Chapman, p. 373. More on Malzac can be found in: Richard Hill (1967) *A Biographical Dictionary of the Sudan*, London: Cass, p. 229; Reda Mowafi (1981) *Slavery, Slave Trade and Abolition Attempts in Egypt and the Sudan 1820–1882*, Malmö: Lund Studies in International History, pp. 48–50, and Robert Joost Willink (2011) *The Fateful Journey: The Expedition of Alexine Tinne and Theodor von Heuglin in Sudan (1863–1864)*, Amsterdam: Amsterdam University Press; John Humphries (2013) *Search for the Nile's Source: The Ruined Reputation of John Petherick, Nineteenth-Century Welsh Explorer*, Cardiff: University of Wales Press, p. 142.
26. Wilson (1901), pp. 28–36.
27. Kathish was abducted in the 1870s. Douglas Johnson (1991) 'Salim Wilson: The Black Evangelist of the North', *Journal of Religion in Africa*, Vol. 21, No. 1, pp. 26–32.
28. Makuei was interviewed in 1973, when he was in his nineties. Francis M. Deng (1995) *War of Visions: Conflict of Identities in the Sudan*, Washington: The Brookings Institution, pp. 73–4.
29. Slatin, pp. 337–9.
30. Napoleon III hoped the 450 Sudanese—from Darfur, Nuba and the South—would cope better with tropical conditions. From 1863–67 they fought France's Mexican wars before returning home. Some later served at Gondokoro trying to stop slavery, others died fighting in the siege of Khartoum. R. Kirk (1941) *The Sudanese in Mexico, Sudan Notes and Records*, Vol. XXIV, Part I, Khartoum (1941), pp. 113–30, and Richard Hill and Peter Hogg (1995) *A Black Corps d'Elite: An Egyptian*

Sudanese Conscript Battalion with the French Army in Mexico, 1863–1867, East Lansing: Michigan State University Press.

31. Sudanese formed the core of Britain's colonial King's African Rifles, helping in the takeover of today's Kenya and Uganda, supporting Germany in Tanganyika (Tanzania), and helping to expand the Belgian Congo. Britain gave the soldiers land in Nairobi they called *Kibra*, 'forest' in Sudanese Arabic, and now the slum of Kibera. Douglas Johnson (2009), 'Tribe or Nationality? The Sudanese diaspora and the Kenyan Nubis', *Journal of Eastern African Studies*, Vol. 3. No. 1 (March 2009), pp. 112–31.
32. Baker (1888), p. 61.
33. Edward Thomas (2015) *South Sudan—A Slow Liberation*, London: Zed Books, p. 57.
34. Baker (1888), pp. 60–62.
35. Elias Toniolo, Richard Leslie Hill (1974) *The Opening of the Nile Basin: Writings by Members of the Catholic Mission to Central Africa on the Geography and Ethnography of the Sudan, 1842–1881*, London: Hurst.
36. Diary notes, quoted by Father Guido Oliana (2014) *Father Angelo Vinco: The Pioneering Missionary of Gondokoro*, Juba: Comboni Missionaries.
37. 'Want of employment, I heard, was the chief operative cause in killing the poor missionaries; for, with no other resource left them to kill time, they spent their days eating, drinking, smoking, and sleeping.' John Hanning Speke (1863) *The Discovery of the Source of the Nile*, Edinburgh: Blackwood, pp. 605–6.
38. Slatin, pp. 338–9.
39. J.A.R. Reid (1937) *The Death of Gordon, Sudan Notes and Records*, Vol. XX, Part 1, pp. 72–3.
40. British army major Edmund Musgrave Barttelot was himself killed by Congolese villagers in revenge. Adam Hochschild (1998) *King Leopold's Ghost*, New York: Houghton Mifflin, p. 98.
41. Henry Morton Stanley (1890) *In Darkest Africa: or, The Quest, Rescue and Retreat of Emin, Governor of Equatoria*, New York: Scribner.
42. Winston Churchill (1930) *Roving Commission: My Early Life*, New York: Charles Scribner, pp. 185–93.
43. Kitchener's reported taking of the skull sparked outrage in London, and it was later buried. Churchill (1930), pp. 228–9.
44. Winston Churchill (1899) *The River War: An Account of the Reconquest of the Sudan*, London: Longman, p. 301.
45. Ibid., p. 311.
46. Sir H.W. Jackson (1920) *Fashoda, 1898, Sudan Notes and Records*, Volume 3, No. 1, pp. 3–9.
47. M.W. Daly, 'Omdurman and Fashoda, 1898: Edited and Annotated

Letters of F.R. Wingate', *British Society for Middle Eastern Studies*, Vol. 10, No. 1 (1983), pp. 21–37.

48. *Punch*, 8 October, 1898, London.

49. In Britain, the Fashoda Incident earned the questionable accolade of being dubbed the 'Pagoda Incident', in the 1930 schoolboy spoof by W.C. Sellar and R.J. Yeatman, *1066 and All That: A Memorable History of England*, and 'remarkable as being the only (memorable) Incident in History'.

50. H. Lincoln Tangye (1910) *In the Torrid Sudan*, London: John Murray, pp. 174–5.

51. Richard Owen (2016) *Sudan Days 1926–1954: A Memoir*, Durham: Matador, p. 169.

3. THE BOG BARONS

1. Quoted by Douglas Johnson, in John Ryle and Justin Willis (2012) *The Sudan Handbook*, London: Rift Valley Institute, p. 122.

2. Sir James Robertson (1974) *Transition in Africa: From Rule to Independence*, London: Hurst, p. 7.

3. H.C. Jackson (1954) *Sudan Days and Ways*, London, p. viii.

4. J.A. Mangan (1982) 'The Education of an Elite Imperial Administration: The Sudan Political Service and the British and the British Public School System', *The International Journal of African Historical Studies*, Vol. 15, No. 4, pp. 671–99.

5. Jackson (1954), p. 15.

6. Philip Bowcock (2016) *Last Guardians: Crown Service in Sudan, Northern Rhodesia and Britain*, London: The Radcliffe Press, p. 110.

7. Richard Wyndham (1936) *The Gentle Savage, A Sudanese Journey in the Province of Bahr-el-Ghazal*, London: Cassell, p. 5.

8. E.H. Nightingale (1994) *Memoirs (Unpublished)*. Nightingale was posted to Blue Nile in 1927. 'One of my tasks in those days was issuing 'freedom papers' to anyone who asked for one,' Nightingale wrote. 'Domestic slavery was common and most slaves were treated more or less as members of the family, but they had the right to demand their freedom and be given a certificate to prove that they were free.'

9. Robertson (1974), p. 104.

10. Edward Thomas (2010) *The Kafia Kingi Enclave: Politics and History in the North-South Boundary of Western Sudan*, London: Rift Valley Institute, p. 14.

11. Letter from Raja District Commissioner 1935, quoted in Thomas (2010), p. 68.

12. Chauncey Stigand (1914) *Administration in Tropical Africa*, London: Constable, p. 40.

13. *Report of the Commission of Inquiry into the Disturbances in the Southern Sudan during August 1955*, Khartoum: McCorquodale, p. 81.

14. By 1953, roughly a quarter of schools were in the South (593 of a total 1,944) but the standards were far lower: 80 percent were the most basic schools. In the North, 97,510 pupils went to government-run schools. In the South, there were only 3,046. *Sudan Almanac* (1953), Sudan Government, Khartoum: McCorquodale, pp. 116–17.

15. Stigand, p. 40.

16. Douglas Johnson (2016) *South Sudan: A New History for a New Nation*, Athens, OH: Ohio University Press, p. 104.

17. V.H. Fergusson (1930) *The story of Fergie Bey; told by himself and some of his friends*, London: Macmillan, p. 221.

18. David Omissi (1990) *Air Power and Colonial Control: The Royal Air Force, 1919–1939*, Manchester: Manchester University Press, p. 88.

19. The great mound of Weideang near Waat in Jonglei was built by the Nuer prophet Ngundeng in the late 19th century and added to by his son Gwek. British officer Percy Coriat, who helped demolish it and kill Gwek, said it was as high as an oak tree, with sides almost too steep to scramble up without a rope. Today, only a low hill remains. Percy Coriat (1939), *Gwek, The Witchdoctor and the Pyramid of Denkgur, Sudan Notes and Records*, Vol. XXII, Part II, Khartoum, pp. 224–6.

20. Lazarus Leek Mawut (1983) *Dinka Resistance to Condominium Rule, 1902–1932*, Khartoum: University of Khartoum, p. 53.

21. E.E. Evans-Pritchard (1986) *Strangers Abroad: Strange Beliefs*, London: Central Television.

22. Richard Lyth, Private Diaries, Boma, 1944.

23. Francis M. Deng and M.W. Daly (1989), *Bonds of Silk: The Human Factor in the British Administration of the Sudan*, Ann Arbor: Michigan State University Press, p. 120.

24. Alexander Maitland (2007) *Wilfred Thesiger: The Life of the Great Explorer*, London: Harper Perennial, p. 123.

25. Ibid., pp. 175–8.

26. Philip Bowcock (2016) *Last Guardians, Crown Service in Sudan, Northern Rhodesia and Britain*, London: Radcliffe, p. 127.

27. Hylton Cleaver (1957) *A History of Rowing*, London: Herbert Jenkins, p. 110.

28. H.M. Kirk-Greene (1982) 'The Sudan Political Service: A Profile in the Sociology of Imperialism', *The International Journal of African Historical Studies*, Vol. 15, No. 1 (1982), Boston, p. 32.

29. *Sudan Almanac* (1953), Sudan Government, Khartoum: McCorquodale, p. 193.

30. Nightingale (1994).

31. Radclyffe Dugmore (1924) *The Vast Sudan*, Bristol: Arrowsmith, pp. 116–17.

32. J.M. Pett and Geoffrey Pett (2015) *White Water Landings*, London: Blurb.

33. Richard Owen (2016), *Sudan Days 1926–1954: A Memoir*, Leicester: Matador, p. 116–17.

34. Robert Collins (1972) 'The Sudan Political Service: A Portrait of the "Imperialists"', *African Affairs*, Vol. 71, No. 284, Oxford: Oxford University Press, p. 300.

35. Robert Collins (1983) *Shadows in the Grass, Britain in the Southern Sudan, 1898–1956*, New Haven: Yale University Press, p. 263.

36. Francis M. Deng, 'In the Eyes of the Ruled', in Robert O. Collins and Francis M. Deng (1984) *The British in the Sudan, 1898–1956*, London: Macmillan, p. 217.

37. Jacob J. Akol (2016) *Long Way to Tipperary: the Story of a 'Lost' Sudanese Boy of the 60s*, published by the author.

38. H.C. Jackson (1954) *The Fighting Sudanese*, London: Macmillan, p. 83.

39. J.S.R. Duncan (1952) *The Sudan: A Record of Achievement*, Edinburgh: Blackwood, p. 183.

40. Report of the Abyssinian Campaigns, quoted by Jackson (1954), p. 83.

41. An Italian force of some 10,000 men attacked from Eritrea at Kassala, facing 600 Sudanese with a handful of machine guns. The battle lasted 12 hours.

42. *Foreign Relations of the United States Diplomatic Papers*, 1940, General and Europe, Volume II, 348 Z.1123.

43. Jackson (1954), p. 66.

44. Collins (1983), p. 396.

45. After hearing news that Italy had entered the war, Thesiger and Laurie did 'a savage war dance' and then opened fire in the direction of Ethiopia. 'We never got a reprimand for our precipitate action, and it has always given me satisfaction I fired the first shots in the Abyssinian campaign,' Thesiger wrote. Maitland (2007), p. 202.

46. Alban, who had won a DFC and a Belgian Croix de Guerre in France in 1918, led soldiers from Akobo into Ethiopia, destroying two Italian outposts. Khartoum officials said that 'like two schoolboys they had rushed out to tackle the post that annoyed them'. Details of the attack are otherwise scant. ('He didn't say much about the war, except to say that he needed the whisky to get through,' Alban's son David told me.) Collins (1983), p. 396; Charles Partee (2000) *An Adventure in Africa: the story of Don McClure*, University Press of America. p. 175.

47. Clifford Geertz (1988) *Works and Lives: The Anthropologist as Author*, Stanford: Stanford University Press, p. 58.

48. Lyth, March 1944, trekking to Kapoeta. Also see Jon Arensen (2013) *The Red Pelican: Life on Africa's Last Frontier*, Old Africa Books. Dick Lyth later joined the church, becoming a bishop in Uganda during Idi Amin's rule. 'Bishop, you're the only man who I allow to stand behind me because I know you won't shoot me,' the bloodthirsty dictator once told him, unaware of his sharpshooting war years.

49. Report of the Abyssinian Campaigns, quoted by Jackson (1954), p. 84.

50. Robertson (1974), p. 110.

51. David Sconyers (1987) 'Servant or Saboteur? The Sudan Political Service during the Crucial Decade: 1946–1956, *Bulletin*', *British Society for Middle Eastern Studies*, Vol. 14, No. 1, p. 7.

52. 'Southern Sudan, 27 April–28 May 1947, Minutes by DMH Riches and DW Lascelles', in Douglas Johnson ed. (1988) *Sudan, The British Documents on the End of Empire Project*, Series B Volume 5, Part I, 1942–1950, London: The Stationery Office, p. 260.

53. Nightingale (1994).

4. A POSTMAN AND AN ARROW

1. CIA, November–December 1954, 'Anticipated Dissension/Susceptibility to Communist Influence', p. 1.

2. Recommendations by J.W. Robertson on the first report of the Sudan Administration 29 July 1947, from Sudan, *The British Documents on the End of Empire Project*, Part I, p. 265.

3. Sir James Robertson (1953) 'The Sudan in Transition', *African Affairs*, Vol. 52, No. 209, p. 326.

4. Proceedings of the Juba Conference on the Political Development of the Southern Sudan, June 1947.

5. Fr. Dellagiacoma (1990) *How a Slave became a Minister: Autobiography of Sayyed Stanislaus Abdallahi Paysama*, Khartoum, quoted by Douglas Johnson (2014) *Federalism in the History of South Sudanese Political Thought*, London: Rift Valley Institute, p. 7.

6. Recommendations by J.W. Robertson on the first report of the Sudan Administration 29 July 1947, from Sudan, *The British Documents on the End of Empire Project*, Part I, p. 265.

7. Severino Fulli Boki Tombe Ga'le (2002) *Shaping a Free Southern Sudan, Memoirs of our Struggle 1934–1985*, Loa: Loa Catholic Mission Council, p. 144.

8. November 1952 Telegram, Yosa Wawa (2008) *Southern Sudanese Pursuits of Self-determination: Documents in Political History*, Kampala: Marianum, p. 81.

9. Prime Minister's Personal Minute, 29 March 1953, to Secretary of State

for Foreign Affairs. Private Papers of Sir Anthony Eden, FO 800/827, 1951–1952, The National Archives, Kew, p. 16.

10. House of Commons, Hansard, 'Sudan (Anglo-Egyptian Agreement)', HC Deb, 12 February 1953, Vol. 511.

11. Douglas Johnson (2014) *Federalism in the History of South Sudanese Political Thought*, London: Rift Valley Institute (RVI), p. 10.

12. Letter from Benjamin Lwoki, 15 November 1954, to British Foreign Minister Sir A. Eden et al., reporting resolutions of the Juba Conference, from Sudan, *The British Documents on the End of Empire Project*, Part II, p. 384–5.

13. *Report of the Commission of Inquiry into the Disturbances in the Southern Sudan during August 1955*, Khartoum: McCorquodale, p. 27.

14. The report is succinct in his failure. 'On 6th August 1955 at Torit, Wakil Buluk Amin (Deputy Company Quartermaster Sergeant) Saturlino shot an arrow at a Northern Assistant Post Master. The arrow missed the Assistant Post Master and injured a Southern soldier instead. During the investigation he confessed that the person whom he was really after was Acting O/C (Officer in Charge) of the Southern Corps, Kaimakam Taher Bey Abdel Rahman.' Ibid., p. 25.

15. Ibid., p. 29.

16. Ibid., p. 34–6.

17. Ibid., p. 35–6.

18. Ibid., p. 50–56.

19. Ibid., p. 56.

20. Ibid., p. 54.

21. Ibid., p. 42.

22. Telegram from Sir Knox Helm to Foreign Office, 28 August 1955, in Sudan, *The British Documents on the End of Empire Project*, Part II, p. 452.

23. Telegram from Churchill to Foreign Secretary Anthony Eden on negotiations with Egypt concerning Sudan, 15 January 1953. Private Papers of Sir Anthony Eden, FO 800/827, 1951–1952, The National Archives, Kew, p. 4.

24. Telegram from Sir Knox Helm to Foreign Office, 28 August 1955 from Sudan, *The British Documents on the End of Empire Project*, Part II, p. 452–3.

25. CIA (1955) 'Comment on Mutiny in Southern Sudan', 21 August 1955, p. 7.

26. Hilary Hook (1987) *Home from the Hill*, The Sportsman's Press, p. 122–3.

27. Ranald Boyle, 'The Great Betrayal', *Daily Mail*, September 1998.

28. Richard Owen (2016), *Sudan Days 1926–1954: A Memoir*, Leicester: Matador, p. 234.

29. Øystein H. Rolandsen (2011) 'A False Start: Between War and Peace

in the Southern Sudan, 1956–62', *The Journal of African History*, Volume 52, No. 1, p. 111.

30. Telegram from Sir Knox Helm to Foreign Office, 28 August 1955 from Sudan, *The British Documents on the End of Empire Project*, Part II, pp. 452–3.

31. Monani Alison Magaya (2014) *The Anya-Nya Movement in South Sudan*, Kampala: Marianum, p. 4.

32. John Howell (1973) 'Politics in the Southern Sudan', *African Affairs*, Vol. 72, No. 287 (1973), p. 165.

33. Kuyok Abol Kuyok reports he was executed; Kuyok Abol Kuyok (2015) *South Sudan: The Notable Firsts*, Bloomington: Author House, p. 34. However, Arop Madut-Arop writes that Oboya escaped, joined the Anya-Nya and refused to be absorbed into the army in the 1972 peace deal. He rejoined battle in 1983 and 'rose to be a commander and died in action fighting in his home area of Acholi land sometime in 1986'. Arop Madut-Arop (2012) *The Genesis of Political Consciousness in South Sudan*, p. 52.

34. Rolandsen p. 108.

35. Notes from Douglas Johnson.

36. Jacob Jiel Akol (2016) *Long Way to Tipperary: The Story of a 'Lost' Sudanese Boy of the Sixties*, published by the author.

37. 'The war we are ending today first broke out in Torit on 18 August 1955,' John Garang said at the signing of the 2005 Comprehensive Peace Agreement.

5. THE VENOM REBELLION

1. 'Sudan African National Union (SANU) newsletter', *Voice of Southern Sudan* (1963), Vol. 1 No. 3, p. 15. Hilaire Belloc's 1898 pithy summary of imperial conquest was also penned about Sudan after the battle of Omdurman: 'Whatever happens, we have got, the Maxim gun, and they have not.'

2. Jacob Jiel Akol (2016) *Long Way to Tipperary: The Story of a 'Lost' Sudanese Boy of the Sixties*, published by the author.

3. *Voice of Southern Sudan* (1964), Vol. 2, No. 1, p. 3.

4. Joseph Oduho and William Deng (1963) *The Problem of the Southern Sudan*, Oxford: Oxford University Press, pp. 53–60.

5. *Voice of Southern Sudan* (1963), Vol. 1 No. 3, p. ii.

6. Poison was also used from tree roots. Samuel Baker treated a man shot in the leg with a poison arrow in 1863 by the Bari people, around modern-day Juba. 'The entire foot had been eaten away by the action of the poison. The bone rotted through just above the ankle, and the

foot dropped off,' he wrote. 'Fortunately, the natives are bad archers.' Baker (1886).

7. Joseph Lagu (2006) *Sudan, Odysseys Through a State: From Ruin to Hope*, Omdurman: Omdurman Ahlia University, p. 111.
8. Madut-Arop, (2012), p. 105.
9. Song recorded by Jean-Francois Chauvel in *Le Figaro*, December 1965, in Storrs McCall, Unpublished Manuscript on the History of the First Civil War in South Sudan, Sudan Open Archive. p. 123.
10. Mike Hoare (1967) *Mercenary*, London: Corgi, p. 175.
11. Richard Holm (2007) *Plane Crash, Rescue, and Recovery, A Close Call in Africa*, CIA, Langley: Center for the Study of Intelligence, p. 2.
12. As many as 120 Cubans fought under CIA orders in Congo, according to Frank R. Villafaña (2009) *Cold War in the Congo: The Confrontation of Cuban Military Forces, 1960–1967*, Piscataway: Transaction Publishers, p. 14.
13. Hank Tester, 'Exiled Cuban Pilots Remember the Congo War', *NBC Miami*, 29 July, 2011.
14. Magaya (2014), p. 37.
15. Che Guevara (2000) *The African Dream, The Diaries of the Revolutionary War in the Congo*, New York: Gove Press.
16. 'SANU newsletter', *Voice of Southern Sudan*, Vol. 1 No. 4 (1963), p. 3.
17. Madut-Arop (2012), p. 127.
18. Testimony of Father Santino Locatelli, quoted in Scopas Poggo (2009) *The First Sudanese Civil War: Africans, Arabs, and Israelis in the Southern Sudan, 1955–1972*, New York: Macmillan, p. 79.
19. 'SANU newsletter', *Voice of Southern Sudan*, Vol. 3, No. 2 (1965), p. 10.
20. Abel Alier, later appointed Vice President, said the massacres were 'authorised' by Khartoum. Abel Alier (1990) *Southern Sudan, Too Many Agreements Dishonoured*, Oxford: Ithaca Press, p. 47.
21. Poggo (2009), p. 84, and Robert Collins (2008) *A History of Modern Sudan*, Cambridge: Cambridge University Press, p. 86.
22. South Sudanese at Khartoum University letter, 14 July 1965, Wawa (2008), pp. 219–20.
23. Neither British planes or US helicopters were meant to be in combat, but rebels said they were used as bombers and gunships against them: 'Sudan helped by RAF pilots', *The Observer*, 21 January 1965, London; 'SANU newsletter', *Voice of Southern Sudan*, Vol. 2, No. 2 (July 1964), p. 15.
24. 'SANU newsletter', *Voice of Southern Sudan*, Vol. 1 No. 3, p. 19; Vol. 1 No. 4, p. 14.

6. TARZAN AND THE ZEBRA BUS

1. Anya-Nya newsletter, No. 4, June 1971.
2. Zvi Zamir, quoted in David Ben-Uziel (2016) *A Mossad Agent in Southern Sudan, 1969–1971: An Operational Log*, Tel Aviv: Ravgon, p. 8.
3. Magaya (2014), p. 71.
4. Allan Reed, 'First Tuesday: The Secret War in the Sudan', *NBC News* (1971).
5. Allan Reed, 'The Anya-Nya: Ten months' travel with its forces inside the southern Sudan', *Munger Africana Library Notes*, Vol. 11 (February 1972), California Institute of Technology, Pasadena, p. 13.
6. Yossi Alpher (2015) *Periphery: Israel's Search for Middle East Allies*, Lanham: Rowman and Littlefield, p. 34.
7. Alpher (2015), p. 36.
8. 'The Anya-Nya Struggle: Background and Objectives', South Sudan Resistance Movement (1971/2).
9. Letter from Lagu to Kaunda, in Wawa (2008), p. 243–5.
10. By 1971, the USSR 'were overwhelmingly the largest military aid supply' to Khartoum, according to the CIA, providing small arms, tanks, artillery, MiG-21 fighter jets and Mi-8 helicopter gunships. CIA, August 1971, Soviet Economic and Military Presence in the Sudan.
11. Kenya's Minister for Agriculture, Bruce Mackenzie, was Mossad's link, later providing information for Israel's 1976 Entebbe raid in Uganda. Two years later, Idi Amin blew Mackenzie up with a gift of a time bomb stuffed inside a mounted lion's head.
12. Hoare (1967), p. 312.
13. 'The Sudan: The Armed Missionary', *Time*, 22 November 1971.
14. Stanley Meisler, '20-Year Sentence in Sudan Ends Wars for a Soldier of Fortune', *The Times*, 10 November 1971.
15. Frederick Forsyth (1974) *The Dogs of War*, London: Hutchinson Random House, p. 105.
16. Forsyth (1974), p. 20.
17. Fola Oyewole (1975) 'Scientists and Mercenaries', *Transition*, No. 48, Indiana University Press, Hutchins Center for African and African American Research. p. 59–65. Forsyth said most mercenaries were 'little more than thugs in uniform' with limited impact. Frederick Forsyth (1977) *Biafra Story: The Making of an African Legend*, London: Penguin, pp. 112–13.
18. Reed (1972), pp. 23–4.
19. Steiner, in a statement under duress to the Ugandan government after arrest in October 1970, said he was delivering medical supplies from the Verona Fathers in Italy. An eyewitness said he was training rebel

forces. Mohamed Omer Beshir (1975) *The Southern Sudan—From Conflict to Peace*, Khartoum: The Khartoum Bookshop, p. 94.

20. The story of the mortar was told by his former recruit, Kerubino Kuanyin Bol, to journalist Till Lincke in 1984.

21. David Robison, 'War on the Nile', *The Observer*, 7 March, 1971, p. 42.

22. Steiner rejects an apparent autobiography as a 'fable', written by Yves-Guy Berges (1978) *The Last Adventurer: from Biafra to Sudan*, London: Weidenfeld and Nicolson.

23. *Voice of Southern Sudan*, No. 5 (May 15, 1969), p. 1.

24. 'Rebels of South Sudan', *The Associated Press*, 1972.

25. Reed (1972), p. 23.

26. 'West German Mercenary Rolf Steiner on Trial', Reuters, Sudan, 3 August, 1971.

27. *Hamburger Abendblatt* newspaper, quoted by Ulli Kulke (2013), 'Rolf Steiner, ein Welt-Krieger in eigener Mission', *Die Welt*, 11 October 2013.

28. 'Sudan: Nimeiri's Problems', CIA, 30 July 1971, No.0381/71.

29. Yossi Alpher, Speech to The Brookings Institution, 2015, Washington, p. 15.

30. Alier (1990), p. 117.

31. Joseph Lagu (1994) 'The struggle for justice without hatred', Speech in Yaounde, Cameroon to the conference 'For a New Africa', p. 3.

32. John Garang (1972) Letter to The Commander in Chief Anyanya National Armed Forces, 24 January 1972.

7. THE MEN TOO TALL FOR TANKS

1. Ryszard Kapuściński (2001) *The Shadow of the Sun*, London: Penguin, p. 197.

2. John Akec (2014) *We Have Lived Too Long to Be Deceived: South Sudanese Discuss the Lessons of Historic Peace Agreements*, London: Rift Valley Institute, p. 8.

3. Nicki Kindersley, 'Subject(s) to control: post-war return migration and state-building in 1970s South Sudan', *Journal of Eastern African Studies*, Vol. 11, No. 2 (2017).

4. CIA Memorandum, 'Peace and Conflict in Sudanic Africa', 19 May 1972.

5. Jack G. Kaikati, 'The Economy of Sudan: A Potential Breadbasket of the Arab World?', *International Journal of Middle East Studies*, Vol. 11, No. 1 (1980), pp. 99–123.

6. South Sudan's eastern Boma plateau is an extension of Ethiopia's south-western highlands. Colonial-era botanists recorded wild *Coffea arabica*

plants reproducing without human help in Boma. 'The proximity of Boma to the parental species (Arabica coffee is a natural hybrid), namely *Coffea canephora* and *Coffea eugenioides*, perhaps makes this area a better candidate for the origin of Arabica, compared to Ethiopia, but no one knows for sure,' said coffee specialist Dr. Aaron Davis from the Royal Botanic Gardens at Kew. Coffee spread from Ethiopia to Yemen, and from there to the rest of the world. Also A.S. Thomas (1942) 'The Wild Arabica Coffee on the Boma plateau of Anglo-Egyptian Sudan', *Journal of Experimental Agriculture*, Vol. 10, pp. 207–212.

7. Malte Sommerlatte, head of the Wildlife Unit at the University of Juba in 1970.

8. CIA, 'The Outlook for Sudan', 16 November 1983.

9. Between 1977–1981, the US provided $342 million in military aid to Sudan, four times more than Kenya, the second biggest recipient in sub-Saharan Africa. CIA, 'US Assistance to Strategically Situated Countries', 1982.

10. Alier (1990), pp. 237–9.

11. A total of 260 kilometres (160 miles) out of 360 km was completed. Paul Howell and Michael Lock (1988) *The Jonglei Canal: Impact and Opportunity*, Cambridge: Cambridge University Press.

12. Joseph Lagu (2006) *Sudan, Odyssey Through a State: From Ruin to Hope*, Omdurman: Omdurman Ahlia University, p. 314.

13. John Garang (1981) 'Identifying, selecting, and implementing rural development strategies for socio-economic development in the Jonglei Projects Area, Southern Region, Sudan, Retrospective Theses and Dissertations', Paper 7413, Iowa State University p. 53.

14. Francis M. Deng (2009) *The Man called Deng Majok: A Biography of Power, Polygyny, and Change*, Asmara: Red Sea Press, p. 317.

15. Oswald Iten (1982) 'Jäger under frevler im Südsudan', *Neue Zürcher Zeitung (NZZ)*, 18 December 1982, pp. 65–8.

16. Arop Madut-Arop (2006) *Sudan's Painful Road to Peace*, Booksurge, p. 47.

17. While some claim plans for rebellion were well advanced, others argue the violence was spontaneous. Peter Adwok Nyaba (2000) *The Politics of Liberation in South Sudan*, Kampala: Fountain, pp. 28–30.

18. Brian D'Silva, Speech at Iowa State University, 2002.

19. Abel Alier met Garang in Bor as fighting broke out. Garang said he was driving north to his home village outside Bor to join his wife and two young children. 'I told him it was risky for him to leave, sandwiched between the retreating and occupying forces,' Alier said. 'He said, with surprising calmness that he would be safe. I never saw him again. He had become a rebel—with a cause.' Alier (1990), p. 267.

20. Alier (1990), p. 267.
21. As recalled by Reuben Thiong.
22. Madut-Arop (2006), p. 51. Conradin Perner, the Swiss ethnographer who knew Kerubino and William Nyuon in the early 1980s, later asked Kerubino why Garang took the leadership. 'It would have been difficult to choose between William and me, we had started the war together and were equal,' Kerubino said, according to Perner. 'But John Garang was more educated than us, and therefore better qualified to take the leadership of a movement which did not only want to be successful militarily but politically as well.' Conradin Perner (2016) *Why Did You Come If You Leave Again? The Narrative of an Ethnographers Footprints Among The Anyuak In South Sudan*, Vol. 2, XLibris, p. 466.
23. Mengistu, who was sentenced to death in absentia for genocide, was speaking from exile in Zimbabwe in 2015. Mengistu Hailemariam, Interview 15 February, 2015, Ajak Deng Chiengkou, SBS Radio.
24. John Garang, speech June 1983, in Paanluel Wel ed. (2014) *The Genius of Dr John Garang: Speeches on the War of Liberation*, Juba: Paanda Media.
25. Perner (2016), pp. 475–6.
26. CIA, 'Sudan: The Southern Insurgency', May 1984.
27. Madut-Arop (2006), p. 98.
28. Letter from Elia Duang Arop to Swiss journalist Till Lincke, 17 November 1983.
29. 'Remarks of President Reagan and President Gaafar Mohamed Nimeiri of the Sudan Following Their Meetings', 21 November 1983, The American Presidency Project (APP), University of California, Santa Barbara.
30. CIA, 'Sudan: The Southern Insurgency', May 1984, and CIA Sudan, 'Roots and Future of the Southern Insurgency', February 1986.
31. Lual Diing Wuol, SPLA commander in Tripoli. Madut-Arop (2006), p. 91.
32. Madut-Arop (2006), p. 92.

8. THE WAR OF THE EDUCATED

1. Sharon Hutchinson (1996) *Nuer Dilemmas, Coping with Money, War, and the State*, Los Angeles: University of California, p. 355.
2. In July 1999, Médecins Sans Frontières (MSF) recorded testimonies of those attacked by 'gas bombs' near Yei, along South Sudan's border with Uganda. Witnesses reported bombings causing 'a nauseating, thick cloud of smoke' with victims vomiting blood and women having miscarriages. MSF (2000) 'Living under Aerial Bombardments:

Report of an investigation in the Province of Equatoria, Southern Sudan', February 2000, Geneva. In Yei, doctors from Norwegian People's Aid (NPA) had similar reports of poison gas bombs, and collected soil samples from the bombing zone, which they handed to British and US intelligence officers in Kenya. NPA chief Halle Jørn Hanssen later claimed CIA officers told him the samples had shown traces of poison, but did not say exactly what. Halle Jørn Hanssen (2017) *Lives at Stake: South Sudan during the Liberation Struggle*, Oslo: Skyline, pp. 230–36. Khartoum denied all claims it used chemical weapons.

3. For example, the hospital in Yei, painted with a Red Cross on its roof, was targeted by bomber aircraft 52 times between 1998–2005, according to Norwegian People's Aid (NPA) who helped run it.

4. By 1985, the SPLA had pushed attacks into the North, into Kordofan and Blue Nile. CIA, 'Sudan: Roots and Future of the Southern Insurgency', February 1986.

5. By 1986, the CIA estimated the SPLA was 'an effective fighting force' between 15,000–20,000 strong. Against them, the 14,000–16,000 government troops in the South were 'poorly equipped and supplied and thinly deployed'. CIA, 'Sudan: Roots and Future of the Southern Insurgency', February 1986, p. 6, and CIA, 'Sudan: Problems and Prospects for the New Civilian Regime', March 1986.

6. Brigadier General Deng Dau Deng, Chairman of the National Commission for War Disabled, Widows and Orphans.

7. CIA, 'Sudan: The Southern Insurgency', May 1984, and CIA, 'Sudan: The Armed Forces in Disarray', September 1986.

8. 'Paratroops flown to U.S. Chevron complex in Sudan', UPI, 3 February 1984.

9. The CIA estimated the oil fields would have brought in at least $275 million annually, or well over $600 million in 2018 terms. CIA, 'Sudan: Roots and Future of the Southern Insurgency', February 1986.

10. Luke Patey (2014) *The New Kings of Crude: China, India, and the Global Struggle for Oil in Sudan and South Sudan*, London: Hurst, pp. 39–43.

11. Human Rights Watch, HRW (1993) 'Civilian Devastation, Abuses by All Parties in the War in Southern Sudan', New York, p. 4.

12. US Embassy diplomatic cable, 'Khartoum: Oil in Southern Sudan— The Story of "Crooks and Nannies"', 13 November 2006.

13. Lincke said no demands were ever made of him or his family for a ransom. The SPLA told Swiss diplomats in Ethiopia the pair were there by their own volition, but refused access to them. Francis Cousin (2016) *Métier sans frontiers—40 ans au service de la diplomatie suisse*, Neuchâtel: Éditions Alphil, pp. 119–21.

14. 'Two Swiss journalists freed by rebels', UPI, 5 February 1985.
15. By March 1986, Sudan's GDP had dropped into negative figures while inflation ran at 50 percent and foreign debt had soared to some $9 billion. CIA, 'Sudan: Problems and Prospects for the New Civilian Regime', March 1986.
16. CIA, 'Sudan: Status of the Southern Insurgency', 1 December 1988.
17. 'Al-Gadhafi Arrives in 'Sisterly Sudan'', Libyan Jamahiriya News Agency, 9 September 1986.
18. Attacks escalated between 1985 and 1988. Traditionally, the *Murahaleen* were warriors who secured the annual '*murhal*' grazing routes of the Baggara people.
19. A US State Department cable describes the train attacks in 1992 and 1993, describing how soldiers reportedly 'killed or captured civilians in their path, burned houses, fields, and granaries, and stole thousands of cattle'. In another attack soldiers also 'captured several hundred women and children', HRW, 1993.
20. HRW documented thousands of Nuba peoples in 1992 being forced from their villages to travel north on daily truck convoys. 'They travel with a military escort,' HRW wrote. 'The trucks are grossly over-crowded and no provisions are made for the undernourished and dis-eased condition of the travelers... a total of over 40,000 people have been relocated to Northern Kordofan to date.' HRW/Africa Watch (1992) 'Sudan: Eradicating The Nuba', Vol. 4, No. 10 (9 September), p. 4.
21. UN (1994) 'Situation of Human Rights in the Sudan, Report of the Special Rapporteur, Gáspár Bíró' (February 1994).
22. Alier (1990), pp. 271–9.
23. SPLA appeal from Garang, 3 March 1984, in Wawa (2008), p. 324.
24. Nyaba (2000), pp. 41–2.
25. CIA, 'Sudan: The Southern Insurgency', May 1984; CIA, 'Sudan: Roots and Future of the Southern Insurgency', February 1986.
26. Kerubino escaped after five years. He returned to battle, switching sides repeatedly, including taking arms from old enemy Khartoum. He was killed by a Khartoum-backed Southern militia in 1999.
27. HRW (1994) 'Sudan: The Lost Boys, Child Soldiers and Unaccompanied Boys in Southern Sudan', Vol. 6, No. 10 (November 1994).
28. Lam Akol (2003), 'Why Garang Must Go Now', in *SPLM/SPLA: The Nasir Declaration*, Khartoum: Khartoum University Press, p. 304.
29. Machar's first wife, Angelina, a strong-willed South Sudanese lady, was in Britain. Emma died in a traffic crash in 1993 in Kenya. Maggie McCune (1999) *Till the Sun Grows Cold: Searching for my daughter, Emma*, London: Headline, p. 189.

30. McCune (1999), p. 197.
31. Lam Akol (2003) *SPLM/SPLA: The Nasir Declaration*, Khartoum: Khartoum University Press, p. 14.
32. Machar's forces reportedly killed about 2,000 Dinka civilians in attacks between September–November 1991, the UN said. There were other attacks. UN Bíró report, February 1994, p. 38.
33. Lam Akol (2003/2011), *SPLM/SPLA: The Nasir Declaration*, Khartoum: Khartoum University Press, pp. 30–2.
34. UN Bíró report, February 1994, pp. 38–9.
35. Rory Nugent, 'Feeding centre destroyed in Sudan massacre', *The Observer*, London, 16 May, 1993, p. 15.
36. Ben Assher and Colin Borradaile (1928) *A Nomad in the South Sudan: Travels of a Political Officer among the Gaweir Nuer*, London: Witherby, p. 168.
37. Hutchinson (2000), 8–12.
38. Richard Owen (2016) *Sudan Days 1926–1954: A Memoir*, Matador, pp. 72–4.
39. Lam Akol (2011) *SPLM/SPLA: Inside an African Revolution*, Khartoum: Khartoum University Press, p. 292.
40. Hutchinson (2000), p. 11.
41. Hutchinson (1996), pp. 353–6.
42. Ibid., p. 355.
43. Nyaba (2000), p. 39.
44. Initially, the SPLA factions were named after their respective headquarters. Machar, based in a riverside town in Upper Nile, led SPLA-Nasir. Garang, in the east, led SPLA-Torit. There were multiple name changes and splits.
45. HRW (1993), p. 12.
46. In 1993, the US Committee for Refugees estimated some 1.3 million people had died. Millard Burr, 'A Working Document: Quantifying Genocide in the Southern Sudan 1983–1993', US Committee for Refugees, Washington, October 1993, p. 2.

9. THE MAN WHO FELL TO EARTH

1. Alex de Waal (2005) *Chasing Ghosts: The Rise and Fall of Militant Islam in the Horn of Africa*, New York: The Social Science Research Council (SSRC).
2. David Lamb, 'Decisive Justice—Amputations—Helped Topple Sudan Regime', *Los Angeles Times*, 19 April 1985.
3. Interview with Rory Nugent, who described Bin Laden as 'a rich kid with a mixed reputation as a fighter'. Also see Rory Nugent, 'The

March of the Green Flag', *Spin*, Vol. 11, No. 2 (May 1995), pp. 68–74, and Nugent, 'My lunch with Osama bin Laden', *Rolling Stone*, October 2001.

4. HRW (2003) 'Sudan, Oil and Human Rights', New York, and IKV Pax Christi (2008) 'Sudan: Whose Oil? Facts and Analysis', 2008 European Coalition on Oil in Sudan, and Fatal Transactions.

5. US embassy cables in 1989 spoke of a government commander crucifying SPLA prisoners of war. Andrew Natsios (2012) *Sudan, South Sudan, and Darfur: What Everyone Needs to Know*, New York: Oxford University Press, p. 78

6. UN Bíró report, February 1994, p. 39.

7. UN Bíró report, February 1994 and January 1995.

8. Declan Walsh, 'The Great Slave Scam', *The Irish Times*, 23 February 2002, and Karl Vick, 'Ripping Off Slave "Redeemers"', *The Washington Post*, 26 February 2002. Also HRW (2002) 'Slavery and Slave Redemption in the Sudan', New York.

9. Lords Hansard text for Monday 18 December 2000, Volume No. 620.

10. Nyaba (2000), p. 14, also Douglas Johnson (2012) 'A New History for a New Nation: The Search For South Sudan's Usable Past', International South Sudan and Sudan Studies Conference Bonn, July 2012, p. 6.

11. Francis M. Deng (2004) *Green Is the Color of the Master. The Legacy of Slavery and the Crisis of National Identity in Modern Sudan*; also, Francis M. Deng, 'The Sudan: Stop the Carnage', *The Brookings Review*, Vol. 12, No. 1 (Winter, 1994), pp. 6–11, and Mohamed Omer Beshir (1975) *The Southern Sudan—From Conflict to Peace*, Khartoum: The Khartoum Bookshop, pp. 130–6.

12. *The Black Book: Imbalance of Power and Wealth in the Sudan* was first published in 2000. Also see Alex Cobham (2005) 'Causes of Conflict in Sudan: Testing the Black Book', QEH Working Paper Series, Queen Elizabeth House, Oxford.

13. Francis M. Deng, (1995) 'War of Visions: Conflict of Identities in the Sudan', The Brookings Institution, Washington, pp. 22–3.

14. UN Bíró report, February 1994, p. 23.

15. John Ashworth (2014) *The Voice of the Voiceless: The Role of the Church in the Sudanese Civil war*, Nairobi: Paulines, p. 100.

16. Seymour M. Hersh, 'The Missiles of August', *The New Yorker*, 12 October 1998 and 'Decision to Strike Factory in Sudan based on Surmise inferred from Evidence', *The New York Times*, 21 September 1998.

17. Sir Samuel White Baker (1888) *The Albert N'Yanza, Great Basin of the Nile, And Explorations of the Nile Sources*, London: Macmillan, pp. 60–62. Baker said the slaver was the father of the American consul in

Khartoum, but others dispute that. *The North American Review*, Vol. 104, No. 214 (January 1867), pp. 270–74.

18. W. Robert Foran (1958) 'Edwardian Ivory Poachers over the Nile', *African Affairs*, Vol. 57, No. 227 (April 1958), pp. 125–34, The Royal African Society.

19. Theodore Roosevelt (1910) *African Game Trails: An Account of the African Wanderings of an American Hunter-Naturalist*, London: John Murray, p. vii, also pp. 445–6.

20. Robertson (1974), pp. 149–50.

21. CIA, 'The Outlook for Sudan', 6 August 1957.

22. CIA Handbook for Special Operations: Sudan. HSO. No. 1, September 1963, p. 42.

23. Rebecca Hamilton, 'The Wonks who sold Washington on South Sudan', Reuters, 11 July 2012.

24. Francis Bok (2003) *Escape from Slavery*, New York: St. Martins, pp. 195–6.

25. Manute popularised but did not, despite urban legend, coin the actual term. See 'Sports Legend Revealed: Did Manute Bol coin the phrase 'My Bad'?', *Los Angeles Times*, 3 May 2011.

26. Blaine Harden, 'The Long Lonely Journey of Manute Bol', *Washington Post*, 22 March 1987.

27. Declan Walsh, 'Pro Basketball; Manute Bol's Fall from Grace', *The New York Times*, 20 June 2001.

28. Evaluation of Norwegian Humanitarian Assistance to the Sudan, COWI, Norway's Royal Ministry of Foreign Affairs, November 1997, p. 45.

29. NPA officials deny any gun running. Investigations by Norwegian journalist Bibiana Dahle Piene suggest that those NPA employees who helped with arms shipments did so as individuals. Bibiana Dahle Piene (2014) *Norge I Sudan: På bunnen av sola*, Oslo: Aschehoug, pp. 220–28.

30. Philip Caputo (2004) *In the Shadows of the Morning*, Guilford: The Lyons Press; Scott Peterson (2000) *Me Against My Brother, At War in Somalia, Sudan and Rwanda*, New York: Routledge, pp. 212–14.

31. Halle Jørn Hanssen (2017) *Lives at Stake: South Sudan during the Liberation Struggle*, Oslo: Skyline, pp. 173–5.

32. HRW (1998), 'Sudan: Global Trade, Local Impact—Arms Transfers to All Sides In The Civil War In Sudan', Vol. 10, No. 4, pp. 59–62.

33. Norman Kempster, 'Albright Takes Aim at Sudan From A Distance As Brutal War Rages On', *Los Angeles Times*, 11 December 1997. Also, James C. McKinley, 'Albright, In Uganda, Steps Up Attack On Sudan's War of Terror', *New York Times*, 11 December 1997.

34. McKinley (1997).

35. Selected Speeches of President George W. Bush, 2001–2008, Address to the Joint Session of the 107th Congress, 20 September, 2001, p. 65.

36. CIA officers met with top Sudanese chiefs in early 2002 in London, where they were told what could be destroyed. Richard Cockett (2010) *Sudan: Darfur and the Failure of an African State*, New Haven: Yale University Press, pp. 163–4.

37. Hilde Johnson (2011) *Waging Peace in Sudan: The Inside Story of the Negotiations that Ended Africa's Longest Civil War*, Khartoum: Madarik, p. 20.

38. Cockett (2010), p. 164.

39. Johnson (2011), p. 16.

40. Ibid., p. 142.

41. George W. Bush, 2002, Statement on Signing the Sudan Peace Act, Washington, 21 October 2002.

42. Francis Bok (2003) *Escape from Slavery*, New York: St. Martins, p. 269.

43. Johnson (2011), p. 142.

44. AFP, 'Garang "was assassinated"', 18 June 2007.

45. US Embassy Cable, Khartoum, Sudan/Uganda: Museveni Visits GoSS, Meets LRA, 26 October 2016. The cable describes how Uganda's Museveni insisted that the crash investigators concluded there was 'nothing wrong with the aircraft'. However, the US National Transportation Safety Board (NTSB), found 'significant shortcomings in the operation of Museveni's helicopter fleet, and concluded that a combination of bad weather, impending darkness, and pilot error caused the crash'.

10. THE LAND OF KUSH

1. Hannah Arendt (1969) *On Violence*, New York: Harcourt, p. 56.

2. Charles Tilly, 'Reflections on the History of European State-making', in Tilly, ed. (1975) *The Formation of National States in Western Europe*, Princeton: Princeton University Press, p. 42.

3. Benedict Anderson (1991) *Imagined Communities: Reflections on the Origin and Spread of Nationalism*, New York: Verso.

4. Victor Lugala (2010) *Vomiting Stolen Food*, Nairobi: Black Rain, p. 3.

5. Government of Southern Sudan, Ministry of Health, 'Neglected Tropical Diseases and Their Control in Southern Sudan: Situation Analysis', February 2008.

6. Arop Madut-Arop (2006), *Sudan's Painful Road to Peace*, Booksurge, p. 68.

7. Natsios (2012), pp. 216–7.

8. Jeffrey Gettleman and Michael R. Gordon, 'Pirates' Catch Exposed

Route of Arms In Sudan', *NewYork Times*, 8 December, 2010; also, US Cable, US–Ukraine Non-proliferation Meetings, 23–24 September, 2009, WikiLeaks.

9. SPLA interviews, also see Richard Rands (2010) 'In Need of Review: SPLA Transformation in 2006–10 and Beyond', Small Arms Survey, HSBA Working Paper 23, Geneva.

10. LRA commanders were based in Juba in the late 1990s, with Khartoum providing weapons training in camps scattered across eastern Equatoria. Ledio Cakaj (2017) *When The Walking Defeats You*, London: Zed.

11. Otti was believed to have been killed around October 2007. Peace talks collapsed, and Uganda sent in airstrikes in December 2008. US Special Operations forces came in late 2011.

12. The 2011 film *Machine Gun Preacher* starred Gerard Butler as Childers.

13. Leni Riefenstahl (1973) *Last of the Nuba*, London: Harper and Row.

14. UN and Sudan Household Survey statistics, 2006.

15. Volker Riehl (2001) 'Who is ruling in South Sudan? The role of NGOs in rebuilding socio-political order', Uppsala: Nordiska Afrikainstitutet, p. 4.

16. World Bank, 2016.

17. Fiona Davies and Gregory Smith, 'Planning and budgeting in Southern Sudan: Starting from Scratch', Overseas Development Institute, October 2010, London.

18. Bashir appeared in public in Khartoum on 14 July 2008, hours after the ICC prosecutor submitted an application for the issuance of an arrest warrant. Bashir's subsequent arrest warrant includes five counts of crimes against humanity (murder, extermination, forcible transfer, torture and rape), two counts of war crimes and three counts of genocide.

19. Kiir speech in Juba, 25 October 2009.

20. The competition for the anthem was announced in August 2010, with the music section in October 2010.

21. Lual A. Deng (2013) *The Power of Creative Reasoning: The Ideas and Vision of John Garang*, iUniverse, p. 3.

11. A LOOTER CONTINUER

1. Mancur Olson (1993) 'Dictatorship, Democracy, and Development', *American Political Science Review*, Vol. 87, No. 3, p. 567.

2. UN Deputy Humanitarian Coordinator Lise Grande, 14 August 2009.

3. The attack on the UN convoy took place in June 2009. The attack in Akobo was in August 2009.

4. Hilde F. Johnson (2016) *South Sudan: The Untold Story, From Independence to Civil War*, London: I.B.Tauris, p. 122. Johnson, the UN chief from

2011–14, calculated the territory in square kilometres to a single sol-dier to be 98:1. In contrast, the UN force in DR Congo, in its main theatre of operations in the east, had a ratio of 17:1.

5. E.E. Evans-Pritchard (1940) *The Nuer*, Oxford: Oxford University Press, pp. 151, 181.

6. Patrick Chabal and Jean-Pascal Daloz (1999) *Africa Works: Disorder as Political Instrument*, Woodbridge: James Currey.

7. Salva Kiir, July 2009.

8. Alex de Waal, 'When Kleptocracy Becomes Insolvent: Brute Causes of the Civil War in South Sudan', *African Affairs*, Vol. 113, No. 452 (1 July 2014), pp. 347–369.

9. The 700 generals commanded, as of 2011, around 200,000 men. African Union (2014) 'Final Report of the African Union Commission of Inquiry on South Sudan', Addis Ababa, p. 281.

10. Victor Lugala (2010) *Vomiting Stolen Food*, Nairobi: Black Rain, p. 3.

11. Hilde Johnson (2016), p. 36.

12. Ibid., p. 23.

13. 'In South Sudan, plunder preserves a fragile peace', Reuters, 20 November, 2012.

14. Jok Madut Jok (2017) *Breaking Sudan: The Search for Peace*, London: Oneworld, pp. 324–6.

15. Total arable land under cultivation in 2011 was 4.5 percent, accord-ing to WFP. Total cattle population was around 12 million in 2011, National Bureau of Statistics.

16. Jok (2017), pp. 325–6, and Johnson (2016), p. 37.

17. Hilde Johnson (2016), p. 41.

18. Clémence Pinaud (2016) 'Military Kinship, Inc.: Patronage, Inter-ethnic Marriages and Social Classes in South Sudan', *Review of African Political Economy*, Vol. 43, No. 148, pp. 243–59.

19. Norwegian People's Aid calculated that between 2007 and 2010 for-eign interests sought or acquired a total of 2.6 million hectares of land, or 6.5 million acres. NPA, 2011, 'The New Frontier, A baseline survey of large-scale investment in Southern-Sudan'.

20. Cherry Leonardi (2007) '"Liberation" or Capture: Youth in between "*hakuma*" and "home" During Civil War and its Aftermath in Southern Sudan', *African Affairs*, Vol. 106, No. 242 (2007), pp. 391–412.

21. 'South Sudan officials have stolen $4 billion: president', Reuters, 4 June 2012.

22. Kiir issued the letter in June 2012, but it referred back to theft since 2005.

23. De Waal (2014), pp. 347–69. Also, Edward Thomas (2015) *South Sudan—A Slow Liberation*, London: Zed Books.

24. Scott Gration (2016) *Flight Path: Son of Africa to Warrior Diplomat*, Mulami Books, pp. 245–6.

25. The Red Cross estimated in 1993 as many as two million could have been laid in Sudan, mainly in the South. UN Bíró report, February 1994, p. 38.

26. There were also around a hundred Lost Girls. While boys got the education needed to the fill application forms in, girls were married off young.

27. Dave Eggers (2006) *What Is the What: The Autobiography of Valentino Achak Deng*, San Francisco: McSweeney's.

28. The White House (2011) Statement of President Barack Obama Recognition of the Republic of South Sudan, 9 July 2011.

12. THE BROWN CATERPILLARS

1. South Sudan's Human Rights Commission (SSHRC) estimated around 2,000 deaths in Bor town. SSHRC Interim Report on South Sudan Internal Conflict, March 2013.

2. HRW (2014) 'South Sudan: Investigate New Cluster Bomb Use', February 2014.

3. The UN base with 43 peacekeepers was attacked on 19 December 2013. Reports of civilian casualties vary; the UN estimated initially that 27 were killed. UN Mission in South Sudan (UMISS) Interim Report on Human Rights Crisis in South Sudan, February 2014, p. 14.

4. Numbers in the camp peaked at around 17,000.

5. Andreas Wimmer, 'States of War: How the Nation-State Made Modern Conflict', 7 November 2013, Foreign Policy, Council on Foreign Relations (CFR), New York. Also, Charles Tilly (1990) *Coercion, Capital, and European States*, Oxford: Blackwell.

6. Douglas Johnson (2010) *When Boundaries become Borders: the Impact of Boundary-making in South Sudan's Frontier Zones*, London: Rift Valley Institute, p. 65.

7. De Waal (2014), pp. 347–69.

8. Alex de Waal, 'South Sudan's Doomsday Machine', *New York Times*, 24 January 2012.

9. Marcelo Guigale, Director of Economic Policy and Policy Reduction Programmes for Africa, World Bank Briefing, Juba, 1 March 2012.

10. Colum Lynch, 'World Bank to South Sudan: Are you out of your freaking mind?!', *Foreign Policy*, 8 May 2012.

11. 'South Sudan to use trucks to export crude', Reuters, Juba, 7 March 2012.

12. Hillary Rodham Clinton (2014) *Hard Choices*, New York: Simon and Schuster.

13. Princeton N. Lyman (2013) 'Sudan–South Sudan: The Unfinished Tasks', *American Foreign Policy Interests*, Vol. 35, No. 6, pp. 333–8.
14. Census figures estimate the Dinka to make up 35 percent of the people, and Nuer, 15 percent.
15. Scott Gration (2016) *Flight Path: Son of Africa to Warrior Diplomat*, Mulami, p. 243.
16. De Waal (2014), pp. 347–69.
17. Jok Madut Jok (2013) 'South Sudan and the Risks of Unrest', The Sudd Institute, 3 December 2013, Juba.
18. Lyman (2013), p. 333.
19. Hilde Johnson (2016), p. 70. Others report Kiir threatened to 'scratch' his enemies' faces. Mahmood Mamdani (2014) 'A Separate Opinion: African Union Commission of Inquiry on South Sudan (AUCISS)', October 20 2014, Addis Ababa, p. 6.
20. There are no exact figures of the ethnic composition of the army, but crude estimates suggest Nuer perhaps made up 40 percent, Dinka some 35 percent, and the rest Equatorians and others. Hilde Johnson (2016), p. 233.
21. Kiir said there were 7,500 members of the militia, but other reports suggested as many as 15,000. Their recruitment in 2012 was explained as a reserve border force in case of invasion by Sudan. Paul Malong, later army chief from 2014–2017, led recruitment. UN Security Council, Panel of Experts on South Sudan, 22 January 2016, S/2016/70, as well as Final Report of the African Union Commission of Inquiry on South Sudan, Addis Ababa, 15 October 2014.
22. Mahmood Mamdani (2016) 'Who's to Blame in South Sudan?', *Boston Review*, 28 June, 2016. The formal AU Commission also said they had reports that Tigers and Mathiang Anyoor were 'deployed around Juba disguised as 'street cleaners' in the weeks leading up to December 15.' AUCISS Final Report (2014), p. 22.
23. The AU inquiry dismissed reports Machar planned to overthrow Kiir. 'From all the information available to the Commission, the evidence does not point to a coup. We were led to conclude that the initial fighting within the Presidential Guard arose out of disagreement and confusion over the alleged order to disarm Nuer members.' AUCISS Final Report (2014), p. 27.
24. Hilde Johnson (2016), p. 181.
25. UNMISS, 'Conflict in South Sudan: A Human Rights Report', 8 May 2014, pp. 16–20.
26. United States Department of State (2013) 'South Sudan 2013 Human Rights Report', Country Reports on Human Rights Practices, Washington, p. 18.

27. 'Those in charge of rounding people up that day had gone to their superiors for instructions. It was only when they returned several hours later that the massacre began. In other words, the mass murder was premeditated, deliberate and authorised, not perpetrated on the spur of the moment by soldiers who had suddenly gone crazy or were fired up by ethnic hatred.' Hilde Johnson (2016), p. 189.

28. Hannah McNeish, 'Massacre, Rapes, Executions carried out in South Sudan', AFP, 23 December 2013; Mamdani (2014), p. 4; HRW, 'South Sudan: Ethnic Targeting, Widespread Killings', 16 January 2014.

29. SSHRC, 2013.

30. UNMISS, 'Conflict in South Sudan: A Human Rights Report', 8 May 2014, p. 53.

31. AUCISS Final Report (2014), pp. 225–6, 298–99.

32. AUCISS Final Report (2014), p. 23, 27, 225–6. AU commission member Mahmood Mamdani issued an additional report providing his dissenting findings. He divided the violence into two stages: the initial bloodshed in Juba from 15–18 December, which he called the 'target violence', and which was responsible for initiating the subsequent fighting. Mamdani argued it was more than a breakdown of law and order, rather that the violence was planned. 'The target violence was organised, not spontaneous,' he wrote. 'It was directed from a centre. Revenge violence followed.' Mamdani (2014), pp. 55–6.

33. Mamdani (2014), pp. 5–6.

34. Hilde F. Johnson, Press Conference on the situation in South Sudan, UNMISS Headquarters, Juba, 26 December 2013.

35. Hilde F. Johnson, 'South Sudan: Past and Present—and the prospects for peace', Royal Norwegian Embassy in Addis Ababa, 13 February 2017.

36. Tristan McConnell, 'From Bosnia to South Sudan: How one man survived a massacre and helped prevent another', Global Post, 22 September 2014.

37. Nicholas Coghlan (2017) Collapse of a Country: A Diplomat's Memoir of South Sudan, Montreal: McGill–Queen's University Press.

38. Carol Berger, 'Old Enmities in the Newest Nation: Behind the Fighting in South Sudan', The New Yorker, 23 January 2014.

39. Rebecca Nyandeng, BBC interview, 17 December 2013.

40. Mamdani (2014), p. 20, also SSHRC (2014), pp. 4–5.

41. US Special Envoy Donald Booth spoke to Kiir on 18 December. Ty McCormick, 'Unmade in the USA', Foreign Policy, 25 February 2015.

42. John Young (2016) 'Popular Struggles and Elite Co-optation: The Nuer White Army in South Sudan's Civil War', Small Arms Survey, Geneva, July 2016, p. 28.

43. Aaron M.U. Church, 'Blood Over Bor', Air Force Magazine, Virginia, October 2015, pp. 34–38.

44. Between 2,500–5,000 Ugandan troops were sent in the initial wave, making up some two-thirds of the attack force that retook Bor. 'Timeline of Recent Intra-Southern Conflict', Small Arms Survey, Geneva, June 2014.

13. THE OTHER CITY

1. Tristan McConnell, 'South Sudan's city of the dispossessed', AFP, 2 October, 2015.
2. Final Report of the African Union Commission of Inquiry on South Sudan (AUCISS), Addis Ababa, 15 October 2014, pp. 298–99.
3. Charles Tripp, 'Review—Sudan: State and Elite', *Africa*, Vol. 67, No. 1 (1997), p. 172, and Cherry Leonardi (2013) *Dealing With Government in South Sudan: Histories of chiefship, community and state*, Woodbridge: James Currey, p. 217.
4. Ibid., pp. 112, 142 and 216, also Mamdani (2014), p. 5, and Amnesty International (2016) 'Our Hearts Have Gone Dark: The Mental Health Impact of South Sudan's Conflict', Nairobi, July 2016; Michelle Nichols, 'Angry Trump envoy to meet South Sudan president to push for peace', Reuters, Addis Ababa, 25 October 2017. The AU said their report of cannibalism was based on multiple reports and backed up by several witnesses, with reasonable grounds to believe the testimonies.
5. AUCISS Final Report (2014), pp. 180, 196.
6. UN Report of the Commission on Human Rights in South Sudan (OHCHR), 23 February 2018, p. 105.
7. Skye Wheeler and Samer Muscati, HRW (2015) '"They Burned it All." Destruction of Villages, Killings, and Sexual Violence in Unity State South Sudan', New York, July 2015.
8. Ibid.
9. United Nations (2014) 'Conflict in South Sudan: A Human Rights Report', 8 May 2014, UNMISS, p. 53.
10. 'All Talk but No Peace: South Sudan's stumbling talks', AFP, 1 February 2015.
11. Interim report of the Panel of Experts on South Sudan, 15 November 2016, and Final report of the Panel of Experts on South Sudan, 13 April 2017.
12. Ilya Gridneff, 'South Sudan Hires Ex-Blackwater Chief to Restore War-Hit Oil', Bloomberg, 18 December 2014.
13. Reports of the UN Panel of Experts on South Sudan: 21 August 2015; 22 January 2016; 19 September 2016; 13 April 2017.
14. Yasmin Sooka, Chair of the Commission on Human Rights in South Sudan, Statement at the 26th Special Session of the UN Human Rights Council, 14 December 2016.

15. UN OCHCR report, 23 February 2018.

16. AUCISS Final Report (2014), pp. 176–8.

17. Ibid.

18. 'Rape in war-torn South Sudan 'worst' UN envoy ever witnessed', AFP, 10 October 2014.

19. Yasmin Sooka, Chair of the Commission on Human Rights in South Sudan at the 26th Special Session of the UN Human Rights Council, 14 December 2016; 'UN Experts call for UN special investigation into epic levels of sexual violence in South Sudan', 2 December 2016.

20. UN Mission in the Republic of South Sudan (UNMISS), 'Attacks on Civilians in Bentiu and Bor, April 2014', 9 January 2015, Juba.

21. Nicholas Coghlan (2017) *Collapse of a Country: A Diplomat's Memoir of South Sudan*, Montreal: McGill–Queen's University Press.

22. By 2018, some 70 percent of the country's children were out of school. One in three schools had been destroyed or occupied by soldiers, according to UNICEF.

23. Amnesty (2016), pp. 1–5; David K. Deng et al. (2015), 'A War Within: Truth, Justice, Reconciliation and Healing in Malakal', South Sudan Law Society.

24. 'South Sudanese President Salva Kiir threatens to kill journalists', Committee to Protect Journalists, 17 August 2015.

25. Global Burden of Armed Violence, Geneva Declaration Secretariat, Geneva, 2008, pp. 30–2; '50,000 and not counting: South Sudan's war dead', AFP, 15 November 2014; 'South Sudan is dying, and nobody is counting', AFP, 11 March 2016; 'UN official says at least 50,000 dead in South Sudan war', Reuters, 3 March 2016.

26. UN OHCHR Report summary, 23 February 2018, p. 5.

27. Leer was taken by government troops in July 2016. Amnesty International (2016) 'Their Voices Stopped: Mass Killing in a Shipping Container in Leer, South Sudan', 10 March 2016.

28. Report of the UN Secretary-General on South Sudan, 30 September 2014.

29. WFP (2017) 'Counting the Beans, The True Cost of a Plate of Food around the World'.

30. Ban Ki-moon, 25 February 2016.

14. THE WAR AMONG OURSELVES

1. Alex de Waal (2017) 'South Sudan 2017: A Political Marketplace Analysis', World Peace Foundation, Tufts University.

2. 'The Position of the Jieng Council of Elders on the IGAD-Plus Proposed Compromise Agreement', 21 July 2015.

3. Reservations of the Government of the Republic of South Sudan, on the 'Comprehensive Peace Agreement on the Resolution of the Conflict in South Sudan,' Juba, 26 August 2015.

4. UN Security Council, 1 July 2015, Sanctions List, Marial Chanuong Yol Mangok.

5. UN Security Council, Sanctions List, Narrative Summaries, 1 July 2015.

6. Colum Lynch, 'Dinner, Drinks and a Near-fatal Ambush for US diplomats', *Foreign Policy*, 6 September 2016.

7. UN, 'A Report on Violations and Abuses of International Human Rights Law and Violations of International Humanitarian Law in the context of the fighting in Juba, South Sudan, in July 2016', UNMISS and the Office of the United Nations High Commissioner for Human Rights (OHCHR), January 2017.

8. Ibid.

9. Jason Patinkin, 'Rampaging South Sudan troops raped foreigners, killed local', Associated Press, 16 August 2016.

10. At least 95 aid workers had been killed by December 2017 in the first four years of war, according to the UN.

11. UN, 'South Sudan: Humanitarian Coordinator condemns the killing of a health worker', 5 May 2016, and HRW, 'South Sudan: Army Abuses Spread West', 6 March 2016.

12. Tito Justin, 'South Sudan President Threatens to Personally Run Military if Road Attacks Continue', *Voice of America*, 20 October 2016.

13. Interim report of the UN Panel of Experts on South Sudan, 21 August 2015.

14. Thomas Cirillo Swaka, Resignation Letter, 11 February 2017.

15. Øystein H. Rolandsen and Nicki Kindersley (2017) 'South Sudan: A Political Economy Analysis', Peace Research Institute Oslo, Norwegian Ministry of Foreign Affairs.

16. Presidential spokesman Ateny Wek Ateny, 'Government reveals a $5 million failed plot to kill Machar', Radio Tamazuj, 10 April 2018.

17. Final report of the Panel of Experts on South Sudan, 22 January 2016.

18. Paul Malong, 9 April 2018.

19. Samantha Power, US Permanent Representative to the United Nations, on a Draft UN Security Council Resolution on South Sudan, 23 December 2016.

20. Oil production had collapsed, slumping from 350,000 barrels per day pre-war in 2012 to some 130,000 barrels per day by 2016. South Sudan owed nothing at independence, but excessive borrowing at punishing rates meant within five years it had racked up domestic debts of at least $4 billion, with external debt spiralling from forward sales of oil. Interim report of the Panel of Experts on South Sudan,

15 November 2016, also Simona Foltyn, 2017, 'How South Sudan's elite looted its foreign reserves', *Mail* and *Guardian*, 3 November 2017.

21. UN OHCHR report, 23 February 2018, p. 120.

22. Princeton Lyman and Kate Almquist Knopf (2016) 'To Save South Sudan, Put it on Life Support', United States Institute of Peace, Washington.

23. UN OHCHR, 23 February 2018, p. 104.

24. Statement to the Security Council by Adama Dieng, UN Special Adviser on the Prevention of Genocide, on his visit to South Sudan, New York, 17 November 2016.

25. Convention on the Prevention and Punishment of the Crime of Genocide.

26. UN OHCHR report, 23 February 2018, p. 17.

27. UN OHCHR report, 6 March 2017.

28. 'UN human rights experts says international community has an obligation to prevent ethnic cleansing in South Sudan', UN, 1 December, 2016.

29. UN OHCHR report, 23 February 2018, p. 104.

30. UN OHCHR report, 6 March 2017.

31. 'There are massacres taking place, people's throats are being slit, people are being killed, villages are being burnt out, there's a scorched-earth policy,' Patel said. 'It is tribal, it is absolutely tribal, so on that basis it is genocide.' Elias Biryabarema, 'UK says killings in South Sudan conflict amount to genocide', Reuters, 12 April 2017; 'War children face starvation in swamp refuge', *The Times*, 18 April 2017.

32. John Kerry, 'Sudan and South Sudan: Independence and Insecurity', US Senate, Committee On Foreign Relations, 14 March 2012.

33. Anne Gearan and Sudarsan Raghavan, 'US appears unable to pull South Sudan back from the brink of civil war', *Washington Post*, 3 May 2014.

34. 'South Sudan's Agony', *New York Times*, 27 June 2015.

35. South Sudan was first ranked worst in the world in the *Fragile States Index* in 2014, published by US-based Fund for Peace. In 2016, it rose to second worst, then slumped back to worst in 2017 and 2018.

36. Adrian Kriesh, 'South Sudan President Salva Kiir downplays refugee crisis', *Deutsche Welle*, 24 August 2017.

37. 'Kiir Won't Step Down', Eye Radio, 24 April 2018.

15. FREEDOM NEXT TIME

1. Andreas Wimmer, 'States of War: How the Nation-State Made Modern Conflict', *Foreign Affairs*, 7 November 2013, Council on Foreign Relations (CFR), New York.

2. UN OHCHR report, 23 February 2018, p. 124.
3. António Guterres, Secretary-General's remarks at the consultative meeting on South Sudan with the African Union, 27 January 2018.
4. February 2018.
5. Michelle Nichols, 'South Sudan's government using food as weapon of war—UN report', Reuters, 10 November 2017.

ACKNOWLEDGEMENTS

This book is based on over a decade of living in and reporting on the Sudans, and I could not have done that without the help of countless people. Many are not named, some cannot be named, but I came as a scared stranger and you welcomed me. Thank you. May one day you have the freedom you struggled so long for, and the time come when you will tell your own stories in peace.

To the brave South Sudan journalists willing to risk all for a principle and a pittance to make sense of the madness, thank you for your friendship; my special thanks to the great Waakhe Simon Wudu. To all those who encouraged, read drafts, listened, offered books, tea, kindness and laughter: Ayuen Panchol, Mabior Philip Mach, Philip Winter, the team at Eye Radio, Makwei Deng, Dianne Janes, Peter Moszynski, Sophie Martell, Till Lincke, Oswald Iten, Kwacakworo Perner, Gabriel Ayuen Mabior, Perdi Martell, Peter and Carissa Nightingale, Hannah McNeish, Daniel Van Oudenaren, Rajiv Golla, Patricia Huon, Elizabeth Spackman, Rebecca Hirst, Jess Hatcher, Tristan McConnell, and the eagle-eyed Zoe Flood. To the courageous MSF teams who got me into places, or got me out. Thanks to all at the South Sudan National Archives, Rift Valley Institute, and the Sudan Archives at Durham University. Silje Heitmann, thank you for the great adventure. In Eritrea, the Sudanese in exile who told me first about the struggle: Taiser Ali, Tigani El-Haj, Sharif Harir and Abdul Wahid al Nur. For all the comrades who watched my back on the wild ride, especially the old Juba crew: Skye Wheeler, Alan Boswell, Matt Richmond, Maggie Fick, Pete Muller, Jenn Warren, Jem Clarke and the massively missed Berenika Stefanska. Jack Kimball, for braving

ACKNOWLEDGEMENTS

the barricades, and Nichole Sobecki, who kept me going in the best and worst of times. Thanks to the BBC teams who always supported, but especially James Copnall, Stephane Mayoux, Martin Plaut, Bola Mosuro and Pete Lewenstein. With AFP, in Khartoum, Jennie Matthew, Guillaume Lavallée, Simon Martelli, and the unfailingly kind Abdelmoniem Abu Idris and Ashraf Shazly. Thanks to Tanya Willmer in Paris, and Jonah Mandel in Jerusalem. In Nairobi, thanks to Mwema Sambulu, the most important person in AFP's East Africa bureau, as well as Jean-Marc Mojon, Stefan Smith, François Ausseill, Roberto Schmidt, Wil Davies, Phil Moore, Boris Bachorz and Matt Lee, who sent me to the South with a fistful of dollars and the advice to 'have fun but borrow a sat-phone' from the LRA to file. For Zanz, who I rescued but who saved me. For Charlotte, who always believed; that meant everything. And for Al Harris, Jonny and Nick Martell, Carolina and Geoff, Rosie and Owen, for always picking up the pieces. Thank you. Most importantly, for my father, so he can read where I have been for so long, with all my love.

INDEX

Abiemnom, South Sudan, 212
Abraham, Isaiah, 216
Abu Idris, Abdelmoneim, 67
Abuk, Joseph, 179
Abyei, 106, 146, 211, 212
Abyssinia, *see* Ethiopia
Achebe, Chinua, 245
Achek, Jacob, 209
Acholi people, 79
Adams, John, 7
Addis Ababa Agreement (1972),
    97–8, 99, 100, 105, 106, 108
Addis Ababa Peace Talks (2014),
    235
Adwok, Peter, 129
Afahal, Salamah, 119–20
Afghanistan, 4, 140, 155, 168, 240,
    277
African Union, 78, 214, 219, 222,
    234, 242, 259, 302, 303
Agreement for the Resolution of
    the Conflict in the Republic of
    South Sudan (2015), 246
Aguer, Philip, 218
AK-47 rifles, 9, 61, 189
    Lord's Resistance Army insur-
        gency (1987–), 171
    Nuer inter-clan conflicts (2010),
        181

South Sudanese Civil War
    (2013–), xviii, 218, 227, 235,
    256
Sudanese Civil War, Second
    (1983–2005), 112, 116, 128,
    135, 136
Akec, John, 100
Akobo, South Sudan, 182, 208, 284
Akol, Jacob, 46–7, 66, 71
Akol, Lam, 132, 133, 134
Akulu, Vicky, 270
Alban, Arthur, 48
Albright, Madeleine, 155
alcohol, 114, 144
Aleu, Aleu Ayieny, 96
Alexandria, Egypt, 28
Algeria, 92
Alier, Abel, 97, 98, 103–4, 129,
    291
Allen, Christopher, 241
Alpher, Yossi, 88–9, 96
Amazon river, 18
American Anti-Slavery Group, 150
Amin, Idi, 89, 95, 285
Amnesty International, 234
Amum, Pagan, 180
Ana Taban, 273
Andrea, Rudolf, 197
Anglo-Egyptian Sudan (1899–

INDEX

INDEX